your
**PROFESSIONAL
QUALIFICATION**

THE TIMES

your
PROFESSIONAL QUALIFICATION

A GUIDE TO PROFESSIONAL QUALIFICATIONS IN THE UK—
WHERE THEY LEAD & HOW TO GET THEM

KOGAN PAGE

First published in 2002 by Kogan Page Limited

Apart from any fair dealing for the purposes of research or private study, or criticism or review, as permitted under the Copyright, Designs and Patents Act 1988, this publication may only be reproduced, stored or transmitted, in any form or by any means, with the prior permission in writing of the publishers, or in the case of reprographic reproduction in accordance with the terms and licences issued by the CLA. Enquiries concerning reproduction outside these terms should be sent to the publishers at the undermentioned address:

Kogan Page Limited
120 Pentonville Road
London N1 9JN
kpinfo@kogan-page.co.uk

© Kogan Page, 2002

British Library Cataloguing in Publication Data

A CIP record for this book is available from the British Library

ISBN 0 7494 3847 9

Typeset by Bibliocraft Ltd, Dundee
Printed and bound in Great Britain by Bell and Bain Ltd, Glasgow

Contents

Part One – Introduction   1

Part Two – Profiles/Directory   9

(all entries in bold have profile)

Christhomas Consortium London	11
Irish International University (European Union)	12
London Executive Schools (International Campus of Irish International University)	13
The Market Research Society	14

Accountancy   15

Association of Accounting Technicians	15
Association of Certified Book-Keepers	15
The Association of Corporate Treasurers	16
Association of Financial Controllers and Administrators	16
The Association of International Accountants	16
CIMA – The Chartered Institute of Management Accountants	17, 18
The Chartered Institute of Public Finance and Accountancy	19
Faculty of Community, Personal and Welfare Accounting	19
The Institute of Certified Book-keepers	19
The Institute of Chartered Accountants in England and Wales (ICAEW)	20, 21
Institute of Chartered Accountants in Ireland	22
The Institute of Chartered Accountants of Scotland	22
The Institute of Company Accountants	23
Institute of Cost and Executive Accountants	23
The Institute of Financial Accountants	24
Institute of Internal Auditors – UK and Ireland	25
International Association of Book-Keepers	25

Advertising and Public Relations   26

Communication Advertising and Marketing Education Foundation	26
Institute of Practitioners in Advertising	27
The Institute of Public Relations	27, 28
London School of Public Relations	27

Aeronautical Engineering   29

The Royal Aeronautical Society	29

Agricultural Engineering — 29
British Agricultural and Garden Machinery Association — 29
The Institution of Agricultural Engineers — 30

Agriculture and Horticulture — 30
The Institute of Horticulture — 30

Arbitration — 30
The Chartered Institute of Arbitrators — 30

Archaeology — 31
The Institute of Field Archaeologists — 31

Architecture — 32
Architects Registration Board — 32
Association of Building Engineers — 32
British Institute of Architectural Technologists — 32
Royal Institute of British Architects — 33

Art and Design — 34
The Association of British Picture Restorers — 34
The Chartered Society of Designers — 34
D&AD (British Design & Art Direction) — 34
The Royal Academy Schools — 35

Astronomy and Space Science — 35
The British Interplanetary Society — 35
Royal Astronomical Society — 35

Automobile Engineering — 35
The Institute of Automotive Engineer Assessors — 35
The Institute of the Motor Industry — 36
Institute of Vehicle Engineers (formerly Institute of British Carriage & Automoblie Manufacturers) — 36

Aviation — 37
The Guild of Air Pilots and Air Navigators — 37
The Guild of Air Traffic Control Officers — 37

Banking — 38
The Chartered Institute of Bankers in Scotland — 38
Institute of Financial Services — 38

Beauty Therapy and Beauty Culture — 39
Association of Therapy Lectures — 39
British Association of Beauty Therapy and Cosmetology Ltd — 39
The British Association of Electrolysists Ltd — 40
The Institute of Electrolysis — 40
International Council of Health Fitness and Sports Therapists — 40
International Federation of Health and Beauty Therapists — 40
International Therapy Examination Council (ITEC) — 41

London College of Fashion 41
Vocational Awards International 41
Vocational Training Charitable Trust (VTCT) 41

Biological Sciences 42

Institute of Biology 42
Institute of Biomedical Science 42
The Linnean Society of London 43
The Zoological Society of London 43

Brewing 43

The Institute & Guild of Brewing 43

Building 44

Architecture and Surveying Institute 44
Association of Building Engineers 44
The Chartered Institute of Building 45
Institute of Asphalt Technology 46
The Institute of Building Control 46
The Institute of Carpenters 47
The Institute of Clerks of Works of Great Britain Incorporated 48
Institute of Maintenance and Building Management 49

Building Services Engineering 50

The Chartered Institution of Building Services Engineers 50

Business Studies 51

The British Association of Communicators in Business 51
The Faculty of Commerce and Industry 51
The Institute of Business Administration & Management 51
The Institute of Chartered Secretaries and Administrators 52
The Institute of Commercial Management 52
The International Faculty of Business Qualifications 53

Catering and Institutional Management 53

British Institute of Innkeeping 53
Confederation of Tourism, Hotel and Catering Management 54, 195
Guild of International Professional Toastmasters 55
Hotel and Catering International Management Association 55

Chemical Engineering 56

The Institution of Chemical Engineers 56

Chemistry 56

The Oil and Colour Chemists' Association 56
The Royal Society of Chemistry 57
Society of Cosmetic Scientists 57

Chiropody 58

The British Chiropody and Podiatry Association 58
The Institute of Chiropodists and Podiatrists 58
Oxford School of Chiropodists and Podiatry 59

The Society of Chiropodists and Podiatrists	59

Chiropractic 60
British Chiropractic Association 60

Cinema, Film and Television 60
British Kinematograph Sound and Television Society (BKSTS)/the Moving Image Society 60

Civil Engineering 61
The Institution of Civil Engineers 61

Cleaning, Laundry and Dry Cleaning 61
British Institute of Cleaning Science 61
The Guild of Cleaners and Launderers 62

Communications and Media 62
Picture Research Association 62

Computing and Information Technology 63
Association of Computer & Operations Management 63
Association of Computer Professionals 63
The British Computer Society 64
Information Systems Examinations Board (ISEB) 66
Institute for the Management of Information Systems 68
Institution of Analysts and Programmers 68
International Association of Business Computing 69

Conference Executives 69
Association for Conferences and Events – Ace International 69

Counselling 70
British Association for Counselling and Psychotherapy 70
Central School for Counselling Training (CSCT Ltd) 70
Counsellors and Psychotherapists in Primary Care 70

Credit Management 71
The Institute of Credit Management 71

Dancing 72
The Benesh Institute 72
The British Ballet Organization 72
Imperial Society of Teachers of Dancing 72
International Dance Teachers' Association Limited 73
The Royal Academy of Dance 73
Royal Ballet School 74

Dietetics 74
The British Dietetic Association 74

Distribution	74
The Institute of Logistics and Transport	74, 75
Dramatic and Performing Arts	76
The British (Theatrical) Arts	76
Equity	77
Electrical, Electronic and Manufacturing Engineering	77
The Institution of Electrical Engineers	77
The Institution of Lighting Engineers	78
Embalming	79
The British Institute of Embalmers	79
National Examinations Board of Embalmers	79
Emergency Services	79
Ambulance Service Institute	79
Employment and Careers Services	80
The Institute of Career Guidance	80
Recruitment and Employment Confederation (formerly The Institute of Employment Consultants)	81
Energy Engineering	81
The Institute of Energy	81
The Institute of Petroleum	82
Engineering Design	82
The Institution of Engineering Designers	82
Environmental Engineering	83
The Chartered Institution of Water and Environmental Management	83
Society of Environmental Engineers	83
Environmental Sciences	84
Institute of Ecology and Environmental Management	84
Export	84
Institute of Export	84
Fire Engineering	85
The Institution of Fire Engineers	85
Fisheries Management	86
Institute of Fisheries Management	86
Floristry	87
The Society of Floristry Ltd	87

Food Science and Nutrition 87
Institute of Food Science and Technology (UK) 87

Forestry and Arboriculture 87
The Arboricultural Association 87
Institute of Chartered Foresters 88
The Royal Forestry Society of England, Wales and Northern Ireland 88

Foundry Technology and Pattern Making 89
The Institute of Cast Metal Engineers 89

Freight Forwarding 89
The British International Freight Association (BIFA) 89

Funeral Directing, Burial and Cremation Administration 90
The Institute of Burial and Cremation Administration 90
National Association of Funeral Directors 91

Furnishing and Furniture 91
National Institute of Carpet and Floorlayers 91

Gas Engineering 91
The Institution of Gas Engineers Managers 91

Gemmology and Jewellery 92
The Gemmological Association and Gem Testing Laboratory of Great Britain (GEM-A) 92
The National Association of Goldsmiths of Great Britain and Ireland 93

Genealogy 93
The Institute of Heraldic and Genealogical Studies 93
Society of Genealogists 94

General Engineering 94
Board for Engineers' Regulation (BER) 94
The Engineering Council 95
Institute of Measurement and Control 96
The Institution of British Engineers 96
The Institution of Incorporated Engineers 97
The Society of Engineers (Incorporated) 97
Women's Engineering Society 98

Geology 99
The Geological Society 99

Glass Technology 99
Society of Glass Technology 99

Hairdressing 99
The Guild of Hairdressers 99
Hairdressing and Beauty Industry Authority (HABIA) 100

Health and Health Services — 100
British Institute of Occupational Hygienists — 100
Chartered Institute of Environmental Health — 100
Institute of Health Record Information and Management (UK) — 101
The Institute of Healthcare Management — 101
The Royal Environmental Health Institute of Scotland — 102
The Royal Institute of Public Health — 102
The Royal Society for the Promotion of Health — 103

Home Economics — 103
Institute of Consumer Sciences incorporating Home Economics — 103

Homeopathy — 104
The Faculty of Homeopathy — 104

Horses and Horse Riding — 104
The British Horse Society — 104

Housing — 105
The Chartered Institute of Housing — 105

Hypnotherapy — 106
British Hypnotherapy Association — 106

Indexing — 107
Society of Indexers — 107

Industrial Safety — 107
British Safety Council — 107
The Institution of Occupational Safety and Health — 108
International Institute of Risk and Safety Management — 108

Insurance and Actuarial Work — 108
Association of Average Adjusters — 108
The Chartered Institute of Loss Adjusters — 109
The Society of Claims Technicians — 109
The Chartered Insurance Institute — 109
The Faculty and Institute of Actuaries — 110

Journalism — 110
The Chartered Institute of Journalists — 110
National Council for the Training of Journalists — 111

Land and Property — 112
The College of Estate Management — 112
The Institute of Revenues, Rating and Valuation — 112
ISVA – the Professional Society for Valuers and Auctioneers — 112
The National Association of Estate Agents — 113
Property Consultants Society — 113
The Royal Institution of Chartered Surveyors — 114

Landscape Architecture 114
The Landscape Institute 114

Law 115
The Association of Chartered Certified Accountants 115
The Law Society of Scotland 116

Leisure and Recreation Management 116
Institute of Groundsmanship 116
Institute of Leisure and Amenity Management 116
Institute of Sport and Recreation Management (ISRM) 117

Librarianship and Information Work 118
CILIP 118
The Institute of Information Scientists 118

Linguistics, Languages and Translation 119
The Greek Institute 119
The Institute of Linguists 119

Management 120
Association for Project Management **120, 121**
The Association of Business Executives 120
Business Management Association 123
Chartered Management Institute **123, 124**
Institute of Administrative Management 125
The Institute of Commercial Management 125
Institute of Directors **126, 127**
Institute of Executives and Managers 128
Institute of Leadership & Management 129
Institute of Management Consultancy 130
Institute of Management Services 130
The Institute of Management Specialists 131
The Institute of Professional Managers and Administrators 131
Institute of Value Management 132
The International Professional Managers Association 132
Professional Business and Technical Management 133
The Society of Business Practitioners 134

Manufacturing 134
The Institute of Manufacturing 134

Marine Engineering 135
The Institute of Marine Engineering, Science and Technology 135

Marketing and Sales 136
The Chartered Institute of Marketing 136
The Institute of Sales and Marketing Management 137
Managing & Marketing Sales Association Examination Board 137
The Society of Sales and Marketing 138

Martial Arts — 138
The Society of Martial Arts/College of Higher Education of Martial Arts — 138

Massage and Allied Therapies — 139
International Council of Holistic Therapists — 139
LCSP Register of Remedial Masseurs and Manipulative Therapists — 140
The Northern Institute of Massage — 140

Materials — 140
The Institute of Materials — 140

Mathematics — 141
Edinburgh Mathematical Society — 141
The Institute of Mathematics and its Applications — 141
The Mathematical Association — 142

Mechanical Engineering — 142
The Institution of Mechanical Engineers — 142

Medical Herbalism — 142
The National Institute of Medical Herbalists — 142

Medical Secretaries — 143
Association of Medical Secretaries, Practice Managers, Administrators and Receptionists — 143

Medicine — 143
British Institute of Musculoskeletal Medicine — 143
British Medical Association (BMA) — 143
The Royal College of Anaesthetists — 144
The Royal College of General Practitioners — 144
The Royal College of Obstetricians and Gynaecologists — 144
The Royal College of Pathologists — 145
The Royal College of Physicians of London — 145
The Royal College of Psychiatrists — 146

Metallurgy — 146
Institute of Corrosion — 146
The Institute of Metal Finishing — 147

Microscopy — 147
The Royal Microscopical Society — 147

Mining Engineering — 148
Institute of Explosives Engineers — 148
The Institute of Quarrying — 149
The Institution of Mining and Metallurgy — 150

Museum and Related Work — 150
The Museums Association — 150

Music 151
The Incorporated Society of Musicians 151

Musical Instrument Technology 151
The Incorporated Society of Organ Builders 151
Pianoforte Tuners' Association 152

Naval Architecture 152
The Royal Institution of Naval Architects 152

Navigation, Seamanship and Marine Qualifications 153
The Nautical Institute 153
The Royal Institute of Navigation 154

Non-destructive Testing 154
The British Institute of Non-Destructive Testing 154

Nuclear Engineering 155
The Institution of Nuclear Engineers 155

Occupational Therapy 156
The College of Occupational Therapists 156

Opticians (Dispensing) 156
The Association of British Dispensing Opticians 156

Orthoptics 157
British Orthoptic Society 157

Osteopathy and Naturopathy 157
The General Council and Register of Naturopaths 157
The London School of Osteopathy 157

Packaging 158
The Institute of Packaging 158

Pension Management 159
The Pensions Management Institute 159

Personnel Management 159
Chartered Institute of Personnel and Development **159, 160**

Pharmacy 161
The College of Pharmacy Practice 161
The Pharmaceutical Society of Northern Ireland 161
The Royal Pharmaceutical Society of Great Britain 161

Photography 162
Association of Photographers (AOP) 162
British Institute of Professional Photography 162

Master Photographers Association	163
The Royal Photographic Society	163

Physics 164
The Institute of Physics 164

Physiotherapy 164
The Chartered Society of Physiotherapy 164

Plant Engineering 165
The Institution of Plant Engineers 165

Plastics and Rubber 165
School of Polymer Technology 165

Plumbing 166
The Institute of Plumbing 166

Population Registration 166
The Institute of Population Registration 166

Printing 167
The Institute of Printing 167

Production Engineering 167
Institute of Operations Management 167
The Institution of Manufacturing Engineers 168

Psychology 168
British Psychological Society 168

Psychotherapy 169
British Association for Counselling and Psychotherapy 169
British Association for the Person Centred Approach (BAPCA) 169
British Association of Psychotherapists (BAP) 170

Public Administration and Local Government 170
The Institute of Public Sector Management 170

Purchasing and Supply 171
The Chartered Institute of Purchasing and Supply **171, 172**

Quality Assurance 171
The Institute of Quality Assurance 171

Radiography 173
The Society and the College of Radiographers 173

Refrigeration Engineering 174
The Institute of Refrigeration 174

Retail 174
The Booksellers Association of Great Britain and Ireland 174
BOSS Federation (British Office Systems and Stationery) 174
The British Antique Dealers' Association 175
The Co-Operative College 175
The Guild of Architectural Ironmongers 175
The Institute of Builders' Merchants 176
Institute of Grocery Distribution 176
The Institute of Masters of Wine 176
The Meat Training Council 177
The Society of Shoe Fitters 177

Road Safety 177
Institute of Road Safety Officers Ltd 177

Road, Rail and Transport Engineering 178
Society of Operations Engineers 178
Institute of Highway Incorporated Engineers 179
The Institute of Road Transport Engineers 179
The Institution of Highways and Transportation 180
Institution of Railway Signal Engineers 180

Security 182
International Institute of Security 182

Shipbroking 182
The Institute of Chartered Shipbrokers 182

Social Work 183
The British Association of Social Workers 183

Sociology 183
The International Institute of Social Economics 183

Speech and Language Therapy 184
Royal College of Speech and Language Therapists 184

Statistics 184
The Royal Statistical Society 184

Stockbroking and Securities 185
The UK Society of Investment Professionals (UKSIP) 185

Structural Engineering 185
The Institution of Structural Engineers 185

Surgical, Dental and Cardiological Technicians 186
The British Institute of Dental and Surgical Technologists 186

Surveying 186
Association of Building Engineers 186

Swimming Instruction — 187
Halliwick Association of Swimming Therapy — 187
The Swimming Teachers' Association — 187

Taxation — 188
The Association of Taxation Technicians — 188
The Chartered Institute of Taxation — 188

Teaching/Education — 189
The College of Teachers — 189
The Educational Institute of Scotland — 190
The Society of Teachers in Business Education — 190
The Society of Teachers of the Alexander Technique — 190

Technical Communications — 191
The British Association of Communicators in Business — 191
The Institute of Scientific and Technical Communicators (ISTC Ltd) — 191

Textiles — 192
The Textile Institute — 192

Timber Technology — 192
Institute of Wood Science — 192

Trading Standards — 193
The Trading Standards Institute — 193

Training — 193
The Chartered Institute of Personnel and Development (CIPD) — 193

Transport — 194
The Institute of Traffic Accident Investigators — 194
Institute of Transport Administration (IOTA) — 194

Travel and Tourism — 195
Confederation of Tourism, Hotel and Catering Management — 195
English Heritage — 196
Institute of Travel and Tourism — 196
The Tourism Management Institute — 196

Veterinary Science — 197
The Royal College of Veterinary Surgeons — 197
Society of Practising Veterinary Surgeons — 197

Wastes Management — 198
Chartered Institution of Wastes Management — 198

Watch and Clock Making and Repairing — 198
The British Horological Institute — 198

Welding 199
The Welding Institute 199

Welfare 200
The Community and Youth Work Association – YDA 200
Institute of Social Welfare 200
Institute of Welfare Officers 201

Part One – Introduction

Gaining a United Kingdom qualification

Whether you want to be a doctor or a dentist, an actor or an actuary, a tree surgeon or a technician, a professional qualification will feature in your career. For some professions in the United Kingdom, it is legally required for you to be qualified, and you would be breaking the criminal law to do the job otherwise. But for most, a professional qualification will almost certainly help your progress.

Your path to qualification in your chosen career will almost inevitably lead you to the professional, trade or craft body concerned with that activity. Some of these have been established for many decades, and others – concerned with more recent areas of work such as information technology – are comparatively new. All have a dual role – to maintain standards and to support their members.

This book lists virtually every professional, trade and craft body in the United Kingdom, with a short summary of what each does and how it can be contacted.

Whatever profession, trade or craft you choose, your British qualification will stand you in good stead. Many British qualifications are accepted in other parts of Europe (through agreements between member states of the European Union), and frequently accepted throughout the world.

The difference between academic and professional qualifications

For many professions, the academic qualifications you gain at school, college or university are a good foundation – but only a foundation. You will need specific knowledge and, often, practical training and experience before you can qualify to do the job. Professional qualifications are about proving your ability to do the job in practice, and not just on paper.

If you go to university and study law, for example, you will graduate with a degree. You may be able to use it in any number of occupations, but you will not be able to practise in either branch of the law profession (as a barrister or a solicitor). Both have set procedures that must be followed before you can be admitted. Likewise, if you take a degree in accountancy, you will not be a qualified accountant until you have taken professional examinations and completed a period of practical experience.

This applies to very many degrees and diplomas in 'professional' subjects. Formal structures exist for qualification, involving both academic education and training. This professional training will consist not just of practical application of the knowledge you have gained so far, but other knowledge you may need.

The stage of a career at which you take professional qualifications varies:

- Some professions require you to undertake a tightly regulated combination of academic study in that subject and practical experience and training during study and afterwards (medicine, dentistry, veterinary science, architecture, many applied uses of psychology).
- Some expect a degree (or considerable practical training plus other examinations) as a basis, but all your professional training will be done after registering with a professional body (accountancy).
- Some will only recognise training done at an accredited college (chiropractic, osteopathy).
- Some allow you to work without formal qualifications, but have a well-established system of professional qualifications (management, leisure management, engineering).

Who should get professional qualifications?

The short answer to this is: everybody who can. There are few occupations in which your progress will not be helped by gaining a professional qualification. And more and more, people in all jobs are expected to have undertaken some sort of formal training.

However, there is an important distinction – some jobs can only be done by people who have formal professional qualifications. These professions often have a professional register held by their governing body and to practise you must have qualified and be on it, and you must remain on it. If you are removed, you can no longer do that work.

Professions that cannot be practised legally without formal qualifications

If you are not formally qualified for the following professions, you may be breaking the law even to call yourself by the relevant title. Below are some of (not all) the professions to which this applies:

- Medicine – you must be registered with the General Medical Council;
- Veterinary science – you must be registered with the Royal College of Veterinary Surgeons;
- Osteopathy – you must be registered with the General Osteopathic Council;
- Chiropractic – you must be registered with the General Chiropractic Council;
- Nursing (not a ward assistant or auxiliary), midwifery and other health professions including health visitor – you must be on the professional register maintained by the United Kingdom Central Council for Nursing, Midwifery and Health Visiting (UKCC);
- Architecture – you must have completed a final examination in professional practice and management and be registered with the Architect's Registration Board;
- Many branches of psychology, for which you have to qualify as a chartered psychologist.

Professions that can legally be practised without a professional qualification

You can describe yourself as many things with no qualification. Counsellor, engineer, interpreter, actor, web designer, interior designer, psychologist (but not chartered psychologist) and many other titles can be used without professional qualifications, and sometimes without academic qualifications.

However, many of these professions have an established professional structure with formal examinations that require you to show an ability to do the job. Membership of the professional body can even affect your ability to work (the Equity card, showing membership of the actors' union, is a passport to much professional work).

Why gain a professional qualification if you don't need one?

Your qualifications, rather than what you call yourself, will determine your career. And while you may not need a qualification legally, you may in many other respects.

Crafts and trades are increasingly striving to set professional standards, and establishing their own professional bodies to maintain them. Without a qualification, you could find your progress hampered. For example, many engineers (in all specialities, including mechanical, electrical and computer engineering) seek to gain the status of chartered engineer. This can only be done through the various engineering professional bodies.

The benefits of a professional qualification include:

- proof that you have reached a certain standard in performing your job;
- readier acceptance by employers and clients of your ability and credentials;
- an indication of your conduct as well as your work;
- easier movement – many professional qualifications are recognised across Europe (through directives now applying to many professions) and throughout the world;
- official letters of attainment can be appended to your professional credentials, which could give you a professional advantage over others.

How academic qualifications can help you to gain a professional qualification

Some degrees allow you to either:

- bypass parts of your professional training (exemption); or
- earn points towards membership of your professional body.

For example, if you take a degree in law in England or Wales, you do not have to take the Common Professional Examination (CPE), a postgraduate diploma in law that must be taken by students whose degree is in another subject. The benefit of exemptions is that they shorten the length of time it takes to qualify.

It is quite common for degrees to earn exemptions from professional training, although impossible to generalise about degrees and subjects. Exemptions could be granted:

- when the degree subject is the same as the profession (accountancy);
- when the degree subject is closely related or has elements in common (maths, business studies, economics and law – exemptions towards accountancy examinations);
- when the student is already professionally qualified in a related profession (medicine and dentistry).

United Kingdom qualifications for overseas students

Why a United Kingdom qualification?

The United Kingdom's reputation for both its education and the calibre of its professions is unsurpassed. A British professional qualification wins respect all over the world. But there are other reasons why you should consider gaining your professional qualifications in the United Kingdom:

- Some British professional bodies – such as the British Computer Society and the Engineering Council – offer the only internationally recognised professional qualification in their field.
- In many professions, you would have ease of movement across Europe through reciprocity of recognition between member states.
- Your British qualification would establish your ability to use English as your working language – not only spoken as a first language in many parts of the world, but increasingly the international language.
- Many British professional bodies have established procedures (including international qualifying exams) for assessing students who have fully or partly qualified overseas, and dedicated postgraduate and international sections.
- You may be able to take professional training under TWES (Training and Work Experience Scheme), which enables overseas professionals to live and gain work experience in the United Kingdom for up to a year without obtaining a work permit.

Is it expensive to gain professional qualifications?

It is impossible to give a general figure for professional bodies' own examinations. But most offer the option of distance or open learning (formerly known as correspondence courses) which reduce the cost considerably. You should find details of costs on the professional bodies' web sites (included in their contact details).

Professions for which the training and academic elements are integrated cost more than conventional university degrees. Approximate costs are:

- Medicine – between £9,000 and £12,000 per annum (pa) for the first two years and around £17,000 pa for the final three years;
- Veterinary science – between £14,000 and £18,000 pa for five years;
- Architecture – £10,800 pa for the five-year recognised programme.

Qualifying in the UK when you are qualified in your own country

Many professional bodies have formal assessment procedures and qualifying examinations specially designed for those who have already qualified in their own country. They will be able to give you help and advice.

Professional bodies in the United Kingdom

Some professions have more than one professional body – how do you choose?

Sometimes there is only one professional body (such as the Royal Institute of British Architects), which usually also acts as the regulator of the profession. But sometimes there are several: accountancy is one example, where there are chartered, certified, management, public sector and international accountants, all with their own established professional bodies.

You may also have to choose between organisations in less formally regulated trades and professions, such as design and some branches of complementary medicine.

There is no definitive way of ensuring you register with the 'best' body, but go through these steps:

- Your choice could be determined by the branch of the profession you want to go into (eg management or public sector accounting).
- If your choice is more complicated (eg chartered or certified accountancy, or even chartered or management accountancy), you need to do some research further down the career line – which will help you to get where you want to go?
- Your choice could be determined by funding: some bodies' students tend to be sponsored by their employers, while others study independently.
- If you are an overseas student (or you want to work overseas), you should find out which professional qualifications carry most weight in the country(ies) in which you want to work.
- Some organisations operate internationally and have branches all over the world, with the wide recognition this confers, which may be high on your priorities.

What is a chartered institute or society, and is it superior to a non-chartered body?

A chartered body will have applied for a Royal Charter through an ancient process called Petition to The Sovereign in Council. For this to be granted it has to meet several criteria, and after it has been granted, the body cannot change its charter or by-laws without approval from the Privy Council (ie the Government). In a nutshell, the grant of a charter confers a degree of esteem, and indicates the calibre of the membership.

To be chartered, a body has to show:

- that its corporate members (usually just called members) are qualified to at least first degree level in a relevant discipline;
- that it is financially sound and can demonstrate a track record of achievement over a number of years;
- that it has 5,000 members or more.

Do professional bodies run their own examinations?

Some do, some do not. Some accredit particular external courses. Some accredit all courses at a particular academic level. Some professions closely supervise the entire training process (eg veterinary science, medicine, architecture), and only approved universities can teach the course.

How to join a professional body

Most bodies allow you to register as a student or an associate if you can show you are studying for the qualifications for membership. But each body has its own constitution and rules for membership, and there are exceptions:

- Organisations such as the Royal Astronomical Society, which admits new members only if they have been proposed by Fellows and elected by the Council (there are no exams, and membership is no guarantee of academic achievement).
- Bodies that assess people on the quality of their work (eg the Association of British Picture Restorers).

What is the difference between a professional body and a trade union?

Both want to protect their members' interests, but professional bodies usually expect a demonstrable level of achievement in your trade, craft or profession, whereas trade unions represent everyone in that trade, craft or profession. There are several areas in common:

- They may try to establish and protect pay rates.
- They may comment on training and welfare.
- They may have a benefit or charitable role (this applies particularly to craft guilds).

However, professional bodies are often the disciplinary and regulatory body for their profession – as opposed to trade unions, which often fight on their members' behalf (this is the distinction between the General Medical Council, the regulatory body, and the British Medical Association, the doctors' organisation).

Using this Guide

You should find no difficulty in using this guide. The professional bodies are listed beneath the profession (or trade or craft) with which they are associated. For example, the entry for 'advertising and public relations' lists four organisations.

The organisations themselves should be able to tell you why you should join them! So go on to their web sites – most have a web site now – and see what they can offer you in your career:

- Start by looking up the profession/trade.
- Read all the relevant entries.
- Take time to read web sites thoroughly – some are excellent, and will tell you practically everything you want to know.
- Bear in mind that some professional bodies are competing with others for your membership.
- Ask questions – ask your peers, ask your college, ask people doing the job, ask employers – to help you to decide which professional body will give you the maximum benefits, prestige and help in your career.

Part Two – Profiles/Directory

CHRISTHOMAS CONSORTIUM LONDON

5 Westminster Bridge Road, London SE1 7XW
Tel: 020 7620 0334, fax: 020 7620 0092,
email: info@christhomasconsortium.co.uk,
website: www.christhomasconsortium.co.uk

Christhomas Consortium London (CCL) is a privately limited educational institution for the benefit of the public to promote, facilitate and raise the standard of continuing professional further higher education and management development. In return this will assist to define, monitor, and improve the standards with the status of independent educational institutions world-wide.

Christhomas' main objective is to be one of the leading independent accrediting educational institutions. The Christhomas' belief is, '*it is not the Institute that counts but the knowledge that you provide*' by offering further higher education and degree programmes from any institute that is totally dedicated to the well being of the candidates.

Christhomas, as an Acreditation Centre for Continuing Professional Further Higher Education assesses, examines and validates in conjunction with the Christhomas' Executive Board of Assessors. Christhomas also validates awards, including the Certificates and Diplomas jointly issued by educational establishments, professional institutions, universities and public and private companies. The accreditation is inspected rigorously and renewed to maintain the expected high standard. Christhomas caters for the busy professional to obtain professional qualifications and professional degrees to enhance their career prospects by designing personalised tailor-made study programmes.

Christhomas is the assessor and examiner for UK accredited professional bodies, namely the Business Management Association, the Institute of Commerce, the Society of Sales and Marketing and the Association of Computer & Operations Management. The accreditation is a unique confirmation and dedication to the attainment of standards.

The accreditation must satisfy Christhomas' Executive Board of Assessors on the following criteria:

a) Staffing and administration;

b) Learning and teaching with professional competence;

c) The health and safety facilities of the premises;

d) Welfare facilities including the provision of counselling and career advice;

e) Quality management including the efficacy of monitoring the programmes provided;

f) The strength of financial and legal viability of the institution.

The assessment system is maintained to a very high standard, as the assessors are well qualified and experienced professionals. All are specialists in their respective profession. The accreditation is inspected rigorously & renewed on a yearly basis to maintain the professional standards of performance.

The following awards can be conferred upon any individuals on the recommendation of their employers, who have satisfied the management in their respective area of employment. This award will boost the morale of the employees and the productivity of the company.

- CERTIFICATE OF PROFICIENCY
- CERTIFICATE OF RECOGNITION
- PROFESSIONAL CERTIFICATE & DIPLOMA

IRISH INTERNATIONAL UNIVERSITY (EUROPEAN UNION)

European Office:
5, Westminster Bridge Road, London SE1 7XW, Great Britain
Tel: +44 (0)20 7620 0334, fax: + 44 (0)20 7620 0092, email: European@iiuedu.ie

International Office:
Unit 213, Block F, Phileo Damansara, Section 16, 46350 Petalying Jaya, Selangor, Malaysia
Tel: +603 7960 2611 / 2608, fax: +603 7960 2613, email: international@iiuedu.ie

Irish International University (IIU) is a privately funded non-profit, further higher international educational institution whose aim is to provide non-traditional professional degrees and post graduate study programmes and qualifications.

These affordable professionally accredited Bachelors, Masters and Doctorate qualifications will enhance the individual's marketability, increase competence, and challenge the intellectuals. To this end, the University seeks to provide a curriculum and degree composition consistent with the needs of students, employers, and society, achieved through a firm commitment to the highest educational standards and principles of integrity.

IIU met the criteria for European status by virtue of its registration in a member state. It is registered in the Republic of Ireland as a corporate company limited by guarantee under the companies Act 1963 to 1999. It operates three main campuses namely On-campus, Off-campus and a Virtual-campus.

The European Office and the International Campus are based in the United Kingdom because the UK is the cradle of academic knowledge and excellence for Europe. The International Office is based in Malaysia due to it being the pre-eminent country in the region for excellence in education.

Each student at Irish International University is expected to grow in areas of personal interest. The academic awards of IIU have gained accreditation and recognition in a number of countries in Europe and internationally by professional educational bodies and public and private companies. The awards are acceptable because the IIU has been granted a number of European and international membership affiliations with educational institutions.

IIU's study plans are accredited by Christhomas Consortium London Limited (CCL) as an Independent Accrediting Educational Institution in compliance with British Professional Qualifications. Therefore, CCL as an independent accrediting body, assesses, examines and validates the study programmes of Irish International University, London Executive Schools and the London School of Law. IIU's Post Graduate qualifications have the special privilege of being awarded British recognised **CERTIFIED MASTERS** and **DOCTORATE MEMBERSHIP** jointly awarded by the UK accredited professional body is the Business Management Association (BMA) and the Christhomas Consortium London (CCL). This will enable the candidates to use the designatory letters of CMBA (UK) and CDBA (UK) respectively after their names.

Irish International University's on campus programmes are delivered by **London Executive Schools (International Campus)**, which is registered as a Non-Profit Education Institution, limited by guarantee in Great Britain.

LONDON EXECUTIVE SCHOOLS (INTERNATIONAL CAMPUS OF IRISH INTERNATIONAL UNIVERSITY)

5 Westminster Bridge Road, London SE1 7XW
Tel: +44 (0) 20 7620 0334, fax: +44 (0) 207 620 0092, email: info@esbca.co.uk,
website: www.esbca.co.uk

London Executive School (LESL) is limited by Guarantee as a Non-Profit Educational Institution and its main objective is to provide the opportunity for international candidates ranging from school leavers to mature students to obtain international professional degree qualifications.

The LESL's aim is to keep all their course fees affordable to accommodate all candidates, especially from developing economies.

As the International Campus, LESL offers courses in the areas of Business Management, Sales and Marketing Management, Information & Communication Technology Management, Business Accounting, Care Management, Hospitality Management and Law Management in association with the regional campus and regional faculties internationally. All courses are available at Certificate, Diploma, Batchelor, Master and Doctorate levels. Syllabus and methodology are structured to assist the integration of theory and practice into related business operations. The international campus' Tutors and Professors endeavor to mould the candidates to meet the demands of today's international business and management challenges.

Continuous assessments are carried out during the study period to monitor the candidate's progress and development. LESL's aspiration is to improve the career and business prospects by enhancing the professional status of a European Community Degree.

The International Campus will provide initial guidance in selecting the study plan together with continuing support, encouragement and a range of counselling to resolve any difficulties faced by the candidate in relation to their individual study method. This will in return help to develop a successful International Business and intellectual Community worldwide.

The International Campus is situated in the heart of London and is not far from the Old Vic Theatre and the Imperial War Museum. Waterloo International Railway Station is only a few minutes away, with its easy access to the channel tunnel taking you directly to Europe. The international mix of students has encouraged worldwide recognition of the International Campus.

The study programmes of LESL are accepted by UK accredited professional bodies such as the Business Management Association (BMA), the Society of Sales and Marketing (SSM) and the Association of Computer and Operation Management (ACOM), which are all highly respected and recognised professional educational institutions in the United Kingdom and are included in the publication "British Qualifications". The International Campus study programmes are internally examined and assessed. Enrolment is in September & April to suit all applicants.

Further information: The Administration Officer at the above address.

THE MARKET RESEARCH SOCIETY

15 Northburgh Street, London EC1V OJR
Tel: Membership helpline: 020 7566 1820,
Email: membership@mrs.org.uk

With over 8,000 members in more than 50 countries, The Market Research Society (MRS) is the world's largest international membership organisation for professional researchers and others engaged in (or interested in) market, social, and opinion research.

It has a diverse membership of individual researchers within agencies, independent consultancies, client-side organisations, and the academic community, and from all levels of seniority and job functions.

All members agree to comply with the MRS Code of Conduct, which is supported by the Codeline advisory service and a range of specialist guidelines on best practice.

MRS offers various qualifications and membership grades, as well as training and professional development resources to support them. It is the official awarding body in the UK for vocational qualifications in market research.

MRS is a major supplier of publications and information services, conferences and seminars, and many other meeting and networking opportunities for researchers.

MRS is 'the voice of the profession' in its media relations and public affairs activities on behalf of professional research practitioners, and aims to achieve the most favourable climate of opinion and legislative environment for research.

Membership Department
The Market Research Society
15 Northburgh Street
London EC1V OJR
Tel: Membership helpline: 020 7566 1820
Email: membership@mrs.org.uk

Accountancy

ASSOCIATION OF ACCOUNTING TECHNICIANS

154 Clerkenwell Road
London
EC1R 5AD
United Kingdom
Tel: 020 7837 8600
Fax: 020 7837 6970
Email: aat@aat.org.uk
Website: www.aat.co.uk

The AAT represents professionals who work in accounting and finance. It has more than 100,000 Members worldwide, and is sponsored by four of the chartered accountancy bodies in the UK.

MAAT: Membership is available to registered Students who may apply if they have demonstrated competence at all three Stages of the AAT Education and Training Scheme NVQ/SVQ Levels 2, 3 and 4, and can provide evidence of the required experience (or part-time equivalent) in an approved accounting function.

FMAAT: Members may apply to become Fellow Members 5 years after they have been admitted to Membership provided that they can supply evidence of either (a) supervisory or management responsibilities held over a prescribed period, or (b) significant specialisation in a relevant area (eg taxation).

MAATs and FMAATs receive a range of services designed to maintain and expand their levels of competence. These include: technical bulletins and courses designed to update, broaden and extend skills gained while qualifying; Branch Network (regionalised groups providing access to technical meetings and other presentations and events); professional support and ethical guidance; and *Accounting Technician*, a monthly magazine.

TRAINING:

Registered Student: Flexible open access for student members to register on the Scheme, although entrants must be numerate and have a good command of English. The Education and Training scheme is competence-based, using a variety of assessment methods. The Scheme is accredited at National and Scottish Vocational Qualification (NVQ/SVQ) Levels 2, 3 and 4 in Accounting (these three Levels are also known as the Foundation, Intermediate and Technician Stages of the AAT's Education and Training Scheme). Students are fully credited for all units successfully completed and NVQ/SVQ Certificates are awarded for each Stage achieved. Students who complete the AAT Education and Training Scheme are eligible to exemptions, should they wish to progress to the senior professional qualifications of all the UK chartered accounting bodies. Further information on entry should be sought from the Institute concerned. Benefits to registered Students include receipt of *Accounting Technician* and access to their local branch.

ASSOCIATION OF CERTIFIED BOOK-KEEPERS

Akhtar House
2 Shepherds Bush Road
London
W6 7PJ
United Kingdom
Tel: 020 8749 7126
Fax: 020 8749 7127
Email: icea@enta.net
Website: www.icea.enta.net

Fellow (FACB): Applicants must pass the ACB's exam or equivalent, be at least 21 and have 5 years' experience.

Associate (AACB): Applicants must pass the ACB's exam or equivalent and have 3 years' experience. The Association provides a single-subject exam in: (1) Book-keeping; (2) Advanced Book-keeping and Accounting; (3) Computer Applications in Accounting.

No formal qualifications are necessary to register as a student, but applicants must have good knowledge of English. The ACB qualifications are ideal for employees at the first and second levels of work in accounting, costing and internal auditing. Members can describe themselves as a Certified Book-Keeper. The qualifications are based on NCVQ competence and the ACB will seek NCVQ recognition in due course.

Exemptions are considered from the applicants who have passed (a) RSA Stage 3, (b) LCC Higher, (c) Pitman Level 2 or similar exam.

Certified Diploma in Computerised Book-keeping & Accounting: This is a single-subject exam in book-keeping and accountancy of 3 hours' duration. One hour for theory and practice and 2 hours for practical assignment to prepare day books/spreadsheets, prepare ledgers and to draw final accounts using a computerised accounts package.

Certified Diploma in Small Business Administration: This is also a single-subject exam of 3 hours' duration in business administration, with special emphasis for small business.

THE ASSOCIATION OF CORPORATE TREASURERS

Ocean House
10/12 Little Trinity Lane
London
EC4V 2DJ
United Kingdom
Tel: 020 7213 9728
Fax: 020 7248 2591
Email: enquiries@treasurers.co.uk
Website: www.treasurers.org

The Association is the only examining body for the profession of corporate treasury management and offers three levels of membership.

1. **Fellow (FCT):** Applicants must satisfy the requirements for membership and should have 5 years' experience of senior responsibility for corporate treasury functions.
2. **Membership Qualification (MCT):** Individuals who successfully complete the Membership qualification are eligible to become Members of the Association and use the designatory letters **MCT**.
3. **Associate Membership Qualification (AMCT):** Individuals who successfully complete the Associateship qualification are entitled to apply for Associate Membership. Once accepted they are entitled to use the designatory letters **AMCT**.

EXAMINATIONS:

1. **The Associate Membership Qualification comprises 6 subjects:** Accountancy Practice and Introductory Economics, Financial Analysis, Corporate Taxation, Business Law, Money Management, Corporate Finance and Funding.
2. **The Membership Qualification comprises 3 subjects:** Corporate Financial Management, Advanced Funding and Risk Management, Treasury Management.
3. **Exemptions:** Exemptions are available on a subject for subject basis from papers I–IV of the Associate qualification with exemption against all four papers for a chartered accountancy qualification. A fast-track route for CIMA students and recently qualified members offers a shortened paper VI (Corporate Finance and Funding), enabling them to qualify at the AMCT level within 5 months.
4. **The Certificate in International Cash Management:** This is a 6 month course with a comprehensive E-learning programme (visit www.treasurers.org/cashmanagement to view the demo). It improves understanding between providers and users of cash management services. Successful completion of the 5 day residential school and examination allows the use of the designatory letters **Cert CM**.

ASSOCIATION OF FINANCIAL CONTROLLERS AND ADMINISTRATORS

Akhtar House
2 Shepherds Bush Road
London
W6 7PJ
United Kingdom
Tel: 020 8749 7126
Fax: 020 8749 7127
Email: icea@enta.net
Website: www.icea.enta.net

Associate (AAFC): Applicants are required to pass the Association's exam or equivalent, be at least 20 and have had 4 years' experience. This qualification is based on NVQ Level 4 competency.

Fellow (FAFC): Applicants must hold a senior position in financial management and must be an Associate. They must have at least 5 years' experience and be over 25.

The Association has a 3-part exam syllabus consisting of 4 papers in each part. Parts 1, 2, and 3 are of first, second and third year degree standard of the British Universities. Only registered students are permitted to sit the exam.

Applicants to be registered as students must be 18 and must have 5 GCE or GCSE passes including 2 at A level or equivalent or 3 years' experience in accounting, finance or allied work.

THE ASSOCIATION OF INTERNATIONAL ACCOUNTANTS

South Bank Building
Kingsway, Team Valley
Newcastle upon Tyne
NE11 0JS
United Kingdom
Tel: 0191 482 4409
Fax: 0191 482 5578
Email: aia@aia.org.uk
Website: www.aia.org.uk

The AIA is one of Britain's five recognised Qualifying Bodies for accountants and company auditors.

Associate (AAIA): Achieved upon passing the AIA professional exams and attaining 3 years' approved accountancy experience. There are no restrictions as to where experience can be gained; in industry, commerce, the public sector or public practice.

Fellow (FAIA): Granted to Associate members following 5 continuous years of post-qualifying accountancy experience.

EXAMINATIONS:

Registration as an AIA student is a prerequisite for entry. Candidates must also be in accountancy employment, or a full-time student on an approved course of accountancy or business studies. The exams comprise three levels:
Foundation Level: *Module A:* Financial Accounting 1, Economics, Cost Accounting; *Module B:* Law, Auditing & Taxation, Statistics & Data Processing;
Professional I: *Module C:* Auditing, Company Law, Management Information; *Module D:* Business Management, Financial Accounting II, Management Accounting;
Professional II: *Module E:* Financial Accounting III, Financial Management; *Module F:* Professional Practice (Auditing), Taxation & Tax Planning.
Local variant papers are available to suit individual national requirements; alternatively, students may opt to follow International Accounting Standards or Islamic Accounting. Members holding the AIA's recognised audit qualification wishing to practice as a registered auditor in the UK may do so under the control of a recognised supervisory body.

ENTRY REQUIREMENTS:

A minimum of 2 A levels and 3 GCSEs (to include Mathematics and English), or the equivalent overseas qualification. Mature students (21 and over) may be admitted to the course on assessment of their general education and accountancy experience, which must be a minimum of five years.

EXEMPTIONS:

Degree holders or those with a BTEC HND in Business Studies (financial stream) are entitled to exemptions from all or part of the Foundation Level. Specific accountancy-related degrees and certain recognised professional qualifications also attract exemptions from Professional Level 1.

CIMA – THE CHARTERED INSTITUTE OF MANAGEMENT ACCOUNTANTS

26 Chapter Street
London
SW1P 4NP
United Kingdom
Tel: 020 7663 5441
Fax: 020 7663 5442
Email: Student-Services@cimaglobal.com
Website: www.cimaglobal.com

We provide our students and members with the skills to achieve even their most ambitious goals. We are internationally renowned for delivering flexible, comprehensive training programmes and for continuing to support CIMA graduates throughout their careers. Consequently they go on to achieve their aims – whether they want to become the Directors and CEOs of the future, or become internationally transferable managers.

MEMBERSHIP:

Registered Student: You need to register in order to sit the exams. Registration requires a minimum of 5 GCE or GCSE passes (any 2 of which must be at A level) including Mathematics and English Language. Alternatively the ATT (NVQ Level 3), BTEC Edexcel NC/ND, or Advanced GNVQ in Business is acceptable. For information on other BTEC Edexcel subjects, please contact the Student Services Centre on Tel: 020 7917 9251.
Associate (ACMA): An applicant is required to pass CIMA's exams comprising 3 stages and to demonstrate a minimum of 3 years' verified, relevant, practical experience in management accounting, basic accounting and financial management. Experience may be gained in industrial, commercial or service organisations in the private or public sector, or may be obtained by any combination of appointments across these sectors.
Fellow (FCMA): As per ACMA, but a minimum of 3 years' experience in a 'senior and responsible position' is required in addition to the 3 years' experience for the Associateship.

EXAMINATIONS:

The syllabus is made up of 3 levels:
Foundation Level: Financial Accounting Fundamentals (FAFN), Management Accounting Fundamentals (FMAF), Economics for Business (FECB), Business Law (FBLW) and Business Mathematics (FBSM). *Please note: FECB, FBLW and FBSM are 2 hour examinations, all other exams allow 3 hours.*
Intermediate Level: Finance (IFIN), Business Taxation (IBTX), Financial Accounting – UK Standards (IFNA) or International Standards (IFAI), Financial Reporting – UK Standards (IFRP) or International Standards (IFRI), Management Accounting – Performance Management (IMPM), Management Accounting – Decision Making (IDEC), Systems and Project Management (ISPM) and Organisational Management (IORG). *Please note: Students can elect to sit Financial Accounting and Financial Reporting with either the UK Accounting Standards format or the International Accounting Standards format.*
Final Level: Management Accounting Business Strategy (FLBS), Management Accounting Financial Strategy (FLFS), Management Accounting Information Strategy (FLIS) and Management Accounting Case Study (FLCS).

CIMA (THE CHARTERED INSTITUTE OF MANAGEMENT ACCOUNTANTS)

26 Chapter Street, London SW1P 4NP, Tel: +44 (0)20 7663 5441, Fax: +44 (0)20 7663 5442
email: student.services@cimaglobal.com, website: www.cimaglobal.com

About Us
With over 78,000 students and 57,000 members worldwide, CIMA is the professional body for Chartered Management Accountants

What is Management Accountancy?
Management Accountancy is concerned with providing financial information and advice essential to managing a business. Management accountants work as part of a management team, dealing with the financial side of business, developing strategies crucial to the running of a business. They look at today's facts and tomorrow's opportunities, not yesterday's accounts. There are over 20,500 companies worldwide such as The Coca-Cola Company, PricewaterhouseCoopers, Greenpeace and MTV employing CIMA students, many of which sponsor students through their training.

CIMA Facts
- Internationally recognised qualification
- Many of the world's most prestigious employers put CIMA at the top of their list of preferred finance qualifications
- Becoming qualified is a highly flexible process which allows you to study at your own pace and to schedule your exams to suit yourself
- CIMA syllabus consists of three levels of examinations
- CIMA members work as Financial Controllers, Chief Accountants, Directors and Managing Directors
- 41 per cent of CIMA members are working in senior positions, earning £50,000 or more

Entry Requirements
Students are welcome from any educational background, although graduates of relevant disciplines may be awarded exemptions from part of the study programme.

Once registered you will take three levels of examinations that help you to gain the skills and experience needed to contribute to the business you are in. The CIMA syllabus has been developed in consultation with employers in order to ensure that it is as relevant to business needs as possible.

Reward
Through studying CIMA, not only will you enjoy a rewarding career with excellent prospects for the future, but you will also be able to witness the value your input has to the organisation. Many members go on to earn in excess of £50,000 within three years of qualifying.

Find Out More
To find out more about CIMA and a career in management accounting, please contact us at the address above.

What does the future hold for you? Visit the CIMA website www.cimaglobal.com to find out more.

THE CHARTERED INSTITUTE OF PUBLIC FINANCE AND ACCOUNTANCY

3 Robert Street
London
WC2N 6RL
United Kingdom
Tel: 020 7543 5718
Fax: 020 7543 5700
Email: choices@cipfa.org
Website: www.cipfa.org.uk/choices

CIPFA is the leading professional body for public services, whether in the public or private sector. Membership is available to those who meet the requirements of the Institute's education and training scheme. Once qualified, members possess a recognised and highly regarded qualification, designated CIPFA.

The CIPFA minimum entry requirements are 3 GCSE passes, and 2 A levels. Subjects must include Maths and English at either level. The equivalent qualifications for Scotland, Northern Ireland and the Republic of Ireland are also accepted. Exemptions are granted for relevant degrees and/or work experience.

CIPFA's Education and Training Scheme consists of a Foundation Stage and 3 Professional Stages: P1, P2 and P3. Subjects studied are: Foundation – Financial Accounting, Cost Accounting and Quantitative Analysis, Law and Effective Management Skills; P1 – Accounting Theory and Practice, Management Accounting, Auditing, Information and Financial Management; P2 – Financial Reporting and Accountability, Accounting for Decision Making, Public Policy and Taxation, Business Strategy and Management; P3 – Finance and Management Case Study Examination, Project.

FACULTY OF COMMUNITY, PERSONAL AND WELFARE ACCOUNTING

22 Parkthorn Road
Preston
PR2 1RX
United Kingdom
Tel: 01457 834 943

The Faculty is a radical professional association for Accountants, Administrators, Secretaries and Financial Consultants in fields related to Community Provision and Consumer Finance. Members are designated Community Finance Accountants/Consultants.

The Faculty is devising a qualification structure based on progressive methods of assessment, cases and practical experience. It is unlikely that the style or content apart from Foundation Accountancy or Administration skills will be similar to that of other bodies. The training programme will include the following: Management of Community Provision; Debt Counselling; Consumer Credit; Assurance and Insurance Studies; Corporate Planning; Accountancy; and Workers Rights. The Faculty now has only a sole designation for all full members, namely **Fellow of the Faculty (FCPWA)**. This is based on individual assessment of the members' ability and experience in the areas outlined above, including 3–5 years' practical experience. All other applicants are enrolled as ordinary members with no designation. Former members of the old Faculty of Community Accountancy and Administration may use their previous single designation.

EXAMINATIONS:

Personal Financial Planning: The Faculty recognises the Financial Planning Certificate of the Chartered Insurance Institute and the requisite levels of the Life Insurance Association by exam.

Accountancy: The Faculty recognises AAT, CIPFA and parts of some other bodies' exams.

Corporate Administration: The Faculty recognises Chartered, Corporate and Certified Public Secretary qualifications.

NVQs: These are accepted at various levels but on an individual basis.

Non-UK Assessment Scheme: A cross-referenced assessment procedure is used for overseas applicants. All assessments, both for UK and overseas applicants, are on an Endowed Membership basis.

Certificate in Community Interviewing: For those who survey financial matters (jointly with YDA).

THE INSTITUTE OF CERTIFIED BOOK-KEEPERS

The Granary
Church Lane
Steveton
Oxon
OX13 6WE
United Kingdom
Tel: 01235 831577
Fax: 01235 831477
Email: info@book-keepers.org

The Institute of Certified Book-keepers is the largest book-keeping organisation in the world with in excess of 10,000 members and students in the UK and in more than a dozen countries around the world. The Institute has its own 'Oscar' awards ceremony where it awards a 'Luca' to winners in each of several categories.

MEMBERSHIP:

Registered Student: Open to any person studying towards the Institute's qualification.

Associate Member (AICB): A person who has passed the ICB Level I Certificate in Financial Record Keeping and the Level II Certificate in Book-keeping (manual or computerised) or its equivalent its eligible to become an Associate Member.

Member (MICB): A person who has passed the ICB Level I Certificate in Financial Record keeping and the Level II Certificate in Book-keeping (manual or computerised) and the Level III Diploma in Manual or Computerised Book-keeping or its equivalent is eligible to become a Member. A Member may use the title 'Certified Book-keeper'.

Fellow (FICB): A Member who is able to demonstrate a minimum of two years' relevant working experience may apply for election to the grade of Fellow. A Fellow may use the title 'Certified Book-keeper'.

QUALIFICATIONS

Level 1: The Certificate in Financial and Basic Book-keeping: This qualification covers the basic record keeping required for a small business. It is based on a cash accounting system and includes the preparation of business documents, the recording of financial transactions in a simple analysed system, the calculation of balances and the profit or loss made during a trading period.

Level 1: The Certificate in Financial Record Keeping: This qualification covers the production of business documents and the posting of those items to the books of original entry, the production of a set of double entry accounts to trial balance for both VAT registered and a non-VAT registered business and the reconciliation of the cash book with the bank statement. There is an additional option unit available in cash and credit handling.

Level 2 (Intermediate) Certificate in Manual Book-keeping: This qualification covers the adjustments to the ledger accounts and the production of final accounts for a sole trader with appropriate adjustments. It also requires the candidate to understand the importance of simple credit control procedures.

Level 2 (Intermediate) Certificate in Computerised Book-keeping: This qualification covers the setting up of a computerised book-keeping system, the input of relevant data, the production of final accounts for a sole trader, and the correction of errors made in the posting of transactions. Please note that if candidates wish to apply for Associate Member based on this qualification they must also complete the certificate in Financial Record Keeping.

Level 3 (Advanced) Diploma in Manual/Computerised Book-keeping: This qualification covers some advanced ledger work including the disposal of fixed assets and the calculation of a selection of provisions. It also requires the production of a set of accounts from incomplete records, for a non-profit making organisation, a partnership and a limited company, and a manufacturing account. The accounts should be presented in management form and are not required for publishing.

EXEMPTIONS:

Associate level: RSA/OCR Stage 1 Book-keeping; IAB Intermediate and Foundation Levels only (Grade A/B only), AAT Foundation and Intermediate Levels. For the Computerised route please apply directly to the ICB.

Member Level RSA/ OCR Stage 2 Book-keeping; IAB Final level (Grade A/B only), AAT Technician level.

OTHER AWARDS:

The Certificate in Payroll Management (PMCert); The Diploma in Payroll Management (PMDip.); The Certificate in Payroll Management (PM.Cert.); The Diploma in Payroll Management (PM.Dip.); The Certificate in Small Business Management (BMCert); The Diploma in Small Business Management (BMDip).

THE INSTITUTE OF CHARTERED ACCOUNTANTS IN ENGLAND AND WALES (ICAEW)

Gloucester House
399 Silbury Boulevard
Central Milton Keynes
MK9 2HL
United Kingdom
Tel: 01908 248040
Email: careers@icaew.co.uk
Website: www.icaew.co.uk/careers

The ICAEW is the largest professional Accountancy Body in Europe with over 120,000 members.

MEMBERSHIP:

Associate Chartered Accountant (ACA): Those who have successfully completed formal training and have passed the Institute's professional exams may apply for admission.

Fellow Chartered Accountant (FCA): Associate members of 10 years' standing who satisfy the requirements for continuing professional education are eligible.

TRAINING:

Training is available in public practice and increasingly in industrial/commercial organisations and the public sector. Students train under a formal training contract with an

THE INSTITUTE OF CHARTERED ACCOUNTANTS IN ENGLAND AND WALES (ICAEW)

Student Support, Gloucester House, 399 Silbury Boulevard, Central Milton Keynes MK9 2HL
Tel: 01908 248040, fax: 01908 248006, email: careers@icaew.co.uk,
website: www.icaew.co.uk/careers

The organisation

The Institute of Chartered Accountants in England and Wales (ICAEW) is the largest professional accountancy body in Europe with over 120,000 ACA-qualified members. Half of our members work in public practice and half in industry and commerce.

The ACA (Associate Chartered Accountant) is widely recognised for its prestige and as an excellent foundation for a successful career in business. Each year thousands of graduates choose to train as Chartered Accountants safe in the knowledge that an additional professional business qualification will not only open doors, it will also set them apart from other applicants.

Type of work

Chartered Accountancy is a dynamic, challenging and highly rewarding profession to enter. It offers a diversity of careers in almost every sector of business. The ACA is recognised throughout the world and members hold senior management positions in firms of accountants, commerce and in the public sector.

Most employers will pay for your examination tuition and will allow you a generous amount of study leave. Starting salaries are competitive and vary enormously depending on the size and location of the organisation.

Training and Exams

The training is challenging but the rewards are high. To succeed you'll need an excellent academic track record, determination, and the ability to inspire confidence and trust in colleagues and clients.

Most students enter into a training contract as soon as they are academically qualified to do so. Training consists of a minimum three-year training contract with an authorised training organisation, combining work experience with academic study and exams.

There are two stages of exams: the Professional Stage comprising six papers, and the Advanced Stage involving a Test of Advanced Technical Competence and an Advanced Case Study.

Chartered Accountancy training develops a valuable blend of technical knowledge, communication skills and commercial awareness, not to mention a broad understanding of the legal implications of the work you do. As you progress through your training, you will be exposed to different areas of business, and will gain a better idea of which area you would like to specialise in. Management Consultancy, Corporate Finance, Information Technology, Insolvency, Financial Management and Taxation are just some of the many career options available to qualified ACAs.

Choice, variety, job satisfaction and excellent financial rewards are all within reach when you choose to become a Chartered Accountant with the Institute of Chartered Accountants in England & Wales.

Key information:

Institute of Chartered Accountants in England and Wales (ICAEW)
Student Support, Gloucester House, 399 Silbury Boulevard, Central Milton Keynes MK9 2HL

authorised training office. Training contracts are of between 3 and 5 years' duration.

ELIGIBILITY FOR ENTRY:

Potential students must meet the following minimum entry requirements:
1) At least 2 GCE A levels plus at least 3 GCSEs or equivalent.

QUALIFYING:

Currently, in order to qualify as a Chartered Accountant, students need to complete these elements of training:
1. Practical work experience in a training office authorised by the Institute;
2. Professional examinations (Professional Stage, Advanced Stage).

PROFESSIONAL EXAMINATIONS:

Professional Stage: Subjects covered are Accounting, Financial Reporting, Audit and Assurance, Taxation, Business Finance and Business Management.

Advanced Stage: Subjects covered are Business Advice, Advanced Technical Knowledge, Advanced Business Management, Acquisition and Management of Knowledge, Communications. (These subjects will be assessed in an Advanced Case Study and a Test of Advanced Technical Competence.)

For further information call the Recruitment and Promotion Section on 01908 248108 or e-mail careers@icaew.co.uk. Alternatively view the Institute's website: www.icaew.co.uk/careers

INSTITUTE OF CHARTERED ACCOUNTANTS IN IRELAND

CA House
87/89 Pembroke Road
Dublin 4
Ireland
Tel: 010 3531 6377200
Fax: 010 3531 6680842
Email: ca@icai.ie
Website: www.icai.ie

Membership – Associate (ACA): In order to be eligible for membership, candidates must have completed satisfactorily the requisite period of service under training contract with a recognised training firm, have passed all requisite parts of the Institute Exam up to and including the Final Admitting Exam and also have completed satisfactorily a special practical computer course designed by the Institute as a prerequisite for membership.

For graduates, the normal period of contract is $3\frac{1}{2}$ years, for Post-Graduates 3 years and for non-graduates it is 4 or 5 years depending on entry route selected. Non-graduates seeking entry into a training contract must be at least 17 and have obtained the requisite standard in the GCE/GCSE or Leaving Certificate Exams. Details on request.

To fulfil the requirements of the EU Directive, members going into the practice are required to meet certain criteria before being granted an auditing certificate.

The Institute's exam: The exam is in 3 parts. The syllabus comprises 2 Professional Exams and a Final Admitting Exam. The core subjects throughout the syllabus comprise Business Law, Financial Accounting, Auditing, Management Accounting, Business Finance, Taxation, Information Technology, Financial Management and Business Information Systems.

The Institute places considerable reliance on FT education for its students and, in addition to the facilities available to non-graduates, Postgraduate (leading to the award of Diplomas/Masters degrees) programmes to meet the needs of business and non-business graduates are also available. PT and block-release study during the student's training contract is carried out under the auspices of the Institute's own Centre of Accounting Studies. Training contracts incorporate periods of paid study leave for this purpose.

THE INSTITUTE OF CHARTERED ACCOUNTANTS OF SCOTLAND

CA House
21 Haymarket Yards
Edinburgh
EH12 5BH
United Kingdom
Tel: 0131 347 0161
Fax: 0131 347 0108
Email: caeducation@icas.org.uk
Website: www.icas.org.uk

Member (CA): To qualify a candidate must have completed a 3 year training contract in a training office authorised by the Institute and have passed the Institute's Test of Competence exam (if applicable), Test of Professional Skills and Test of Professional Expertise (compulsory).

CA Student: The minimum entry qualification for CA training is a UK university degree (or equivalent qualification from overseas), or membership of the Association of Accounting Technicians. The Institute distinguishes two categories of degree – fully accredited (degree in accounting which gives exemption from the first-level Test of Competence Course and Exams) and Qualifying (non-relevant degrees). Qualifying graduates take the Institute's Test of Competence Course and Exam during the 1st year of the training contract but may be given single subject exemptions depending on degree content.

EXAMINATIONS:

Test of Competence: The syllabus includes Financial Accounting, Principles of Auditing and Reporting, Business Management, Finance, Business Law. Exam is by multiple-choice and narrative questions. (Fully accredited graduates exempt.)

Test of Professional Skills: The syllabus includes Financial Reporting, Assurance and Business Systems, Advanced Finance, Taxation. Exam is by case studies, narrative and computational questions.

Test of Professional Expertise: One multi-discipline case study designed to test candidates' ability to apply their theoretical knowledge and practical skills to problems of the type likely to be encountered by the newly qualified accountant. Additional syllabus material includes Corporate Planning, Corporate Strategies and Management, Business Improvement, Management of Financial Structures, Ethics.

THE INSTITUTE OF COMPANY ACCOUNTANTS

40 Tyndalls Park Road
Clifton
Bristol
BS8 1PL
United Kingdom
Tel: 0117 9738261
Fax: 0117 9238292

The Institute traces its origins to the year 1923. Associateship is gained only through registered studentship, practical experience and the passing of entrance exams. Although the majority of members occupy positions of responsibility in commerce and education, the Institute has also a highly successful practising arm. Institute practitioners, who are required first to qualify for a practising certificate, specialise in providing accountancy services to smaller businesses and private individuals.

Fellow (FSCA): Associates of at least 3 years' standing, who hold positions of suitable responsibility, may apply for election to Fellowship.

Associate (ASCA): On successful completion of the exams, students with at least 3 years' approved practical experience may apply for admission to Associateship and use the designation **Incorporated Company Accountant**.

Registered Student: one who is studying for the qualifying exams of the Institute. Applicants must have obtained a degree from an approved university; or GCE/GCSE in 5 subjects, including English and Mathematics and 2 at A level, or the equivalent; or by acceptable work experience.

EXAMINATIONS:

The exams are at four levels. The 12 papers comprising Levels 1, 2 and 3 may be attempted in any combination and order. At each diet up to 4 papers may be attempted as allowed by the exam timetable. The 4 papers of Level 4 must be attempted at one diet after all other papers have been passed. Each paper is of 3 hours' duration and there are 4 sittings over 2 days.

Level 1: Financial Accounting 1; Quantitative Techniques; Cost Accounting; Business Law.

Level 2: Economics and the Business Environment; Business Organisation and Management; Information Technology; Taxation 1.

Level 3: Financial Accounting 2; Management Accounting; Company and Partnership Law; General Principles of Auditing and Basic Receivership and Liquidations.

Level 4: Financial Accounting 3; Financial Management or Professional Practice; Internal Auditing; Taxation 2.

Exemptions: Limited exemptions from individual subjects at Levels 1, 2 and 3 may be available in respect of passes at comparable professional exams or through relevant work experience. No exemptions granted at Level 4.

INSTITUTE OF COST AND EXECUTIVE ACCOUNTANTS

Akhtar House
2 Shepherds Bush Road
London
W6 7PJ
United Kingdom
Tel: 020 8749 7126
Fax: 020 8749 7127
Email: icea@enta.net
Website: www.icea.enta.net

Fellow (FCEA): Applicants are required to pass the Institute's exam, be at least 21 and have at least 5 years' experience with competence. No one is granted exemption from the Fellowship exam.

Associate (ACEA): Applicants must pass the Institute's exams or equivalent, be at least 20 and have had 4 years' appropriate experience and competence as required by NCVQ.

Technician (TCA): The Certificate of Technician in Costing and Accounting is issued to those applicants who passed the Associateship Level I and Level II exams and have had appropriate experience for at least 3 years and competence as required by NCVQ.

CMA: The Institute will issue the Certificate in Management Accountancy to a member, Fellow or Associate, who holds the position of a financial executive, controller or director of a standing organisation approved by the Council, has completed the Institute's training course and is at least 30.

DipEMA: Diploma in Executive and Management Accountancy is restricted to Fellows of the Institute who must pass the Diploma Exam. The Diploma Holder, subject to the standard of achievement being acceptable, will get the opportunity to register with several British Universities to study for MA, MSc, MBA and then PhD in accountancy. Many overseas universities give preference to diploma holders for postgraduate study.

DipEF: Diploma in Executive Finance for non-accountants is designed for executives who are not accountants or do not have any accounting qualifications. This diploma provides non-accountant executives with the background knowledge and awareness of financial terms which will assist them to understand financial information and to communicate effectively with financial personnel.

Registered Students: Only registered students may sit the exam. The applicant must be 18 and have 5 GCE or GCSE passes, including 2 at A level or equivalent or 3 years' experience in accounting, costing or allied work. The Institute recognises appropriate NCVQ qualifications for admission and for exemption.

The Institute has a 4-part exam syllabus, consisting of 4 papers in each part. The Associateship Levels 1, 2 and 3 are equiv. to degree standard, whereas Fellowship is equiv. to honours degree standard of the British universities. The Institute's qualifications are recognised by the Local Government Management Board for appointments. The Institute issues a 'Practising Certificate' for its practising members, covered by professional indemnity insurance and under the control of the professional and ethical guide for members, registered with the Office of Fair Trading.

THE INSTITUTE OF FINANCIAL ACCOUNTANTS

Burford House
44 London Road
Sevenoaks
Kent
TN13 1AS
United Kingdom
Tel: 01732 458080
Fax: 01732 455848
Email: mail@ifa.org.uk
Website: www.ifa.org.uk

The Institute of Financial Accountants, established in 1916, is the largest professional body of its type in the world. It represents members and students in more than eighty countries and provides a qualification and continuous professional development for those who want to become financial accountants. It sets standards within the profession, both technically and ethically. Financial Accountants are employed in senior positions within industry, commerce and practice. They are professionals who take an active role in financial management.

EXAMINATION STRUCTURE:

Pre-Professional: Financial Accounting 1, Cost Accounting, Business Law & Business Taxation.
Associate Membership: Financial Accounting 2, Management Accounting, Management Information Systems & Principles of Management.
Fellow Membership: Advanced Financial Accounting, Financial Management & Strategic Management.

ENTRY REQUIREMENTS:

The following qualifications will be accepted for admission to the Pre-professional Level: 4 GCSEs including English Language and a quantitative subject plus one A level or Scottish Higher in an academic subject, NVQ3 in Accounting, GNVQ Advanced, BTEC National Certificate/Diploma, SCOTVEC National Certificate, or IAB Final Examination. Students over 21 with at least 4 years' relevant experience may be admitted to the pre-professional level.

EXEMPTIONS:

Pre-professional level: HNC Business and Finance with the relevant 'pathway' or non-relevant degree.
Associate Membership level: HNC 2/HND 2 Business and Finance (Management Accounting and Financial Accounting modules must be taken from the financial 'pathway'), Business degree with Financial and Management Accounting modules, AAT Technician Level, S/NVQ4 in Accounting, CIMA Stage 2 or ACCA Papers 1–6.
Fellow Membership level: Accounting Degree, CIMA stage 3 or ACCA Certificate.

MEMBERSHIP:

Associate: A person shall be eligible for admission as an Associate member when he/she has passed either the Associate Level of professional examinations, or received exemption.
Fellow: A person shall be eligible for admission as a Fellow when, in addition to five years' experience in a senior accountancy capacity, he/she has passed the Fellowship exams, or has received exemptions.

INSTITUTE OF INTERNAL AUDITORS – UK AND IRELAND

13 Abbeville Mews
88 Clapham Park Road
London
SW4 7BX
United Kingdom
Tel: 020 7498 0101
Fax: 020 7978 2492
Email: info@iia.org.uk
Website: www.iia.org.uk

The Institute of Internal Auditors – UK and Ireland is the only body whose prime objectives are to represent all internal auditors and to further the profession of internal auditing.
Entry to full membership is through professional qualifications achieved through examinations.

EXAMINATIONS:

The syllabus covers every aspect of the discipline of internal auditing proving a broad coverage of management, accounting and finance, with a detailed study of the corporate control process and the means of monitoring that process.
PIIA – the practitioner level, which covers: Organisation and Management – Concepts and Practices, Accounting and Financial Systems, Internal Auditing, Business Information Systems, Auditing and Corporate Governance and Risk Management.
MIIA – the professional level, which covers: Advanced Management, Financial Management and Business Analysis, Advanced Information Systems, Auditing and Advanced Internal Auditing.
The **QICA** specialist qualification in computer auditing. The QICA qualification comprises two levels each with its own examination paper. The first level examination paper is Business Information Systems Auditing and the second level paper is Specialist Information Systems Auditing.

INTERNATIONAL ASSOCIATION OF BOOK-KEEPERS

Burford House
44 London Road
Sevenoaks
Kent
TN13 1AS
United Kingdom
Tel: 01732 458080
Fax: 01732 455848
Email: mail@iab.org.uk
Website: www.iab.org.uk

The IAB is the longest established professional body for book-keeping. It was formed in 1973, and is committed to maintaining the highest standards in book-keeping. It holds its examinations in over 90 countries throughout the world.
The IAB's qualifications are wholly relevant to individuals working at the first levels of financial accountancy. The syllabuses and examinations are constantly updated to meet current business needs.

MEMBERSHIP:

Fellowship (FIAB): After successful completion of the exam requirements, or their equivalent, and 2 or more years' practical book-keeping experience in a senior capacity. Fellows are entitled to use the designation **Registered Book-keeper**.
Membership (MIAB): After successful completion of the Intermediate examination or its equivalent.

EXAMINATIONS:

The Association offers examinations at three levels, *Foundation, Intermediate and Final*. The exams are open access; therefore anyone of any experience or qualifications may become a registered student to allow them to study towards the Association's examinations. The exam structure is aimed at giving students a practical knowledge of book-keeping and accounting skills.

The Association also offers a:

Diploma in Computerised Book-keeping, which is an assessment of book-keeping skills using accountancy software; **Diploma in Small Business Financial Management**, which covers the basic records and requirements of a small business and how that information may be used to control the business; **Diploma in Payroll Administration**, which covers all aspects of payroll, including the requirements of the Inland Revenue.

EXEMPTIONS:

Foundation: Holders of RSA Stage 1 & 2 Practical Book-keeping, SCOTVEC Financial Record Keeping 1, 2 & 3, NVQ 2 in Accounting or equivalent qualifications in Book-keeping or Accounts. Candidates who have attained the age of 19 and have at least three years' approved book-keeping experience may also be exempt.

Intermediate: Holders of GCSE Accounting (grades A–C), RSA Book-keeping & Accounts Level II, LCCI Book-keeping or Accounts.

Final: Holders of RSA Book-keeping & Accounts Level III, LCCI Book-keeping & Accounts Higher, A level Accounting (grades A–C) or their equivalent in Book-keeping and Accounts.

Advertising and Public Relations

COMMUNICATION ADVERTISING AND MARKETING EDUCATION FOUNDATION

Abford House
15 Wilton Road
London
SW1V 1NJ
United Kingdom
Tel: 020 7828 7506
Fax: 020 7976 5140
Email: info@camfoundation.com
Website: www.camfoundation.com

CAM is the examining body for the principal UK trade and professional associations of the marketing communication industry. The CAM qualifications are industry examined and controlled, developing candidates' careers by giving the essential practical skills and knowledge. Candidates may study through a UK network of colleges providing FT, PT, evening, intensive and distance-learning options.

WHAT THE QUALIFICATIONS COVER:

Advanced Diploma in Communication Studies: This is broad based and can be regarded as an induction for those who work in the marketing communication industry. To achieve the qualification candidates study, and must pass, the following 6 subjects: Marketing; Advertising; Public Relations; Media; Direct Marketing and Sales Promotion; Research and Consumer Behaviour. (An Advanced Certificate is awarded for each subject passed.)

Higher Diploma in Integrated Marketing Communication: This is management orientated for those wishing to develop their career to senior practitioner level. All candidates must pass the Higher Certificate in Management and Strategy and the Higher Certificate in Planning, Implementation and Evaluation. CAM also offers specialist Higher Diploma options in Advertising, Public Relations, Direct Marketing and Sales Promotion.

Entry Requirements: All candidates applying for **Advanced Diploma** registration must be at least 18 years of age and have a minimum of 5 GCSEs including Maths and English at grade C or above, or the equivalent qualifications. Where English is not the first language, evidence of English language competence to IELTS 6.5 is required. Those with industry experience but without formal qualifications may apply through discussion with the Registrar.

Entrance to the **Higher Diploma** is normally by completion of the Advanced Diploma. Experienced practitioners may gain direct entry if they can prove their experience and competence.

Exemptions: Applications for exemptions from one or more Advanced Certificate modules are considered on the basis of previous educational qualifications that substantially cover the CAM syllabi.

Qualifications: On successful completion of the Advanced Diploma, candidates can apply for Associate membership of the CAM Foundation and use the designation **AmCAM**. On completion of the Higher Diploma candidates can apply for full membership of the CAM Foundation and use the designation **MCAM**. Honorary Fellowships (**FCAM**) are only awarded to those who have made an outstanding contribution to the marketing communication industry.

National Vocational Qualifications (NVQs): (at Levels 3 and 4) for Advertising, Direct Marketing and Public Relations were launched at the end of 1994. (Those for Sales Promotion are expected to follow.) To meet the special requirements for awarding NVQs CAM has entered into an agreement with the RSA Examinations Board and formed a new Joint Organisation which has now been accredited.

INSTITUTE OF PRACTITIONERS IN ADVERTISING

44 Belgrave Square
London
SW1X 8QS
United Kingdom
Tel: 020 7235 7020
Fax: 020 7245 9904
Email: mark@ipa.co.uk
Website: http://www.ipa.co.uk

Fellow (FIPA): Fellows are elected by the Council from among Members of at least 5 years' standing and after outstanding service to advertising.

Member (MIPA): Those eligible as Members must satisfy the IPA's Council that they have obtained and can evidence a minimum of 3 year's Continuous Professional Development (CPD) accreditation as recognised by the Institute, and that they continue to meet these requirements. In addition, all applicants must be endorsed by the Chief Executive, or equivalent, from the member-agency concerned.

Agencies involved in the creating and/or placing of advertising and marketing communications are admitted as Incorporated Practitioners in Advertising. As the Institute is the trade and professional organisation solely for advertising and marketing communications agencies, only people working in member-agencies of the Institute are eligible to apply for personal membership.

THE INSTITUTE OF PUBLIC RELATIONS

The Old Trading House
15 Northburgh Street
London
EC1V 0PR
United Kingdom
Tel: 020 7253 5151
Fax: 020 7490 0588
Email: info@ipr.org.uk
Website: www.ipr.org.uk

Membership criteria
Member (MIPR): Members hold the IPR Diploma in Public Relations
or, have four years' experience in public relations and an approved IPR qualification
or, have six years' experience in public relations and commit to provide a twelve-month CPD record one-year after joining
or, have ten years' experience in public relations

Associate (AMIPR): Associates hold the Advanced Certificate in Public Relations
or, hold an IPR approved qualification
or, have three years' experience in public relations.

Affiliate: Open to individuals who are working or interested in public relations or who are carrying out a specialist role in public relations, and do not qualify for any other grade of membership. Applications must be accompanied by a full CV or career history.

Affiliate Studying: Open to full-time students in the UK studying non-IPR approved qualifications who wish to keep up to date with developments in the PR industry and use IPR membership services.

Student: Individuals who, at the time of application, are registered on an IPR approved qualification.

LONDON SCHOOL OF PUBLIC RELATIONS

David Game House
69 Notting Hill Gate
London
W11 3JS
United Kingdom
Tel: 020 7221 3399
Fax: 020 7243 1730
Email: lsp@easynet.co.uk
Website: www.pr-school-london.com

Provides training for those wishing to enter public relations as a career or for those already in PR or an information/communications job who require some formal training. The Diploma issued by the School is a heavyweight introduction for graduates and is backed by leading consultancies.

Courses on offer: An Integrated Approach to Public Relations (15 wk evening Diploma).

An Advisory Board of Fellows of the Institute of PR act to monitor course standards and the setting of exam papers. The course is also recognised by the National Union of Journalists (NUJ). The School is a recognised training provider by the Public Relations Consultants Association (PRCA).

the Institute of Public Relations

INSTITUTE OF PUBLIC RELATIONS

The Old Trading House, 15 Northburgh Street, London EC1V 0PR
Tel: +44 (0)20 7253 5151, fax: +44 (0)20 7490 0588, email: Info@ipr.org.uk, website: www.ipr.org.uk

Public relations is the discipline which looks after reputation, with the aim of earning understanding and support and influencing opinion and behaviour. It is the planned and sustained effort to establish and maintain goodwill and mutual understanding between an organisation and its public.

Public relations encompasses many different types of activities and like many jobs you will realise your suitability through experience. However, certain qualities are required; these include, among others, ability to counsel management, analyse management needs, identify causes of problems, plan and organise tasks and communicate effectively with others, as well as having common sense, energy, creativity, organisational skills and of course literacy.

The Institute of Public Relations (IPR) is the UK's leading public relations industry professional body. Founded in February 1948, it today has over 7000 members.

The IPR is the largest association of its kind in Europe. It is a member of the European PR federation CERP (Confédération Européenne des Relations Publiques) and a founding member of the Global Alliance for Public Relations and Communications Management.

The Institute is about developing skills, raising awareness, rewarding excellence, supporting members and giving public relations a voice at the highest levels. We frequently speak at national and international conferences, provide comments to the press and take an active part in influencing new regulation concerning the industry, both nationally and internationally.

We're specialists in PR training and experts on conference management and seminars. In addition we offer the post-graduate vocational IPR Diploma and Foundation courses in public relations, and approve PR courses at undergraduate and postgraduate level at universities throughout the UK.

The IPR's main aims are;

- To provide a professional structure for the practice of public relations;
- To enhance the ability and status of our members as professional practitioners;
- To represent and serve the professional interests of our members;
- To provide opportunities for members to meet and exchange views and ideas;
- To raise standards within the profession through the promotion of best practice – including the production of best practice guides, case studies, training events and our continuous professional development scheme 'Developing Excellence'.

As a member of the IPR you will have access to a wide range of free services and discounts on products of professional and personal benefit. These include; regularly being kept up to date with PR issues, networking opportunities with others in your business and support for you and your career development.

Types of Membership – Six grades of membership (Fellow, member, associate, affiliate, affiliate studying and student)

Qualification required/supplied – IPR Diploma, IPR Advanced Certificate, IPR approved courses

Institute of Public Relations
The Old Trading House,
15 Northburgh Street, London EC1V 0PR
Tel: +44 (0)20 7253 5151
Fax: +44 (0)20 7490 0588
Email: Info@ipr.org.uk   Web site: www.ipr.org.uk

Aeronautical Engineering

THE ROYAL AERONAUTICAL SOCIETY
4 Hamilton Place
Hyde Park Corner
London
W1J 7BQ
United Kingdom
Tel: 020 7670 4300
Fax: 020 7499 6230
Email: iain.mackrory-jamieson@raes.org.uk
Website: www.aerosociety.com

The Royal Aeronautical Society is the focal point for today's global aerospace community. Founded in 1866 to further the science of Aeronautics, the Royal Aeronautical Society has been at the forefront of developments in aerospace ever since. Today, the Royal Aeronautical Society works on it's members behalf to *promote the highest professional standards in all aerospace disciplines; provide specialist information and act as a central forum for the exchange of ideas; and play a leading role in influencing opinion on aviation matters.* As a nominated body of the Engineering Council it is also able to nominate suitably qualified engineers for registration in all three sections of the Register.

CORPORATE MEMBERSHIP:

Fellow (FRAeS): Must have the qualifications necessary for Membership, have made outstanding contributions in the profession, attained a position of high responsibility or have had long experience of high quality.

Member (MRAeS): Must be over 25 yrs of age, have passed an approved exam (normally of the level of a UK Honours degree), and have a minimum of 4 years' experience, including 2 years training and 2 years in a position of responsibility. Alternatively, a person without a degree is eligible to become a Member on reaching 35 if that person can demonstrate adequate additional experience and responsibilities within the aerospace industry.

NON-CORPORATE MEMBERSHIP:

Companion (CRAeS): Applicants must be the calibre for Fellowship but do not, for one reason or another, meet the requirements for that grade.

Associate Member (AMRAeS): Must be over 23, have passed an approved exam (eg BTEC HNC) and had a minimum of 5 years' satisfactory experience of which 2 years have been devoted to practical training. A person of at least 30 yrs of age, with 10 years' relevant experience may also be eligible for Associate Membership if they can demonstrate adequate additional experience and responsibilities within the aerospace industry. Alternatively, a graduate who has completed the training for full membership may also join at this level.

Associate (ARAeS): Applicants must be over 21 years of age, have passed an approved qualification and have had a minimum of 3 years' satisfactory experience of which 2 years have been devoted to practical training.

Graduate (GradRAeS): Applicants must be between the ages of 21 and 32. They must have an academic qualification acceptable for Corporate membership.

Student: Applicants must be in full-time education and have the objective of becoming engaged in the profession of aeronautics.

Affiliate: This class is open to those ineligible for other classes but who are associated with or have an interest in aeronautics.

Agricultural Engineering

BRITISH AGRICULTURAL AND GARDEN MACHINERY ASSOCIATION
14–16 Church Street
Rickmansworth
Hertfordshire
WD3 1RQ
United Kingdom
Tel: 01923 720241
Fax: 01923 896063
Email: info@bagma.com
Website: www.bagma.com

BAGMA Management Diploma: The course is designed to introduce potential and junior managers in agricultural and garden machinery dealerships to the modern management skills needed to operate a successful business.

Part A: 1. Financial Aspects: Cost Accounting, Management Accounting, Financial Planning and Control; 2. Legal Aspects: The Law of Contract, Torts of Importance in Business, Business and Transport Law.

Part B: Dealership Management Functions and Services: General, Sales and Personnel Management, Marketing and Stock Control.

After the conclusion of the course candidates will also be required to attend an interview with the Diploma Board and to submit a project on a case study.

BAGMA have also published Occupational Standards for Service Engineering which have recently been accredited by QCA as NVQ Level 2 and 3 for Agricultural and Garden Machinery retail trades. BAGMA have also developed National Traineeships for service and partsales staff and a Modern Apprenticeship for service engineers. Supervisors of the future are likely to have come through the NT/MA route, both of which include N/SVQ qualifications and key skills.

THE INSTITUTION OF AGRICULTURAL ENGINEERS

West End Road
Silsoe
Bedford
MK45 4DU
United Kingdom
Tel: 01525 861096
Fax: 01525 861660
Email: secretary@iagre.org
Website: www.iagre.org

CORPORATE MEMBERS:
Fellow (FIAgrE); Member (MIAgrE).

NON-CORPORATE MEMBERS:
Associate Member (AMIAgrE); Associate (AIgrE)

ENGINEERING COUNCIL REGISTRATION:
Members with appropriate academic qualifications, training and experience are eligible to apply to the Institution for Eng Council registration as Chartered Engineer, Incorporated Engineer or Engineering Technician. Full particulars of requirements for membership are obtainable from the Secretariat.

Agriculture and Horticulture

THE INSTITUTE OF HORTICULTURE

14/15 Belgrave Square
London
SW1X 8PS
United Kingdom
Tel: 020 7245 6943
Fax: 020 7245 6943
Email: ioh@horticulture.org.uk
Website: www.horticulture.org.uk

Membership of the Institute affords recognition of professional status and achievement in horticulture. Membership is available to those working wholly or substantially in horticulture (or in a branch of science or arts directly linked with horticulture) and having the appropriate combination of qualifications and experience. There are membership grades to match the successive stages reached in the career progression of all horticulturists.

Fellowship (FIHort): Attained by nomination and election by those Members who have made an outstanding contribution to horticulture.
Corporate Membership (MIHort): Open to those who have reached a high level either by qualification or achievement in a particular field of experience. The qualification expected is a university degree, Botanic Gardens Diploma, MHort (RHS), HND, NVQ Level 4 or ND with suitable experience.
Associate Membership: Open to holders of an ND, C&G Phase III or IV, RHS Diploma, NVQ Level 3 or C&G Phase I or II, but with considerable industry experience.
Affiliate Membership: Granted to those whose main occupation or involvement is in horticulture, but who are not yet deemed eligible to become an Associate or Corporate Member.
Student Membership: Available for those studying for horticultural qualifications.
Qualifying Exams
The Institute does not have its own exams, but expects Members to have obtained qualifications in horticulture or highly related subjects either from a university or from a horticultural college. The Institute can provide details of universities and colleges that offer appropriate courses.

Arbitration

THE CHARTERED INSTITUTE OF ARBITRATORS

International Arbitration Centre
12 Boomsbury Square
London
WCA 2LP
United Kingdom
Tel: 020 7421 7446
Fax: 020 7404 4023
Email: info@arbitrators.org
Website: www.arbitrators.org

The Institute exists to promote and facilitate the settlement of disputes by arbitration and alternative dispute resolution.
Associate (ACIArb): Associates shall: (a) satisfy the Council that he/she is in all respects a fit and proper person for admission to the Institute; (b) be engaged in a profession, occupation or calling in which recourse to arbitration is directly or indirectly involved; (c) be not less than 21; (d) possess a general standard of education conforming with the requirements of the Council; and (e) (i) have passed Part I of the exam of the Institute, or (ii) have passed any other exam accepted by the Council as the equivalent, or (iii) have such knowledge and experience of the law and

practice of arbitration as the Council may approve.

Member (MCIArb): Members shall be elected by the Council and every candidate for election shall: (a) be an Associate of the Institute and be not less than 25 years of age; (b) satisfy the Council that he/she is in all respects a suitable person for election as a Member; (c) either have passed or been exempted from Part I of the examinations or assessment of the Institute and have passed Part II or any other examination accepted by the Council as the equivalent to Part II. Alternatively the person may be a full member of another association of arbitrators or practitioners of alternative means of dispute resolution which has standards of knowledge of arbitration and alternative dispute resolution law, practice and procedure which are in the opinion of the Council equivalent to those of the Institute for election to membership and satisfy the Council that he/she has achieved those standards.

Fellow (FCIArb): Fellows shall be elected by the Council and every candidate shall: (a) be a member of the Institute and be not less than 35 years of age; (b) satisfy the Council that he/she is in all respects a suitable person for election as a Fellow; (c) have completed and passed the Institute's personal assessment for Fellowship to the satisfaction of the Council; (d) have passed or been exempted from Part I of the examinations of the Institute and Part II of the examinations of the Institute and have passed or been exempted from Part III of the examinations of the Institute and thereafter have completed and passed the Assessment for Fellowship Programme to the satisfaction of the Council. Upon election to Fellowship by the Council of the Institute, in accordance with (a) and (e) above, the member will be entitled to describe himself as a 'Chartered Arbitrator'.

Individual Affiliate/Corporate Affiliate: The Council may elect a person who is not professionally qualified but has an interest in arbitration.

Retired Member: Associates, Members and Fellows, on reaching the age of 60, who are not practising in any occupation directly or indirectly concerned with arbitration, may request to be transferred.

Honorary Member: The Council may elect a person of eminence for services rendered to the Institute and/or arbitration.

Archaeology

THE INSTITUTE OF FIELD ARCHAEOLOGISTS

University of Reading
2 Earley Gate, PO Box 239
Reading
RG6 6AU
United Kingdom
Tel: 0118 9316446
Fax: 0118 9316448
Email: admin@ifa.virgin.net
Website: www.archaeologists.net

Member (MIFA): Open to graduate members with at least 3 years' continuous experience who can demonstrate they have satisfactorily exercised responsibility for a substantial archaeological project. Also open to non-graduates and those with a non-relevant degree whose experience and achievements are considered to confer equivalent qualification.

Associate (AIFA): Open to graduate members with at least 12 months' continuous experience who can demonstrate they have satisfactorily exercised delegated or part responsibility for a substantial archaeological project. Also open to non-graduates and those with a non-relevant degree whose experience and achievements are considered to confer equivalent qualification.

Practitioner (PIFA): Open to graduate members with at least 6 months' experience in field archaeology. Also open to non-graduates and those with a non-relevant degree whose experience and achievements are considered to confer equivalent qualification.

Affiliate: Open to those studying archaeology or actively involved in field archaeology who support the Institute's aims and activities.

EXAMINATIONS:

Candidates for all categories of membership must agree to abide by the Institute's Code of Conduct and are examined on the basis of documented evidence of academic qualifications, experience, levels of responsibility held, and demonstrable achievements (e.g. publications), supported by references from appropriate referees. There is a formal appeals procedure.

Architecture

ARCHITECTS REGISTRATION BOARD

8 Weymouth Street
London
W1W 5BU
United Kingdom
Tel: 020 7580 5861
Fax: 020 7436 5269
Email: info@arb.org.uk

The Architects Registration Board is the regulatory body for architects in the United Kingdom. Only those individuals registered with the Architects Registration Board can use the title architect. In order to be admitted to the Register, it is necessary to have passed recognised exams at a school of architecture in the UK and to have obtained at least two years' practical training experience working under the supervision of an architect. Provision also exists for entry onto the Register for those with non-UK qualifications in architecture and practical training experience.

ASSOCIATION OF BUILDING ENGINEERS

Lutyens House
Billing Brook Road
Weston Favell
Northampton
NN3 8NW
United Kingdom
Tel: 01604 404121
Fax: 01604 784220
Email: building.engineers@abe.org.uk
Website: www.abe.org.uk

The Association was founded in 1925 under the name of The Incorporated Association of Architects and Surveyors and is the professional body for those specialising in the technology of building.

Fellow (FBEng): Must not be less than 32 years of age and must have held a senior appointment in the construction industry for a period of at least 5 years.

Member (MBEng): Graduates holding an accredited classified Honours degree on satisfying the ABE Evaluation of Professional Competence (EPC). Exemption from the EPC is granted to corporate members of certain related professional bodies and to those over 35 years of age, holding a responsible position in a relevant organisation, having substantial experience, who satisfy an interview panel.

Graduate Member (Grad BEng): Must have at least one year's relevant experience and hold an accredited degree or one with classified Honours in a relevant discipline.

Associate Member (ABEng): Must have at least 2 years' experience in a professional office and hold a qualification of an academic standard not less than that of a BTEC HNC in Construction.

Student: Open to those enrolled on approved courses of study leading to MBEng.

NB **Corporate Members (Fellows and Members)** are eligible to register as professional engineer (PEng) with the Society of Professional Engineers and thus entitled to register with the Union Internationale des Ingenieurs Professionnels and use the designation Ingenieur Professionnel Européen (IngPEur).

BRITISH INSTITUTE OF ARCHITECTURAL TECHNOLOGISTS

397 City Road
London
EC1V 1NH
United Kingdom
Tel: 0800 731 5471
Fax: 020 7837 3194
Email: careers@biat.org.uk
Website: www.biat.org.uk

Member (MBIAT): Open to those applicants who satisfy the Institute that they meet its academic and professional requirements. This grade is only open to those upgrading from Profile, Technician or Associate membership. Standard route: to have obtained a degree in Architectural Technology or in a technically based subject in the Built Environment or an approved HNC/HND in Building Studies including the design options or an alternative BIAT approved higher-level qualification. Must then have completed a Professional and occupational performance record under supervision of an approved supervisor and have passed a professional interview.

Associate (ABIAT): Open to all applicants who have obtained a qualification as listed in the standard route above.

Technician (TBIAT): Open to all applicants who have successfully completed the appropriate professional and occupational performance record and are not self employed.

Profile Membership: Open to applicants with non-standard qualifications or who are self-employed.

Student Membership: Open to all further and higher education students following an approved course and to school students following relevant GCSEs and A levels or GNVQs, who intend to pursue a career in architectural technology.

ROYAL INSTITUTE OF BRITISH ARCHITECTS
66 Portland Place
London
W1B 1AD
United Kingdom
Tel: 0906 302 0400 (calls cost 50p per minute)
Fax: 0207 631 1802
Email: info@inst.riba.org
Website: www.architecture.com

Non-Corporate Membership – Student: Candidates may enrol as a Student member if they are bona fide students of Architecture studying for the RIBA Exam in Architecture or for an exam providing exemption from the RIBA Exam.

Corporate Membership: A person may qualify for election if he/she has passed or received exemption from Parts 1 and 2 of the RIBA Examination in Architecture and the RIBA Exam in Professional Practice, or has obtained a qualification in architecture outside the UK which in the opinion of the admission panel indicates possession of the requisite knowledge and experience of architectural practice. The designation **FRIBA (Fellow)** and **ARIBA (Associate)** are still used but only by those who were members of the Institute before the present charter came into effect in 1971. It is now more common for members of the Institute to use the suffix RIBA, as there is now only one class of corporate membership.

Honorary Membership: By election.

Subscriber Membership: Open to anyone with a personal or professional interest in architecture and who is ineligible for corporate or student membership.

EXAMINATIONS:

The RIBA recognises courses at 36 schools of architecture. All students must spend at least 2 years in practical training in addition to the academic course before qualifying for RIBA membership. One year of this must be after completing the course, but the other year is generally taken in the middle of the course. Most schools provide a year's break after the third academic session. The final year of the practical training must be spent in an architect's office, but the first practical training period can be spent in other sectors of the building industry such as with contractors, manufacturers, quantity surveyors, engineers, and planners. At least one of the practical training years must normally be spent in a UK architectural practice.

Min entry requirements to the RIBA course:

The General Certificate of Education (England, Wales, Northern Ireland): Candidates should have at least 5 GCSE passes and 2 academic A level passes, or 1 subject at A level with 2 AS levels of the GCE. This is a min, and is no guarantee for admission to every school of architecture, many of which will demand higher entrance qualifications and ask for specific A levels. Both the GCE A level subjects should be drawn from the academic field of study. English, Mathematics, Physics and Chemistry are considered to be core subjects. Students with BTEC (or SCOTVEC) Certificate in Building Studies may be considered if they also have GCSE English Language. Some schools may also require 3 additional subjects to include Mathematics. In Scotland the qualifications are similar, except that at least 3 subjects must be passed at Higher grade and 2 at Ordinary grade. Those without A level art would be expected to prepare a portfolio.

Universities with a recognised course of architecture: Robert Gordon University, Aberdeen; University of Bath; The Queen's University of Belfast; *University of Central England in Birmingham; *University of Brighton; University of Cambridge; University of Wales College of Cardiff; *De Montfort University, Leicester; University of Dundee; Heriot-Watt University, Edinburgh; University of Edinburgh; University of Strathclyde, Glasgow; *Glasgow University and Glasgow School of Art; University of Huddersfield; *University of Humberside; *Leeds Metropolitan University; University of Liverpool; *Liverpool John Moore's University; University College London; University of East London; *University of Greenwich, London; *Kingston University, London; *University of North London; *South Bank University, London; University of Westminster, London; University of Manchester; University of Newcastle upon Tyne; University of Nottingham; Oxford Brookes University, Oxford; University of Plymouth; University of Portsmouth; University of the West of England and the University of Sheffield.
* PT courses available.

Other recognised schools of architecture: Canterbury School of Architecture, Kent Institute of Art and Design; Architectural Association, London; School of Architecture and Interior Design, Royal College of Art, London (Part 2 exemption only).

The *Description and Regulations* (for the RIBA Exam in Architecture) contains details of the external exam syllabus and may be purchased from the RIBA Education Department. Further information can be found in the careers section of the website.

Art and Design

THE ASSOCIATION OF BRITISH PICTURE RESTORERS

PO Box 32
Hayling Island
PO11 9WE
United Kingdom
Tel: 023 9246 5115
Fax: 023 9246 5115
Email: apbrlondon@aol.com
Website: www.abpr.co.uk

MEMBERSHIP:

Fellowship: Open to practising picture restorers whose work and studio have been examined by the Council of the Association and found to be of a sufficiently high standard.
Associate Membership: Open to practising picture restorers who are in agreement with the aims of the Association. Students of picture restoration may belong as Associate members at a reduced subscription.

EXAMINATIONS:

Before an application is approved the applicant must have at least 7 years' full-time experience. After approval of the application and when the applicant has sufficient work for consideration, two members of the Council visit the applicant's studio to assess both work in progress and finished work. They then report to the Council, which comes to a decision on whether or not to admit the applicant as a Fellow of the ABPR. Although the main emphasis will be on assessing their ability, the examiner will also be considering the applicant's attitude, background knowledge, studio and past experience.

THE CHARTERED SOCIETY OF DESIGNERS

5 Bermondsey Exchange
179–181 Bermondsey Street
London
SE1 3UW
United Kingdom
Tel: 020 7831 9777
Fax: 020 7831 6277
Email: csd@.org.uk

Corporate membership of the Society is a recognised professional qualification and entitles members to use the affix **Fellow (FCSD):** Granted to members who have had at least 5 years' standing and whose work demonstrates a high degree of competence. Fellowship may also be offered to designers of distinction, or to others appropriately qualified, who are not already Society members and who have had at least 7 years' practice or experience.
Member (MCSD): Open to all practising designers who have had at least 4 years' practice or experience and who have the necessary standard of education and professional competence. Evidence of technical skill and creative ability in one or more of the Society's recognised categories of membership must be submitted. Candidates are assessed by interview together with submission of a portfolio of relevant work.
Graduate Membership: On the completion of an accredited degree or BTEC HND course in Design, students are eligible for Graduate Membership of the Society without assessment interview. Candidates for Graduate Membership who do not have approved qualifications must submit for an assessment interview. There is no affix.
Student Membership: Open to all students following a degree or BTEC HND course in Design.

D&AD (BRITISH DESIGN & ART DIRECTION)

9 Graphite Square
Vauxhall Walk
London
SE11 5EE
United Kingdom
Tel: 020 7840 1111
Fax: 020 7840 0840
Email: info@dandad.co.uk
Website: www.dandad.org

Founded in 1962, D&AD is a professional association and educational charity with a membership of more than 2000, working on behalf of the design and advertising communities. Our mission is to set creative standards, educate and inspire the next creative generation and promote the importance of good design and advertising to business as a whole.

MEMBERSHIP:

Full: This category is open to creatives whose work is judged to be of sufficiently high standard to be included in the D&AD Annual. Full members take an active part in running the organisation, elect the Executive and form part of D&AD's constitution. They are drawn from a wide range of disciplines and include art directors, copywriters, designers, photographers, typographers and illustrators.
Associate: This is open to those who are not actively employed in a creative design or advertising function, but are recognised as encouraging and supporting D&AD aims and ideas. Typically Associate members are clients, educators, or are involved in the management

of creative projects – for example, marketing or account directors.

New Blood: This is open to students and young creatives who have successfully completed one of our education programmes, ie the advertising and design workshops and the Student Awards. Creatives whose work is featured on the D&AD Getty Images Bloodbank are also eligible to become New Blood members.

D&AD also offers workshops, Students Awards, and a Professional Development programme (up to 18 months) which allows individuals to work towards their IPA Continuous Professional Development in Advertising.

THE ROYAL ACADEMY SCHOOLS

Royal Academy of Arts
Burlington House
Piccadilly
London
W1V 0DS
United Kingdom
Tel: 020 7300 5920
Fax: 020 7300 5856
Website: www.royalacademy.org.uk

Prospectus orderline tel: 020 7300 5857
The RA Schools award the Royal Academy Schools Postgraduate Diploma **(PGDipRA)**. The course lasts for 3 years FT in Fine Art, Painting or Sculpture. Candidates for the postgraduate course must have a BA Hons degree or a university degree in Fine Art.

Astronomy and Space Science

THE BRITISH INTERPLANETARY SOCIETY

27–29 South Lambeth Road
London
SW8 1SZ
United Kingdom
Tel: 020 7735 3160
Fax: 020 7820 1504
Email: bis.bis@virgin.net
Website: bis-spaceflight.com

The Society bases its requirements for its Fellowship grade on recognised professional and scholastic qualifications. Its Membership grade is open to all persons interested in space or astronautics.

Fellows (FBIS): Fellowship is a Corporate Membership grade of the Society and is open to suitably qualified persons. Election to Fellow may be based on one of the following: an outstanding contribution to the work of the Society or to Astronautics or, 5 years' continuous membership at the time of application and additionally either a relevant university degree in Science, Mathematics, Engineering or Medicine plus 5 years' relevant scientific, technical or other professional experience; or at least 10 years' relevant scientific, technical or other professional experience.

Members (non-Corporate Grade): No special qualifications are required.

ROYAL ASTRONOMICAL SOCIETY

Burlington House
Piccadilly
London
W1J 0BQ
United Kingdom
Tel: 020 7734 4582/3307
Fax: 020 7494 0166
Email: info@ras.org.uk
Website: www.ras.org.uk

The Society conducts no examinations and Fellowship of the Society (FRAS) implies no kind of professional qualification. New members are proposed by Fellows and elected by Council.

Automobile Engineering

THE INSTITUTE OF AUTOMOTIVE ENGINEER ASSESSORS

Stowe House
Netherstowe
Lichfield
Staffs
WS13 6TJ
United Kingdom
Tel: 01543 251346
Fax: 01543 415804
Email: secretary@iaea.demon.co.uk

CORPORATE MEMBERSHIP:

Fellow (FInstAEA): A Member who has rendered special services to the Institute may be elected to Fellowship by a resolution passed at a General Meeting of the Institute.

Member (MInstAEA): A Member shall be an Incorporated Member who is not under 30 years of age and has satisfied the Council that he has been engaged for at least 5 years in assessing work in connection with automobile claims as an Incorporated Member.

Incorporated Member (IMInstAEA): This class of Member shall be a person who is not under 25 years of age and has an Automotive Engineering or Motor Vehicle Body Repair apprenticeship or equivalent training and has passed the Institute's written and practical estimating examinations and satisfied the Council that they have at least 2 years assessing experience in connection with automobile claims.

EXAMINATIONS:

Written and practical exams for Corporate Membership. Candidates must satisfy the examiners in all 4 sections of the Institute's written and practical exams.

Exemption in respect of training or qualification may be granted by the Institute in exceptional circumstances.

THE INSTITUTE OF THE MOTOR INDUSTRY

Fanshaws
Brickendon
Hertford
SG13 8PQ
United Kingdom
Tel: 01992 511521
Fax: 01992 511548

Fellow (FIMI): A person qualified by training and experience to hold a senior management position (relevant NVQ Level 5 or equivalent qualification).

Member (MIMI): A person qualified by training and experience to hold a middle management position (relevant NVQ Level 4 or equivalent qualification).

Associate Member (AMIMI): A person qualified by training or experience to industry vocational level (relevant NVQ Level 3 or equivalent qualification).

Affiliate (AffIMI): A person over the age of 18 who is employed in the industry but not qualified for corporate membership (relevant NVQ Level 2 or equivalent qualification).

Graduate: A person over 21 studying for an Institute recognised qualification meeting or contributing to entry criteria for corporate membership.

Student: A person aged 16 to 21 registered as working towards an Institute vocational qualification.

The Institute also awards two vocational engineering qualifications subject to experience as well as academic and skill competence. These are **Certificated Automotive Engineer (CAE)** for suitably qualified vehicle technicians and **Licentiate Automotive Engineer (LAE)** for master technicians.

The Institute certificates the following management qualifications which lead to membership at the levels shown in brackets: Supervisory Studies (AMIMI); Certificate of Management (MIMI); Diploma in Motor Industry Management (FIMI).

The Institute is an Awarding Body for a comprehensive range of NVQs covering vehicle mechanical, body repair and refinishing, sales, customer service, parts, administration, management and training/ development.

INSTITUTE OF VEHICLE ENGINEERS (FORMERLY INSTITUTE OF BRITISH CARRIAGE & AUTOMOBLIE MANUFACTURERS)

31 Redstone Farm Road
Hall Green
Birmingham
West Midlands
B28 9NU
United Kingdom
Tel: 0121 778 4354
Fax: 0121 702 2615
Email: info@ivehe.org
Website: www.ivehe.org

The Institute of British Carriage and Automobile Manufacturers changed its name to the Institute of Vehicle Engineers by special resolution and was incorporated with Companies House on 12 January 2000.

Fellowship (FIVehE): Open to persons, minimum age 40, who have been members (MIVehE) for not less than 5 years and who submit a precis describing any significant contribution(s) to the Institute and/or vehicle manufacturing or any branch thereof.

Membership (MIVehE): Open to persons, minimum age 25, who are registered as CEng or IEng or meet the Institute's academic requirements. Alternatively those who have completed non-technical professional training and held a responsible position of direction in a practical, technical, administrative, commercial or any branch of vehicle construction industry for not less than 2 years.

Associate Membership (AMIVehE): Open to persons, minimum age 23, who are registered as EngTech or meet the Institute's academic requirements. Alternatively those who have received a good general education and have completed relevant approved courses. They shall have been formally trained and hold or have held a responsible position in practical, technical, commercial, administration or any branch of the vehicle construction industry.

Associate (AIVehE): Open to persons, minimum age 21, with a basic level of academic achievement, training and experience in vehicle construction or any branch thereof.

Licentiate or Certified Vehicle Technologist (LVT or CVT): Additional qualifications for complying with the Institute's technical requirements.

EXAMINATIONS:
Potential members are expected to be registered with the Engineering Council or to hold a BEng degree, HND, ONC or equivalent NVQ or have served an appropriate apprenticeship with the relevant NVQ Level 3 or above.

Aviation

THE GUILD OF AIR PILOTS AND AIR NAVIGATORS
Cobham House
9 Warwick Court
Gray's Inn
London
WC1R 5DJ
United Kingdom
Tel: 020 7404 4032
Fax: 020 7404 4035
Email: gapan@gapan.org
Website: www.gapan.org

A Livery Company of the City of London. Application for admission as Upper Freeman or Freeman is welcomed from Pilots or Navigators who meet the criteria given below. Admission is subject to approval by the Court of the Guild.
Upper Freemen: Within the preceding 10 yrs shall have engaged in the profession of air pilot or air navigator for a period or periods totalling not less than 5 yrs, and shall be or shall have been the holder of a professional pilot's licence, a flight navigator's licence, a full instructor's rating, or test pilot qualifications. Professional pilots include both civil and military pilots.
Freemen: Hold the qualifications described for Upper Freemen but without having completed the prescribed period of engagement in the profession of air pilot or air navigator (ie from the date of attaining a full commercial rating or obtaining military wings), or hold or have held for not less than 2 yrs a private pilot's licence and have substantial experience as a pilot, or have qualifications and experience as a pilot of airships, balloons, gliders or hang gliders.
Associate: The membership is intended for those pilots or navigators who do not, as yet, meet the above requirements.
Note: At the discretion of the Court, persons who have contributed or are likely to contribute to the advancement of the profession may be admitted.
The Guild administers charitable trusts to improve air safety and aviation education and works for the improvement of standards and the encouragement of those entering the profession. Each year it awards several flying scholarships. In conjunction with the Triservice Aircrew Selection Centre at RAF Cranwell, aptitude tests for potential commercial aviators are arranged as required. It also administers the Guild of Air Pilots Benevolent Fund and is responsible for several aviation trophies and awards which are presented annually.
Application forms can be obtained by contacting the Membership Secretary at the above address.

THE GUILD OF AIR TRAFFIC CONTROL OFFICERS
24 The Greenwood
Guildford
Surrey
GU1 2ND
United Kingdom
Email: caf@gatco.org
Website: www.gatco.org

Full Member: Candidates shall be a British Subject, over the age of 18, actually engaged in the profession and the holder of a current licence or certificate of competency recognised or issued by Her Majesty's Government which enables them to carry out one or more of the functions of the Air Traffic Control Service or, by being an Associate Member for at least 3 years and, in the opinion of the Executive Board, have merited the status of Full Membership by virtue of their professional conduct and experience.
Associate Member: Candidates shall be over the age of 18, not otherwise qualified for Full Membership and shall have previously held a licence or certificate of competency recognised or issued by Her Majesty's Government which enabled them to carry out one or more of the functions of the Air Traffic Control Service or, can prove to the Executive council that they had carried out one or more of the functions of the Air Traffic Control Service for which at the time no licence or certificate was required or, be able to satisfy the Executive Council that they are closely allied to and sincerely interested in the profession of Air Traffic Control and that, because of their special qualifications and/or appointment, can contribute to the aims of the Guild.
Student Member: Shall be a British Subject over the age of 18 and be able to prove to the Executive Council or the Membership Secretary that they are engaged in a course of training for the Profession approved by the Executive Board.
Corporate Member: Any company, partnership, association or organisation from any country whose activities concern aviation, and who is able to satisfy the Executive Council of its suitability for membership.

Banking

THE CHARTERED INSTITUTE OF BANKERS IN SCOTLAND

Drumsheugh House
38B Drumsheugh Gardens
Edinburgh
EH3 7SW
United Kingdom
Tel: 0131 473 7777
Fax: 0131 473 7788
Email: info@ciobs.org.uk
Website: www.ciobs.org.uk

MEMBERSHIP:

Fellow (FCIBS): Fellowship is open to Members of at least 10 years' standing, currently holding a managerial position in banking and elected by Council for a significant contribution to banking and/or the Institute.

Member (MCIBS): Membership is awarded to Associates who have passed the Final exams, which place particular emphasis on management skills and theory.

Associate (ACIBS): Associateship is awarded to Student Members who have gained 9 credits from a selection of the following subjects: Core Introduction to Financial Services, Banking Practice, Banking and the Law, Financial Economics, Business Accounting, Marketing Financial Services, Optional Investment, International Business, Taxation, Business Banking, Management, Mortgage Lending, Call Centre Management, Financial Services Sales Management, Corporate Finance.

EXAMINATIONS:

Diploma in Financial Services (DipFS): Awarded to students who have passed 6 exams from the following list: Core Introduction to Financial Services, Optional Legal Environment, Economic Environment, Basic Accounting and Taxation, Introduction to Insurance, Sales and Service, Team Development, Banking Operations, Information Technology, Introduction to Insurance and Telephone Banking, Introduction to Investment, International Services.

Entry is open to all employees in the financial services sector. There is a fast track route for those who possess university entry level qualifications and those with a university degree can go directly to the Associateship course.

INSTITUTE OF FINANCIAL SERVICES

IFS House
4/9 Burgate Lane
Canterbury
Kent
CT1 2XJ
United Kingdom
Tel: 01227 018609
Fax: 01227 763788/479641/453547
Email: institute@ifslearning.com
Website: www.ifslearning.com

The Institute of Financial Services **(ifs)** is the official brand of the Chartered Institute of Bankers **(CIB)**, one of the leading bodies for the provision of education and life-long career support services to the financial services industry.

Through a process of innovation and a desire to provides 'winning' solutions, the **ifs** provides a range of products and services that meet the needs of the wider financial services community. Through its faculty structure the **ifs** develops and delivers a range of appropriate qualifications, for which the **CIB** continues to act as the assessing and awarding body.

The Faculties allow for the provision of targeted services and specialist educational programmes to particular sectors, including the areas of Banking and Finance, Regulatory and Retail and E-Commerce and Technology.

MEMBERSHIP:

Fellow (FCIB): Fellows must have previously been elected to Associateship (or hold a comparable qualification), hold a management position and have given service to the Institute and/or financial services education, above normal work commitments.

Associate (ACIB): Have completed the Associateship qualification, which is linked to the simultaneous award of the BSc (Hons) degree in Financial Services.

Member: This grade of membership is open to anyone over the age of 18 yr.

QUALIFICATIONS:

MA in E-Commerce: A pioneering management qualification, developed in collaboration with Canterbury Business School, a department of the University of Kent at Canterbury. This qualification has been designed to put candidates at the cutting-edge of tomorrow's business models.

BSc (Hons) in Financial Services and Associateship: This programme is designed to be relevant and practical, and allows candidates to follow a specialist or generalist route depending on their individual needs and interests. Direct entry for those holding a degree or the Diploma in Financial Services Management (replacing the Banking Certificate).

Diploma in Financial Services Management (DFSM): A flexible, portable qualification designed to equip candidates with the essential skills and knowledge to help 'fast-track' their management careers. The DFSM also acts as the foundation element for the BSc/Associateship.

Certificate for Financial Advisers (CeFA): A regulatory 'benchmark' qualification for financial advisers and intermediaries. CeFA qualification must be achieved to 'practice' unsupervised.

Certificate in Mortgage Advice and Practice (CeMAP): CeMAP has been developed with the co-operation of the Council of Mortgage Lenders (CML) to meet the needs of those following the standards of good practice defined by the CML's Code of Mortgage Lending Practice. Candidates with CeFA/FPC or equivalent can take a special 'Bridge' paper to complete the qualification.

Certificate in Financial Services Practice (CFSP): An adaptable, flexible qualification particularly relevant to, and valued by, those in a customer care or front of office role, across the whole financial services industry

Contact Centre Professional (CCP): A new qualification designed to recognise the key role played by contact centres and to reward staff operating in the contact centre environment with a professional qualification.

Professional Investment Certificate (PIC): An advanced qualification, building on existing statutory examinations for financial advisers (CeFA, FPC or Investment Advice Certificate (IAC)). It is designed to meet the specialist needs of individuals giving financial advice to clients.

National Vocational Qualifications (NVQs): The CIB is an awarding body for a wide range of NVQs directly relevant to the financial sector.

Free-standing Qualifications: A range of specialist awards based upon papers drawn from both the BSc (Hons) degree programme and from the MA in E-Commerce, providing credits towards those qualifications.

Beauty Therapy and Beauty Culture

ASSOCIATION OF THERAPY LECTURES

3rd Floor, Eastleigh House
Upper Market Street
Eastleigh
SO51 9FD
United Kingdom
Tel: 023 8048 8900
Fax: 023 8048 8970
Website: www.fht.org.uk
(Part of the Federation of Holistic Therapists)

This is the largest professional association supporting lecturers in Beauty Therapy, Holistic Therapies and Health & Fitness subjects. Membership is open to those currently teaching in Colleges, public or private. Fellowship is open to those with more than 5 years' teaching experience.

BRITISH ASSOCIATION OF BEAUTY THERAPY AND COSMETOLOGY LTD

Secretariat, Babtac House
70 Eastgate Street
Gloucester
Gloucestershire
GL1 1QN
United Kingdom
Tel: 01452 421114
Fax: 01452 421110
Email: manager@babtac.com
Website: www.babtac.com

Full Member: A person who has gained a recognised qualification in Facial & Body Treatments (minimum) approved by the Association. Covered by group insurance and entitled to vote.

Student Member: A person undergoing a course of training at an establishment approved by the Association. Covered by limited group insurance while working under direct supervision of a Full member. Not entitled to vote.

Specific Skills Member: A person who has gained a recognised qualification approved by the Association. Covered by group insurance and entitled to vote.

Overseas Member: A person working with the Beauty Profession abroad. Not covered by group insurance. Not entitled to vote.

Associate Member: A person who has a business or profession related to beauty therapy. Not covered by group insurance. Not entitled to vote.

Overseas Associate Member: Not covered by group insurance. Not entitled to vote.

Non-Practising Member: A person no longer practising beauty therapy. Not entitled to vote. CIBTAC International is recognised worldwide. CIBTAC is the Awarding Body of BABTAC and offers an international qualification.

THE BRITISH ASSOCIATION OF ELECTROLYSISTS LTD

40 Parkfield Road
Ickenham, Uxbridge
Middlesex
UB10 8LW
United Kingdom
Tel: 0870 1280477
Fax: 0870 1330407
Email: sec@baeltd.fsbusiness.co.uk

Full Membership (MBAE): By exam only. Candidates may apply after they have completed the required Syllabus of Training or if they are qualified electrolysists. All candidates must sit the oral and practical exams. DRE members, electrolysists who have worked continuously for 5 years, candidates participating in the BAE Epilation course and those who hold a C&G Certificate in Electrical Epilation, a BTEC National Diploma in Beauty Therapy or Confederation of International Beauty Therapy & Cosmetology Certificate, NVQ Level 3, will all be granted exemption from the theory paper unless otherwise stated.

THE INSTITUTE OF ELECTROLYSIS

138 Downs Barn Boulevard
Downs Barn
Milton Keynes
MK14 7RP
United Kingdom
Tel: 01908 695297
Fax: 01908 695297
Email: institute@electrolysis.co.uk
Website: www.electrolysis.co.uk

The professional organisation for practising Electrolysists and Therapists.
There are two categories of membership:
Full, for holders of the **Diploma in Remedial Electrolysis (DRE)** and **Associate (AIE).** Candidates may apply for entry to the Institute after successfully completing a recognised course in Epilation. If applying after this basic training, having passed the entry requirements, the candidate becomes an Associate member. Associates then accrue 2 years in practice to qualify for Full membership.
Or, an experienced qualified Electrolysist may produce evidence of being in practice for 2 years and on passing the full entrance examination would be directly admitted to Full membership.

EXAMINATIONS:
Consist of a Practical, Oral and Sterilisation paper to qualify for either category of membership. All of these sections, plus a further General Written paper are required for Full membership. Sections may be taken separately and the qualification accumulated.
The Certificate in The Treatment of Dilated Capillaries: This is a new qualification open to Institute members who treat broken capillaries. The high standard of the Practical and Oral examination ensures that referrals from the public are passed on to members practising to a very high standard.

SUPPORT:
The Institute offers a network system of Mentors and Tutorial support for candidates contemplating or revising for the entry examinations in order to achieve a high rate of success. Workshops and seminars are held regularly to update members of the Institute.

INTERNATIONAL COUNCIL OF HEALTH FITNESS AND SPORTS THERAPISTS

3rd Floor, Eastleigh House
Upper Market Street
Eastleigh
SO51 9FD
United Kingdom
Tel: 023 8048 8900
Fax: 023 8048 8970
Email: info@fht.org.uk
Website: www.fht.org.uk
(Part of the Federation of Holistic Therapies)

This professional association supports therapists in the health and fitness industry. Membership is open to those qualified through awarding bodies such as IIST, S/NVQs, and C&G.

INTERNATIONAL FEDERATION OF HEALTH AND BEAUTY THERAPISTS

3rd Floor, Eastleigh House
Upper Market Street
Eastleigh
SO51 9FD
United Kingdom
Tel: 023 8048 8900
Fax: 023 8048 8970
Email: info@fht.org.uk
Website: www.fht.org.uk
(Part of the Federation of Holistic Therapies)

This professional association supports therapists in the Health & Beauty industry. Membership is only open to those qualified through awarding bodies such as VTCT, S/NVQs, BTEC and C&G. Exemptions are granted only for those who have other acceptable qualifications and experience.

INTERNATIONAL THERAPY EXAMINATION COUNCIL (ITEC)

10/11 Heathfield Terrace
Chiswick
London
W4 4JE
United Kingdom
Tel: 020 8994 4141
Fax: 020 8994 7880
Email: info@itecworld.co.uk

EXAMINATIONS:

The ITEC exams are divided into three groups:

1. **Beauty Therapy:** Diplomas in Beauty Therapy (Aestheticienne plus Physiatrics), Beauty Specialist. Entry requirements: 5 GCSEs including English language or equivalent as determined by school/college principal. Minimum age 16 yrs. Certificates in Beauty Specialist, Facial Make Up, Manicure and Pedicure.
2. **Complementary Therapy:** Anatomy, Physiology and Body Massage, Anatomy and Physiology Theory. Diplomas in Aromatherapy, Nutrition, Reflexology, Sports Therapy. Certificates in Nutrition and Diet (theory only), Sports Therapy, Sports Massage, Sports Equipment, Stress Management.
3. **Sport Therapy:** Certificates in Aerobic Exercise, Spa, Steam and Sauna Therapy, Sports Massage, Sports Injury Equipment and Gym Instruction. Diplomas awarded in Fitness (Gym) Instruction, Aerobic Exercise and Aerobic Teaching.

LONDON COLLEGE OF FASHION

20 John Prince's Street
London
W1G 0BJ
United Kingdom
Tel: 020 7514 7407
Fax: 020 7514 8388

VOCATIONAL AWARDS INTERNATIONAL VOCATIONAL TRAINING CHARITABLE TRUST (VTCT)

3rd Floor, Eastleigh House
Upper Market Street
Eastleigh
Hampshire
SO50 9FD
United Kingdom
Tel: 023 8068 4500
Fax: 023 8065 1493
Email: info@vtct.org.uk
Website: www.vtct.org.uk

S/NVQ QUALIFICATIONS:

S/NVQ in Beauty Therapy at Levels 2 & 3
S/NVQ in Hairdressing at Levels 1, 2 & 3
NVQ in Customer Service at Levels 2 & 3
Key and core skill units at Levels 1, 2, 3 & 4

NON-S/NVQ QUALIFICATIONS:

Diploma in Business Essentials for Therapists
Assesor Award
Verifier Award
Diploma in Anatomy & Physiology
Diploma in Nutrition
Emergency First Aid Certificate
Receptionist Diploma
Therapist's First Aid Diploma

INTERNATIONAL HEALTH & BEAUTY COUNCIL (IHBC)

Beauty Consultant Diploma
Beauty Specialist Diploma
Colour Consultancy Diploma
Cosmetic Make-Up Certificate
Depilation Certificate
Diploma in Advanced Nail Techniques
Diploma in Electrology
Diploma in Epilation
Ear Piercing Certificate
Face and Body Painting Diploma
Fashion/Photographic Make-Up Diploma
Foundation Certificate in Beauty Therapy
International Beauty Therapist Diploma
International Sugaring Certificate
Make-Up Artiste Diploma
Make-Up Certificate
Make-Up and Manicure Certificate
Manicure Certificate
Manicure and Pedicure Certificate
Mendhi/Henna Skin Decoration Diploma
Nail Art Diploma
Theatrical and Medial Make-Up Diploma
Threading Depilation Certificate
Wax Depilation Certificate

INTERNATIONAL INSTITUTE OF HEALTH & HOLISTIC THERAPIES (IIHHT)

Massage Qualifications

Baby Massage Certificate
Body Massage Certificate
Body Massage Diploma
Indian Head Massage Diploma
Remedial Massage Diploma
Diploma in Workplace Massage

Holistic and Complementary Qualifications

Foundation Certificate in Complementary Therapies
Diploma in Clinical Practice for Complementary Therapists
Counselling by a Therapist Certificate
Diploma in Aromatherapy
Diploma in Advanced Aromatherapy
Diploma in Aromatherapy for Carers
Diploma in Holistic Therapies
Diploma in Holistic Consultation Techniques
Diploma for Reiki Practitioners
Thermal Ausicular Therapy Certificate
Diploma in Holistic Colour Therapy
Diploma in Holistic Crystal Therapy
Diploma in Reflexology
Advanced Diploma in Reflexology
Diploma in Stress Management
Red Vein Treatment Diploma
Remedial Camouflage Diploma
Diploma in Special Needs Exercise

Health and Fitness and Activity Therapy Qualifications

Foundation Certificate in Health and Fitness Studies
Diploma in Health and Fitness Studies
Advanced Diploma in Health and Fitness Studies
Master's Diploma in Health and Fitness Studies
Diploma in Sports Therapy
Advanced Diploma in Sports Therapy
Master's Diploma in Sports Therapy
Management of Activity Injuries Diploma
Personal Trainer Diploma
Sports Event Massage Certificate
Sports Massage Certificate

Biological Sciences

INSTITUTE OF BIOLOGY

20–22 Queensberry Place
London
SW7 2DZ
United Kingdom
Tel: 020 7581 8333
Fax: 020 7823 9409
Email: info@iob.org
Website: www.iob.org

Chartered Biologist (CBiol): This designation may be used by Fellows and Members of the Institute.
European Biologist (EuroProBiol): This pan-European professional title may be awarded to Fellows and Members of the Institute with appropriate experience.
Fellow (CBiol FIBiol): The senior grade reserved for biologists who have achieved distinction. **Member (CBiol MIBiol):** The main grade for professional biologists. The usual entry requirement is a good honours degree in a biological subject followed by at least 3 years' experience in responsible work in biology.
Graduate (GIBiol): The first step towards Chartered Biologist status for biologists who do not yet have sufficient professional experience for the Member grade.
Associate: For those with a third class honours or pass degree or HND/HNC in a biological subject.
Student: For those over 17 yrs of age and studying for a qualification in Bioscience.
Affiliate: For those who share an interest in the advancement of biology and who do not fulfil any of the above criteria.

INSTITUTE OF BIOMEDICAL SCIENCE

12 Coldbath Square
London
EC1R 5HL
United Kingdom
Tel: 020 7713 0214
Fax: 020 7436 4946
Email: mail@ibms.org
Website: www.ibms.org

Fellow (FIBMS): Must possess an IBMS accredited MSc or individually approved higher degree or have passed the IBMS Exam by Thesis. Candidates must have been Associate members for 2 years.
Associate (AIBMS): Must possess an IBMS accredited BSc honours degree or individually approved BSc honours degree. Holders of other qualifications should consult the Institute.

Graduate applicants must have at least 1 year's acceptable professional experience.
Student Member: Must be on a course directly leading to Associateship, or must have obtained a qualification acceptable for Associateship and be obtaining or intending to obtain the required professional experience.
Affiliate: Must possess a suitable level of educational attainment and further appropriate vocational attainment. Candidates are assessed individually.
Company Member: Suitable organisations and institutions involved in Biomedical Science can apply.
The Institute recommends an annual achievement of credits for Continuing Professional Development, and it is possible to achieve a CPD Diploma.
(See note on State Registration. To be state registered, medical laboratory scientific officers must by law hold a qualification and have completed a form of training approved by the Health Professional Council.)

THE LINNEAN SOCIETY OF LONDON

Burlington House
Piccadilly
London
W1J OBF
United Kingdom
Tel: 020 7434 4479
Fax: 020 7287 9364
Email: john@linnean.org

This is a learned society which provides a meeting point for many biological disciplines, particularly systematic biology and evolution, and publishes scientific journals, symposia volumes and Synopses of the British Fauna. It possesses a large library and the collections of Carl Linnaeus.
Fellow (FLS): People of any nationality, 21 or over, who take an active interest in any branch of biological science may be considered for election on the proposal and recommendation of at least 1 Fellow.
Associate (ALS): Restricted to persons aged 18–29. Associates may retain Associateship until 30. Eligible to apply for election to Fellowship on reaching 21.
Student Associates: Student Associates must be between 16 and 24 on election and may retain this status until 25. They must be registered as FT or PT students at a university or other IHE.

THE ZOOLOGICAL SOCIETY OF LONDON

Regent's Park
London
NW1 4RY
United Kingdom
Tel: 020 7449 6261
Email: marion.hoyland@zsl.org
Website: www.zsl.org

Membership of the Society does not confer professional status.
Ordinary Fellowship: This grade is open to persons of at least 18 who are able to satisfy the Council as to their interest in the purposes and activities of the Society.
Scientific Fellowship: Applicants must submit evidence that they are making or have made a contribution to the advancement of Zoology. For example, the following are qualifications which may prove acceptable:
(a) possession of an approved honours degree in Zoology or Veterinary Science or an equivalent qualification, or
(b) possession of a degree or equivalent qualification taken partly in Zoology with a professional position in zoological work (including a post teaching Zoological Science up to GCE A level standard), or
(c) an original contribution to zoological knowledge of a standard judged adequate by the Council, published in a recognised scientific journal, or
(d) proven practical experience in animal conservation.

Brewing

THE INSTITUTE & GUILD OF BREWING

33 Clarges Street
London
W1J 7EE
United Kingdom
Tel: 020 7499 8144
Fax: 020 7499 1156
Email: enquiries@igb.org.uk
Website: www.igb.org.uk

Student Member: person engaged in the study of the principles and practices of the brewing, fermentation, distillation and related industries with the object of qualifying for subsequent admission to the category of Associate Member.
Member: person who by virtue of their knowledge of the scientific and technical aspects of brewing, fermentation, distillation and related industries are able to further the objects of the Institute.

Associate Member: Person who has passed the prescribed exam.
Associate Membership Exam: Candidates must be members of the Institute.
Exemptions: Exemption may be granted in respect of BSc Hons in Brewing and Distilling, MSc in Brewing and Distilling, and Postgraduate Diploma in Brewing and Distilling (Heriot-Watt University).
Diploma Member: Associate Member who has passed the prescribed exam.

Building

ARCHITECTURE AND SURVEYING INSTITUTE

St Mary House
15 St Mary Street
Chippenham
Wilts
SN15 3WD
United Kingdom
Tel: 01249 444505
Fax: 01249 443602
Email: mail@asi.org.uk
Website: www.asi.org.uk

The Institute offers appropriate membership grades to construction professionals in all areas of the built environment including private practice, Local and Central Government, Mechanical Engineering Services and vocational education. Chartered and Incorporated Engineers are also contained within the various specialist disciplines of Membership. Architect members are required to be registered with the Architects Registration Board.

CORPORATE GRADES:

Fellow (FASI): Open to existing members who have satisfied the requirements for Member level plus additional experience at senior level or those who hold an exempting qualification (minimum age 35).
Member (MASI): Entry is by honours degree-level examination only. Qualified members are entitled to the designation Corporate Surveyor. Exemption given to relevant qualifications.

NON-CORPORATE GRADES:

Associate Member (AMASI): Primarily reserved for applicants over 23 with a wealth of practical industry experience but whose technical/educational qualifications do not meet the standard for corporate membership.

EXAMINATIONS:

Stage I: Requirements are satisfied by a BTEC HNC in Building Studies or other approved course.
Stage II: Subjects include Technology, Measurement, Law, Contract Documentation, Financial Management, Property Maintenance and Rehabilitation, and Economics of Industry. A BTEC/SCOTVEC HND may give exemption, with the candidate being permitted to progress to Corporate Membership by means of experience, a log book and a case study.
Stage III: Subjects are dependent on the Institute's divisions namely Design, Construction, Engineering, Property, Measurement and Specialism. This is set at honours degree level and the candidate is then required to demonstrate suitable experience and may attend a professional interview.
Direct Member Examination: Open to mature candidates with considerable experience in the industry. A case study-type exam tests ability to handle complex situations such as may be expected throughout a Surveyor's career.

ASSOCIATION OF BUILDING ENGINEERS

Lutyens House
Billing Brook Road
Weston Favell
Northampton
NN3 8NW
United Kingdom
Tel: 01604 404121
Fax: 01604 784220
Email: building.engineers@abe.org.uk
Website: www.abe.org.uk

The Association was founded in 1925 under the name of The Incorporated Association of Architects and Surveyors and is the professional body for those specialising in the technology of building.
Fellow (FBEng): Must be not less than 32 years of age and must have held a senior appointment in the construction industry for a period of at least 5 years.
Member (MBEng): Graduates holding an accredited classified Hons degree on satisfying the ABE Evaluation of Professional Competence (EPC). Exemption from the EPC is granted to corporate members of certain related professional bodies and to those over 35 years of age, holding a responsible position in a relevant organisation, having substantial experience, who satisfy an interview panel.
Graduate Member (Grad BEng): Must have at least one year's relevant experience and hold an accredited degree or one with classified honours in a relevant discipline.

Associate Member (ABEng): Must have at least 2 years' experience in a professional office and hold a qualification of an academic standard not less than that of a BTEC HNC in Construction.
Student: Open to those enrolled on an approved course of study leading to an MBEng.
NB **Corporate Members (Fellow and Member)** are eligible to register as a professional engineer (PEng) with the Society of Professional Engineers and thus entitled to register with the Union Internationale des Ingenieurs Professionnels and use the designation Ingenieur Professionnel Européen (IngPEur).

THE CHARTERED INSTITUTE OF BUILDING

Englemere
Kings Ride
Ascot
Berkshire
SL5 7TB
United Kingdom
Tel: 01344 630700
Fax: 01344 630777
Email: memenquiry@ciob.org.uk
Website: www.ciob.org.uk/

The CIOB is the leading body for professionals in building-related disciplines and is committed to the highest possible standards for its members in construction-related education.
Fellow (FCIOB): Fellowship is the highest class of Institute membership and is awarded only to those members who have reached senior positions in the industry.
Member (MCIOB): A Member must be not less than 23 years of age, have passed or be exempt from the CIOB's written examinations, have had a minimum of 3 years professional-level experience, and have passed the Professional Interview or undertaken the Professional Development Programme (PDP).
Mature candidates may be accepted for Corporate membership through the Direct Membership Examination route.
Incorporated (ICIOB): For those who have either a minimum of an HND (195 credits) in a construction-related area, or who are fully exempt from all the Institute's examinations and are preparing for the interview by undertaking either the Professional Development Programme or the Professional Interview.
Associate: An applicant must be not less than 21 years of age, have passed or be exempt from Level 1 (minimum HNC) of the Education Framework examinations, and have a minimum of 2 years' experience at higher technician level.
Student: An applicant must be at least 16 years of age and have been accepted for, or engaged in, a course of building studies recognised by the Institute.

EXAMINATIONS:
The content of the CIOB exams assesses candidates' understanding of both technological and managerial aspects of the building process. The new Educational Framework comprises:
Formation Studies: Design and Technology 1; Science for Building Materials; Site Surveying; Business Environment 1; Information and Decision Making; Structures; Assessed Experiential Learning.
Core Studies: Design and Technology 2; Business Environment 2; Legal Studies; Management; Management of Building Production; Building Services; Pre-Contract Studies; Assessed Experiential Learning.
Professional Studies: The candidate must choose four modules from the following: Facilities Management, Commercial Management, Project Management, Construction Management, Production Design Management and Complete Project Evaluation and Development, Assessed Experiential Learning or Dissertation. Mature candidates with at least 10 years' professional experience have the opportunity of applying for a Direct Membership Examination leading to Chartered Builder Status. Part A requires the candidate to prepare a report on their professional experience, which forms the basis of their Professional Interview. At the interview a panel of senior Members/Fellows will asses the relevance and the extent of the person's practical achievements. In part B the candidate has the option of either sitting examinations or writing a thesis.
The CIOB also accredits a number of construction-related degree programmes, which provide exemptions for their own examinations. Details of these are available on request.
Professional Competence: On gaining a recognised qualification, candidates for membership are required to prove professional competence through the completion of a vocational award. This may be either the CIOB's own Professional Development Programme (PDP), or a recognised Level 4 NVQ.
Where no formal academic qualifications are held, entrance to corporate membership may be gained through successful completion of a recognised NVQ Level 5.
Details of these routes can be obtained from the CIOB.
Professional Commitment: On completion of their examinations and a vocational programme, the candidate is required to attend a Professional Interview. The interview focuses on a 20 minute presentation by the candidate

that highlights their commitment to the profession, and their past and future personal development. A panel of three senior Members/Fellows will question the candidate further on the content of the presentation, and assess their eligibility for Chartered Builder status.

INSTITUTE OF ASPHALT TECHNOLOGY

Office 5, Trident House
Clare Road
Stanwell
Middlesex
TW19 7QU
United Kingdom
Tel: 01784 423444
Fax: 01784 423888

The Institute provides membership as follows:
Fellow (FIAT): Must be over 40, have been a Member for 5 years, and have reached an eminent position in asphalt activities.
Member (MIAT): Must be over 25, be an Associate member and have 5 years' asphalt experience, or be over 30, have 10 yrs' asphalt experience, and have reached a sufficiently responsible position.
Associate Member (AMIAT): Must have passed relevant exams approved by the Institute.
Associate (AIAT): Must be over 18 and have employment associated with bituminous products.
Student: Must be over 16, with 4 GCSE grades or equivalent, and be training in asphalt technology.

Qualifications:
1. IAT Professional Exam (HNC)
2. Quarry and Roadsurfacing (Degree)

THE INSTITUTE OF BUILDING CONTROL

92–104 East Street
Epsom
Surrey
KT17 1EB
United Kingdom
Tel: 01372 745577
Fax: 01372 748282
Email: admin@instobc.demon.co.uk
Website: www.demon.co.uk/instobc

MEMBERSHIP:

There are five classes of membership of the Institute:
Fellow (FIBC): This grade is awarded to members who are engaged in a Building Control capacity and have shown outstanding service, either to the Institute or to the Building Control profession.
Member (MIBC): Applicants must be not less than 23 years of age and must have successfully completed, or be exempt from, the Institute's Incorporated examination, Parts I and II, and have completed the Assessment of Professional Competence (APC). This grade represents Corporate Membership of the Institute.
Incorporated (IMIBC): Applicants must be not less than 21 years of age, employed in a Building Control capacity (and/or be pursuing an approved* course of study), and have sucessfully completed, or be exempt from, the Incorporated examinations, Parts I and II.
Associate (AMIBC): Applicants must be not less than 21 years of age, employed in a Building Control capacity (and/or be pursuing an approved* course of study), and have achieved an HND or HNC pass in a construction-related subject, or an equivalent qualification as determined by the Institute's Education & Development Committee. Persons awarded Associate Membership may proceed directly to the Incorporated examination, Part I.
Student: Students joining the Institute and progressing through the membership route will be required to satisfy the criteria and regulations in force at the time of registration.
Applicants registering as students of the Institute must be in possession of one of the following academic awards:
(a) GCSE or CSE passes in 5 subjects, including Mathematics, a science subject and a subject requiring the use of descriptive English; two GCSE passes at A/S or A level or two SCE passes in Highers or two SQA passes in Higher Still;
(b) an appropriate ONC or OND in a Construction related course;
(c) BTEC National Certificate in Building Studies or Civil Engineering;
(d) City and Guilds Final or Technical Certificate Parts I and II;
(e) a National Vocational Qualification (NVQ) in the Built Environment – Level 3.
Additionally students must be not less than 17 years of age and must be in approved* employment and/or undertaking an approved* course of study.
Mature Entrants: Mature candidates, ie Associate Members of 35 years and above with a minimum of 5 years' Building Control experience, will be exempt from the Incorporated examination but will be required to produce a Critical Analysis of a Major Task and a Professional Studies module, or to complete the Advanced Building Control Surveying and Fire Safety Studies examinations at Incorporated Part II level before proceeding to the Assessment of Professional Competence.

Mature candidates who have successfully completed a Critical Analysis of a Major Task and either the Professional Studies Module or the Advanced Building Control Surveying and Fire Studies examinations at Part II can apply to be upgraded to Incorporated Membership.
Exemptions: An exemption list of qualifications accepted by the Institute is available on application from the Institute's headquarters.
Specimen Examination Papers: Specimen past papers may be obtained from the Institute.

PROFESSIONAL EXAMINATIONS:

Following a review of its examination structure and syllabus, the Institute introduced new examinations in June 1995. The scheme comprises an Incorporated examination, Parts I and II. Candidates must be registered at the appropriate class of membership and be in possession of the prerequisite qualifications at the time of application. Applicants may register for membership examinations with the Institute at any time of the year. The Part I and II examinations are held annually each June. The closing date for examination entry is 1 March of the year in which the examination is to be taken. Late entries will be accepted up to 31 March but the appropriate late entry fee will be levied. The Assessment of Professional Competence (APC) is a separate element and will be held annually.
Notes:
1. Cognate degrees are defined as accredited degrees in Building Control or accredited degrees with a Building Control option or conversion course.
2. Non-cognate degrees are defined as construction-related courses, eg building, building surveying, building management, building engineering, construction management, fire engineering, building technology, built environment or other approved derivatives.
3. Guidance notes on the requirements in respect of the Critical Analysis of a Major Task, Professional Studies Module, Career Critique submission, and the path to corporated membership for 'professionals with other appropriate qualifications' are set out in Appendix One.
4. Any candidate who has satisfied fully the requirements of the Construction Industry Council (CIC) and has successfully completed the Assessment Interview conducted by the CIC as the Designated Body for Approved Inspectors will be admitted at Corporate Member level.

THE INSTITUTE OF CARPENTERS
35 Hayworth Road
Sandiacre
Nottingham
NG10 5LL
United Kingdom
Tel: 0115 949 0641
Fax: 0115 949 1664
Email: mail@central-office.co.uk
Website: www.central-office.co.uk

Fellow (FIOC): Open to a Member who is 21 or over, who has passed the Institute's own exam, or other qualifications approved by the Institute.
Member (MIOC): Candidates who are *bona fide* craftsmen or women, who have passed the Institute's own Advanced Craft exam, or other qualifications approved by the Institute, and who are trained as Carpenters, Joiners, Shopfitters, Cabinet Makers, or Wood Machinists.
Note: Wood Machinists require a pass in the practical paper of the Institute's Member exam.
Licentiate (LIOC): Candidates who are *bona fide* craftsmen and women who have passed the Practical paper of the Institute's Advanced Craft Exam, or other qualifications approved by the Institute, and who are trained as Carpenters, Joiners, Shopfitters, or Cabinet Makers.
Affiliate: Candidates who are *bona fide* craftsmen and women, who have passed the Institute's Intermediate Exam and are trained or training as Carpenters, Joiners, Shopfitters, or Cabinet Makers.

EXAMINATIONS:

Fellowship: Performance Criteria provides for the requirements of organisation and supervision in the Woodworking industry. The exam consists of 2 papers, each of 3 hours duration: (i) Joiner or Carpentry Practice; (ii) a general paper relating to workshop and site supervision organisation.
Advanced Craft: Performance Criteria requires a knowledge of carpentry and joinery to an advanced stage (NVQ Level 3). The exam consists of: a 7 hour predetermined practical task and a 3 hour Associated Vocational Technology (Job Knowledge) paper relating to Joinery/Shopfitting and Carpentry.
Advanced Craft Practical: The 7 hour practical task as stated above.
Intermediate: Performance Criteria requires a basic knowledge of Carpentry and Joinery as required for NVQ Level 2. The exam consists of a 4 hour predetermined practical task and a 1 hour Associated Vocational Technology (Job

Knowledge) paper relating to Joinery and Carpentry.

Foundation Certificate: For those in secondary school education, or NVQ Level 1/2 wood occupation trainee, the syllabus is designed to be incorporated into the secondary school, college/training centre curriculum and is approved by SCAA3. Certification requires success in each of the following elements: (a) A 1 hour job knowledge paper; (b) a 3 hour practical task; (c) course-work assessment.

THE INSTITUTE OF CLERKS OF WORKS OF GREAT BRITAIN INCORPORATED

The Old House, The Lawns
33 Thorpe Road
Peterborough
PE3 6AD
United Kingdom
Tel: 01733 564033
Fax: 01733 564632
Email: info@icwgb.co.uk
Website: www.icwgb.com

Fellow (FICW): Any person of 40 who has been a Member for more than 10 years and who:
(a) has been a practising Clerk of Works for more than 15 years and is also practising; or (b) has been a Lecturer at a recognised educational establishment concerned with subjects connected with the profession of Clerks of Works for more than 15 years and is still practising; or (c) has been engaged partly as a Clerk of Works and partly as a Lecturer for an aggregate of more than 15 years and is engaged in either of those professions as at the date of his/her election.

Member (MICW): Any person practising as a Clerk of Works and who: (a) is 23 and has passed the Final Exam of the Institute comprising Part 1, Part 2 and Professional Practice Exam Part III, and has been recommended by the Examination Board for election as a Member of the Institute; or (b) is at least 40 and has passed the Mature Entrants Exam set by the Institute and is practising as a Clerk of Works and has been recommended by the Examination Board for election as a Member of the Institute; or (c) is 45, a Licentiate at the time of application having held that grade of membership for not less than 5 years and can produce evidence of having practised as a Clerk of Works for not less than 8 consecutive years immediately preceding application (or 10 years not immediately preceding application) and has been recommended for election as a Member of the Institute; or (d) is at least 50 and can produce evidence of having practised as a Clerk of Works for not less than 10 consecutive years immediately preceding the application (or a total period of 12 years not immediately preceding the application) of which not less than 5 years must have been in a capacity which at the discretion of the Examination Board shall be deemed to require a level of practical experience and responsibility at least comparable with the technical ability of a person in sub-clauses (a), (b) and (e) hereof and has been so interviewed by the Examination Board and recommended for election as a Member of the Institute; or (e) is at least 30, is qualified by exam and experience and is lecturing at a recognised education establishment in subjects connected with the profession of Clerk of Works and has done so for a period not less than 2 years and has been interviewed by the regional examining board and recommended by the Examination Board for election as a Member of the Institute.

Licentiate (LICW): (a) Any person of 22 who has passed the Part I Final Exam and has been recommended for election as a Licentiate; or (b) any person of 23 who has passed an exam accepted by the Examination Board as being equivalent to the Part I Final Exam and whose application is supported by evidence of not less than 2 years' supervisory experience in the construction industry; or (c) any person of 30 who is practising as a Clerk of Works and can produce evidence of having so practised for at least 3 consecutive years immediately preceding the application plus has 3 years' supervisory experience (or for a total period of 8 years not immediately preceding the application). (d) any person of 25 who is a lecturer at a college or teaching establishment and is teaching subjects considered suitable by the Examination Board as related to the profession of Clerk of Works.

Probationer: (a) Any person of 21 who has passed the Intermediate Exam and in the opinion of the Examining Board possesses adequate experience of a supervisory or practical nature; or (b) any person of 22 who has passed an exam accepted by the Examination Board as being equivalent to the Intermediate Exam and whose application is supported by evidence of not less than 1 year's supervisory experience in the construction industry; or (c) any person of 30 who is practising as a Clerk of Works and can produce evidence of having so practised for not less than 1 year preceding the application plus has 2 years' supervisory experience (or supervisory experience for a period of 5 consecutive years not immediately preceding the application); or (d) any person of 40 who has been accepted as a candidate for the Mature Entrants Exam, and recommended for election as a Probationer of the Institute.

Student: Any person of 18 following a course of instruction recognised by the Institute

Examination Board as a suitable preparatory course leading to the Institute's Exam.

EXAMINATION:

The Intermediate Exam is common to all candidates and consists of 4 papers: Construction Technology 1, Materials Science 1, Surveying and Levelling/Calculations 1, Site Procedures and Administration 1. Candidates may not take the Final Exam until they have passed or been exempted from the Intermediate Exam. Final Part I consists of 4 papers common to all candidates: Construction Technology 2, Construction Services 1, Contractors' Plant and Equipment 1 and Construction Science 1; plus papers in Construction Technology 3 (choice of Building, Civil Engineering, Engineering Services 1, Landscaping), Concrete Technology (common to all except Engineering Services) and Engineering Services 2. Final II is common to all candidates and is divided into 2 Groups. Group A consists of papers on Professional Practice and Procedure, and Elements of Law and Maintenance and Repair. Group B comprises papers on Measurement and Specification, and Materials Inspection and Testing. Final III is a Professional Practice Exam which comprises an oral and practical identification of materials. Mature Entrants: Group A: Surveying and Levelling, Professional Practice and Procedure/Elements of Law. Group B: Measurement and Specification, Materials Inspection and Testing.

Exemptions: Total exemption is granted from the Intermediate and whole or partial exemption from the Final Exam in respect of certain qualifications, including the following: HND, HTD (Building or Civil Engineering) and HNC, HTC (Building or Civil Engineering); OND, TED and ONC, BTEC (Intermediate only); C&G Construction Technician's Certificate; C&G Full Technological Certificate; Certificate of the National Examining Board for Supervisory Studies; NVQ/SVQ Level 3 Site Inspection (New Works).

INSTITUTE OF MAINTENANCE AND BUILDING MANAGEMENT

Keets House
30 East Street
Farnham
Surrey
GU9 7SW
United Kingdom
Tel: 01252 710994
Fax: 01252 737741
Email: imbm@btconnect.com

Fellows (FIMBM): They will have been Corporate Members of the Institute for at least five consecutive years, have appropriate qualifications and experience and have a proven record of service to the Institute or to the industry at regional, national or international level.

Member (MIMBM): Members are persons whom the Executive Council deem to have the appropriate building management or maintenance experience and knowledge. The roles and responsibilities of Members will fall within the following parameters:
(a) Managerial responsibility for organisation operation, management function or department concerned with the management, maintenance and modification of property and its services; (b) responsible for/contribute to the formulation of policy for the management, maintenance and modification of property and its services; (c) responsible for the planning/or execution and/or monitoring of operations concerned with the management, maintenance and modification of property and its services; (d) responsible for the design of products, artefacts, methods and systems used/required for the management, maintenance and modification of property and its services; (e) responsible for the provision and/or utilisation of management services to enable the management, maintenance and modification of property and its services (may include financial, contractual, personnel, information, marketing, public relations and research responsibilities); (f) responsible for the delivery and/or development and/or management of qualifications at advanced management or technical levels relating to the management, maintenance and modification of property and its services.
Members should possess an Honours degree level education.

Associate (AIMBM): Associates are persons whom the Executive Council deem to have the appropriate building management or maintenance experience and knowledge. The roles and responsibilities of Associates will fall within the following parameters:
(a) Contribute to the management of organisation operation; responsible for contributory responsibility for management function or department concerned with the management, maintenance and modification of property and/or its services; (b) responsible for/contributory responsibility for the execution and/or monitoring of operations concerned with the management, maintenance and modification of property and/or its services; (c) responsible for/contributory responsibility for the provision and/or utilisation of management services to enable the management, maintenance and modification of property and/or its services (may include financial, contractual, personnel, information, marketing, public relations and

research responsibilities); (d) responsible for the supervision of management, administrative and technical personnel (within level and scope of responsibility) concerned with the management, maintenance and modification of property and/or its services; (e) responsible for the delivery and/or management of qualifications at trade, technical or supervisory levels relating to the management, maintenance and modification of property and its services.
Associates should hold a relevant degree, HND, HNC or an appropriate NVQ at Level 3/4.

Technician (TIMBM): Technicians are persons whom the National Council deem to have appropriate building management or maintenance experience and knowledge. The roles and responsibilities of Technicians will fall within the following parameters:
(a) Responsible for the supervision of personnel involved in administration and/or technical operations relating to the management, maintenance and modification of property and/or its services; (b) contribute to the execution and/or monitoring and/or administration of operations concerned with the management, maintenance and modification of property and/or its services; (c) responsible for the execution and/or monitoring and/or administration of discrete and/or small works relating to the management, maintenance and modification of property and/or its services.
Technicians should hold an ONC/SND/HNC or an appropriate NVQ at Level 2. Applicants following approved courses/qualifications will also be considered for membership.

Affiliate: Affiliates are persons not employed in building or building maintenance organisations but having an interest in building or building maintenance invited by the Council to join the IMBM.

EXAMINATIONS:

The Institute is the professional body for the establishment of standards of competence and conduct for those employed in Building Maintenance and Estates Services in both the private and public sectors.

NVQs: The Institute recognises a broad range of construction-related qualifications at levels appropriate to the membership grades. The Institute is the Standards Setting Body for Building Maintenance and Estates Services and has developed NVQs at Levels 3 & 4 which correspond to the Technician and Associate grades of membership respectively.

PQS: The Institute has also developed a course-based Honours degree programme – the Professional Qualification Structure (PQS). The PQS/BSc(Hons) Building Maintenance Management is a part-time programme consisting of three individually examined and certified stages. Completion of Parts 1 and/or 2 enables students to be considered for Associate Membership. Completion of Part 3 allows students to be considered for full Membership. The PQS has an entry requirement of HNC, which may be achieved through APL/APEL. Credit transfers are available between the PQS and the Building Maintenance and Estates Service S/NVQS.

Offers of membership (all levels): Applicants should note that qualifications AND industry experience are taken into account when assessing membership applications.

Building Services Engineering

THE CHARTERED INSTITUTION OF BUILDING SERVICES ENGINEERS

Delta House
222 Balham High Road
London
SW12 9BS
United Kingdom
Tel: 020 8675 5211
Fax: 020 8675 5449
Email: kanderson@cibse.org
Website: www.cibse.org

The activities of the Institution embrace the whole field of Building Services Engineering which is concerned with the human, scientific and technical aspects of the design, construction, operation and maintenance of all the engineering elements associated with the built environment other than its structure, as well as similar elements associated with certain industrial processes. Such engineering services include heating, ventilation, air conditioning, refrigeration, lighting, electrical power and utilisation, lifts and passenger conveyors, fire protection, gas utilisation, fuel efficiency and energy conservation.

CIBSE is a joint awarding body for an NVQ Level 5 in Construction Project Management and Level 3/4 in Building Services.

The Institution is a full nominating and authorising body of the Engineering Council, thus able to register members as CEng (Member), IEng (Associate) and Eng Tech (Licentiate) and authorised to accredit degree courses in Building Services Engineering.

Fellow (FCIBSE): The senior grade of membership. Minimum age at least 35.

Member (MCIBSE): Applicants must be at least 25, have received practical training and obtained appropriate professional experience in Building Services Engineering. To satisfy the academic requirements, applicants must have obtained an approved 3 year BEng (Hons). Those who began their studies in 1999 or after need to take a further year of study or an approved 4 year MEng degree.

Associate (ACIBSE): Applicants must be at least 23, have received 2 years' appropriate training and have a minimum of 3 years' experience. The academic requirements can be satisfied by completing exams at HNC level in an acceptable engineering subject, or equivalent. For those who began their studies in 1999 or after the academic requirement will be a 3 year BEng degree in an appropriate subject.

Licentiate (LCIBSE): Applicants must be over 21 and possess an acceptable BTEC National Certificate with certain specified units in Mathematics. Applicants must also have had appropriate training and experience.

Graduate: Applicants must have acceptable qualifications at degree level. Applicants must also be receiving practical training and experience in Building Services Engineering.

Student: Applicants must be enrolled on a recognised course of study leading to the award of a qualification appropriate to Building Services Engineering.

Business Studies

THE BRITISH ASSOCIATION OF COMMUNICATORS IN BUSINESS

42 Borough High Street
London
SE1 1XW
United Kingdom
Tel: 020 7378 7139
Fax: 020 7378 7140
Email: enquiries@bacb.org
Website: www.bacb.org

MEMBERSHIP GRADES:

Fellow (FCB): Fellows are elected by the Council and must be of the highest standing in the field of internal corporate communication.

Member (MCB): One who has been engaged in internal corporate communications for at least 10 years and has demonstrated his or her professional ability and competence to the satisfaction of the Membership Committee. Experience must include having had management responsibilities.

Associate Member: A person who is engaged in corporate communication.

Student: Must be enrolled in a formal course of relevant further education and/or be studying by on-the-job training or otherwise for a relevant exam.

THE FACULTY OF COMMERCE AND INDUSTRY

52 Market Street
PO Box 99
Wigan
Lancashire
WN1 1HX
United Kingdom
Tel: 01695 622226
Fax: 01695 627199

The Faculty, established in 1982 to provide a bridge between commerce and industry, is international in scope and dimension with members in over 30 countries. Membership is open to all those engaged in management and senior supervisory positions in Commerce and Industry. The Faculty publishes the *International Management Focus*, holds social and business functions, and provides an international forum to bring together those engaged in Commerce and Industry.

ENTRY QUALIFICATIONS:

Fellow (FFCI): Applicants must be over the age of 25 at the time of application, already be an Associate of the Faculty, and have at least 5 years' experience in a management or senior supervisory position considered appropriate by the Council of the Faculty.

Associate (AFCI): Applicants must be over the age of 20 at the time of application, and have passed or been exempted from the entrance examination of the Faculty and have at least 2 years' experience in a management or senior supervisory position considered appropriate by the Council of the Faculty.

Student: Applicants must be over the age of 16 at the time of application, and have passed such examinations as the Council of the Faculty consider appropriate for admission to the Faculty's entrance examination programme.

THE INSTITUTE OF BUSINESS ADMINISTRATION & MANAGEMENT

16 Park Crescent
London
W1B 1AH
United Kingdom
Tel: 020 7612 7028
Fax: 020 7612 7012
Email: Info@ibam.org
Website: www.ibam.org

Promotes professional standards of administration and management in small and medium-sized organisations.

MEMBERSHIP:

Fellow (FInstBA): Candidates must be at least 25, be a member or have Associate status in the IBA and have at least 5 years' relevant work experience at senior level within an organisation.

Member (MInstBA): Candidates must be at least 21, have Associate status in the IBA, at least 3 years' relevant work experience in an administrative capacity and have completed an approved programme of study.

Associate (AInstBA): Candidates must be at least 19 and have successfully completed an approved programme of study.

Licentiate: Candidates must be registered on to a suitable course relating to a junior-level business administration role and be interested in further developing their personal professional studies.

PROGRAMMES OF STUDY:

The IBA syllabus covers a variety of topics important to administrators of small and medium-sized enterprises and includes Business Operations Administration, Business Law, Marketing Management, Business Accounting, Human Resource Administration, Managing Change, Management in the Organisation, Business Communications, Business Finance, Total Quality Management and Premises/Facilities Administration. Each module carries its own award – **IBAM Certificate of Professional Studies**; on completion of 5 modules the candidate is awarded an **IBAM Diploma in Business Administraton**; on completion of a further four modules (nine all together), the **IBAM Advanced Diploma in Business Administration** is awarded.

IBAM qualifications also provide advanced entry onto higher-level programmes including those of charted bodies such as the ICSA and University degree (BBA) and Masters (MBA) programmes.

The IBAM is an operating division of the ICSA and is the recommended qualifying scheme for IBA membership.

THE INSTITUTE OF CHARTERED SECRETARIES AND ADMINISTRATORS

16 Park Crescent
London
W1B 1AH
United Kingdom
Tel: 020 7612 7022
Fax: 020 7323 1132
Email: info@icsa.co.uk
Website: www.icsa.org.uk/

ICSA is the body through which Chartered Secretaries are qualified and supported. The Institute provides a broad-based professional qualification focusing on business practice, law, accountancy, finance and regulation. Members are employed in a variety of sectors including business, local government, charities and universities, with the core membership employed as Company Secretaries.

MEMBERSHIP:

Associate (ACIS): Successful completion of the exams plus 3 to 6 years' relevant experience is required for this grade of membership.

Fellow (FCIS): Fellows must be at least 25, and have 8 years' relevant experience, 3 of which must have been at senior level.

EXAMINATIONS:

The qualifying scheme consists of three programmes – Foundation, Pre-Professional and Professional, encompassing the four core themes of Corporate Finance, Corporate Law, Administration and Management. The Institute operates a policy of open entry onto the Foundation programme and exemptions are available from some qualifying scheme modules for holders of relevant degrees and professional qualifications.

THE INSTITUTE OF COMMERCIAL MANAGEMENT

50 Burnhill Road
Beckenham
Kent
BR3 3LA
United Kingdom
Tel: 020 8663 3577
Fax: 020 8663 3212
Email: ioc@wadetrade.com

EXAMINATIONS:

Diploma in Business Studies (DBS): Economics, Business Law, Business Organisation, Managing the Finance Function, Introduction to Information Technology and Statistics.

Certificate in Management Studies (CMS): Marketing, Business Planning, Business Principles, Organisational Behaviour.

Diploma in Management Studies (DMS): Management Practice, Marketing Management, Operations Management, Human Resource Management.

Diploma in International Business (DIB): Practice and Procedures in International Business, International Marketing, Business Development in Overseas Markets, Import/Export Agency Management.

THE INTERNATIONAL FACULTY OF BUSINESS QUALIFICATIONS

Laurom House, The Oaks Business Village
Revenge Road
Lordswood
Kent
ME5 8UD
United Kingdom
Tel: 01634 869200
Fax: 01634 869149
Email: ifbq@aol.com

The International Faculty of Business Qualifications was formed to fulfil two main objectives:
1. To provide business qualifications through coaching, assessment and review.
2. To validate the awards of professional institutes and centres of learning and training which offer qualifications and awards in business subjects.
The Faculty places special emphasis on accreditation of prior learning. Assessment of skills gained through life and work experience is an essential feature of our programmes, providing a route to recognised business qualifications for applicants who may not have had the opportunity to study or train, but who have acquired the necessary skills through experience and proven ability. Assessment of skills and recognition awards already achieved leads to the granting of certificates and diplomas in the appropriate subjects.
The Faculty also assesses the skills of tutors and trainers and can award individual certification to deliver approved courses.
The validation of the awards of professional institutes is carried out through an assessment of entry requirements and procedures which should comply with international standards and practices. The differing business practices in different countries of the world can be accommodated.

MEMBERSHIP GRADES

Student: Applicants must achieve success in appropriate subjects at a level which, in the opinion of the Council of the Faculty, is satisfactory for the purposes of admission to Student Membership Grade.
Associate (AIFBQ): Applicants for 'Associate' grade must have passed the examinations of the Faculty incorporating all of the subjects included in the syllabus. Exemption on a subject-for-subject basis will be granted, at the discretion of the Board, to applicants who hold degrees and qualifications from universities and/or awarding bodies approved for this purpose by the Faculty, or can demonstrate competence in the practice of specific skills.

Fellow (FIFBQ): Applicants must have passed the examinations of the Faculty as for Associate membership or have been exempted and must have at least 5 years' experience in the practice of skills approved by the Council of the Faculty.

Catering and Institutional Management

BRITISH INSTITUTE OF INNKEEPING

Wessex House
80 Park Street
Camberley
Surrey
GU15 3PT
United Kingdom
Tel: 01276 684449
Fax: 01276 23045
Email: info@bii.org
Website: www.bii.org

Founded in 1981, the Institute is the professional body for the licensed retail sector.

MEMBERSHIP:

There are a wide range of grades available allowing membership of the British Institute of Innkeeping – from those who have just started their careers in licensed retailing to those who have been in the industry for many years. The grade of membership awarded depends on both experience and qualifications taken and is determined by a points system. Members can benefit from a wide range of services offering business, personal and financial benefits.

EXAMINATIONS:

National Vocational Qualifications: With the Hospitality Awarding Body, BIIAB awards On-Licensed Premises Management (Level 4) and On-Licensed Premises Supervision (Level 3). The parallel Scottish Vocational Qualifications (Levels 3 & 4) are also awarded.
National Licensee's Certificate: Aimed at applicants and holders of a Justices' Licence (On, Off and Part IV), the certificate seeks to instil the knowledge of basic licensing law and the social responsibilities of selling alcohol.
Entertainment Licensee's National Certificate: Designed to assist those who run premises with a Public Entertainment Licence, by providing the basic knowledge of licensing law and the social responsibilities attached.
Licensee's National Drugs Certificate: A qualification intended to provide licensees and managers with knowledge of the prevailing drugs scene, legislation associated with the

misuse of drugs and licensed premises and the operational guidelines for identifying drug misuse, dealing and drug strategies.

Induction Examination Certificate: An intensive introduction aimed at entrants to the licensed trade via tenancy, leasehold or freehold; incorporating the National Licensee's Certificate. It covers 8 units, including financial management, marketing cellar management and employment law.

Qualifying Examination Certificate: This covers the technical, operational and administrative aspects of licensed house management, control and development. It incorporates the National Licensee's Certificate and 16 Units including financial management, health and safety at work, cellar management and catering.

Door Supervisor's National Certificate: A two-stage benchmark outlining the role of the door supervisor and aimed at those working in door supervision. Stage One is knowledge based and incorporates licensing law, procedures in dealing with searches, use of force, health and safety and social skills. Stage Two comprises 5 skill based modules: first aid, fire safety, drugs awareness, conflict management and physical interventions.

Advanced Qualifications: These are aimed at licensees, managers and senior staff working in pubs, bars and pub/restaurants and are intended to develop the business and the individual. They are Catering Management, Practical Trainer Financial Management, Business Development, Customer Service Management, Leadership and Motivation, Cellar and Beer Quality Management, Spirit Retail and Wine Retail are available nationwide via BIIAB's network of approved training centres. The AQ Diploma in Licensed Retailing is now available. Candidates must achieve 5 prerequisite Advanced Qualifications from which they will take action points and an action plan, then demonstrate application, understanding, success and evaluation. All BIIAB qualifications carry points, which count towards initial membership and progression through the Institute's membership grades.

CONFEDERATION OF TOURISM, HOTEL AND CATERING MANAGEMENT

CONFEDERATION OF
TOURISM · HOTEL · CATERING
MANAGEMENT

118–120 Great Titchfield Street
London
W1W 6SS
United Kingdom
Tel: 020 7612 0170
Fax: 020 7612 0170
Email: info@cthcm.com
Website: www.cthcm.com

The Confederation of Tourism Hotel and Catering Management was established in 1982 to provide recognised standards of management training appropriate to the needs of the hotel and travel industries, via its syllabi, examinations and awards. Those studying for the examinations of the Confederation are offered a structured learning process, encompassing both the theoretical and practical aspects of the industry, together with a clearly defined path of development through progressive grades of membership.

The Confederation offers four externally examined Diploma training programmes, each of which will normally take an academic year to complete, and four grades of membership each indicating a level of personal development.

TRAINING PROGRAMMES:

Diploma in Hotel Management: Aims to provide students with a broad understanding of the operational aspects of the international hotel industry, and a knowledge of the underlying principles involved. **Syllabus content:** food and beverage operations, food science, hygiene and nutrition, front office operations, facilities and accommodation operations, hospitality costing and control, supervisory management, marketing, tourism, computing, business communication.

Advanced Diploma in Hotel Management: Aims to provide an understanding of the managerial, decision-making and leadership aspects of the international hotel industry and to develop independent research and study skills which will be required when working at senior managerial level in the industry. **Syllabus content:** food and beverage management, food and beverage production, facilities and accommodation management, management accounting, human resource management, management research report.

Diploma in Travel Agency Management: Aims to provide students with a broad understanding of the operational aspects of travel agency management and airline ticketing, along with an understanding of the tourism industry. **Syllabus content:** travel geography, the tourism industy, travel agency operations, fares and ticketing levels one and two, computer reservations systems, travel agency law, business computing, sales and marketing, finance for the travel industry.

Advanced Diploma in Tour Operation Management: Aims to provide an understanding of the managerial, decision-making and leadership aspects of the international tour operation industry and to develop the independent research skills which will be required when working as a senior manager in the industry. **Syllabus content:** tour operations, tour management, resort representation, advanced fares calculation, advanced computer reservation systems, brochure and website design.

ADMISSION REQUIREMENTS:

The selection of students for admission to the courses at Diploma level is at the discretion of individual educational establishments. No specific educational qualifications are required, although it is desirable for applicants to have completed formal secondary education.

For selection on to a course at Advanced Diploma level the applicant must have been successful in, or exempted from, the Diploma level course. Exemptions are granted at the discretion of the Confederation on the basis of previous education and experience.

Examination results and certificates: Each candidate will receive a record of performance in one of four grades for each component of the examination. The grades are Distinction, Credit, Pass and Referral. Qualifications are awarded to those candidates who achieve at least a pass grade in all components of their course.

GRADES OF MEMBERSHIP:

Student Member: This classification is for those who have enrolled on a CTHCM course at a registered CTHCM centre.

Associate Member (AMCTHCM): Awarded to those who have passed or been exempted from the Diploma level examination. Holders of equivalent qualifications acceptable to the Confederation may also be granted Associate Membership.

Member (MCTHCM): Awarded to those who have passed or been exempted from the Advanced Diploma level examinations, and hold at least 2 years' experience in the industry. Holders of equivalent qualifications acceptable to the Confederation may also be granted Membership, as may those who have at least 10 years' relevant experience.

Fellow (FCTHCM): Awarded at the discretion of the Confederation to those who have achieved positions of significant responsibility in the industry, or who have made notable contributions to the work of the Confederation.

GUILD OF INTERNATIONAL PROFESSIONAL TOASTMASTERS

Life President: Ivor Spencer
12 Little Bornes
Alleyn Park
London
SE21
United Kingdom
Tel: 020 8670 5585
Fax: 020 8670 0055
Email: ivor@ivorspencer.com
Website: www.ivorspencer.com

Applicants must be professional toastmasters. They are required to complete a questionnaire, after which they may be invited to an oral exam conducted by the Executive Committee; menu cards must be submitted as evidence that applicants have been engaged as toastmasters. In general, candidates must be of a calibre to enable them to officiate at major (e.g. royal and civic) occasions and to manage many types of public and social function. Successful candidates are placed on a year's probation, at the end of which there is a final exam consisting of written and oral tests. The Guild also awards its trophy to the Best After Dinner Speaker of the Year. Ivor Spencer created The Guild of International Professional Toastmasters Best After Dinner Speaker Award of the Year, which has been established for 30 years. Its recipients have been former Prime Minister Baroness Thatcher, Lord Tonypandy, Bob Monkhouse, Sir Peter Ustinov and other eminent speakers. The Award still continues, but the name has been changed to THE IVOR SPENCER BEST AFTER-DINNER SPEAKER AWARD OF THE YEAR.

HOTEL AND CATERING INTERNATIONAL MANAGEMENT ASSOCIATION

191 Trinity Road
London
SW17 7HN
United Kingdom
Tel: 020 8772 7400
Fax: 020 8772 7500
Email: pds@hcima.co.uk
Website: www.hcima.org.uk

Founded in 1971 from the merger between the Hotel and Catering Institute and the Institutional Management Association, the HCIMA is the professional body for managers in all sectors of the 'Hospitality' industry worldwide.

Fellow (FHCIMA): Captains of Industry – Members (MHCIMA) who have been members of the Association for over 10 years may apply to become HCIMA fellows.

Member (MHCIMA): Established managers – senior managers who have a considerable background of experience and a moderate amount of structured learning or graduates with appropriate management experience.

Associate (AHCIMA): Managers – experienced supervisors and managers with some structured learning or recent graduates with limited experience.

Intermediate: Aspiring Managers – supervisors with little or no structured learning or those with an appropriate qualification and limited experience.

Student: Students following HCIMA-accredited courses of study, GNVQ Intermediate/Advanced, NVQ Level 3 and above.

HCIMA Programme of Study: This programme is intended for hospitality professionals who wish to gain a qualification while continuing with full-time employment.

The **HCIMA Professional Certificate** is designed for those working at supervisory level in the hospitality industry, with at least 2 years' previous experience.

Courses are available at colleges in the UK, with the option of studying part-time or by distance learning.

The programme has been developed to provide a framework for continuing professional development. That is, experience and knowledge are consolidated to assist in decision-making and optimising job performance. Skills and competencies are recognised in each area of the hospitality industry and subject areas are designed to be accessible to all individuals working in this sector.

Further details may be obtained from the HCIMA direct.

Chemical Engineering

THE INSTITUTION OF CHEMICAL ENGINEERS

165–189 Railway Terrace
Rugby
Warwickshire
CV21 3HQ
United Kingdom
Tel: 01788 578214
Fax: 01788 560833
Email: memserv@icheme.org.uk
Website: www.icheme.org

The Institution of Chemical Engineers (IChemE) is the qualifying and professional body for chemical engineers and has over 25,000 members worldwide.

The IChemE Vision: 'To be at the forefront of chemical engineering as a leading international body, qualifying, serving and representing chemical engineers and promoting the advancement of the discipline.'

Worldwide Representation: About 30% of IChemE's members are based outside the UK, in over 80 countries. The satellite office in Melbourne looks after IChemE's 3,000 Australian members.

MEMBERSHIP:

There are 4 grades of membership which cater for every age, qualification and range of experience. Those in the Corporate grades of Member and Fellow are recognised as Chartered Chemical Engineers.

Fellow (FIChemE): Have met the requirements for the grade of Member and have held an *important* post of responsibility in chemical engineering for a period of time.

Member (MIChemE): Must reach the required standards of academic achievement (usually an accredited Honours degree), training and experience and hold a post of responsibility in chemical engineering.

Associate Member (AMIChemE): A grade recognising practising professional chemical engineers who hold a degree-level qualification but who do not fully satisfy the requirements for the grade of Member. Indidivudals who fully satisfy the Engineering Councils' requirements for Incorporated Engineer (IEng) registration may also join at this grade.

Affiliate: The general grade for those who wish to associate themselves with the work of the IChemE but do not, as yet, have the necessary qualifications or experience for the grade of Associate Member. There will be a subset of this grade exclusively for student members who will be able to use the title 'Affiliate Student'.

Chemistry

THE OIL AND COLOUR CHEMISTS' ASSOCIATION

Priory House
967 Harrow Road
Wembley
Middlesex
HA0 2SF
United Kingdom
Tel: 020 8908 1086
Fax: 020 8908 1219
Email: Enquiries@occa.org.uk

Fellow (FTSC): Must be not less than 33, have been an Ordinary Member for not less than 10 years, be engaged in a position of superior responsibility in the coatings industry, *either* have been an Associate of the professional grade for at least 8 years *or* have not less than 15 years' experience in the science or technology of coatings in a position of superior responsibility. They must have made an outstanding contribution to the field or have reached a position of eminence in the industry.

Associate (ATSC): May be appointed from among those who are or are not already Licentiates. The former must have practised the science or technology of surface coatings for at least 3 years, have superior skill and maturity in the profession, hold the CGLI Insignia Award *or* submit written evidence of work at an acceptable standard. Such candidates may be required to take an oral exam.

Candidates who are not already Licentiates are considered in 2 categories. Those not less than 24 must be an Ordinary Member and have been an Ordinary Member or Student for 2 years, hold the GRSC or GInstP or an exempting degree, have approved experience and may be required to take an oral exam. Candidates not less than 30 must be an Ordinary Member and have been an Ordinary Member or Student for 2 years, have been engaged in relevant practice for at least 7 years, have attained a position of considerable standing in the industry and must usually take an oral exam.

Licentiate (LTSC): Must be an Ordinary Member and have been an Ordinary Member or Student for 1 year, be at least 22 and satisfy 1 of the several specified requirements. Candidates may be required to take an oral exam and will be required to submit written evidence on a subject directly associated with the science and technology of surface coatings.

Student: Usually less than 25 and engaged on a relevant course of training.

Ordinary Member: A chemist or other scientifically trained person, or someone technically trained in the oil and colour industries who complies with the standard of competence laid down by the Council.

THE ROYAL SOCIETY OF CHEMISTRY

Burlington House
Piccadilly
London
W1J 0BA
United Kingdom
Tel: 020 7437 8656
Fax: 020 7437 8883
Email: education@rsc.org
Website: www.rsc.org or www.chemsoc.org

All members of the Society will be in the category of Member (MRSC) unless they are not yet qualified for this category or they have sought and have been accorded recognition for their outstanding achievements and have become Fellows. The award of the Chartered Chemist designation will be separated from admission to categories of membership, which are as follows:

Fellow (FRSC): Fellows must have sufficient experience in a senior position since being admitted as a Member (or since being qualified for admission). Non-members who do not possess the necessary academic qualification but who have made outstanding contributions to the promotion, advancement or application of the chemical sciences or the advancement of the profession, or the management or direction of organisations in which the chemical sciences are important may be admitted to Fellowship.

Member (MRSC): Requirements are Graduateship or training based on the chemical sciences. Members should also have acquired and practised key skills through professional activity

Chartered Chemist (CChem): Is awarded to an experienced practising Member or Fellow, who has specialist skills relevant to their practice, in-depth knowledge, made a significant personal contribution and maintained chemical expertise through continuing professional development.

Associate Member (AMRSC): This is a transistional category of membership for new entrants to professional practice. Entry requirements are Graduateship or training based on the chemical sciences.

Affliate: For those not yet qualified for any other category.

EXAMINATIONS:

Since July 1994, exams for GRSC are no longer available. **Master in Chemical Analysis (MChemA)** is for intending public analysts and their deputies. The Society offers specialist qualifications for Qualified Persons in relation to the Pharmaceutical Directive 75/319/EEC, and also in chemistry through a registration function.

For further details email education@rsc.org

SOCIETY OF COSMETIC SCIENTISTS

GT House
24/26 Rothesay Road
Luton
Beds
LU1 1QX
United Kingdom
Tel: 01582 726661
Fax: 01582 405217
Email: ifscc.scs@btinternet.com
Website: www.scs.org.uk

The object of the Society, formed in 1948, is to promote the status of the cosmetic industry, by means of lectures, symposia, publications and education.

Honorary Member: They are elected.

Member: At the date of their election Members must possess the following qualifications: a degree granted by a British university in Chemistry, Chemical Engineering, Pharmacy, Medicine, Biology, Physics or a related science; or the Diploma in Cosmetic Science awarded by the Society; or an equivalent of such degrees as recognised by Council (advice on degree equivalents will be sought from other scientific bodies, eg University of London, Royal Society of Chemists, Pharmaceutical Society of Great Britain); at least 1 year's experience essentially devoted to some scientific aspect(s) of cosmetics and/or technologically closely related products.

Associate: At the date of their election Associates must possess one of the following qualifications: BTEC higher certificate or BTEC higher diploma in an appropriate scientific subject; or a recognised equivalent, together with at least 1 year's experience essentially devoted to some scientific aspect(s) of cosmetics and/or technologically closely related products; or an educational standard in 2 scientific subjects of the GCE A level or a recognised equivalent of such qualifications, together with at least 3 years' experience essentially devoted to some aspect(s) of cosmetics and/or technologically closely related products; or an educational standard in 2 scientific subjects of the GCE O level or GCSE together with at least 5 years' experience essentially devoted to some scientific aspect(s) of cosmetics and/or technologically closely related products; or at least 7 years' experience in cosmetics and toiletries or closely related products; or any other qualification which, in the opinion of Council, makes the candidate worthy of Associate Membership.

Student: Students are those pursuing the Society's Diploma or other educational course leading ultimately to Membership or Associate Membership of the Society; or those who, in the opinion of the Membership Committee, have the required academic qualifications and who are gaining, or actively seeking to gain, approved experience and expecting admission to Membership or Associate Membership of the Society at the time of their election to Student Membership. Students must have a minimum qualification of 2 scientific subjects of the GCE O level or a recognised equivalent. Membership of this grade is temporary: it covers only the period that a candidate for membership is under training. All Student Memberships are reviewed at the end of 3 years. Re-election is only permitted if the Membership Committee is satisfied of the Student's ultimate intention to become a Member; all Bye-Laws concerning Student Membership are subject to the discretion of Council.

Diploma: The Society runs a Certificate Course in Cosmetic Science, in conjunction with the London College of Fashion, leading to the Diploma in Cosmetic Science, available by distance-learning only.

Chiropody

THE BRITISH CHIROPODY AND PODIATRY ASSOCIATION

New Hall
Bath Road
Maidenhead
Berkshire
SL6 4LA
United Kingdom
Tel: 01628 632440
Fax: 01628 674483

Fellow (FSSCh): A fellow has to have been in practice for 5 years and completed the Advanced course on Orthotics and Biomechanics. He or she must also be elected by the appropriate Council of the Association.

Member (MSSCh): Obtained by having completed both the theory and practice of chiropody in accordance with The Open College of Chiropody and Podiatry's curriculum.

Any member, MSSCh or FSSCh, automatically becomes a Member of the British Chiropody and Podiatry Association (MBChA).

THE INSTITUTE OF CHIROPODISTS AND PODIATRISTS

27 Wright Street
Southport
Merseyside
PR9 0TL
United Kingdom
Tel: 01704 546141
Fax: 01704 500477
Email: secretary@inst-chiropodist.org.uk
Website: www.inst-chiropodist.org.uk

Institute Chiropody Course: The theory is conducted by distance learning with the practical element totalling 6 weeks full time at the Institute School in Sheffield. Students have access to a tutor helpline, attend a seminar and pass theoretical examinations before commencing the practical. Successful candidates are eligible for full membership (MInstChP) of the Institute. The Institute of Chiropodists and Podiatrists is the only body offering Chiropody courses that are accredited by the Open and Distance Learning Quality Council.

Applications for **Membership (MInstChP)** are also considered from state registered chiropodists, persons who have been in full-time practice for at least 3 years and pass a written, practical and oral exam, and from graduates of the Institute Chiropody Course.

The **Diploma in Chiropodial Medicine (DChM)** is granted to Members who have completed 6 modules on chiropodial subjects, including Physical Therapy and Biomechanics. Each of Modules 1 to 4 has at least 1 seminar (optional) and modules 5 and 6 have 2 weekend seminars with practical studies (compulsory). A recognised First Aid Certificate must be obtained for Module 4. Modules 1 to 4 have written exams and Modules 5 and 6 have practical and written exams.

OXFORD SCHOOL OF CHIROPODISTS AND PODIATRY

6 Wesley Lane
Bicester
Oxon
OX26 6JU
United Kingdom
Tel: 01869 248538
Fax: 01869 248538

Membership: All successful students are eligible to become full members of The Institute of Chiropodists and Podiatrists.

Exams/Qualifications: Students have to sit three theory examinations (Preliminary, Intermediate and Final). The Final exam is set and conducted by the Institute of Chiropodists and Podiatrists. Students also have to take a Final Practical Assessment which is also conducted by an Inspector from the Institute of Chiropodists and Podiatrists. All successful students gain the qualification **Diploma in Surgical Chiropody – DSCh(Ox).** Exemptions are possible where prior learning is given credit.

The training course covers both theoretical and practical aspects of chiropody and takes 18 months to complete. The theoretical part of the course is completed by distance learning as well as attendance of training days at the school. Students must complete a minimum of 300 hours' practical training, including not only clinical work but training in other environments.

THE SOCIETY OF CHIROPODISTS AND PODIATRISTS

1 Fellmongers Path
Tower Bridge Road
London
SE1 3LY
United Kingdom
Tel: 020 7234 8620
Fax: 020 7234 8621
Email: enq@scpod.org
Website: www.feetforlife.org

Member (MChS): To gain membership of the Society, applicants must have completed the Society's 3 year FT course of training leading to the award of its Diploma in Podiatric Medicine (DPodM) coupled with a first degree in Podiatry or Podiatric Medicine approved by the Society (usually a BSc (Hons) Podiatry) and by the Chiropodists Board of the Council for Professions Supplementary to Medicine; or, in the case of those holding foreign qualifications, they must have successfully applied for, and have received, state registration from the said Chiropodists Board (SRCh).

Fellow (FChS): Awarded solely on the grounds of superior professional ability and experience and is attainable by exam only. Candidates are not eligible to sit the final clinical exam for Fellowship until they have completed a minimum of 4 assessed modules of post-registration study approved by the Society's Fellowship Panel.

Fellow of the Surgical Faculty of the College of Podiatrists (FCPodS): Members of the Society of Chiropodists and Podiatrists who complete the Society's PG course of training in foot surgery are awarded Fellowship of the Surgical Faculty of the Society's College of Podiatrists when they pass their final practical exam. Fellows of the Surgical Faculty are qualified to undertake more advanced skin and soft-tissue surgery than are non-Fellows as well as a range of surgical procedures on the foot involving bone and tendon.

Teacher's Certificate of the Society of Chiropodists: This qualification is for State Registered Chiropodists and Members of the Society and consists of 2 written papers and oral tests on the principles of teaching and theory of chiropody. Exemption from the teaching section will be granted to those who hold a C&G Teachers Certificate or other qualification deemed appropriate by the Faculty of I+Undergraduate Education and who have been employed in a School of Chiropody on a regular basis for at least 1 year.

Training: All the schools now teach a BSc (Hons) in Podiatry. All the schools are departments of universities or colleges of higher education. Students should be at least 18 at the start of the course and should have attained 5 GCE or GCSE passes (grades A, B or C) to include English language and preferably 2 science subjects. Normally, 2 of the passes should be at A level (or 4 at Advanced Supplementary level). Students with the Scottish Certificate of Education should have attained 5 standard grade passes (grades 1 to 3) of which 3 should be higher grade passes (grades A to C). Where students have passes in excess of the minimum requirements, the number together with the grades of the passes, may be taken into account in assessing their entry qualifications. Qualifications deemed to be equivalent may be taken into account.

NB: These are minimum requirements. Individual institutions may lay down higher entry requirements, and prospective students are advised to make early contact with the listed institutions of their choice. Institutions have their own requirements for mature students, whose qualifications and experience are judged on their merits.

Courses of training are offered at the following:

England
Birmingham School of Podiatry, Matthew Boulton College; Department of Podiatry, Brighton University; Directorate of Podiatry; Durham School of Podiatric Medicine; Huddersfield School of Podiatry, University of Huddersfield; London Foot Hospital and School of Podiatric Medicine, University College London; Northampton School of Podiatry, University College, Northampton; University of Salford; Plymouth School of Podiatry, University of Plymouth; Wessex School of Podiatry, University of Southampton.

Wales
The Centre for Podiatric Studies, University of Wales Institute, Cardiff.

Scotland
Edinburgh School of Podiatry, Queen Margaret University College; Glasgow School of Podiatric Medicine, Glasgow Caledonian University.

Northern Ireland
Centre for Podiatric Medicine, University of Ulster at Jordanstown.

Chiropractic

BRITISH CHIROPRACTIC ASSOCIATION

Blagrave House, 17 Blagrave Street
Reading
Berkshire
RG1 1QB
United Kingdom
Tel: 0118 950 5950
Fax: 0118 958 8946
Email: enquiries@chiropratic-uk.co.uk
Website: www.chiropractic-uk.co.uk.

Chiropractors are accepted as members of the Association after qualifying from a FT course of at least 4 years at an accredited college of chiropractic. Members are categorised in Full, Semi-Active, Provisional, or Associate gradings and have to abide by the Association's Code of Ethics and Bye-Laws.

TRAINING:

There are two internationally recognised training institutions in the UK, the Anglo European College of Chiropractic, Parkwood Road, Bournemouth, Dorset BH5 2DF, tel: 01202 436 200, and the Welsh Institute of Chiropractic leads to the award of a BSc (Hons) Chiropractic. Courses commence in September of each year and a prospectus can be obtained from each of the institutions concerned. The profession is now regulated by statute by the General Chiropractic Council (GCC) which opened a register in June 1999. The register closed in June 2001 and it is now illegal for any practitioner to practice as a chiropractor without first being registered with the GCC.

Cinema, Film and Television

BRITISH KINEMATOGRAPH SOUND AND TELEVISION SOCIETY (BKSTS)/THE MOVING IMAGE SOCIETY

5 Walpole Court, Ealing Studios
Eailing Green
London
W5 5ED
United Kingdom
Tel: 020 8584 5220
Fax: 020 8584 5230
Email: movingimage@bksts.demon.co.uk
Website: www.bksts.com

Fellowship: Conferred upon those who have contributed outstanding service to the industries. The award of the Fellowship is at the discretion of the Council and differs from all other grades in this respect.

Full Membership (MBKS): Is for those aged at least 25 and/or employed for 5 years in the technical areas of film, television, sound or related industries. Members are entitled to use the designatory letters MBKS. All applicants must be proposed by a paid-up Full Member.

Associate Membership: Is open to those over the age of 18 who are engaged or interested in the technical areas of film, sound, television or related industries.

Interim Membership: Is for applicants who have completed their training and/or are beginning a career in the industry. Interim Members may apply for Associate Membership when they have gained experience.

Student Membership: Is for anyone over the age of 16 undergoing recognised industrial or HE training relevant to Society's activities.

Civil Engineering

THE INSTITUTION OF CIVIL ENGINEERS

1 Great George Street
Westminster
London
SW1P 3AA
United Kingdom
Tel: 020 7665 2200/2135
Fax: 020 7233 0515
Email: membership@ice.org.uk
Website: www.ice.org.uk

The Institution of Civil Engineers is a UK-based international organisation with 80,000 members from Students to Fellows. Its membership is mainly UK based, although about 20% is overseas. The ICE is a centre of learning and offers a wide range of activities to enable members continually to update their competence. It assesses and qualifies Civil Engineers to the highest standards throughout the world. There are various grades of membership as described below.

Fellow (FICE): This is the highest level of membership and is a mark of the position and expertise that has been acquired. Fellows will normally have a achieved a position of responsibility in the promotion, design, construction, maintenance and management of important engineering work; hold high educational qualifications and have either made some outstanding or notable contribution to the science of engineering or materially advanced the practice of engineering from the academic, research, technical or management standpoint. They will normally have completed a programme of at least 7 days continuing education.

Member (MICE): Should normally hold an approved academic qualification to MEng level, have completed an Approved Training Scheme or a period of experience in lieu, have undertaken a programme of at least 30 days' continuing education, have had responsible experience in one of the many branches of civil engineering, be at least 25 and have passed the relevant Professional Review.

Associate Member (AMICE): Should normally hold an approved academic qualification to IEng degree level, have completed an Approved Training Scheme or a period of experience in lieu, have undertaken a programme of at least 15 days' continuing education, have had responsible experience in a branch of civil engineering, be at least 23 and have passed the relevant Professional Review.

Technician member: Must hold an approved academic qualification, have completed an Approved Training Scheme or a period of exerperience in lieu and have passed the relevant Professional Review.

Graduate: Must hold an approved academic qualification leading to one of the professional qualification classes and be engaged in an acceptable form of approved training or practical experience or in suitable postgraduate studies.

Student: Must be at least 16 and be studying for the profession on a course approved by the Institution.

Cleaning, Laundry and Dry Cleaning

BRITISH INSTITUTE OF CLEANING SCIENCE

3 Moulton Court, Anglia Way
Moulton Park
Northampton
NN3 6JA
United Kingdom
Tel: 01604 678710
Fax: 01604 645988
Email: info@bics.org.uk
Website: www.bics.org.uk

The Institute is a body of individuals and companies who support the objective of improving the opportunities for Education, Training and Qualification through the cleaning industry. It offers appropriate qualifications at all levels and successful completion of these will entitle the individual to membership in the appropriate grade. It is possible to join as a student member prior to qualification.

The Institute works closely with City & Guilds both in regard to their City & Guilds 764–1 and 764–2 Certificates in Cleaning Science and as a Joint Awarding body for NVQ Cleaning and Support Services Levels 1 and 2.

The Institute also offers qualifications for the Cleaning Operators Proficiency Certificate, the Food Premises Cleaning Certificate and the Car Valeting Certificate. The Cleaning Operators Proficiency Certificate and the Food Premises Cleaning Certificate are both approved prior to learning for NVQ qualifications.

THE GUILD OF CLEANERS AND LAUNDERERS

Secretariat, 1 Wellfield Road
Offerton
Stockport
Cheshire
SK2 6AS
United Kingdom
Tel: 0161 483 4655
Fax: 0161 483 4655

Fellow (FGCL): Entrance to the College of Fellows is by election.
Associate Membership (AGCL): (a) *By Exam:* the applicant should have satisfied the requirements for Licentiateship as indicated below, and should have a minimum of 5 years' managerial or technical experience in the textile care of associated industry, and have been a Guild Member for at least 1 year. (b) *By Exemption:* applicants should have at least 5 years' managerial or practical experience in textile care associated industries. They should also be able to demonstrate to the Guild Examination Board that they hold appropriate equivalent qualifications of the type required for Licentiateship.
Licentiateship (LGCL): Open to any member of the Guild, of any age, who has qualified by exam only in: Advanced Laundry or Advanced Drycleaning Technology; plus 3 practical subjects from Stain Removal, Dry Cleaning Practice, Garment Finishing, Silk Finishing, Leather Cleaning, and has relevant certificates in or experience of management.
Membership: Open to people who are directly employed in the drycleaning and laundry industry and allied trades.
The Guild also has **Honorary Members** and **Overseas Members**.
National Diploma in Laundry and Cleaning Technology: The Diploma is awarded to students who have obtained Advanced Certificates in Laundry and Dry Cleaning plus certain other practical exams.

CERTIFICATES:

Laundry Management and Technology; Advanced Laundry Technology; Advanced Dry Cleaning Technology; Intermediate Dry Cleaning Technology; Principles of Laundering; Introduction to Dry Cleaning; Business Administration; Customer Relations; Stain Removal; Garment Finishing; Advanced Garment Finishing; Suede and Leather Cleaning; Commercial and Industrial Dry Cleaning. Candidates seeking to qualify at Advanced Laundry or Dry Cleaning Technology level would normally have GCSEs in English, Mathematics and a science subject or an equivalent or higher qualification.
Some of the above qualifications are superseded by NVQ/SVQs at Levels 1 and 2.

Communications and Media

THE PICTURE RESEARCH ASSOCIATION

2 Culver Drive
Oxted
Surrey
RH8 9HP
United Kingdom
Tel: 01883 730123
Fax: 01883 730144
Email: pra@lippmann.co.uk
Website: www.picture-research.org.uk

Founded in 1977, The Picture Research Association is a professional organisation for picture researchers, picture editors and managers, and all those specifically involved in the research, management and supply of visual material to all forms of the media worldwide. The purpose of The Picture Research Association is to promote the interest and specific skills of its members and the international recognition of professional people involved in the business of researching, editing, managing and distributing pictures. The organisation has been involved in the extensive developments influencing the picture industry. The Picture Research Association offers its members numerous services and information, aiming to continually improve the recognition and communication of those that play such vital roles in the production of all media publishing.

AIMS:

To promote the recognition of picture research, management, editing, buying and supplying as a profession requiring particular skills and knowledge.
To bring together all those involved in the picture profession and provide a forum for information exchange and interaction.
To advise those specifically wishing to embark on a profession in the research and supply of pictures for all types of visual media information, providing guidelines and standards in so doing.

MEMBERSHIP:

Full Member: Applicants must have more than 2 years' full-time experience in tpicture research. Membership entitles them to vote, receive all the information and services the Association provides and freelance Full Members are eligible to join the Freelance Register as soon as they have received their membership card.

Introductory Member: This grade is open to those who have less than 2 years' experience working as a picture researcher or picture editor. It enables the applicant to vote, receive all the Association's publications and attend all meetings. It does not provide eligibility to join the Freelance Register.

Computing and Information Technology

ASSOCIATION OF COMPUTER & OPERATIONS MANAGEMENT

5 Westminister Bridge Road
London
SE1 7XW
United Kingdom
Tel: 020 7620 0334
Fax: 020 7620 0090

The Association of Computer & Operations Management (ACOM) was incorporated by guarantee as the computer professional body in England and Wales. ACOM is an independent non-political and non-profit-making professional body. The aim of the ACOM is the promotion and the advancement of efficient information engineering through computing in industry, commerce and the public service.

The main purpose of the Association in designing its educational and examination programme is to provide practitioners in computing with the opportunity of studying for a relevant professional qualification.

EXAMINATIONS:

Certificate in Computer and Operations Management: This covers data processing organisation and information processing management, operating systems and systems software management, and principles of programming and program writing and analysis.

Diploma in Computer and Operations Management: This covers the principles of computer operations management, principles and theory of systems analysis and design, and the concept of computer management, practice and information systems.

Advance Diploma in Computer and Operation Management: This covers computer architecture and systems programming, software engineering and applied information technology in computer management, and programming design techniques.

MEMBERSHIP GRADES:

Membership of the Association is open to those who meet the Association's requirements. Applicants must be at least 17 years of age. The grades and designatory letters are as follows:
Fellow (FACOM)
Associate (AACOM)
Graduate (GradACOM)
Application for membership should be made the Chief Executive of the Association at the above address.

ASSOCIATION OF COMPUTER PROFESSIONALS

204 Barnett Wood Lane
Ashtead
Surrey
KT21 2DB
United Kingdom
Tel: 01372 273442
Fax: 01372 277778
Email: acp@btinternet.com
Website: www.acpexamboard.com

PROFESSIONAL EXAMINATIONS:

Flexible examinations to ACP courses is offered to both complete beginners and mature students and our structured teaching programmes deliver the practical training and skills that now play a vital role in modern business practices. The ACP Advanced Diploma continues to serve as an entry to the second or third year of undergraduate studies, or for many students, as direct entry on Master of Sciences courses at British universities. The Association's examinations comprise three levels: Certificate, Diploma and Advanced Diploma.

Certificate in Information Technology and Programming: Information Technology Fundamentals, Computer Applications and Operations, Applied Programming, and Programming Project.

Diploma in Information Systems Analysis and Design: System Analysis and Design, Software Engineering, and Business Information Systems.

Advanced Diploma in Computer Science: Information Systems Principles and Networking, Information Systems Analysis and Design, Advanced Programming, Information Systems Management, Project Work.

In addition to the professional syllabi, we offer a range of specialist single-subject qualifications to complement the current office skills subjects in word processing, spreadsheets, databases and operating systems.

MEMBERSHIP:

In considering an application for membership, the Council will evaluate the individual's recognised qualification(s) and/or employment experience. The nature, quality and quantity of an individual's formal study, specialised training and/or employment experience will be the grading criteria used by the Council. As members progress in experience and skills, they may apply for a higher grade of membership than that which is currently held.

Fellow (FACP): Awarded selectively by the Association to one who has made a significant contribution the the Association or to the ICT industry in general.

Member (MACP): One who is employed within ICT and who has a minimum of 8 years' approved experience within the industry.

Associate Member (AACP): One who is employed within ICT and who has a minimum of 4 years' approved experience* within the industry.

Licentiate Member: (LACP): One who is employed within ICT and who has a minimum of 2 years' approved experience* within the industry.

Graduate Member (GradACP): Reserved for one who has passed the Association's examinations and has attained the ACP Advanced Diploma or an equivalent qualification(s).

Practitioner Member: One who is employed within ICT but whose employment experience is not (*as yet*) sufficient for admisson to Licentiate or higher status within the Association.

Student Member: One who is studying for an ACP qualification but who (*ordinarily*) has no employment experience within ICT.

* This figure may be reduced, depending on any relevant qualification(s) held by the individual.

THE BRITISH COMPUTER SOCIETY

1 Sandford Street
Swindon
Wilts
SN1 1HJ
United Kingdom
Tel: 01793 417424
Email: bcshq@bcs.org.uk
Website: www.bcs.org

The Society has a range of membership grades designed to accommodate almost everyone with an active interest in computers and computer systems.

PROFESSIONAL MEMBERSHIP:

Fellow (FBCS): A Chartered Professional grade. For election to Fellow applicants should be at least 30 and have been an MBCS for at least 1 year. A minimum of 8 years of practical experience are also required, 5 of them in a position of substantial responsibility. Fellows of the Society are entitled to use the post-nominal letters FBCS and the title Chartered Information Systems Practitioner.

Member (MBCS): A Chartered Professional grade. Eligibility is dependent on age (minimum 24), academic qualifications, experience and current level of responsibility. Eligibility to apply for the Professional grade is determined by a simple points system – points are awarded for academic qualifications, training and relevant work experience. Further information is available via our website www.bcs.org/membership. Routes are also available for those with no formal academic qualification. Members are entitled to use the post-nominal letters MBCS and the title Chartered Information Systems Practitioner.

Associate Member (AMBCS): A Professional but non-chartered grade. Eligibility is dependent upon age (minimum 22), academic qualifications, experience and current level of responsibility. Requirements for academic qualifications and responsibility are lower than those of Member, but the experience required is similar.

OTHER GRADES:

Companion (CompBCS): The Companion grade is intended to cover senior members of other professions who, although not qualifying as Information Systems Engineers, do have significant involvement within IT. Eligibility is dependent on age (minimum 30), academic qualifications, experience and eminence or authority in a particular discipline. Those elected to this grade are entitled to use the post-nominal letters CompBCS and to describe themselves as a Companion of The British Computer Society.

Graduate: For those who have achieved the necessary academic qualification for one of the Professional grades and are gaining the required training and experience.

Student: Open to those who have embarked in a course of study for an appropriate academic qualification leading to one of the Professional grades of membership.

Affiliate: Affiliate membership is open to anyone with an interest in computing.

INSTITUTIONAL MEMBERSHIP:

Business Affiliate: Open to business and public organisations.

Educational Affiliate: Open to institutions of further and higher education.
Schools Affiliate: Open to UK schools.

ENGINEERING COUNCIL QUALIFICATIONS:

The British Computer Society is a Chartered Engineering Institution and professional members who meet the Engineering Council requirements may apply for the qualifications of Chartered Engineer (CEng) and Incorporated Engineer (IEng). The criteria for registration are set out in the Engineering Council policy document *Standards and Routes to Registration (SARTOR)* and, in terms of training and experience, are similar to those for BCS Professional membership. However, with certain limited exceptions, applicants must have an academic qualification which has been accredited for CEng or IEng by one of the Engineering Institutions. The qualifications now include 250 computing-related degree courses, which are accredited by the BCS.

European Engineer: Members registered as Chartered Engineers may also apply for the qualification 'European Engineer', awarded by the Federation Européene d'Association Nationales d'Ingenieurs (FEANI). It entitles those registered to use the letters Eur Ing.

For further details about membership requirements and annual subscriptions, please contact Customer Services on 01793 417424. Abated rates are available for retired members and those in full-time education.

The BCS Professional Examination

The BCS Professional examination has a modular structure set in three stages: Certificate, Diploma and Professional Graduate Diploma, plus a Professional Project at Diploma or Professional Graduate level. Combined with the right amount of work experience, successful completion of the Diploma (equivalent to HND level) can provide a route to Associate Member of the BCS and achievement of the Professional Graduate Diploma (equivalent to Honours degree level) can provide a route to full Member status.

Certificate: Considered equivalent to the first year of an HND. It consists of a 2 hour written paper on each of the compulsory modules: Information Systems, Software Development, Technology.

Diploma: Examined at an academic level equivalent to an HND. It consists of a 2 hour written paper on the compulsory core module – Professional Issues in Information Systems Practice – PLUS a 2 hour written paper on each of 3 modules from the following list: Architecture, Computer Networks, Database Systems, Multimedia, Object-Oriented Programming, Project Management, Services Management, Software Development, Systems Analysis, Systems Design, Systems Software.

Professional Graduate Diploma: Examined to the level of a university Honours degree. It consists of a 3 hour written paper on each of 4 of the following modules: Advanced Database Management Systems, Computer Graphics, Computer Services Management, Distributed and Parallel Systems, Knowledge-Based Systems, Management Information Systems, Network Information Systems, Programming Paradigms, Safety Critical and Realtime Software, Software Engineering, Systems Design Methods, User Interface Design.

Alternatively, candidates can take the Professional Graduate Diploma by submission of a dissertation on a topic that has been agreed by the BCS. Such candidates may also be required to undergo an oral examination.

In addition, candidates undertake a **Professional Project**, at either **Diploma** level (examined to the level expected of an HND project) or **Professional Graduate Diploma** level (examined to the level expected of a university Honours degree project). The purpose of the Professional Project is to demonstrate an appropriate level of Professional competence in the development of a suitable computer-based system.

There are no formal entry requirements for the examination and candidates must determine their own suitability for each module they want to enter. However, candidates will be expected to have general education to GCE A level equivalent, have ability to communicate in English, and to draw practical experience when answering examination questions. A formal course of instruction is not mandatory, but the examination should not be undertaken without adequate preparation. The examiners recommend 140 hours of study time per module for the Certificate and Diploma, and 200 hours per module for the Professional Graduate Diploma. These are total hours and include tuition, self-study, assignments and exercise.

INFORMATION SYSTEMS EXAMINATIONS BOARD (ISEB)

The British Computer Society
1 Sanford Street
Swindon
Wilts
SN1 1HJ
United Kingdom
Tel: 01793 417462
Fax: 01793 480270
Email: iseb@hq.bcs.org.uk
Website: www.iseb.org.uk

Business Systems Development

The scheme has been defined to cover the general aspects of business systems development; the topics emphasise the personal and business-oriented aspects of analysis and design. The technical areas in the syllabus are intended to test analysts' and/or designers' understanding rather than expert knowledge. Individual modular certificates are available in the following areas: Analysis and Design Techniques, Behaviour and Process Modelling, Business Activity Modelling, Business Organisation, Business Systems Investigation, Data Management Essentials, Data Modelling, Database and Physical Process Design, Estimating for Structure Development, Evaluating and Processing Software Packages, Function Modelling, Graphical User Interface Design, Information and Communications Technology, Object-Oriented Modelling, RAD and Prototyping Essentials, Requirements Engineering, SSADM Essentials, System Design and Implementation, User-Centred System Development, Website design.

How is the qualification structured? There are two types of qualification available:

1. Certificates in Business Systems Development.
2. Diplomas in Business Systems Development.

The modular Certificates are assessed by 1 hour written examinations, the majority of which are 'open book'. All modules count as a single credit towards achieving a Diploma, unless otherwise specified. Diplomas are available in 5 specialised areas: Systems Analysis and Design, Data Management, SSADM 4+, Business Analysis, Rapid Application Development.

To achieve a Diploma, candidates must obtain the appropriate core module(s), any required optional modules and pass an oral examination.

Entry requirements: These qualifications are aimed at practitioners with a basic knowledge of Information Systems and Technology. Although there are no formal examination entry requirements, ISEB recommends that candidates have:

1. General education to GCE A level or equivalent;
2. At least 6 months' experience in a business or administration environment;
3. Attended a training course offered by an accredited training provider.

Note: It may be that training suppliers will impose their own course entry criteria.

Project Management for Information Systems

The **Certificate in Project Management for Information Systems** is awarded on the basis of the candidate assessment, a written examination and an oral examination. The **Diploma in Project Management** is awarded upon successful completion of 5 written projects (minimum 3,000 words each) and an oral examination. Candidates must have the requisite number of years' work experience, which varies depending on whether they want to attempt the Certificate through an accredited training course (normally 2 week residential) or the direct entry route, or the Diploma through achievement of the Certificate or direct entry route. In addition, holders of the Open University M865 or the APMP qualification can apply for exemption from the written examination.

These qualifications are aimed at practitioners with previous experience or training in people management, motivation and control. The syllabus reflects the general and well-established techniques of managing highly technical and often complex projects; these techniques may apply to any type of project but are related here to the particular problems experienced within IS developments. The Diploma also focuses on the behavioural competence necessary to effect good project management.

IT SERVICE MANAGEMENT

Foundation Certificate in IT Service Management: Awarded on the basis of a multiple-choice paper with 40 questions, lasting 1 hour. Candidates should have a basic working knowledge of IT and attend an accredited training course, which normally lasts 3 days.

Manager's Certificate in IT Service Management: Awarded upon successful completion of two 3 hour written examination papers based on a case study. This qualification is aimed at experienced IT professionals involved in the implementation and/or management of service management functions. Candidates should have at least 5 years' practical experience, have had substantial decision-making responsibility affecting the support or delivery of IT services, and have attended an accredited training course (normally two 1 week courses). The Foundation Certificate is a prerequisite for entrance to the examination leading to the Manager's Certificate.

The syllabus for both these qualifications is based on Service Support & Service Delivery booked in the CCTA's IT Infrastructure Library (ITIL) and complies with the terms of the ISO9001 Quality Standard. The 2 papers of the Manager's Certificate correspond accordingly.

Certificate in Business and Management Skills: Awarded on the basis of course assessment through individual and group case studies, and the independent review of a portfolio and video evidence submitted to ISEB at the end of the course. Candidates must attend an accredited training course.

This qualification is aimed at IT professionals, particularly those responsible for the delivery and support of key IT services, who are looking to expand their knowledge and understanding of wider business and management issues. The course is based upon wide experience and best practice within the IT industry.

Information Communications Technology: These Diplomas are set in 2 stages. Stage One is in three parts: Part A (Certificate in Business Strategies) and Part C (Certificate in Resource Management), which are both compulsory and Part B, the candidate's choice for which will determine the Diploma awarded. The choices are Certificate in Call Centre Management, Certificate in Network Services Management, Certificate in Telecommunications Management and Certificate in E-Business Management. Certificates are awarded upon successful completion of a 3 hour written examination. Diplomas are awarded on the basis of Stage Two: a project demonstrating assimilation of all the course material.

The available course Diplomas are: **Management Diploma in Telecommunication**, **Management Diploma in E-Business**, **Management Diploma in Network Services** and **Diploma in Call Centre Management**.

Candidates must have the requisite level of education and number of years' work experience. Stage One of the Diploma reflects the knowledge required to manage a complex operation using technical and human resources; Stage Two demonstrates the application of all the elements from Stage One.

Foundation Certificate in Software Testing: Awarded on the basis of a multiple-choice paper with 40 questions, lasting 1 hour. Candidates should attend an accredited training course leading to the Certificate, although a direct entry route is available.

This qualification is for anyone with an IT background and an interest in testing, including software developers, testers, test analysts, test engineers, test consultants, test managers, project managers and quality managers. It will ensure candidates understand the basics of software testing.

There will eventually be 3 levels of Software Testing qualifications; the additions will be a Practitioner Certificate and a Practitioner Diploma.

Certificate in Information Security Management Principles: Awarded on the basis of a multiple-choice paper with 100 questions, lasting 2 hours. Candidates must have a minimum of 12 months' experience in IT and attend an accredited training course leading to the Certificate. However, if 6 months of that experience was spent in security control activity (eg closely related to one or more of the 10 sections of BS7799), a direct entry route is available.

This qualification is designed to provide the foundation of knowledge necessary for individuals who have security responsibility as part of their role, or who are thinking of moving into a security-related function. The syllabus reflects the general and well-established techniques of Information Security, incorporating the latest technological principles.

DSDM Certificates: The **DSDM Essentials** qualification is awarded on the basis of a multiple-choice paper with 60 questions, lasting 1 hour. The **DSDM Practitioners Certificate** is awarded by ISEB under the guidance and development of the DSDM Consortium. Candidates must submit an application to the DSDM secretariat, including their CV and copies of DSDM Course Attendance Certificates (if applicable). The Practitioners Certificate is awarded on the basis of a project synopsis of 2000 words and an oral examination. Candidates should have at least 2 years' practical experience, including 6 months on RAD projects, and attend a 3 day accredited training course. There is also an experienced route available.

The DSDM Consortium also offer the following courses: **DSDM Aware** (1 day) and **Managing DSDM Projects** (2 days). Contact them direct for more details:

DSDM Secretariat, Kent House, 81 Station Road, Ashford, Kent TN23 1PP; Tel: 01233 661003; Fax: 01233 661004; Email: secretariat@dsdm.org.uk, Website: www.dsdm.org.uk

European Computer Driving Licence (ECDL): This is the international computer skills qualification recognised in over 50 countries worldwide, which enables candidates to demonstrate their competence in computer skills. Testing is carried out at audited test centres, and consists of written and practical tests. Automated tests are also available at some test centres. ECDL is open to anyone regardless of age, education or experience, and attendance on a training course is not mandatory.

The syllabus is designed to cover the key concepts of computing, its practical applications and their use in the workplace and society in general. It is divided into 7 modules, all of which must be passed before the ECDL Certificate is awarded. The modules are Basic Concepts of Information Technology, Using the Computer and Managing Files, Word Processing, Spreadsheets, Databases, Presentation, Information and Communication.

For more information visit our website: www.ecdl.co.uk or contact customer support on 01793 417530 or email ecdlenq@hq.bcs.org.uk

INSTITUTE FOR THE MANAGEMENT OF INFORMATION SYSTEMS

5 Kingfisher House
New Mill Road
Orpington
Kent
BR5 3QG
United Kingdom
Tel: 0700 00 23456
Fax: 0700 00 23023
Email: central@imis.org.uk
Website: www.imis.org.uk

MEMBERSHIP:

Fellow (FIMIS): An applicant must hold an appropriate senior position, in his/her company and/or profession.
Full Member (MIMIS): Requires a minimum of 8 years' appropriate experience (excluding training).
Associate Member (AIMIS): Requires a minimum of 4 years' appropriate experience (excluding training), depending on academic background.
Licentiate Member (LIMIS): Awarded to applicants with less than 4 years' appropriate experience and with certain approved professional qualifications.
Student Member: Available to those studying for a recognised qualification in IS. Four syllabus levels.
Practitioner Member: Available to those who are not full-time students for the Institute's examinations but spend a substantial amount of their working week in some aspect of IS.

EXAMINATIONS:

Foundation: No prerequisites for this course. Each module is designed to introduce the student to the basic elements of IS and management practices.
Diploma: Continues on from the Foundation level, although entry is also available to candidates who comply with the 4 GCSE entrance requirements. The general standard equates to Ordinary National Certificate/Diploma.
Higher Diploma: Extends and compliments the Diploma course, equating to HNC/Diploma.

Graduate Diploma: Honours degree level standard and recognised by the University of Greenwich, London. This qualification enables graduates to participate as fully qualified professionals in the development of computer-based systems.

INSTITUTION OF ANALYSTS AND PROGRAMMERS

Charles House
36 Culmington Road
Ealing
London
W13 9NH
United Kingdom
Tel: 020 8567 2118
Fax: 020 8567 4379
Email: dg@iap.org.uk
Website: www.iap.org.uk

The Institution is the leading international organisation for professional Analysts and Programmers. Its membership includes some of the world's most influential computer professionals.

MEMBERSHIP:

There are 4 grades of membership: Fellow (FIAP), Member (MIAP), Associate Member (AMIAP) and Graduate (GradIAP). The Student category provides an opportunity for those starting out in the profession to associate themselves with the Institution and to receive some of the benefits of membership. It carries no designatory letters.
Applications for admission to the Institution are evaluated by a system of points, which takes account of the quantity and quality of the applicant's formal training and working experience in what the IAP regards as the essential Core Subjects of Analysis, Programming and Business. Points may be gained in all of these subjects through formal courses, distance learning, private study and in the workplace.
Student: For admission as a Student an applicant should be training for the profession and intend to apply for one of the grades of membership of the Institution as soon as he or she is qualified to do so.
Graduate (GradIAP): For admission as a Graduate an applicant will need at least 250 points. All 250 of these points must have been gained from a course of formal study and examination approved by the Institution. This total must include at least 100 points in Analysis and 100 points in Programming.
Associate Member (AMIAP): For admission as an Associate Member an applicant will need at least 350 points. This total must include at least 100 points in Analysis or Programming.

The balance may be made up with further points gained in the Core Subjects, Additional Subjects or by workplace experience. Typically these requirements can be met by applicants with either a good Honours degree (or equivalent) in computer science, or with a minimum of 4 years' work experience.

Member (MIAP): For upgrading to Member an applicant needs at least 650 points, including at least 100 points each in Analysis or Programming, with a total of at least 400 points in these two subjects, plus at least 50 points in Business. The balance may be made up with further points in these Core Subjects or Additional Skills, but at least 150 points must have been gained in the workplace. Those seeking direct admission as a Member will need at least 700 points. Typically these requirements can be met by applicants with a degree (or its equivalent) in Computer Science and four years' relevant workplace experience, or with at least 8 years' workplace experience.

Fellow (FIAP): Applicants who are considered to have exceeded the requirements for a Member by a substantial margin, and who have spent a considerable part of their working time in positions of substantial responsibility, may be considered by the Council of the Institution for admission to the grade of Fellow. Only the most outstanding professionals can meet the standards required for admission to the Institution's most senior grade, and applications are subject to the most vigorous scrutiny.

INTERNATIONAL ASSOCIATION OF BUSINESS COMPUTING

PO Box 2158
Swindon
SN5 3GY
United Kingdom
Tel: 01793 772254
Fax: 01793 772254
Email: admin@iabc.demon.co.uk
Website: www.iabc.demon.co.uk

AIMS:

The Association is a non-profit making, independent and apolitical body whose aim is to provide vocational qualifications in business computing and information systems, offering equal opportunities to all through open access courses available for anyone considering pursuing an academic or commercial career in computing, or wishing to enhance their present situation with additional qualifications.

EXAMINATIONS:

Courses are assessed by exams which take place twice yearly in June and December. There are 2 levels: Certificate and Diploma. No prior educational qualifications required to enter at Certificate level.

Certificate: Comprises Introduction to Computer Systems, Computer Programming, Information Technology, Word Processing.

Diploma: Comprises Systems Analysis, Program Design & Implementation, Computers for Managers, Practical Project. (King's College London); London (University College (UCL)); Loughborough; Luton; Manchester; Manchester Metropolitan.

Conference Executives

ASSOCIATION FOR CONFERENCES AND EVENTS – ACE INTERNATIONAL

Riverside House
High Street
Huntingdon
Cambridgeshire
PE29 3SG
United Kingdom
Tel: 01480 457595
Fax: 01480 412863
Email: ace@martex.co.uk
Website: www.martex.co.uk/ace

Membership of the Association exists in over 30 countries outside Great Britain and it is open to all those concerned with the organisation and administration of conferences, business events, meetings, seminars, symposia, study tours and incentive travel in addition to those who supply services and various facilities for the industry. The Association organises professional training in conference-related skills for members and non-members, as well as working with colleges in joint training initiatives. ACE initiated the establishment of occupational standards and the development of a framework of NVQs for the Events Industry. These are now accredited and awarded by the City and Guilds Institute. The Association also operates the secretariat of the Events Sector Industry Training Organisation (ESITO).

Counselling

BRITISH ASSOCIATION FOR COUNSELLING AND PSYCHOTHERAPY

1 Regent Place
Rugby
Warwickshire
CV21 2PJ
United Kingdom
Tel: 0870 443 5226
Fax: 0870 443 5160
Email: bac@bac.co.uk
Website: www.bacp.co.uk

MEMBERSHIP:

BAC membership is open to those practising counselling or psychotherapy, using counselling skills within another role or training in counselling. All BACP members are required to work in accordance with the Codes of Ethics and Practice. Membership alone is not a qualification.
There are currently 4 codes: for counsellors, for supervision of counsellors, for trainers and for counselling skills.

ACCREDITATION:

Accreditation as an individual counsellor will be awarded to individual members who successfully demonstrate that they meet one of the following criteria: (a) 450 hours of formal counsellor training comprised of 250 hours of theory and 200 hours of skills training and at least 450 hours of supervised counselling practice over a minimum of 3 years; (b) completion of a BAC accredited course plus supervised counselling practice as (a) above; (c) 10 unit combination of counsellor training (1 unit = 75 hours) and years of supervised practice (1 unit = 150 hours minimum per year); (d) 10 years of supervised counselling practice with a minimum of 150 practice hours per year. In all cases members must have an agreed ongoing arrangement for counselling supervision of $1\frac{1}{2}$ hours individual or equivalent monthly, have undertaken 40 hours of personal therapy or an equivalent activity, and give evidence of serious commitment to ongoing personal and professional development. This could be indicated by regular participation in further training, support study, etc. Accreditation is renewed on an annual basis.
United Kingdom Register of Counsellors:

CENTRAL SCHOOL FOR COUNSELLING TRAINING (CSCT LTD)

9 Telfords Yard
6–8 The Highway
London
E1W 2BS
United Kingdom
Tel: 020 7977 7999; 0800 243 463 (freephone enquiries)
Fax: 020 7977 7990
Email: info@csct.ltd.uk
Website: www.counsellingtraining.com

CSCT Ltd has been running counselling training programmes for over 22 years. Courses are offered part time at over 130 FE colleges and other training centres in London, throughout the UK and abroad. All courses are nationally approved qualifications within the National Qualifications Framework with the awarding body, The Counselling and Psychotherapy Central Awarding Body (CPCAB).
Introductory (Level 2 NQF, not mandatory): Certificate in Introductory Counselling Skills (ICSO2) or plus Descriptor: Working with Addiction, Working With Young People (ICSO2).
Foundation (Level 2 NQF): Intermediate Certificate in Counselling Skills (CSO2) or plus Descriptor: Working With Addiction, Working With Young People (CSO2) or Intermediate Certificate in Counselling Studies (CO2).
Intermediate/Advanced (Level 3 NQF): Advanced Certificate in Counselling Skills (CSO3) or plus Descriptor: Working With Addiction, Working With Young People (CSO3); Advanced Diploma in Therapeutic Counselling: humanistic/psychodynamic/integrative (TCO3); or plus Descriptor: Working With Addiction, Working With Young People (TCO3) (available September 2003); Advanced Certificate in Consultancy Supervision (CSUO3) (available September 2003).

COUNSELLORS AND PSYCHOTHERAPISTS IN PRIMARY CARE

Queensway House
Queensway
Bognor Regis
West Sussex
PO21 1QT
United Kingdom
Tel: 01243 870701
Fax: 01243 870702
Email: cpc@cpc-online.co.uk
Website: www.cpc-online.co.uk

Professional membership association for individual practitioners. Also welcome to join are relevant organisations and subscribers interested in the developments in Primary Care Counselling.

AIMS:

The aims of the association are to represent counsellors and psychotherapists working in Primary Care. We also aim to lead the way in establishing national standards and guidelines for further development of the profession and effective counselling throughout NHS Primary Health Care.

MEMBERSHIP:

Registered Members: must be BACP accredited or UKCP registered or have a postgraduate level Diploma/Masters Degree in Counselling or Psychotherapy or a Diploma in Counselling (minimum 450 hours training including skills and theory). They must also have had at least 3 years' (or 450 client hours) experience working in Primary Care, as well as at least 1.5 hours per month individual supervision and have undertaken 40 hours' personal individual therapy.

Intermediate Members: Are those who do not currently meet all the criteria for full Registered Membership, in one or two of the following respects: they have less than 3 years' experience in Primary Care Counselling; they have between 200 and 450 hours of generic core training but have at least 5 years' experience in Primary Care; they have undertaken less than 40 hours' personal therapy.

Credit Management

THE INSTITUTE OF CREDIT MANAGEMENT

The Water Mill
Station Road
South Luffenham
Oakham
Leicestershire
LE15 8NB
United Kingdom
Tel: 01780 722900
Fax: 01780 721333
Email: info@icm.org.uk

MEMBERSHIP:

Fellow (FICM): There is no direct admittance to Fellowship: applicants must be current Members of the Institute. They must also meet any two of the following three criteria: (a) be able to prove 7 years in senior management positions; (b) be able to demonstrate that they have made a notable contribution to the credit profession over a number of years; (c) show evidence of active participation in Institute national or branch affairs by having held office over a number of years.

Member (MICM): Entry to this grade is open to those who are able to demonstrate a minimum of 5 years' management-level experience in the credit profession or its ancillary services.

Graduate Member (MCIM(Grad)): Entry is by successful completion of the Institute's Certificate and Diploma examinations.

Associate Member (AICM(Cert)): Entry is by successful completion of the Institute's Certificate examinations.

Affiliate: Entry to this grade is open to those who: (a) are at least 21; (b) have experience in credit management. This is a non-professional grade without designatory letters and without the right to vote on the Institute's affairs at national level.

Student: The Institute has an open entry policy and does not require applicants to satisfy any age or educational criteria before being admitted.

PROFESSIONAL EXAMINATIONS:

Certificate: A candidate for the Certificate examinations must be registered as a Student of the Institute.

The subjects are: Business Environment; Accounting; Business Law; Introductory Credit Management.

Diploma: A candidate for the Diploma must normally have passed or been exempted from all Certificate subjects. The subjects are: Advanced Credit Management; Practical Credit Management; Credit Management Law; Legal Proceedings and Insolvency.

In both qualifications candidates may take any number of subjects at one sitting.

The Foundation Award in Credit Management: This is a stand-alone qualification that is awarded to students who successfully complete the Certificate subject Introductory Credit Management. Students are only eligible for this award when on registration with the Institute they confirm that, initially at least, it is their intended end-point qualification.

EXEMPTIONS:

Exemption from Certificate subjects may be granted to students holding passes in comparative subjects in schemes of equivalent or higher standard, eg ONC or OND Business Studies, a BTEC National Award, NVQs or a SCOTVEC equivalent.

Exemptions are granted from Diploma subjects to students who have successfully completed comparable subjects in degree courses, in BTEC Higher National Awards, SCOTVEC equivalents, or in the Final Stages of the exams of recognised professional bodies.

Dancing

THE BENESH INSTITUTE

36 Battersea Square
London
SW11 3RA
United Kingdom
Tel: 020 7326 8031
Fax: 020 7326 8033
Email: beneshinstitute@rad.org.uk
Website: www.rad.org.uk/www.benesh.org

The Benesh Institute fosters and co-ordinates developments in Benesh Movement Notation in all its applications, trains Benesh choreologists and clinical notators, conducts exams, maintains a library of movement scores and registers works for copyearight protection.

AWARDS:

Proficiency Certificates: Elementary, Intermediate and Advanced levels.
Teachers' Certificates: Elementary, Intermediate and Advanced levels.
Fellowship: Awarded for outstanding work in the furtherance and development of Benesh Movement Notation.
Associateship: Awarded on the successful completion of study programmes recognised by major dance companies as the professional qualification.

THE BRITISH BALLET ORGANIZATION

39 Lonsdale Road
Barnes
London
SW13 9JP
United Kingdom
Tel: 020 8748 1241
Fax: 020 8748 1301
Email: info@bbo.org.uk
Website: www.bbo.org.uk

MEMBERSHIP:

Membership is by exam. Three levels of membership: Student, Executant and Teaching. Teachers from recognised societies may apply for provisional registration.

EXAMINATIONS:

Teaching Qualifications by exam in Ballet, Tap and Jazz, Teacher Training Scheme and Ballet Scholarship Scheme for BBO students. Exams in the BBO syllabus from Pre-Primary to Advanced Standards in Ballet, Tap, Jazz and Modern Dance.

IMPERIAL SOCIETY OF TEACHERS OF DANCING

Imperial House
22/26 Paul Street
London
EC2A 4QE
United Kingdom
Tel: 020 7377 1577
Fax: 020 7247 8979
Email: admin@istd.org
Website: www.istd.org

MEMBERSHIP:

Fellowship Membership (FISTD): Holders of the Licentiate Diploma may enter for the highest qualification of the Society from the age of 28 and after 8 years' teaching experience. Successful candidates may apply to train as an examiner of the faculty.
Licentiate Diploma (LISTD Dip): The Licentiate Diploma is granted on successful completion of written papers in the History and Development of Western Dance, Anatomy and Physiology.
Licentiate Membership (LISTD): Candidates may enter for the Licentiate exam from the age of 23 and after 5 years' teaching experience.
Associate Diploma (AISTD Dip): Candidates aged 21 and upwards may enter for the Associate Diploma exam after 3 years' teaching experience. Associate Diploma status permits the teacher to become fully registered.
Associate Membership (AISTD): Students aged 18 and upwards may enter for the Associate exam to gain a teaching qualification and provisional registration.
Student Membership: Can be applied for by candidates who have been successful in the Intermediate, Advanced 1 or Advanced 2 exams in any of the Theatre Faculties.
The Associate, Licentiate, Fellowship and Diploma examinations are qualifications which are recognised and approved by the Council for Dance Education and Training.

EXAMINATIONS:

Grade/Class Exams: Can be taken in Classical Ballet (Cecchetti and Imperial Methods), Classical Greek Dance, Modern Theatre Dance (including Tap), National Dance (including Scottish Dancing) and South Asian Dance. There are 8 levels of exam from Pre-Primary to Grade VI, although the content varies from faculty to faculty.
Medal Tests: Can be taken in Ballroom, Latin American, Sequence, Disco, Classical Greek, Jazz, National, and Scottish Country and Highland Dancing. The levels ascend from Bronze to Silver, Gold, Gold Star and Supreme Award in up to 4 divisions.

Professional Exams: Can be taken in all faculties and are linked with Membership of the Society as detailed above.

INTERNATIONAL DANCE TEACHERS' ASSOCIATION LIMITED

International House
76 Bennett Road
Brighton
BN2 5JL
United Kingdom
Tel: 01273 685652
Fax: 01273 674388
Email: info@idta.co.uk
Website: www.idta.co.uk

This Association is the result of mergers between various teachers' organisations. The Association conducts professional exams at **Associate (AIDTA)**, **Member (MIDTA)**, and **Fellow (FIDTA)** level in Ballet, Ballroom, Latin, Modern Jazz, Freestyle, Rock and Roll, Classical, Sequence, Theatre Craft, Line Dancing and Tap Dancing and minor (amateur) exams in the same branches plus Gymnastic Dance, Line Dancing and Dance Exercise. The Association is an Awarding Body recognised by the DfEE. It has developed a National Curriculum programme for Dance in Physical Education, that meets all Key Stage requirements.

THE ROYAL ACADEMY OF DANCE

36 Battersea Square
London
SW11 3RA
United Kingdom
Tel: 020 7223 0091
Fax: 020 7924 3129
Email: info@rad.org.uk
Website: www.rad.org.uk

A teaching, training and examining body of classical ballet.

MEMBERSHIP:

Affiliate Membership as a Student: Optional for students who have passed Grade 8, Intermediate Foundation, Intermediate, Advanced Foundation.
Full Membership: Optional for students who have passed Advanced 1, Advanced 2.
Teaching Membership: Mandatory for teachers who enter candidates for exams or assessments.

REGISTRATION:

A Register of Teachers, who enter children and students for exam, is held by the Academy.

GRADED EXAMINATIONS:

For children from the age of 5, starting at Pre-Primary and Primary, and progressing through 8 grades.

VOCATIONAL GRADED EXAMINATIONS:

For students who study Classical Ballet, possibly with a view to either performing or teaching. Five levels: Intermediate Foundation, Intermediate, Advanced Foundation, Advanced 1, Advanced 2.

TEACHING PROGRAMMES AND QUALIFICATIONS FOR THE FACULTY OF EDUCATION:

BA(Hons) in the Art of Teaching of Ballet – a 3 year practical teacher training programme validated by the University of Durham, combining Performance, Education, Dance History and the contextual disciplines of Music and Labanotation. Faculty of Education, Royal Academy of Dance.
BA (Hons) in Dance Education – a full-time (3 years) or part-time (6 years) distance-learning teacher training programme validated by the University of Durham with exit levels at such as The Healthy Dancer, Music for Dance Teaching, Dance Notation, The Freelance Dance Teacher and Dance in the National Curricula. Faculty of Education, Royal Academy of Dance.
Professional Dancers Teaching diploma – a 3 month intensive programme for ex-professional dancers. Faculty of Education, Royal Academy of Dance.
RAD Teaching Certificate – Shortly being revised, a 3 year distance-learning programme comprising teaching experience, course attendance, assessment and monitoring, and a final exam. Faculty of Education, Royal Academy of Dance.
Certificate in Benesh Movement Notation – a full-time (1 year) or part-time (2 years) distance-learning programme providing a thorough grounding in the principles and usage of the Benesh system. Faculty of Education, Royal Academy of Dance.

ROYAL BALLET SCHOOL

155 Talgarth Road
London
W14 9DE
United Kingdom
Tel: 020 8748 6335
Fax: 020 8563 0649
Email: info@royalballetschool.co.uk
Website: www.royalballetschool.co.uk

The Royal Ballet School (RBS) takes senior students from the ages of 16 to 18.
It also has a Lower School at White Lodge, Richmond Park, Surrey, where entry is at 11, with occasional places at 12 and 13 years, and provides a specialist education in ballet combined with general education. Many of the Lower School pupils graduate to the Upper School, where they are trained with other students who have been successful in the entrance auditions held in London and the regions. General education continues to A level standard.

Dietetics

THE BRITISH DIETETIC ASSOCIATION

5th Floor, Charles House
148–149 Great Charles Street
Queensway
Birmingham
B3 3HT
United Kingdom
Tel: 0121 200 8080
Fax: 0121 200 8081
Email: info@bda.uk.com
Website: www.bda.uk.com.

For registration with the Dietitians Board of the Council for Professions Supplementary to Medicine, a candidate must hold a recognised qualification in Dietetics. To qualify for membership of The British Dietetic Association one must be eligible for state registration.
State Registered Dietitians (SRD): May use the letters SRD.
Affiliate Membership: May be granted to graduates with a qualification in Nutrition who are working in the field of Applied Human Nutrition.
Honorary Associates: Are elected for distinguished contributions to the field of Human Nutrition and Dietetics.

Distribution

THE INSTITUTE OF LOGISTICS AND TRANSPORT

Logistics Transport Centre
Earlstrees Court, Earlstrees Road
Corby
Nothants
NN17 4XQ
United Kingdom
Tel: 01536 74100
Fax: 01536 740101
Email: enquiry@iolt.org.uk
Website: www.iolt.org.uk

MEMBERSHIP GRADES:
Fellow (FCIT, FILT): Fellowship of the Institute is open to those Chartered Members who have at least 7 years' experience in a position or positions of high responsibility in the management of logistics or transport. Fellowship is also granted to people who have attained a position of eminence in logistics or transport.
Member (MILT): Candidates for election or transfer to the grade of Member should hold an approved qualification at Level 3 or 4* in the logistics or transport and have management responsibility which involves planning, making decisions, directing and accountability for the use and performance of resources. Candidates with a Level 3 qualification should have at least 3 years' relevant work experience; candidates with a Level 4 qualification should have at least one year's relevant work experience. Candidates are required to provide evidence that they meet the above criteria, either by a CV or though the application form. Candidates without a Level 3 or 4 qualification but with management responsibility over an extended period (at least 5 years) may submit a portfolio of evidence for consideration under the Accreditation of Prior Achievement (APA) process.
Chartered Member (MCIT, MIILT): Candidates for election or transfer to the grade of Chartered Member should hold the Institute's Advanced Diploma or an exempting qualification (usually an approved degree) and have at least 5 years' relevant experience in the logistics of transport, including at least 2 at a senior level. A postgraduate programme is available to candidates whose qualifications meet only part of the requirements for exemption from the Institute's Advanced Diploma. The Professional Route enables experienced logistics or transport professionals who do not fully meet the academic requirements for Chartered Membership to demonstrate that they broadly satisfy the Institute's criteria. Alternatives include writing a professional

THE INSTITUTE OF LOGISTICS AND TRANSPORT

The Institute of Logistics and Transport

Earlstrees Court, Earlstrees Road, Corby, Northants NN17 4XQ
Tel: + 44 (0)1536 740100, fax: + 44 (0)1536 740101, email: enquiry@iolt.org.uk,
website: www.iolt.org.uk

The Institute of Logistics and Transport (ILT) is the professional body for transport, logistics and integrated supply-chain management. It aims to be the focus for professional excellence and the development of the most modern techniques in logistics and transport and to encourage the adoption of policies which are both efficient and sustainable. ILT has 23,000 members involved in a variety of sectors including manufacturing, distribution, passenger transport, retail, import and export, national and local government, purchase and supply, warehousing, education, research and the armed forces.

Members receive *Logistics & Transport Focus*, the exclusive members-only journal. Published 10 times a year, the Journal provides a wealth of information and articles which embrace all aspects of logistics and transport, the total supply-chain, as well as news about the Institute and its activities. It also contains job vacancies and career opportunities.

The Institute's bookshop offers over 100 logistics, transport, business and management related titles, with up to 40 per cent discount to ILT members. To request a copy of the new 2002 brochure, or to make an enquiry, email: bookshop@iolt.org.uk

ILT's library houses one of the largest collections of logistics and transport information in Europe. Now totaling over 10,000 references, this comprehensive source of information includes leading publications, trade journals, videos, CD-ROMS, reports, conference papers, case studies, Acts of Parliament and other Government papers. Members of the Institute have FREE access to the Library and Information Service.

Members can also attend National and Regional events, including:
- Lecture series
- Local Branch activities
- Annual Convention and Exhibition
- Annual awards

The Institute has a comprehensive and progressive qualifications programme designed to enhance your knowledge and range of skills within the dynamic areas of logistics and transport. Suitable for new entrants through to strategic management, the Institute offers excellent career progression potential.

ILT has 13 **Special Interest Groups** (SIGs). Each group proactively debates and implements strategies to benefit its particular sector. Each SIG provides members with real opportunities to enhance their professional development, technical knowledge and expertise.

Not a member – Join Today – call + 44 (0)1536 740104 with your credit card details.

essay, delivering a professional paper, submitting previously published works and/or undergoing a professional interview. Candidates are required to provide evidence of their experience either by a CV or through the application form.
Affiliate: Affiliate Membership is open to those who are interested in the logistics or transport and who support the aims of the Institute but who may not, for a variety of reasons, qualify for Membership. This grade includes those studying for educational qualifications in logistics or transport.
*Level 3 qualifications include relevant N/SVQs at Level 3 and the ILT Certificate or ILT Higher Certificate qualification. Level 4 qualifications include relevant N/SVQs at Level 4, relevant HNC/HNDs and the ILT Diploma.

EXAMINATIONS

ILT Higher Certificate: A programme for new managers working in logistics and transport, providing an understanding of the practical art of Logistics and Transport Management through a range of optional units. The logistics units of this competency-based qualification are recognised by the European Board of Logistics (ECBL). Candidates successfully completing the programme may be able to apply to become 'European Junior Logistician' and use the globally recognised letters 'EJLog' after their name.
Diploma in Logistics: A choice of a modular, competence-based programme for middle managers with functional responsibilities in warehousing, transport, inventory or materials management; or the alternative programme demonstrating knowledge and understanding application to transport at the operational management level. Also suitable for graduates entering the profession.
ILT Diploma in Transport: This Diploma provides managers currently involved in all aspects of transport with the increased sector-specific knowledge and expertise required by today's successful operational managers. The course incorporates core skills such as Economics and Finance, Human Resource Management and aspects of Transport Management. Students then have the added benefit of choosing to specialise in their area of expertise – the multi-modal Movement of either Goods or People – designed to help their current career and progress through their chosen career path.
Advanced Diploma in Logistics: A choice of a competence-based programme for senior managers covering all aspects of supply-chain strategy and management or the alternative programme addressing the strategic management of transport.
ILT Advanced Diploma in Transport: The Advanced Diploma in Transport gives aspiring leaders a tactical insight into what will be required of them at the next stage of their professional development and prepares the next generation of business champions for this important transition. Two core units deal with the development of Transport Policy at local, national and international levels coupled with Business Strategy and Policy. Students then study either Transport Planning, Transport and Society or other relevant units specific to their chosen specialism and career path.
NVQ and SVQ assessment: All of the qualifications listed above are linked to N/SVQs and candidates therefore have the opportunity to gain additional qualifications.
BSc and MSc opportunities: The Diploma and Advanced Diploma provide a fast-track approach to academic qualifications. The MSc in Logistics or Passenger Transport Management is a degree validated by Aston University, with distance-learning materials and support provided by the Institute of Logistics and Transport. This 3 year programme for professionals addresses strategic issues in passenger/transport management or logistics. Those achieving the Certificate, Diploma or Advanced Diploma with logistics options are eligible for accreditation by the European Certification Board for Logistics (ECBL). Studies for all these qualifications can be followed by attending a registered or approved training centre or by distance learning.

Dramatic and Performing Arts

THE BRITISH (THEATRICAL) ARTS

12 Deveron Way
Rise Park
Romford
Essex
RM1 4UL
United Kingdom
Tel: 01708 756263

The organisation, which conducts exams in Dramatic Art, Classical, Stage Ballet, Mime, Tap, Musical Theatre and Modern Dance, has the following grades of membership:
Fellow (FBA): This grade is reserved for teacher members of at least 10 years' standing who have presented students gaining teacher membership. The Art's examiners and adjudicators are drawn from this group.
Advanced Teacher Member
Teacher Member (TMBA)
Member, Non-Teaching Member (AMBA)
Companion (CBA), Student Member
Exams are conducted at Elementary, Intermediate and Advanced standards for teachers

and performers. There are Bronze, Silver and Gold Medal tests for Preliminary-Advanced and non-professional adult students.
Further details on application.

EQUITY

Upper St Martins Lane
London
WC2H 9EG
Uniterd Kingdom
Tel: 020 7379 6000
Fax: 020 7379 7001
Email: info@equity.org.uk
Website: www.equity.org.uk

Equity is the only Professional Association to represent artists from across the entire spectrum of arts and entertainment. Membership includes actors, singers, dancers, choreographers, stage managers, theatre directors and designers, variety and circus artists, television and radio presenters, walk-on and supporting artists, stunt performers and directors, and theatre fight directors.

The main aim of Equity is to promote the interests of its members, negotiating minimum terms and conditions of employment throughout the world of entertainment and to endeavour to ensure these take account of social and economic changes. Equity also offers the Equity card to all members. This is the universally recognised symbol of status as a professional in the entertainment industry. Members' details are also included on a large number of specialist registers which are made available to casting directors and employers.

MEMBERSHIP:

Full Membership: Open to those who are currently professionally employed in the field of entertainment.
Student Membership: Available to those on a full-time higher education course lasting for one year or more which prepares them to work in the entertainment industry. If applicants are on a NCDT or CDET accredited course or studying theatre design or studying singing at a conservator or on the musical theatre course at the Royal Academy of Music, they can acquire full membership on graduating without having to provide proof of work. If they are on a non-accredited course, then they can continue student membership for up to two years after graduating, which enables them to gain professional employment and become eligible for Full Membership.
Youth Membership: Applicants aged between 14 and 16 years who are performing professionally and earning at least half of the adult rate for the job in question can become a Youth Member and are eligible to acquire Full Membership upon turning 16.

Electrical, Electronic and Manufacturing Engineering

THE INSTITUTION OF ELECTRICAL ENGINEERS

Savoy Place
London
WC2R 0BL
United Kingdom
Tel: 020 7240 1871
Fax: 020 7497 3609
Website: www.iee.org.uk

CORPORATE MEMBERSHIP:

Honorary Fellow (HonFIEE): Honorary Fellows are elected by the Council. There are corporate and non-corporate Honorary Fellows.
Fellow (FIEE): Fellows are members of the profession who have met the requirements for MIEE and have carried superior responsibility for at least 5 years.
Member (MIEE): Must have satisfied the educational requirements of an accredited MEng or equivalent and have provided evidence that they are (a) competent to practise as a Chartered Engineer and (b) committed to professional development throughout their career in engineering. Member and Fellow candidates have to be, disregarding temporary unemployment, engaged in or associated with any branch of engineering.

NON-CORPORATE MEMBERSHIP:

Companion (Companion IEE): Not normally an Engineer by profession but must satisfy the Council that they have rendered important services to electrical/electronic/software/systems/information or manufacturing engineering. They are not eligible for election as Fellows.
Associate Member (AMIEE): A person who has a minimum of a Pass degree on an Honours degree course or its equivalent, and is working in an activity relevant to the interests of the Institution as illustrated by IEE's Professional Networks.
Associate: Must be aged at least 21, of good education (at least that necessary for enrolment for tertiary education) and be interested in the advancement of electrical/electronic/software/systems/information or manufacturing engineering and its applications.
Student: Must be studying for the profession and intending to satisfy the requirements for AMIEE.

Comprehensive information on the IEE including membership application forms can be found on the internet at www.iee.org.uk/

THE INSTITUTION OF LIGHTING ENGINEERS

Lennox House
9 Lawford Road
Rugby
CV21 2DZ
United Kingdom
Tel: 01788 576492
Fax: 01788 540145
Email: ile@ile.co.uk
Website: www.ile.co.uk

MEMBERSHIP:

Fellow: A person who (a) (i) is at least 35, and (ii) has been in the grade of Member for at least 5 years, and (iii) has made a substantial contribution towards furthering the objectives of the Institution or (b) has, in the opinion of the Council, such experience and eminence in the profession, that his/her admission as a Fellow would be conducive to the interests of the Institution.

Member: A person who is at least 25 and (a) (i) has obtained a degree in an approved engineering/science subject, and (ii) has received at least 2 years' training in lighting installations or equipment, and (iii) has 3 years' approved experience, or (b) complies with all the requirements of (a) but with an academic qualification in a non-engineering field acceptable to the Council, or (c) (i) has obtained a qualification not less than a BTEC HNC in an approved engineering/science subject, and (ii) has at least 2 years' training in the industry, and (iii) has 5 years' approved experience, or (d) complies with all the requirements of (c) but with an academic qualification in a non-engineering field acceptable to the Council, or (e) (i) a person who is at least 30, and (ii) is a Corporate Member of an Engineering Council approved professional body authorised to register Chartered Engineers, and (iii) has 3 years' approved experience in the industry, or (f) a person who is at least 35, and (i) has attained a satisfactory level of general education, and (ii) has received at least 2 years' training and satisfies the Council of this by submission of evidence in the form of a written thesis, and (iii) has at least 10 years' experience in the lighting industry, and (iv) attends a professional interview, and (v) has been a non-Corporate member of the Institution in the grade of Affiliate for a minimum of 5 years.

Note: A person elected to the grade of Member by route (b), (d) or (f) is not eligible for registration with the Engineering Council as a CEng or IEng.

Associate Member: A person who is at least 23 and (a) (i) has obtained a qualification not less than BTEC HNC in an approved engineering/science subject, and (ii) has at least 2 years' training in the industry, and (iii) has at least 3 years' experience in the industry, or (b) complies with all the requirements of (a) but with an academic qualification in a non-engineering field acceptable to the Council, or (c) (i) has obtained a qualification not less than BTEC NC in an approved engineering/science subject, and (ii) has 2 years' training in the profession, and (iii) has a minimum of 5 years' experience in the industry, or (d) complies with all the requirements of (c) but with an academic qualification in a non-engineering field acceptable to the Council, or (e) a person over 35 who (i) has attained a satisfactory level of general education, and (ii) has a minimum of 15 years' experience in the industry and can satisfy the Council of this by submission of a written thesis, and (iii) attends a professional interview, and (iv) has been a non-Corporate Member of the Institution in the grade of Affiliate for a minimum of 3 years.

Note: A person elected to the grade of Associate Member by route (b), (d) or (e) is not eligible for registration with the Engineering Council as an IEng or an EngTech.

Affiliate: (a) A person of 21 or more who has obtained an ILE Final Certificate in Lighting Technology, or (b) a person at least 30 who has a minimum of 10 years' experience in the industry and show, by presentation of a thesis, that his/her knowledge of lighting or associated subject is equivalent to that gained in an ILE Final Certificate in Lighting Technology.

Associate: A candidate for election or transfer to the grade of Associate shall be interested in the objects of the Institution and over 21.

Student: A candidate for election to the grade of Student shall be under 26 and satisfy the Council that he/she has obtained a satisfactory standard of general education and is undergoing an approved training in lighting or the design or development of lighting installations or equipment.

Embalming

THE BRITISH INSTITUTE OF EMBALMERS

21c Station Road
Knowle
Solihull
West Midlands
B93 0HL
United Kingdom
Tel: 01564 778991
Fax: 01564 770812
Email: info@bioe.co.uk
Website: www.bioe.org.uk

Fellow (FBIE): Fellowship is granted by the National Council of the Institute upon invitation from the Fellows themselves. It is given for exceptional services to the Institute or the science in general.

Member (MBIE): Membership is authorised by the National Council of the Institute, which demands certain qualifications from the applicant. Information may be obtained from the National Office.

NATIONAL EXAMINATIONS BOARD OF EMBALMERS

39 Poplar Grove
Kennington
Oxford
OX1 5QN
United Kingdom
Tel: 01865 735788
Fax: 01865 730941
Email: nebe@btinternet.com

The Board examines candidates who wish to become qualified members of the British Institute of Embalmers (which is not itself an examining body).

Registration: Information packs (available from the above office and the International Office of the British Institute of Embalmers, 21c Station Road, Knowle, Solihull, West Midlands B97 0HL) contain lists of approved schools and tutors. The Board only accepts Candidates from these accredited Tutors, so it is essential to register with one of these Tutors initially.

Candidates are then taught through a Modular Programme, with the Board setting a first (Foundation) Module, which must be passed prior to continuing on the course.

After successfully completing the Foundation Module, Candidates need to apply for registration with the British Institute of Embalmers, as a Student Member.

Examinations: The Board sets 'school-based' tests at the conclusion of each of the 5 modules, and the marks attained in these tests count towards the Board's final exam.

The **final exam:** consists of a theoretical exam and a practical exam; the former must be passed before the latter may be attempted. The theoretical exam contains questions from the whole syllabus covering Anatomy and Physiology, (elementary) Pathology, Bacteriology and Chemistry, and a comprehensive understanding of the theory of Embalming. The practical exam consists of the embalmment of a subject. Applicants for the practical exam must already have performed 30 complete embalmments, 12 of which have been subjected to a post mortem exam.

Emergency Services

AMBULANCE SERVICE INSTITUTE

2 Appletree Close
Oakley
Near Basingstoke
Hampshire
RG23 7HL
United Kingdom
Fax: 01256 782650 (24 hour)
Email: ambservinst.uk@virgin.net
Website: www.asi.ac.uk or
www.asi-international.com

Official Publication: 'asi INTERNATONAL' ®™ No: 2170635

Hon. Secretary & Treasurer: Mr W. R. Jones FASI (Hon)

Membership of the Ambulance Service Institute is open to all employees of an NHS Ambulance Service. There is also a section for Non-NHS personnel such as Voluntary Aid, First Responders, Non-NHS Ambulance Services, Military Medical and Industrial First Aid/Medical personnel, etc, who hold a current First Aid certificate or higher qualification issued by a recognised body such as the British Red Cross Society and/or the St Johns Ambulance and who are being regularly trained in Ambulance or First Aid duties.

Fellow (FASI): Open to Graduate Members who submit a paper on their research area to the Board of Management on one or more aspects of Ambulance Service development that may improve the professional care given to patients and/or the way in which the service is provided.

There is no prescribed examination for the Fellowship grade.

Graduate (GASI): Open to Associate Members in order to enable them to further develop and expand their knowledge of Clinical and/or Management/Training skills for the benefit of patients and the general public at large and who have sucessfully passed the prescribed examination. This grade is also available for Membership by exemption to Ambulance personnel who can comply with the criteria.

Associate (AASI): Available in Pre-Hospital Care, Control and Communications, and Management/Training. Open to Licentiate Members who have sucessfully passed the prescribed examination. This grade is also available for Membership entry by exemption to IHCD qualified Ambulance Paramedics who are able to comply with the criteria.

Licentiate (LASI): Available in Pre-Hospital Care, Control and Communications, and Management/Training. This grade is also available for Membership entry by exemption to IHCD qualified Ambulance Technicians who are able to comply with the criteria.

Student: Open to all employees of an Ambulance Service, Voluntary First Aid/First AED Responders, Military Medical and Industrial First Aid/Medical personnel, etc, who hold a current First Aid/First Aid at Work Certificate or higher qualification issued by a recognised body such as the British Red Cross Society and/ or the St Johns Ambulance and who are being regularly trained in Ambulance and/or First Aid duties. There are no designatory letters for the Student grade of membership.

Affiliate (ASI Affil): Open to individuals, companies and bodies who support the Institute's aims, objectives and activities without claim to membership by examination or other means.

EXAMINATIONS:

Graduate Grade: The syllabus includes standards of performance and quality control, contractual procedures – standards-applications and management, major incident planning – all hazards, human relations, the law and developments in relation to Ambulance Services, budgetary control within the Ambulance Services, equipment design and evaluation including vehicles, information technology and communication systems, and existing and proposed European and British legislation applicable to the Ambulance Services of Great Britain.

Associate Grade: *Pre-Hospital Care* includes papers on anatomy/physiology, advanced resuscitation, drug administration, neonatal conditions, emergency childbirth, trauma, and multiple casualty management.

Associate Grade: *Control Communications and Management* includes papers on communication and computer technology, standards of performance, health and safety and welfare at work Act, personnel management, identification of training needs and development, patient complaints evaluation, Departmental and Service reports, and contractual procedures and contract management.

Licentiate Grade: *Pre-Hospital Care* includes papers on anatomy/physiology, patient care and examination and diagnosis, resuscitation, emergency childbirth, infectious diseases, trauma management, personal hygiene, use and maintenance of ambulance equipment, road traffic law, advanced driving, health and safety, and patient complaints procedures.

Licentiate Grade: *Control Communications & First Line Management* includes papers on communication systems and procedures, control of emergency and priority dispatch cases, non-emergency cases control and journey pre-planning, health and safety, personnel management, training, reports, contract procedures and management and major incidents, patient complaints procedures.

Employment and Careers Services

THE INSTITUTE OF CAREER GUIDANCE

27a Lower High Street
Stourbridge
West Midlands
DY8 1TA
United Kingdom
Tel: 01384 376464
Fax: 01384 440830
Email: hq@icg-uk.org
Website: www.icg-uk.org

MEMBERSHIP CATEGORIES

Full Member: Subscribes to Code of Ethics and Standards. Commitment to Continuous Professional Development. DCG Parts 1/ S/ NVQ Level 4 in Advice or Guidance (or equivalent) or QCG qualifications in careers guidance.

Associate: Subscribes to Code of Ethics and Standards. Commitment to Continuous Professional Development. S/NVQ Level 3 in Guidance or Working in Guidance.

Student: Studying FT for DCG, new Qualification in Careers Guidance (QCG) or PT whilst unemployed.

Affiliate: Subscribes to Code of Ethics and Standards. Interest in Guidance.

Fellow (Qualified): 10 years' Practice + Full Membership.

Fellow (Academic): Research (recognised by Council).

Fellow (Honorary): Good Works (elected at final Council meeting of the year).

RECRUITMENT AND EMPLOYMENT CONFEDERATION (FORMERLY THE INSTITUTE OF EMPLOYMENT CONSULTANTS)

3rd Floor, Steward House
16a Commercial Way
Woking
Surrey
GU21 6ET
United Kingdom
Tel: 020 7462 3260
Fax: 01483 714979
Email: info@rec.uk.com
Website: www.rec.uk.com

MEMBERSHIP:

Fellow (FREC): Candidates for Fellowship must be recruitment consultants of at least 10 years' standing, able to show evidence of the highest standards of professional conduct throughout their career. They must have been members of the REC for 3 years and need sponsorship from 2 Fellows of the REC.
Member (MREC): Candidates must show evidence of *one* of the following qualifications: Foundation Vocational Award plus $\frac{1}{2}$ years' proven relevant experience *or* Certificate in Recruitment Practice plus 2 years proven relevant experience *or* successful completion of 5 REC-approved training courses plus 3 years' proven relevant experience. Candidates with 6 years' relevant experience *or* 5 years' relevant experience plus a degree are exempt from these conditions.
Associate Member (AREC): Candidates must show evidence of *one* of the following qualifications: Foundation Vocational Award plus 6 months' proven relevant experience *or* Certificate in Recruitment Practice *or* successful completion of 3 REC-approved training courses plus 2 years' proven relevant experience. Candidates with 4 years' relevant experience *or* 3 years' relevant experience plus a degree are exempt from these conditions.
Affiliate Membership: Granted to anyone supporting the purpose and objects of the Institute.
Student Membership: Granted to anyone enrolled on an educational course recognised by the Institute.

EXAMINATIONS:

Foundation Vocational Award in Employment Agency Practice: Run by the REC.
Certificate in Recruitment Practice (Cert RP): Run jointly by the REC and the AQA (Assessment & Qualifications Alliance).

Energy Engineering

THE INSTITUTE OF ENERGY

18 Devonshire Street
London
W1G 7AU
United Kingdom
Tel: 020 7580 7124
Fax: 020 7580 4420
Email: info@instenergy.org.uk
Website: www.instenergy.org.uk

The Institute of Energy (InstE) is the professional body representing the Energy, Environment and Engineering sectors in the UK and overseas. It is a learned society and licensed to recognise individuals at Chartered Engineer, Incorporated Engineer and Engineering Technician levels.
The InstE's aim is to promote the cost-effective and environmentally responsible provision and management of energy in all its forms. This is accomplished through services provided to individuals and organisations in membership, and to the benefit of the wider society. The InstE's services include:
- Education, training and life-long learning;
- Policy debate and influence;
- Consultancy;
- Knowledge and information through events, publications and website;
- Regional, national and international networks.

ACADEMIC/VOCATIONAL QUALIFICATIONS:

The InstE's Qualifications Database houses information about Energy, Environment and Engineering undergraduate, postgraduate, and continuing professional development courses and seminars operated on a FT, PT and/or DL basis in the UK and overseas. Contact the Education Office by email at education@instenergy.org.uk for information on courses and guidance on your professional development. The Education Office can also provide information about the Training in Energy Management through the Open Learning (TEMOL) course, the Level 4 NVQ in Managing Energy and various professional development courses in Energy and Environmental Management.

PROFESSIONAL QUALIFICATIONS:

Individual membership grades reflect an individual's qualifications, training and experience in the Energy, Environment and Engineering sectors. All members are required to make a commitment to their professional development to ensure that they maintain their skills, knowledge and competencies. The InstE's professional membership grades include:

Fellow (FInstE): Aged 33 or over, with an Honours degree or equivalent academic qualification and a minimum of 5 years' senior Energy/Energy Engineering experience. Fellows with the appropriate Engineering qualification, training and experience can be registered at Chartered Engineer level.

Member (MInstE): Aged 25 or over, with an Honours degree or equivalent academic qualification and a minimum of 4 years' training and experience in an Energy/Energy Engineering/Environment field. Members with the appropriate Engineering qualification, training and experience can be registered at Chartered Engineer level.

Associate Member (AMInstE): Aged 23 or over, with an HNC/D, NVQ Level 4 in Managing Energy or equivalent qualifications and a minimum of 5 years' training and experience in an Energy/Energy Engineering/Environment field. Associate Members with the appropriate Engineering qualification, training and experience can be registered at Incorporated Engineer level.

Technician Member (TMInstE): Aged 21 or over, with an Advanced GNVQ, NC/D or equivalent qualification and a minimum of 4 years' training and experience in an Energy/Energy Engineering/Environment field. Technician Members with the appropriate Engineering qualification, training and experience can be registered at Engineering Technician level.

Other membership grades include **Students** completing Energy, Environmental or Engineering academic courses; **Graduates** who have completed Energy, Environmental or Engineering qualifications; and **Affiliates** who have an interest in the Energy, Environmental and Engineering sectors.

THE INSTITUTE OF PETROLEUM

61 New Cavendish Street
London
W1G 7AR
United Kingdom
Tel: 020 7467 7100
Fax: 020 7255 1472
Email: ip@petroleum.co.uk
Website: www.petroleum.co.uk

Membership of the Institute of Petroleum is open to all individuals, companies and other associations wishing to further its aims, which are 'the advancement of technical knowledge relating to the international oil and gas industry'. It is a non-qualifying body. The Institute will increase the knowledge and understanding of the oil industry by young people so that they see it as providing stimulating and fulfilling opportunities.

Honorary Fellow: Person of eminence, who may or may not be actively engaged in the petroleum industry. These positions shall normally be for life, but the Council may at its discretion elect a person for the period of their tenure of some particular official position.

Fellow (FInstPet): A Member for not less than 5 years who satisfies the Council that he has appropriate professional, technical, scientific or academic qualifications and that he has held, for not less than 5 years, a position of responsibility concerned with petroleum.

Member (MInstPet): Shall be not less than 18 and shall satisfy the Council that he or she is a fit and proper person to belong to the Institute and is desirous of furthering its objects.

Student Member (SInstPet): A Student Member shall be not less than 18 and shall satisfy the Council that he or she is undertaking an FT or S course of study, approved by the Council, and intends to become a Member of the Institute.

Collective Membership: Companies and other associations which are interested in and desirous of assisting in the work of the Institute may be elected Collective Members under the conditions laid down in the Institute's By-laws.

Engineering Design

THE INSTITUTION OF ENGINEERING DESIGNERS

Courtleigh
Westbury Leigh
Westbury
Wiltshire
BA13 3TA
United Kingdom
Tel: 01373 822801
Fax: 01373 858085
Email: ied@ied.org.uk
Website: www.ied.org.uk

DIVISIONAL STRUCTURE:

The Institution is organised into three separate sections: Engineering Design Division, Product Design Division and CADD Division. Membership to these divisions is based on the following requirements.

CORPORATE MEMBERSHIP:

Fellow (FIED): By portfolio assessment for persons of outstanding ability in the profession who have at least 10 years' experience, of which 6 years were devoted to Engineering Design, Product Design or CADD and who hold an HNC or equivalent, and are not less than 30.

Members (MIED): Must have at least 3 years' experience, of which 2 years were devoted to Engineering Design, Product Design or CADD and hold a qualification of HNC or equivalent, and are not less than 23.

NON-CORPORATE MEMBERSHIP:

Associates: Must have at least 2 years' drawing office experience and hold a qualification not less than ONC equivalent, and are not less than 22.

AFFILIATE MEMBERSHIP:

Graduate & Diplomat Membership: Available for persons with appropriate educational qualifications but without adequate experience/responsibility for admission to an appropriate Corporate or Non-Corporate grade.
Students: Must be actively or prospectively engaged in engineering/product/CAD as apprentices or trainees, be engaged in a suitable course of study, and are not less than 18.

ENGINEERING COUNCIL REGISTRATION:

Corporate Members to the Engineering Division may be nominated for Registration as Chartered Engineers or Incorporated Engineers and Non-Corporate Members as Engineering Technicians, depending on their qualifications, training and experience.

Environmental Engineering

THE CHARTERED INSTITUTION OF WATER AND ENVIRONMENTAL MANAGEMENT

15 John Street
London
WC1N 2EB
United Kingdom
Tel: 020 7831 3110
Fax: 020 7405 4967
Email: admin@ciwem.org.uk
Website: www.ciwem.org.uk

CIWEM, founded in 1895, is the leading Professional Body in Water and Environmental Management, in recognition of which the Institution was granted a Royal Charter in 1995.
In the Royal Charter granted to CIWEM, Water and Environmental Management is defined as the application of engineering, scientific or management knowledge and expertise to the provision of works and services designed to further the beneficial management, conservation and improvement of the environment. This includes: Environmental management; Resource protection, development, use and conservation; Integrated pollution control; Public health, water and sanitation services; Flood defence and land drainage; and Recreation, amenity and conservation activities.

EXAMINATIONS:

PG Certificate in Water & Environmental Management: Provides the broad understanding of water and environmental management issues needed by those active in all facets of the industry.
PG Diploma in Water & Environmental Management: Provides a high standard of knowledge in a series of specially chosen options tailored to industry needs.
The courses are all modular and may be taken singly or in combinations. The Certificate will be awarded after successful completion of all 4 compulsory modules and the Diploma after the successful completion of a further 4 optional modules.

SOCIETY OF ENVIRONMENTAL ENGINEERS

The Manor House
High Street
Buntingford
Hertfordshire
SG9 9AB
United Kingdom
Tel: 01763 271209
Fax: 01763 273255
Email: see@owles.demon.co.uk
Website: www.environmental.org.uk

This is a learned society formed in 1959 to cover the whole field of Environmental Engineering and to provide a forum for the dissemination and discussion of knowledge in that field. The major subjects covered by the Society's current work are the testing of industrial and military equipment, the development and use of packaging materials and methods, safety and comfort in road, rail, sea and air travel and contamination control.
Membership is confined to those of professional status whose main responsibilities are environmental research, testing or the manufacture of equipment for such research and testing.
The SEE has nominated body status with the ETB and is able to assess the competence of environmental engineering candidates for registration to CEng, IEng and Eng Tech.
The requirements for **Membership** are an Honours degree in an Engineering subject plus at least 2 years' training and experience in Environmental Engineering. **Associate Members** are required to have an academic qualification plus at least 3 years' training and

experience. Those with no qualifications may join the SEE as **Associates**. **Student Membership** is also available.

Environmental Sciences

INSTITUTE OF ECOLOGY AND ENVIRONMENTAL MANAGEMENT

45 Southgate Street
Winchester
Hampshire
SO23 9EH
United Kingdom
Tel: 01962 868626
Fax: 01962 868626
Email: enquires@ieem.demon.co.uk
Website: www.ieem.org.uk

IEEM was established in 1991 and now represents over 1000 Ecologists and Environmental Managers in the UK and abroad. It provides professional services to its membership, produces a quarterly journal and other publications, and organises workshops and conferences which are open to all.

MEMBERSHIP:

Membership is open to all individuals who are practising ecologists, graduates and students of ecology and environmental disciplines and to those who are interested in the profession of Ecology and Environmental Management. The categories of membership are as follows:
Fellow (FIEEM): Must have been a Member for at least 5 years and have made an outstanding contribution to the field.
Full Member (MIEEM): Those who hold at least a relevant second class Honours degree (or equivalent) plus a minimum of 3 years' suitable professional practice.
Full members may be elected as Fellows if they can demonstrate that they have made a substantial contribution to the professional practice of Ecology and Environmental Management.
Associate Member (AIEEM): This grade is open to individuals who currently lack the necessary professional experience.
Those wishing for Full or Associate Membership but who do not possess sufficient qualifications may be considered for these grades if they have accumulated their skills and knowledge vocationally (e.g. through work experience, part-time education or other training). These applicants may present a portfolio of work which will be examined and considered for membership.

Affiliate Member: Affiliate Membership is open to Ecologists and Environmental Managers without the necessary qualifications; or amateurs with an interest in the field.
Student Member: For those enrolled on a relevant course leading to an examined Honours degree, HND or equivalent.

Export

INSTITUTE OF EXPORT

Export House
Minerva Business Park
Lynch Wood
Peterborough
PE2 6FT
United Kingdom
Tel: 01733 404400
Fax: 01733 404444
Email: education@export.org.uk
Website: www.export.org.uk

QUALIFICATIONS:

Professional Qualification in Export: The Institute provides a 2 year PT nationally taught professional qualification in International Trade. Tuition is provided through colleges of Further and HE, and through the Institute's Home Study programme. Part 1, The Advanced Certificate in International Trade consists of 4 subjects: Operating in the Global Economy, the Business Environment, International Physical Distribution and the Finance of International Trade. Part 2 (2nd year) consists of 4 subjects: International Market Planning, International Logistics and Purchasing, Management of International Trade and Practical Global Trading. Completion of both Part 1 and Part 2 entitles eligibility for graduate membership of the Institute. Candidates for Part 1 must be at least 18; for Part 2 they must have passed Part 1. Exemptions from individual subjects may be granted for equivalent qualifications. Each case is considered individually.

MEMBERSHIP:

Membership: Open to any individual engaged in international trade. Full Membership is dependent on appropriate educational qualifications, experience and career achievements. All members have to be elected by the Council, and the grades of membership are as follows:
Fellow (FIEx): By application from any person who can demonstrate outstanding achievements and has reached a position of eminence in their career. No one may join the Institute at this grade.

Companion (CIEx): By invitation to any person who has demonstrated outstanding achievements at the highest level.

Member by Experience (MIEx): By application from any person who has the requisite number of years' experience in international trade and holds a position of responsibility.

Associate Member (AMIEx): By application from any person who does not qualify for Full Membership by experience or educational qualifications yet has obtained a sufficient level of achievement to justify their election to this grade.

Graduate Member (MIEx (Grad)): By application from any person who has passed the Institute's professional exams or their equivalents, as agreed by the Institute's Education Committee.

Affiliate: By application from any person who is seeking to improve their knowledge and understanding of overseas trade and international business administration and management.

Student Member: By application from any person of at least 18 years of age with 4 O level qualifications, including English Language, or 4 GCSE passes at grades A, B or C or an acceptable equivalent and 1 A level pass, or equivalent, or ITAS Level 2 S/NVQ. Candidates aged 21 years and over who lack formal academic qualifications but have had 3 years' practical experience in overseas trade may be accepted at the Institute's discretion. All students of the Institute are required to pass the professional exams within 4 years of the date of their registration unless a special extension is granted. Overseas students must demonstrate competence in English and comparable qualifications.

Business Membership: Available to all businesses wishing to be, or already involved in, international trade with an annual turnover of up to £8 million. Any business within this bracket may apply with the aid of one trade referee.

Corporate Membership: Available to large companies with an annual turnover exceeding £8 million. Any company may apply with the aid of one trade referee. The size and experience of these companies will be a valuable addition to the membership base.

Fire Engineering

THE INSTITUTION OF FIRE ENGINEERS

148 Upper New Walk
Leicester
LE1 7QB
United Kingdom
Tel: 0116 255 3654
Fax: 0116 247 1231
Email: info@ife.org.uk
Website: www.ife.org.uk

CORPORATE MEMBERSHIP:

Fellow (FIFireE): Applicants must be a member of at least 3 years' standing, hold a recognised Honours degree in Fire Engineering or a relevant subject, have at least 4 years' acceptable training and responsible experience and 3 years' continuing professional development. Fire Engineers who meet these requirements but do not hold the relevant formal qualifications may gain Membership via the Mature Candidate Route. Such applicants will need to demonstrate at least 15 years of increasing responsibility and their knowledge and competency will be assessed through the submitting of a technical paper.

Member (MIFireE): Applicants must hold a recognised degree or equivalent in a relevant subject, or the Membership examination or recognised equivalent, have at least 4 years' acceptable training and responsible experience and 2 years' continuing professional development, and have their application supported by three corporate members of the Institution. Fire Engineers without the relevant formal qualifications may gain membership via the Mature Candidate Route by demonstrating at least 15 years of increasing responsibility and their knowledge and competency will be assessed through the submission of a technical paper.

Associate (AIFireE): Applicants must have successfully completed the required modules of study, or hold a relevant Honours degree required to progress to Fellow but cannot fulfil the training and experience for that grade, and be able to demonstrate at least 1 year of continuing professional development and have their application supported by 3 corporate members of the Institution.

NON-CORPORATE MEMBERSHIP:

Graduate (GIFireE): Applicants must either pass the Graduateship examination, the UK station officers examination, an HNC/D, or an Institute recognised and accredited course. In addition, the applicant must have at least 3 years of acceptable training/experience in Fire

Engineering. Fire Engineers without formal academic qualifications may gain Graduate Membership via the Mature Candidate Route. They should and have at least 12 years of increasing responsibility and their knowledge and competency will be assessed through the submission of a technical paper.

Technician (TIFireE): Applicants must hold the Institution's intermediate examination and have at least 2 years' acceptable training and responsible experience in Fire Engineering. Alternatively, applicants can be registered as Engineering Technicians with the Engineering Council in the UK, or international equivalent.

Student: Applicants must be engaged as a PT or FT student of Fire Engineering (which may include vocational workplace-based training) or be PT or FT employment in Fire Engineering. The Institution may also elect Honorary Fellows.

EXAMINATIONS:

The Institution conducts a Preliminary Examination, which qualifies for the award of a Preliminary Certificate, and an Intermediate Examination which qualifies for the award of an Intermediate Certificate.

The Institution also conducts a Graduate Examination which has a reciprocity arrangement with the Fire Service Examination Board statutory Station Officers' Examination. Candidates for this exam must have completed 3 years in a fire engineering capacity approved by the Institution.

The Membership Exam is open to Graduate members of the Institution.

For further details of these examinations or any other aspect of the Institution of Fire Engineers please contact the Secretariat at the above address.

Fisheries Management

INSTITUTE OF FISHERIES MANAGEMENT

22 Rushworth Avenue
West Bridgford
Nottingham
NG2 7LF
United Kingdom
Tel: 0115 9822317
Fax: 0115 9826150
Email: chris@randall.force9.co.uk
Website: www.ifm.org.uk

The Institute of Fisheries Management is an international organisation of fisheries professional, lay and student members sharing a common interest in the modern management of recreational and commercial fisheries.

Fellow (FIFM): Persons who are qualified as Members and who, in the opinion of the Council, have made a significant contribution to fisheries management in the field of research, development or otherwise, and/or in furthering the interests and objectives of the Institute, may be invited to become Fellows.

Honorary Member (Hon MIFM): A person who has rendered special services to Fisheries Management or to the Institute, or who is distinguished in some other sphere.

Registered Member (MIFM): A person who has been engaged in, or involved with, Fisheries Management for at least 5 years and who: (a) holds the Diploma of the Institute; or (b) holds an appropriate university degree or CNAA degree; or (c) holds such alternative qualifications as the Council may from time to time deem appropriate.

Licentiate Member (LMIFM): A person who has been engaged in, or involved with, Fisheries Management for at least 2 years and who: (a) holds the diploma or a Certificate of the Institute; or (b) holds an appropriate degree as in (b) above; or (c) holds such alternative qualifications as the Council may from time to time deem appropriate.

Associate Members: A person employed in Fisheries Management (whether in an FT or PT capacity and whether in a paid or honorary capacity) not eligible as a Members or Licentiate Member.

Subscriber Member: A person or body not qualifying for membership in any other category and appearing to have an interest in Fisheries Management.

Student Member: A person who is interested in Fisheries Management, who are in FT or PT education and who is not in regular paid employment.

The IFM runs 3 correspondence courses: The **Certificate and Diploma in Fisheries Management and the Certificate in Fish Farming** are accepted qualifications by employers such as the Environment Agency. Details from V. L. Holt at above address.

The Certificate courses can each be completed in one year. The duration of the Diploma course is two years, and it has been credit-rated by the Open University Validation Service. Persons gaining the Diploma are now entitled to 60 credit points at Level 1 and 15 credit points at Level 2, which can be used to contribute towards an Open University degree.

Floristry

THE SOCIETY OF FLORISTRY LTD

Meadowside Hall Road
West Bergholt
Colchester
Essex
CO6 3DU
United Kingdom
Tel: 0870 241 0432
Fax: 0870 241 0432
Email: info@societyofflorestry.org
Website: www.societyofflorestry.org

Fellowship is only granted to paid-up persons holding the National Diploma of the Society of Floristry Limited. Membership is open to all persons engaged in the floral industry.

EXAMINATIONS

Intermediate Certificate of the Society of Floristry (ICSF): Intermediate exams are held annually and are open to students taking a recognised course of floristry training or the equivalent 3 years' relevant experience in the industry.

National Diploma of the Society of Floristry (NDSF): The National Diploma exam is also held annually. This is the highest award for professional floristry in the UK. Entry qualification is the Intermediate Certificate of the Society of Floristry.

Attending a seminar is a compulsory component for both exams.

Food Science and Nutrition

INSTITUTE OF FOOD SCIENCE AND TECHNOLOGY (UK)

5 Cambridge Court
210 Shepherds Bush Road
London
W6 7NJ
United Kingdom
Tel: 020 7603 6316
Email: info@ifst.org
Website: www.ifst.org

MEMBERSHIP:

Fellow (FIFST): Fellows (not less than 33) have the necessary qualifications for Membership and not less than 7 years' appropriate experience in Food Science or Technology in addition to the relevant period of qualifying experience for Membership (see below). They must *either* have made a substantial contribution to Food Science and Technology *or* have reached a position of suitable seniority and authority in the profession.

Member (MIFST): Members *either* have an appropriate degree with first or second class Honours or an equivalent academic or professional qualification together with at least 3 years' suitable experience if the qualification is in Food Science or Food Technology, or at least 4 years' if a major element of Food Science & Technology is included; *or* have an acceptable degree or academic or professional qualification, together with at least 4 to 6 years' appropriate experience, depending on the nature and subject of the qualification.

Licentiate: Must *either* have an appropriate degree or academic or professional qualification; *or* an acceptable academic or professional qualification (minimum level HND).

Student Member: Must be in an approved course of study in the UK or Europe.

Affiliate: A person, while ineligible for any other grade of membership, qualifies for this grade by virtue of their activities relating to Food Science and Technology.

Academic requirements for membership: University, academic or professional qualifications acceptable by the Institute include not only those in Food Science or Food Technology, but also those in any other relevant discipline, eg Chemistry, Microbiology, Biochemistry, Engineering, Chemical Engineering, etc.

EXAMINATIONS:

Higher Certificate in Food Premises Inspection: Issued by IFST, the Higher Certificate meets the requirements of the Department of Health Code of Practice No 9, that Inspections of Food Premises should only be undertaken by officers who are suitably qualified and experienced.

Forestry and Arboriculture

THE ARBORICULTURAL ASSOCIATION

Ampfield House
Ampfield, Nr Romsey
Hampshire
SO51 9PA
United Kingdom
Tel: 01794 368717
Fax: 01794 368978
Email: treehouse@dial.pipex.com
Website: www.trees.org.uk

MEMBERSHIP:

Fellow: Fellows are professional arboriculturists with qualifications to Professional Diploma in Arboriculture (or equivalent), or higher qualification, experience and proficiency to standards approved by the Association. Applicants for Fellowship must have held associate membership for at least 5 years, and supporting statements from 2 sponsors who are Fellows.

Associate: Associates are persons professionally concerned with arboriculture and who hold the Professional Diploma in Arboriculture (or equivalent) or a higher qualification.

Affiliate: All others with a professional involvement in arboriculture, including members of related professions with an interest in arboriculture.

Corporate Member: Corporate members are civic amenity societies, associations, Local Authorities, companies, partnerships, institutions, public bodies, Government Departments, and similar bodies having sympathy with the objectives of the Association.

Ordinary Member: Any other person interested in the planting, care and conservation of amenity trees and woods.

Student: A person engaged in FT/S training or education with a maximum time limit of 3 years of membership in this category unless extended at the discretion of the Council.

INSTITUTE OF CHARTERED FORESTERS

7A St Colme Street
Edinburgh
EH3 6AA
United Kingdom
Tel: 0131 225 2705
Fax: 0131 220 6128
Email: icf@charteredforesters.org
Website: www.charteredforesters.org

MEMBERSHIP:

Fellow: Holds a degree or diploma in forestry or a related science and has passed the Institute's Professional Exams, has been engaged in forestry in Britain in a professional capacity for at least 5 years and has been a member for at least 10 years. (Forestry is defined in its broadest context and includes professionals practising in all aspects of tree management, including forest management, arboriculture, urban forestry and environmental forestry.)

Ordinary Member: Has similar academic qualifications, has passed the Institute's Professional Exams and has been engaged in forestry in a professional capacity for at least 2 years.

Associate: Engaged in forestry and intend to qualify for full membership.

Affiliate: Not a professional forester but interested in the objectives of the Institute and includes some corporate bodies.

Student: Enrolled for a course in forestry approved by Council.

EXAMINATIONS:

Entry to Corporate Grades (ie Fellow and Ordinary Membership) is open to Associates who have obtained an approved qualification in forestry, and have passed the Institute's Professional Exams, which consist of theory papers, a project, field work and an oral exam.

THE ROYAL FORESTRY SOCIETY OF ENGLAND, WALES AND NORTHERN IRELAND

102 High Street
Tring
Hertfordshire
HP23 4AF
United Kingdom
Tel: 01442 822028
Fax: 01442 890395
Email: rfshq@rfs.org.uk
Website: www.rfs.org.uk

Certificate in Arboriculture: The syllabus for the written exam covers Botany, Nursery Work, Planting, Maintenance, Pests, Tree Surgery, Legal Questions, and Care and Use of Tools. The award is in association with the Awarding Body Consortium, and is dependent upon the candidate holding specified arboricultural proficiency tests offered by the National Proficiency Tests Council. This is a craftsman level award, equivalent to an NVQ Level 2.

Professional Diploma in Arboriculture: The syllabus covers the same general field as the Certificate, but in much greater depth. Candidates should be at least 23 and must have been in arboriculture-related industries for 3 years. This equates to NVQ Level 4, a supervisory or consultant level qualification.

Both the Certificate and the DipArb(RFS) are taken by private study or at various colleges, often on a day-release basis. They are suitable for those employed in botanical gardens, woodlands, local authority work and tree surgery companies.

Foundry Technology and Pattern Making

THE INSTITUTE OF CAST METAL ENGINEERS
Bordesley Hall
The Holloway
Alvechurch
Birmingham
B48 7QA
United Kingdom
Tel: 01527 596100
Fax: 01527 596102
Email: info@icme.org.uk
Website: www.icme.org.uk

Formed 1904, granted first Royal Charter in 1921; Third Supplemental Charter granted in 1994. The Institute is a Nominated Body of the Engineering Council and the granting of the Third Supplemental Charter has aligned its own membership requirements with those required by the Engineering Council. The Charter has also introduced the new grade of Affiliated Member. In line with the changing nature of the castings industry the Institute changed its name to The Institute of Cast Metals Engineers in August 2001.
Fellow (FICME): A person wishing to apply for the grade of Fellow has to be 35 years of age or over and to have the required academic qualifications. They must also prove that they have obtained a position of eminence within the industry and have held this position for at least 3 years.
Member (MICME): Should be at least 25 years of age and have achieved the required academic standard, and have held a position of responsibility within the industry for at least 3 years.
Associate Member (AMICME): Applicants with suitable qualifications may apply to join at this grade of membership at the age of 21 years. Associate Members who are registered Incorporated Engineers may use the deignatory letters **I Eng AMIBF** after their name.
Associate: Available to anyone not less than 18 years of age who can satisfy the General Council that they have a bona fide interest in the cast metals industry.
Affiliate Member: Have to prove they have attained a responsible position within their Company.
Student: This grade is available to anyone under the age of 23 years who is studying on a course related to Cast Metals Technology.
The Institute is a Nominated Body of the Engineering Council and may nominate its members for Chartered Engineer (CEng), Incorporated Engineer (IEng) and Engineering Technician (EngTech) status. It can also make submission for those suitably qualified members to become a Registered European Engineer (EurIng).
Fellows and Members who are registered as Chartered Engineers may call themselves 'Chartered'. Those who are registered as Incorporated Engineers may refer to themselves as an 'Incorporated Cast Metal Engineer'.

Freight Forwarding

THE BRITISH INTERNATIONAL FREIGHT ASSOCIATION (BIFA)
Redfern House
Browells Lane
Feltham
Middlesex
TW13 7EP
United Kingdom
Tel: 020 8844 2266
Fax: 020 8890 5546
Email: bifa@btconnect.com
Website: www.bifa.org

MEMBERSHIP:

BIFA membership is corporate, open to forwarding and international freight services companies which satisfy strict entrance criteria. Individual Membership is open to anyone working within any sector of the freight industry. The IFP professional qualification centres around a required level of appropriate experience and knowledge, and all relevant learning, whether by traditional or vocational qualification, higher or further education or specialised short courses, is accredited according to its level.
There are 4 categories of membership to accommodate those in the freight industry throughout their career development.
Affiliate: Caters for those at the beginning of their career and no special entrance criteria are needed. It also applies to those who interface with the industry and do not seek professional qualification in it.
Associate: Those at this level have already achieved a mid-point in learning and/or experience.
Full Professional Membership: Awarded to those who have a high enough proven level of experience and learning to be considered a professional.
Fellow: Conferred by status, experience and time.

EXAMINATIONS:

Exams may be taken if this is the chosen learning method, but are no longer essential.

The Advanced Certificate in International Trade (ACIT) is taken at FE colleges. There are also IFP modules available by correspondence, followed by a comprehensive tender project. These courses may be done in their entirety or as selected modules. Each is a stand-alone subject that is individually accredited.

Qualification by NVQs is becoming very popular, the most relevant being International Trade and Services. Any NVQ with appropriate operational or business knowledge is accredited according to level and direct relevance.

Because of the wider scope of knowledge now needed by the forwarder, there can be no single qualification that will cater adequately for all sector needs. The qualifications of the specialist sector institutes such as the Institute of Export, the Institute of Logistics and Transport, the Institute of Chartered Shipbrokers, the United Kingdom Warehousing Association and the like are therefore also accredited as appropriate.

Another pathway towards professional qualification is higher education and these courses too are accredited as appropriate.

Funeral Directing, Burial and Cremation Administration

THE INSTITUTE OF BURIAL AND CREMATION ADMINISTRATION

Kelham Hall
Newark
Nottinghamshire
NG23 5QX
United Kingdom
Tel: 01636 708311
Fax: 01636 708311

MEMBERSHIP:

Fellow (FInstBCA): Elected from those Members on whom, in the opinion of the Institute's Council, it would be in the interest of the Institute to confer the status of Fellow. The primary requirement shall be that such person shall have: (a) upon some subject with which the Institute is concerned in its objects, prepared and submitted to the Council or had published a paper or thesis, or prepared and delivered at a general meeting or conference of the Institute or similar organisation an address or lecture, which in the opinion of the Council is of value and interest to the Institute in any of its objects; or (b) performed any service which in the opinion of the Council has been of outstanding importance to the Institute or was in connection with matters relating to any of the objects of the Institute.

Member (MInstBCA): Elected from those who: (a) are holders of the Final Diploma of the Institute; or (b) have held Associate Membership for a period of 5 years, and are in FT employment in a senior managerial capacity or hold any other appointment of a senior administrative or supervisory character in a burial or cremation undertaking.

Associate Member (AInstBCA): Elected from 2 groups of applicants: (a) those who have for at least 2 years been employed in a supervisory or administrative appointment in a burial or cremation undertaking or a public service ancillary thereto for the disposal of the dead; and (b) Registered Licentiates or Students of the Institute who have passed 5 modules of the Institute's Diploma course.

Registered Licentiate (LInstBCA): Elected from those employed FT or PT in the service of a burial or cremation undertaking or a public service ancillary thereto for the disposal of the dead, but are not eligible for any other category of membership.

Student: Must be gainfully employed in a burial or cremation undertaking or a public service ancillary thereto for the disposal of the dead; may be required to pass an approved exam before enrolling for the Institute's Exams.

EXAMINATIONS:

The Institute administers a Diploma Course which is studied by correspondance and supplemented by attendance at a seminar at Stoke Rochford Hall in Lincolnshire. For further details contact: Gary Marshall, Education and Training Officer, Institute Education Service, 18 Albert Crescent, Keresley, Coventry CV6 2GG, tel: 01203 832260. The Institute also administers a course for the training of cemetary operatives titled the COTS scheme, in partnership with Berkshire College of Agriculture. For further details contact: Tim Morris 107 Parlaunt Road, Langley, Slough SL3 8BE, tel 020 8546 4463, 0374 973712 (mobile).

NATIONAL ASSOCIATION OF FUNERAL DIRECTORS

618 Warwick Road
Solihull
West Midlands
B91 1AA
United Kingdom
Tel: 0121 711 1343
Fax: 0121 711 1351
Email: info@nafd.org.uk
Website: www.nafd.org.uk

MEMBERSHIP:

Full Member (Category A): Business engaged in (but not necessarily exclusively) the practice of Funeral Directing within the United Kingdom, the Isle of Man and the Channel Islands. The nominated representative may be the proprietor or a senior executive. Member firms are required to pass an entrance exam consisting of an inspection of premises and facilities; also an assessment of the knowledge and capability of the senior representative, unless he or she holds the Diploma in Funeral Directing.
Full Member (Category B): Business engaged in (but not necessarily exclusively) supplying goods or services to the funeral profession as set out below:
(a) A proprietor or director of cemetery and/or crematoria (not being a public authority) or their nominee; (b) Manufacturers and suppliers of funeral directors' merchandise and equipment; (c) Manufacturers and main distributors of hearses, but not their agents; (d) A proprietor or director of an embalming service; (e) A person, firm or company that hires to Funeral Directors, operates or owns a hearse or hearses and a passenger car or cars, if accepted into membership after 3rd May 1978.
Overseas Member: A Funeral Director, ancillary business or allied professional association that operates outside the United Kingdom.

EXAMINATIONS:

Diploma in Funeral Directing (DipFD): The Diploma is awarded only to Registered Students who have passed a written exam based on the Association's *Manual of Funeral Directing* and a practical oral exam on funeral arranging and have also been working in a funeral director's business for at least 2 years, carried out 25 funeral arrangements and are over the age of 18. Holders of the Diploma may advance to the Higher Diploma, details of which are available for the National Office.
NVQ in Funeral Services: This qualification is for persons employed within the funeral profession. The programme offers assessment in the workplace with minimum disruption to day-to-day activities. For those who do not wish to take a formal examination.

Furnishing and Furniture

NATIONAL INSTITUTE OF CARPET AND FLOORLAYERS

4d St Mary's Place
The Lace Market
Nottingham
NG1 1PH
United Kingdom
Tel: 0115 958 3077
Fax: 0115 941 2238
Email: nicf@cfa.org.uk
Website: www.nicf.carpetinfo.co.uk

MEMBERSHIP:

There are 5 levels of membership in the Institute:
Master Fitter (MInstCF): Obtained by the completion of a written exam and an assessment of past work by a regional assessor.
Approved Fitter: Obtained by the completion of a written exam; business references are also required.
Associate Membership: For those not actively involved with carpet fitting but who have an interest in the profession.
Trainee Membership: For students and apprentices.
Patron Membership: For manufacturers and large retail outlets.

Gas Engineering

THE INSTITUTION OF GAS ENGINEERS MANAGERS

21 Portland Place
London
WIN 3AF
United Kingdom
Tel: 020 7636 6603
Fax: 020 7636 6602
Website: www.igaseng.com

HONORARY MEMBERSHIP:

Honorary Fellow (HonFIGasE): Elected at the Council's invitation.

CORPORATE MEMBERSHIP:

Honorary Fellow: Elected at the Council's invitation. Allows use of abbreviated title

'MIGEM' and, in addition, of 'Chartered Gas Engineer' and registration as Chartered Engineer (CEng), or 'Incorporated Gas Engineer' and registration as Incorporated Engineer, or 'Engineering Technician' and registration as Engineering Technician.
Fellow: Suitably senior Chartered Engineer Member or non-Member over 30.
Chartered Member: Over 25, with MEng degree level qualification (MEng or BEng plus further learning), practical training and/or responsible experience.
Incorporated Member: Over 23, with engineering degree level qualification, practical training and/or responsible experience. Allows registration as Incorporated Engineer (IEng).
Technician Member: Over 21 with National Certificate or NVQ Level 3 or equivalent in Engineering, practical training and/or responsible experience. Allows registration as Engineering Technician (EngTech).
Professional Associate Member: Non-engineers, academically or professionally qualified at NVQ Level III or above and engaged in a senior management position in the gas industry for a minimum of 6 years.

NON-CORPORATE MEMBERSHIP:

Companion (CompanionIGEM): Elected at the Council's invitation.
Graduate Member (GradIGEM): Over 21, holding MEng degree level qualification.
Associate Member (AMIGEM): Non-engineers, holding a management position in the gas industry and with a minimum of 10 years' work experience in the gas industry.
Associate (AIGEM): Over 21 with sufficient professional experience to participate.
Student: Between 16 and 29 and studying for a suitable academic qualification to Corporate Membership.

COMPANY MEMBERSHIP:

Industrial Affiliate: Firm or other un-incorporated associate, limited company, public authority or institutions, or other body corporate in or associated with the gas industry.

NOTE:

Mature routes to CEng and IEng available for over 35s.

Gemmology and Jewellery

THE GEMMOLOGICAL ASSOCIATION AND GEM TESTING LABORATORY OF GREAT BRITAIN (GEM-A)

27 Greville Street
London
EC1N 8TN
United Kingdom
Tel: 020 7404 3334
Fax: 020 7404 8843
Email: gagtl@btinternet.com
Website: www.gagtl.com

MEMBERSHIP:

Fellow (FGA): Fellowship is granted to those who are successful in the Diploma Exam in Gemmology and who are approved for membership by the Council of Management.
Member: Ordinary membership is open to all who support the aims and objectives of the organisation and who are approved by the Council of Management.
Diamond Member (DGA): This membership is granted to those who are successful in the Gem Diamond Diploma Exam and who are approved for membership by the Council of Management.

EXAMINATIONS:

The Diploma Exam in Gemmology: Taken after a correspondence course run by the Association or at classes run by the Association and at FE Colleges. It is necessary to qualify in the Preliminary Exam before taking the Diploma Exam. The Diploma Exam, taken at the end of the course, is theoretical and practical. The syllabus includes Elementary Crystallography, Physical and Optical Properties of Gems, Occurrence, Identification and Fashioning of Gemstones. Successful students are awarded the Diploma in Gemmology.
The Gem Diamond Exam: May be taken after study of the Correspondence Course run by the Association or at classes run by the Association and at FE Colleges. The Exam is theoretical and practical, and the syllabus includes Physical and Optical Properties of Diamond, Grading of Gem Diamond, Occurrence, Fashioning, Identification, and Appraisal of Diamond. Successful students are awarded the Gem Diamond Diploma. The practical component of this course and exam is offered as a separate certificate qualification.

THE NATIONAL ASSOCIATION OF GOLDSMITHS OF GREAT BRITAIN AND IRELAND

78A Luke Street
London
EC2A 4XG
United Kingdom
Tel: 020 7613 4445
Fax: 020 7613 4450
Email: nag@jewellersuk.com
Website: www.jewellers.org

Professional Jewellers' Diploma: This correspondence course is taken over an 18 month period. The syllabus includes Jewellery Merchandise, Gemstones, Hallmarks, Horology, Salesmanship and Business subjects. Candidates successful in the theory and practical examination are entitled to style themselves **P.J.Dip**.

Professional Jewellers' Gemstone Diploma: This 1 year correspondence course provides those in the industry with an understanding of the appearance, properties and major features of the gemstones most likely to be encountered. Candidates successful in the exam are entitled to style themselves **P.J.Gem.Dip**. The exam includes theoretical and practical tests.

Professional Jewellers' Management Diploma: Along with other subjects this 1 year correspondence course covers Time Management, Dealing with Complaints, Appraisal and Interview Techniques, Leadership and Motivation, and Delegation. Successful candidates are entitled to style themselves **P.J.Man.Dip**.

Professional Jewellers' Valuation Diploma: This 1 year correspondence course, is a structured educational framework in which fundamental methodologies of jewellery valuation can be defined and specialist aspects discussed. All applicants must hold a recognised gemstone qualification. Successful candidates are entitled to style themselves **P.J.Val.Dip**.

Genealogy

THE INSTITUTE OF HERALDIC AND GENEALOGICAL STUDIES

79–82 Northgate
Canterbury
Kent
CT1 1BA
United Kingdom
Tel: 01227 768664
Fax: 01227 765617
Email: ihgs@ihgs.ac.uk
Website: www.ihgs.ac.uk

A registered charity constituted as an incorporated educational trust to make provision for training, study and research in family history and related disciplines. Full library, archive and research facilities are provided at the above address, where a wide range of courses leading to qualification in genealogical research is conducted. PT, correspondence and residential courses.

Fellowship (FHG): Normally awarded to those members and honorary members with broadly based knowledge and extensive experience of heraldry and genealogy whose high degree of expertise is deemed worthy of recognition.

Licentiate (LHG): Has completed a prescribed course of study and research over not less than 4 years, is over 25, has passed the exams prescribed by the examining board and has submitted an approved dissertation or thesis. They are expected to have had not less than 5 full years' experience in research. Licentiateship is not determined by membership continuity.

Those following approved courses elsewhere may apply for admission to exams.

A series of graded assessments and certificate exams are offered, leading the student from the beginning of study, through **Record Agent** to the higher levels of qualification in **Genealogy**. Courses are suitable for those who wish to study Genealogy, Heraldry and related subjects auxiliary to history either as a vocation or an academic discipline.

Associate: Unqualified supporting member with use of library, etc.

SOCIETY OF GENEALOGISTS

14 Charterhouse Buildings
Goswell Road
London
EC1M 7BA
United Kingdom
Tel: 020 7251 8799
Fax: 020 7250 1800
Email: info@sog.org.uk
Website: www.sog.org.uk

The Society (founded 1911) is a registered educational charity, established to encourage and foster the study, science and knowledge of genealogy. This it does chiefly through its library, publications, lectures and courses. It does not hold exams.

MEMBERSHIP:

Honorary Fellow (FSG(Hon)): Any person, Member or not, may be elected to Honorary Fellowship for very distinguished services to genealogy by the existing Fellows. Their number is limited to 10.
Fellow (FSG): Member of not less than 5 years' standing may be elected to Fellowship for distinguished services to the Society or to genealogy by the existing Fellows. Their number is limited to 100.
Members: Members are elected by the Executive Committee. The number is unlimited and there are presently over 14,700.

General Engineering

BOARD FOR ENGINEERS' REGULATION (BER)

Engineering Council
10 Maltravers Street
London
WC2R 3ER
Tel: 0207 240 7891
Fax: 0207 379 5586
Website: www.engc.org.uk
United Kingdom

The principal task of the BER is to determine the standards and criteria for the education, training, competence and commitment required for the registration of engineers and technicians. Having set the standards, the Institutions accredit relevant courses at universities and colleges, and approve programmes of training and experience. The criteria set out below took effect in 1999, following a major review.

Registration provides a recognised guide to the competence of an engineer and as in other professional fields of medicine, law or accountancy denotes a qualification of national – and international – currency, known and understood by employers.

The BER is concerned also with the standards of professional conduct which engineering institutions stipulate for their members and which define a level of high integrity in all aspects of the work of qualified engineers.

The Register and Registration

The Register is designed to maintain an up-to-date and detailed record of qualified engineers. It has 3 sections: Chartered Engineer, Incorporated Engineer and Engineering Technician, and registration, can be achieved in 2 Stages in each of these sections as follows:

Initial Stage – Achieving the required academic qualification;

Final Stage – Satisfying the requirements for Initial Professional Development (IPD), which incorporates training and responsible experience.

Registration is undertaken through an engineering institution which is a nominated body of the Engineering Council. An annual registration fee is payable and each registrant receives a Certificate of Registration.

The standards required for registration in each of the sections and their 2 Stages are set out below:

Chartered Engineer section

An engineering education exemplified by an accredited MEng degree in Engineering followed by initial professional development (IPD) incorporating training and experience at an appropriate level or completion of The Engineering Council Examination. IPD is followed by a Professional Review with interview. The total period of IPD will vary according to the candidate and the type of training and experience.

Those entered on the Register at the Final Stage are authorised to use the style or title of Chartered Engineer and the designatory letters **CEng**.

Incorporated Engineer section

An engineering education to a standard exemplified by an accredited degree followed by initial professional development incorporating training and experience at an appropriate level. IPD is followed by a Professional Review with Interview. The total period of IPD will vary according to the candidate and the type of training and experience.

Those entered on the Register at the Final Stage are entitled to ·use the style or title Incorporated Engineer and the designatory letters **IEng**.

Engineering Technician section

Initial Stage – An engineering education which provides a level of understanding of engineering principles broadly equivalent to that required for an EDEXEL or SQA-SCOTVEC National Award or Advanced GNVQ.

Final Stage – as above, but the Professional Review may not involve an interview.

Those entered on the Register at the Final Stage are entitled to use the style or title Engineering Technician and the designatory letters **EngTech.**

Movement from one section of the Register to another is possible for those seeking progressive career opportunities.

EXAMINATIONS:

The Engineering Council Examination sets the academic standard for initial registration in the Chartered Engineer section of the Council's Register (although most registrants meet this standard by the award of a degree that is accredited as being at least equivalent in standard to the Examination).

The Council conducts its Examination worldwide for those whose circumstances prevent them from pursuing an accredited degree programme, and for those who have non-accredited degrees and wish to undertake a further qualification to meet the required standard. Prospective candidates for the Examination must confirm their eligibility for entry by completing Form ECX(Q), available from the address given below.

The Part 1 Examination: The scope and standard of the Part 1 Examination is not less than that of an examination set at a point about 12 months through a 3-year FT UK degree course. Candidates must satisfy the examiners in 6 subjects: 4 compulsory subjects and 2 subjects from a list of 4 optional ones. The minimum entry requirement is two GCE A level passes or an equivalent qualification. Exemption may be gained from Part 1 by those holding relevant qualifications, eg a Higher or Advanced Diploma in an appropriate engineering discipline.

The Part 2 Examination: This Examination is in 2 parts: Part 2(A) consists of 6 subjects chosen from 30 normally available. Candidates are advised to choose subjects appropriate to the particular engineering discipline they wish to pursue. Part 2(B) consists of a project. The standard of the Part 2 Examination is that of a BEng (Hons) degree in Engineering as awarded by a UK university. The entry requirement is a pass in Part 1 or an equivalent exempting qualification.

The Part 3 Examination: This Examination is in 2 parts: Part 3(A) consists of 4 papers. One of these is a compulsory paper on Engineering Systems; one is a technical paper, from a choice of six; and two further papers should be taken from the Part 2(A) diet. Candidates are strongly advised to seek advice from their relevant professional institution when choosing the papers to be sat. Part 3(B) consists of a project. The exit level of the Part 3 Examination is that of an accredited MEng degree in Engineering as awarded by a UK university.

Full details of the examination are published in: *Guidance and Rules for Candidates* (May 1990) and *Subsequent Examinations Syllabuses* (May 1999) and *Subsequent Examinations*. An order form for these and other publications together with a full information pack on the Examinations may be obtained from: The Engineering Council Examinations Department, 10 Maltravers Street, London WC2R 3ER; tel 020 7240 7891, fax 020–7379 5586, e-mail Exams@engc.org.uk

National & Scottish Vocational Qualifications: N/SVQs may be accepted as evidence of learning and competence required for registration. At present, each award is assessed for the contribution it makes by a procedure published by the Council in *Guidance for Institutions and Awarding Bodies on Occupational Standards, N/SVQ and Registration.*

THE ENGINEERING COUNCIL

10 Maltravers Street
London
WC2R 3ER
United Kingdom
Tel: 020 7240 7891
Website: www.engc.org.uk

The Engineering Council was established by Royal Charter in 1981, augmented by a new Supplemental Charter in January 1996. The mission of the Engineering Council is to enhance the standing and contribution of the UK engineering profession in the national interest and to the benefit of society. A vital aspect of the work of the Engineering Council is to stimulate awareness of the importance of registered engineers and technicians as central figures in the competitiveness of British industry and commerce and therefore essential to the wealth of the nation. Equally important is the task of promoting among young people the idea of the Engineering profession as a desirable and interesting career and encouraging them to study relevant subjects. The nominated Institutions of the Engineering Council are as follows: Institute of Acoustics; Royal Aeronautical Society; Institution of Agricultural Engineers; Chartered Institution of Building Services Engineers; Institute of Cast Metal Engineers; Institution of Chemical Engineers; Institution of Civil Engineers; British Computer Society; Association of Cost Engineers; Institution of Electrical Engineers; The Institution of Incorporated Engineers; Institute of Energy; Institution of Engineering Designers; Institution of Fire Engineers; Institution of Gas Engineers; Institute of Healthcare Engineering and Estate Management; Institute of Highway Incorporated Engineers; Institution of Lighting Engineers; Institute of Marine Engineers; Institute of Materials; Institute of Measurement and Control; Institution of Mechanical Engineers; Institution of Mining and Metallurgy; Royal Institution of Naval Architects; British Institute of Non Destructive Testing; Institution of Nuclear Engineers; The Society of Operations Engineers; The Society of Environmental Engineers; Institute of Physics; Institute of Physics and Engineering in Medicine; Institute of Plumbing; The Institution of Railway Signal Engineers; Institution of Structural Engineers; Chartered Institution of Water and Environmental Management; Institution of Water Officers; Welding Institute.

INSTITUTE OF MEASUREMENT AND CONTROL

87 Gower Street
London
WC1E 6AF
United Kingdom
Tel: 020 7387 4949
Fax: 020 7388 8431
Email: records@instmc.org.uk
Website: www.instmc.org.uk

CORPORATE MEMBERS:

Honorary Fellow (HonFInstMC): Election is at the discretion of the Council.
Fellow (FInstMC): Must be at least 33 and have had at least 8 years' professional experience, involving superior responsibility for at least 5 years.
Member (MInstMC): Must be at least 25 and have been awarded a degree accredited by the Engineering Council; *or* passed The Engineering Council's Exams; *or* have an equivalent qualification in science or mathematics. They must also have had at least 4 years' FT experience practising measurement and control technology, which may include 2 years' professional training approved by the Council.
There is a route for candidates who do not satisfy the academic requirements.

NON-CORPORATE MEMBERS:

Companion: Must be 33 and have acquired national distinction in an executive capacity in the field of measurement and control.
Graduate: Must have obtained the educational qualifications required for Membership.
Licentiate (LInst.MC): Must be 23 and have obtained a BTEC or SCOTVEC Higher National Award or equivalent. They must have had 5 years' relevant experience.
Associate: Must be 21 and have obtained an appropriate qualification such as BTEC or SCOTVEC National Certificate.
Student: Must be at least 16 and be engaged on a recognised course of study complying with the educational requirements for the class of Graduate, Licentiate or Associate.
Affiliate: Open to anyone interested in measurement and control.
Companion Company: Organisations with an interest in measurement and control.

THE INSTITUTION OF BRITISH ENGINEERS

Clifford Hill Court
Clifford Chambers
Stratford upon Avon
Warwickshire
CV37 8AA
United Kingdom
Tel: 01789 298739
Fax: 01789 294442
Email: info@britishengineers.com
Website: www.britishengineers.com

Vice President: Vice Presidents are normally the chair of the Institution's Active Regional Branch in a particular area/country. These VPs form the IBE International Council.
Fellow (FIBE): Sales and marketing directors of Engineering companies and directors in other disciplines are awarded this grade.
Member (MIBE): Sales and marketing managers of Engineering companies and managers in other disciplines are awarded this grade.
Associate Member (AMIBE): Persons below the level of manager who are employed in Engineering companies are awarded this grade.
Graduate Member (GradIBE): For persons studying for a career in Engineering or desirous of entering the engineering profession, but who do not have the necessary experience and understanding of Engineering to qualify for Associate Membership. Graduate Members will be currently undertaking a level of study or training equivalent or similar to NVQ Level 2 or above. On achieving the necessary experience and understanding they would normally be required to seek upgrading to AMIBE.
Qualified Sales Engineer (SEng): Persons in FT employment in Engineering companies at any level who have the technical qualifications and experience necessary are awarded the designatory letters SEng. The minimum requirements are: (a) a minimum academic standard in Engineering, eg BTech, HND, HNC or equivalent; (b) at least 5 years' FT training including 2 years' practical training; and (c)

proven performance over at least 5 years in selling, sales management or marketing within the industry.

Bi-Lingual Engineer (BLEng): The Institution has introduced its BLEng qualification because the Engineering Industries are chronically short of Engineers with foreign language capabilities. BLEng is for persons who can satisfy all the requirements for Associate Membership of the IBE and who are fluent both orally and in writing, with a high technical bias, in at least 2 modern languages, one of which must be English. The designatory letters BLEng precede the membership designatory letters: ie BLEng, AMIBE.

Diploma in Business Engineering: The DBE is a new qualification at bachelor degree level for Engineers who are involved in the senior management of engineering companies. It assumes that engineering training to HND, HNC or CGLI Full Technological Certificate or equivalent has been achieved and focuses on the elements of Strategy, Planning, Finance, Marketing and Human Resources that are essential to the ongoing growth and profitability of an engineering enterprise. The designatory letters DBE precede the membership designatory letters: ie DBE, FIBE.

Cetificate of Competence in Engineering Practice: The Institution has introduced its GradIBE qualification to encourage young Engineers and will be granted to Graduate Members who attain a qualification at, or equivalent to, NVQ Level 2 standard.

THE INSTITUTION OF INCORPORATED ENGINEERS

Savoy Hill House, Savoy Hill
London
WC2R 0BS
United Kingdom
Tel: 020 7836 3357
Fax: 020 7497 9006
Email: info@iie.org.uk
Website: www.iie.org.uk

Incorporated Engineers form the mainstream of professional Engineering practitioners and act as exponents of today's technology. They provide leadership and control in a managerial role, combined with a practical approach and a detailed understanding of particular technologies.

CORPORATE MEMBERSHIP:

Fellow (FIIE); Member (MIIE): Candidates must satisfy the technical education requirements governing Graduateship and have suitable industrial training and experience. They meet the criteria for registration with the Engineering Council in the professional engineering section as Incorporated Engineers (IEng).

NON-CORPORATE MEMBERSHIP:

Associate (Associate IIE): Associates of the Institution benefit from the full range of member support available to all members. They are committed to developing their career in association with IIE, or are working towards achievement of other classes of membership.

Associate Member (AMIIE): Contact the IIE for up-to-date details of qualifications. Associate Members meet the criteria for registration with The Engineering Council as Engineering Technicians (EngTech) or in the academic qualification criteria for IEng registration.

THE SOCIETY OF ENGINEERS (INCORPORATED)

Guinea Wiggs
Nayland
Colchester
Essex
CO6 4NF
United Kingdom
Tel: 01206 263332
Fax: 01206 262624
Email: secretary@society-of-engineers.org.uk
Website: www.society-of-engineers.org.uk

The Society of Engineers is the third-oldest engineering body in the UK (established in 1854) and is a Professional Affiliate Member of the Engineering Council of the UK. It was the first to be established on a truly multidisciplinary basis. SOE is a learned body which arranges technical lectures/visits, sponsors medals and prizes, publishes a twice yearly journal called *Engineering World* and runs its own examinations.

MEMBERSHIP:

Entry to The Society of Engineers is by qualification plus experience.

Student (StudSE): The candidate must be at least 17 years of age and must be studying for an engineering qualification at any academic level.

Engineering Associate (ASE): The minimum age for this grade is 21 years. It is essential that the candidate meets one of the following qualification requirements for entry: BTEC, HNC, HND or GNVQ/NVQ/SNVQ Level 4 in engineering or similar approved qualification. The candidate must also have had at least 3 years' engineering training/experience including 1 year's practical or site work.

Associate Member (AMSE): Must be at least aged 23 and hold an ASE plus Cert. Eng *or*

BEng/BSc, GNVQ/NVQ/SNVQ Level 5 in Engineering or similar approved qualification. The candidate must have 5 years' engineering training/experience, including 2 years' practical or site work.

Member (MSE): (corporate member) minimum age for entrance: 26 years. Must have acquired an AMSE plus DipEng *or* BSc (Hons), BEng (Hons) plus Project Paper or similar approved qualification plus project paper. Experience requirements: 5 years' Engineering training/experience, including 2 years' practical or site work plus holding a position of professional responsibility for at least 3 years *or* MEng with approved project study at a participating university leading to Diploma (DipEng). A professional interview will also be held.

Fellow (FSE): (Corporate Member) The candidate must be at least 33 years of age and also a Corporate Member (MSE) of at least 7 years standing, who in the opinion of the Membership Elections Committee, endorsed by the Council, is deemed to have had sufficient experience, and who can also demonstrate continued career development. Sufficient experience includes having major responsibility for the design, research or execution of engineering works. Services rendered to the Society in particular, or to the profession of Engineering generally, are also taken into account.

Or: Direct entry is by a thesis of approximately 30,000 words leading to an Honours Diploma (Dip Eng (Hons). (See Section 8 of the *Examinations & Membership Structure – Qualifying Examinations Syllabus* for details).

MATURE CANDIDATE ROUTE:

Associate Member (AMSE): Candidates must be at least 30 years of age and submit a documented 'Job at Work Project' showing their role (including responsibility, experience and training). This is followed by a Professional Review (see Section 7 of the *Examinations & Membership Structure – Qualifying Examinations Syllabus* for details).

Member (MSE): (Corporate Member) The candidate must be at least 35 years old. Entrance for this grade requires the submission of a dissertation on Engineering specialisation of approximately 20,000 words. Entrants are granted 12 months to complete this, with reviews every 3 months by the Engineering Supervisor appointed by The Society of Engineers. This is followed by a Professional Review (see Section 7 of the *Examinations & Membership Structure – Qualifying Examinations Syllabus* for details).

Note: Academic qualifications are accepted subject to the Council's approval.

WOMEN'S ENGINEERING SOCIETY

2 Queen Anne's Gate Buildings
Dartmouth Street
London
SW1H 9BP
United Kingdom
Tel: 020 7233 1974
Fax: 020 7233 1973
Email: info@wes.org.uk
Website: www.wes.org.uk

Honorary Membership (HonMWES): Open to men or women distinguished in science or engineering or whom the Society wishes to honour for services rendered to the Society or to causes in which it is interested.

Membership (MWES): Open to women over 25 who have received recognised education and training in the theory and practice of engineering or related sciences and are occupying or have occupied in a professional or administrative capacity positions of responsibility associated with engineering. In cases of exceptional responsibility the education and training requirements may be waived.

Associate Membership (AMWES): Open to women with qualifications similar to those for membership but the required standard of responsibility and seniority is not so high.

Student Membership: Open to women who are engaged upon work of an engineering or scientific character and/or are undergoing a course of education or training with a view to qualifying for election to the class of Associate Member.

Junior Membership: Open to women aged between 16 and 19 who are undergoing FT education with the intention of entering a course of training in engineering or science.

Associateship: Open to men or women aged at least 24 who are of good education and who, by their connection with engineering, the sciences, arts or otherwise, will by their association with the Society assist in the general advancement of its work and its aims and objects.

Group Member: The Council may elect to this class universities, polytechnics, technical colleges and other such organisations where women are under training to become engineers.

Company Member: The Council may elect to this class companies, corporations and other organisations which employ engineers and are interested in supporting the aims of the Women's Engineering Society.

Geology

THE GEOLOGICAL SOCIETY
Burlington House
Piccadilly
London
W1J 0BG
United Kingdom
Tel: 020 7434 9944
Fax: 020 7439 8975
Email: enquiries@geolsoc.org.uk
Website: www.geolsoc.org.uk/

MEMBERSHIP:

Candidate Fellow: If you are still at school but aged over 16 and can provide evidence of your intention to study Geology or a related subject at university, you may join as a Candidate Fellow. This category also applies if you are currently registered for an Honours degree (first degree) in Geology. You can remain a Candidate Fellow for up to one year after graduation. Membership dues for Candidate Fellows are heavily discounted, especially if you choose to pay up-front for the duration of your undergraduate course.

Fellow: Fellows will have a degree or equivalent qualification in Geology (or a related subject), *or* have not less than 6 years' relevant experience in Geology or a related subject (e.g. membership of another learned society, either in the UK or overseas). If you are currently studying for an MSc or PhD you should inform the Membership department when you apply.

Chartered Geologist: If you are a Fellow of the Society with not less than five years' relevant postgraduate experience in the practice of Geology, you have the opportunity to apply for Chartered Geologists status.

Glass Technology

SOCIETY OF GLASS TECHNOLOGY
Don Valley House
Savile St East
Sheffield
S4 7UQ
United Kingdom
Tel: 0114 263 4455
Fax: 0114 263 4411
Email: info@sgt.org
Website: www.sgt.org

Honorary Fellow (HonFSGT): Elected in recognition of conspicuous service to the Society or distinguished contributions to knowledge in Glass Technology. The number of Honorary Fellows is limited, at any one time, to 12.

Fellow (FSGT): Elected, having rendered special service to the Society and having been a Member for at least 5 years. The other requirements for Fellowship are: (a) a degree or other qualifications acceptable to the Society, (b) having been engaged in the Glass or an allied industry or in a technical institution associated with Glass for a period of at least 7 years, (c) having either made a noteworthy contribution to knowledge in some branch of Glass Technology or attained a position of responsibility in the industry or in a teaching institution coupled with positive and adequate service to the Council through one of the Committees.

Ordinary Member: A person interested in the objects of the Society.

Hairdressing

THE GUILD OF HAIRDRESSERS
Unit 1E, Redbrook Business Park
Wilthorpe Road
Barnsley
S75 1JN
United Kingdom
Tel: 01226 786 555
Fax: 01226 208 300

National Diploma of Hairdressing Ladies and Men's (formerly known as the **General Certificate in Ladies and Men's Hairdressing):** Awarded by the Guild of Hairdressers. The qualification is open to all hairdressers and to those in training who have completed 85% of any course recognised by the Examination Council or have certification by the Hairdressing Training Board (until certification is in operation those completing a 2 year NVQ course may take this exam). It is not confined to Guild Members. Holders of the Certificate are accepted by the Hairdressing Council for admission as Registered Hairdressers. The Diploma will be awarded to all successful candidates who obtain 60% or more of the maximum marks in each section; those candidates who show a high standard throughout the whole exam and gain more than 70% in each section will receive a 'Credit' or more than 80% in each section will receive an 'Honours' Diploma. The exam includes a one-day practical exam and 1.5 hours' theory paper.

HAIRDRESSING AND BEAUTY INDUSTRY AUTHORITY (HABIA)

Fraser House
Netherhall Road
Doncaster
DN1 2PH
United Kingdom
Tel: 01302 380000
Fax: 01302 380028
Email: enquiries@habia.org.uk
Website: www.habia.org.uk

HABIA is recognised by the Government as the National Training Organisation for the Hairdressing and Beauty Therapy industries in the UK.
It is responsible for improving upon the already high, professional standing of the British Hairdressing and Beauty industries through the development of high-quality standards tailored to the present and future needs of employers. The National Occupational Standards for Hairdressing and Beauty that HABIA develops form the basis for the National Vocational Qualifications (NVQs) and Scottish Vocational Qualifications (SVQs).
HABIA develops learning programmes for Hairdressing and Beauty Therapy, ranging from guidance for dyslexic hairdressing students and Modern Apprenticeship frameworks to the latest in management practice for salon owners. It researches and communicates industry training needs and works with awarding bodies to design qualifications for delivery in over 700 hairdressing and beauty schools.
HABIA has partners in Italy, Spain and the USA, and welcomes other countries to participate. It also runs a membership programme, open to everyone in the Hairdressing and Beauty industry, offering members the chance to vote on issues affecting them plus the opportunity to receive a whole range of advice, information and benefits.
Level 1: Assesses skills needed to assist salon staff (hairdressing only).
Level 2: Covers basic skills required to be a competent junior hairdresser or beauty therapist.
Level 3: Expands on technical skills needed at Level 2 and reflects responsibilities undertaken by senior salon staff.
Level 4: Accredits competencies demonstrated in managing a salon.

Health and Health Services

BRITISH INSTITUTE OF OCCUPATIONAL HYGIENISTS

Suite 2, Georgian House
Great Northern Road
Derby
DE1 1LT
United Kingdom
Tel: 01332 298087
Fax: 01332 298099
Email: admin@bioh.org
Website: www.bioh.org

AWARDS:
Modules in specified aspects of Occupational Hygiene
Certificate of Operational Competence in Comprehensive Occupational Hygiene (CertOccHyg)
Diploma of Professional Competence in Comprehensive Occupational Hygiene (DipOccHyg)
Examinations for the Modules are open to candidates who meet stated minimum educational requirements or who attend a course in the subject.
Candidates for Certificate and Diploma awards are required to produce evidence of having been engaged in the practice of occupational hygiene at an appropriate level, and over an appropriate range of activities, for a specified time before they can be considered for an award. Exams for these two awards are designed to assess the candidate's ability to practise at the appropriate level and are therefore different from each other in scope. Each exam consists of a written exam and an oral exam. The written exam may be taken before the specified period of time has elapsed, but the award of competency will not be given until the oral exam has also been passed.

CHARTERED INSTITUTE OF ENVIRONMENTAL HEALTH

Chadwick Court
Hatfields
London
SE1 8DJ
United Kingdom
Tel: 020 7928 6006
Fax: 020 7928 0353
Email: education@cieh.org.uk
Website: www.cieh.org.uk

The Institute is a chartered professional and educational body dedicated to the promotion of environmental health.

MEMBERSHIP:

Corporate membership: Full membership is open only to persons who are qualified for appointment as Environmental Health Officers in England, Wales and Northern Ireland and who have passed an assessment of professional competence.

Graduate membership: For persons who hold a Diploma in Environmental Health, or the Certificate of Registration of the Environmental Health Officers Registration Board.

Affiliate membership: For persons working in the field of Environmental Health.

Associate membership: For graduates working in the field of Environmental Health.

EXAMINATIONS:

The Certificate of Registration of the Environmental Health Officers Registration Board is awarded to persons who successfully complete a degree or MSc course in Environmental Health which is approved by the Institute, and complete a 12 month period of assessed practical training during the course, or a 1 year period of assessed work experience at the end of the course and the CIEH professional examinations.

The Diploma in Environmental Health is no longer offered. Persons who hold the Certificate of Registration, or the Diploma, are considered to be fully qualified to practice as Environmental Health Officers.

The Assessment of Professional Competence (APC) may be taken by fully qualified Environmental Health Officers who have at least 2 years' post-qualification experience and who have been a Graduate member of the Institute for at least a year. The APC is a test of professional skills, not technical knowledge.

The Royal Environmental Health Institute of Scotland (q.v.) administers the qualification of Environmental Health Officers in Scotland.

INSTITUTE OF HEALTH RECORD INFORMATION AND MANAGEMENT (UK)

141 Leander Drive
Rochdale
Lancashire
OL11 2XE
United Kingdom
Tel: 01706 868481
Fax: 01706 868481
Email: ihrim@zen.co.uk

MEMBERSHIP:

Fellow (FHRIM): A distinction awarded by the Association to those Associates who have made a significant contribution within the Health Records field.

Associate (AHRIM): A member holding the full professional qualification.

Certified Member (CHRIM): First-level professional qualification, for those who have passed the certificate exam, acknowledged by the letters CHRIM.

Licenciate: A class of membership open to affiliates after 2 years' membership, giving the option to play an extended role in the Association at local level.

Students: A class of membership for those wishing to take the Association's professional exams.

Affiliate: Open to those not wishing to study for a professional qualification but wishing to belong to a professional organisation.

EXAMINATIONS:

Certificate Exam: Candidates must be registered students of the Association and have GCSE passes at grades A–C or equivalent in at least 5 subjects.

Exemptions: Registered Students who have passed recognised alternative exams may apply for exemption from the Certificate Exam.

Diploma Award: Candidates must have passed the Certificate Exam or hold an equivalent qualification and have GCSE passes at grades A–C in 5 subjects.

National Clinical Coding Qualification: Designed to encourage the development of accurate disease and therapeutic coding and consistency of quality and practice throughout the UK. Holders of this qualification become Accredited Clinical Coders (ACC).

Certificate of Technical Competence: A workplace assessment of competence of the individual (open to non-members).

Certificate of Technical Competence at Supervisory Level: A work-based assessment for supervisors (open to non-members).

THE INSTITUTE OF HEALTHCARE MANAGEMENT

46–48 Grosvenor Gardens
London
SW1W 0WN
United Kingdom
Tel: 020 7881 9235
Fax: 020 7881 9236
Email: enquiries@ihm.org.uk
Website: www.ihm.org.uk

MEMBERSHIP:

Full Membership (MIHM): Open to persons who have 2 years' healthcare management experience, or 5 years' senior management experience outside of the health sector *and a recognised professional or managerial*

qualification or demonstrable relevant experiential learning.
Associate Membership: Open to persons who do not yet satisfy all the criteria for full membership.
Further information on membership benefits and qualifications are available from the Membership and Education Departments at the Institute.

THE ROYAL ENVIRONMENTAL HEALTH INSTITUTE OF SCOTLAND

3 Manor Place
Edinburgh
EH3 7DH
United Kingdom
Tel: 0131 225 6999
Fax: 0131 225 3993
Email: rehis@rehis.org.uk
Website: www.rehis.org

Member: Membership of the Institute is open to those holding appropriate qualifications. Associate membership is available to others who have an interest in the objectives of the Institute.
Environmental Health Officer (EHO) Training in Scotland: The qualification for appointment as an EHO in Scotland is the Institute's Diploma in Environmental Health. Qualified EHOs from other countries may be accepted by the Institute as equivalent.
Candidates for the Diploma must be in possession of a BSc (Hons) in Environmental Health from Edinburgh or Strathclyde University. Each University has its own specific entry requirements. In addition candidates must complete an approved course of 48 weeks' practical training with a local authority. This training, which is monitored by the Institute, can be carried out during the university holiday periods or end-on after completing the degree.
Diplomas in the Inspection of Red Meat, White Meat and Other Foods: Candidates for these qualifications must complete an approved course of training with Glasgow College of Food Technology in conjunction with Glasgow University Veterinary Department. Each applicant must satisfy the entrance qualifications of the College and the Meat Hygiene Service. In addition each candidate must complete an approved period of 'in-plant' practical training under the supervision of the Meat Hygiene Service.

THE ROYAL INSTITUTE OF PUBLIC HEALTH

28 Portland Place
London
W1B 1DE
United Kingdom
Tel: 020 7580 2731
Fax: 020 7580 6157
Email: info@riph.org.uk
Website: www.riph.org.uk

The Royal Institute of Public Health is an independent organisation promoting public health through education, training, information, quality testing and policy development. The Royal Institute runs courses and symposia on topical health issues and is an accredited awarding body for nationally recognised qualifications in Food and Hygiene, HACCP, Nutrition, Salon Hygiene and Anatomical Pathology Technology.

QUALIFICATIONS:

The Royal Institute has over 40 years' experience as an awarding body, offering a portfolio of qualifications which are directly relevant to the workplace and is acknowledged by the UK Government and the food industry as one of five organisations providing appropriate standards for training in food hygiene and safety. Nearly 80,000 candidates take Royal Institute or Royal Institute accredited qualifications annually. Examinations are available throughout the UK and overseas in the following subjects:

Level 1 Foundation Certificate in Food Hygiene and Safety, Level 2 Intermediate Certificate in Food Hygiene and Safety, Level 3 Advanced Diploma in Food Hygiene and Safety. A wide range of *sector specific* examinations are available at all levels.
Level 2 Intermediate Certificate in Applied HACCP Principles, Level 3 Advanced Diploma in HACCP Principles.
Level 2 Certificate in Nutrition and Health, Level 3 Diploma in Nutrition and Health.
Level 2 Certificate in Salon Hygiene – Beauty Therapy, Level 2 Certificate in Salon Hygiene – Hairdressing.
Level 2 Certificate in Anatomical Pathology Technology, Level 3 Diploma in Anatomical Patholgy Technology.
All food hygiene and HACCP examinations are available on demand.

Further information regarding the Royal Institute's qualifications and registered training centres is available from the Royal Institute's Examination Department – email exams @riph.org.uk

MEMBERSHIP:

The Royal Institute has an international membership representing a cross-section of health professionals and hygiene specialists whose work involves the protection and improvement of the public health. **For full criteria and further information on the Royal Institute's Membership Department email membership@riph.org.uk**

THE ROYAL SOCIETY FOR THE PROMOTION OF HEALTH

38A St George's Drive
London
SW1V 4BH
United Kingdom
Tel: 020 7630 0121
Fax: 020 7976 6847
Email: rshealth@rshealth.org.uk
Website: www.rsph.org.

The Royal Society for the Promotion of Health acts to promote the health of the population through the provision of information to the public, professions and government. As an awarding body it offers qualifications in Food Hygiene (including Meat Inspection and HACCP), Health and Safety, Nutrition, Pest Control, Environmental Protection, Health Promotion and Couselling. Members of the Society, from a wide variety of professions and occupations, participate in a growing regional branch network, and the work of policy advisory groups. They benefit from a lively journal, a full conference programme, membership benefits and use of the designation Fellow/Member/Associate Member of the Royal Society for the Promotion of Health (FRSH, MRSH, AMRSH).

Home Economics

INSTITUTE OF CONSUMER SCIENCES INCORPORATING HOME ECONOMICS

Lonsdale House
52 Blucher Street
Birmingham
B1 1QU
United Kingdom
Tel: 0121 616 5188
Fax: 0121 616 5188
Email: icsc@btclick.com
Website: www.institute-consumer-sciences.co.uk

CORPORATE MEMBERSHIP:

Corporate Membership (MICSc): You have full voting powers and may use the letters MICSc after your name. You are eligible if: (a) you have a minimum of 3 years' work experience in the field of consumer sciences, home economics and allied technologies plus a first degree or its equivalent at Ordinary or Honours level in a title recognised for membership by the Institute; (b) you have a minimum of 4 years' work experience plus a BTEC Higher National Diploma/Certificate or SQA or equivalent in a title recognised for membership by the Institute, or degrees/diplomas recognised for corporate membership in other disciplines where the holder is currently employed within the field of home economics and allied technologies, including social work; (c) you are in a position of responsibility or have extensive freelance/other experience within consumer sciences allied employment. You may not have a particular consumer science or home economics qualification but may be offered membership at the discretion of the Standards Board or those it delegates.

NON-CORPORATE MEMBERSHIP:

Associate (AICSc): You are a holder of a degree or a HND or equivalent in the subject discipline or a related accepted discipline. If you are a registered postgraduate research student you will probably be eligible for associate membership. AICSc is awarded for members with a degree or equivalent working towards membership.
Professional Affiliate: You are ineligible for any other grade of membership but are involved in appropriate activities relating to the subject discipline.
Student: You are a full-time student on any course in the UK or overseas which could lead directly to any qualification accepted for Associate Membership.

Corporate Forum: Organisations which educate or employ consumer scientists, or have a declared interest in the theory and practice of consumer science.

DEGREES:
Courses related to the field of Consumer Sciences and Home Economics are widely available, and include the following: consumer studies; food studies; textiles and clothing; design; development; manufacturing; psychology; marketing and business studies; consumer education and social policy. Degree courses also exist which allow greater specialisation in particular areas such as: food science; food technology; food and nutrition; food marketing management; textiles; textile design; fashion management; clothing design and manufacture; hotel management; catering management; hospitality management; retail management; retail design management and food retail management. There are degree courses in consumer protection/consumer and trading standards, which can lead to employment as a Trading Standards Officer or to related work in consumer advice. Postgraduate qualifications include: diplomas and higher degrees in such subjects as food technology, textile technology and marketing; professional qualifications for social workers and dieticians; teaching qualifications BEd in Design and Technology, and a PGCE (postgraduate certificate in education).

Homeopathy

THE FACULTY OF HOMEOPATHY
15 Clerkenwell Place
London
EC1R 0AA
United Kingdom
Tel: 020 7566 7810
Fax: 020 7566 7815
Email: info@trusthomeopathy.org
Website: www.trusthomeopathy.org

The Faculty (incorporated by Act of Parliament) is responsible for maintaining standards of training and education in homeopathic medicine for doctors, veterinary surgeons, dental surgeons, podiatrists, midwives, nurses, pharmacists and other statutorily registered health care professionals.
Accredited postgraduate education and training courses are run at 5 centres in the UK – Bristol Homeopathic Hospital, Glasgow Homeopathic Hospital, the Royal London Homeopathic Hospital, Tunbridge Wells Homeopathic Hospital and the Homeopathic Physicians Teaching Group, Oxford. Training at all these centres is structured towards the Faculty's examinations leading to the primary care qualification LFHom and – for doctors and veterinary surgeons – medical/veterinary membership of the Faculty and the qualification of MFHom/VetMFHom. There is also a diploma course for dentists and pharmacists leading to the qualification DFHom. Details of the exams and membership schemes are available from the address above.

Horses and Horse Riding

THE BRITISH HORSE SOCIETY
Stoneleigh Deer Park
Stareton
Kenilworth
Warwickshire
CV8 2XZ
United Kingdom
Tel: 01926 707700
Fax: 01926 707800
Email: enquiry@bhs.org.uk
Website: www.bhs.org.uk

All exams are practical and oral. The Certificates are officially recognised within the UK and internationally.

HORSE KNOWLEDGE AND RIDING EXAMINATIONS:
Minimum age is 16 years. Candidates are required to take these exams in progression from Stage I upwards. *Riding* and *Care* sections of the exams may be taken separately.

RIDING INSTRUCTORS:
Fellowship of the British Horse Society (FBHS): Open to Gold BHS members, minimum age 25, open to holders of the BHSI Certificate. The exam covers Equitation, Training the Horse, and ability in instructing over a very broad field at an advanced level **(International Level 4)**.
Instructor's Certificate (BHSI): Must be a Gold BHS member, minimum age 22. Candidates must pass the BHS Stable Manager's Certificate and the Equitation and Teaching section **(International Level 3)**.
Intermediate Instructor's Certificate (BHSII): Must be a Gold member of the BHS, minimum age 20 years. Candidates must pass the Riding and Care sections of Stage 4 and the Intermediate Teaching Test to obtain the Intermediate Instructor's Certificate. They must also hold a current Health & Safety First

Aid at Work Certificate. A current Equine Specific First Aid Certificate will be accepted in the place of a First Aid at Work Certificate. Full details on the Equine Specific First Aid Certificate are available from the BHS. **(International Level 2.)**

Assistant Instructor's Certificate (BHSAI): Must be a Gold member of the BHS and have reached the age of 17 years 6 months. Candidates under 18 years must hold 4 GCSEs, A, B or C (or equivalent), 1 of which must be English. Candidates passing the Stage 2 and Preliminary Teaching Test have been awarded the Preliminary Teacher's Certificate. They must log 500 hours of teaching experience and also hold a current Health & Safety First Aid at Work Certificate and complete Stage 3 to gain the BHSAI Certificate **(International Level 1)**.

STABLE MANAGERS:

BHS Groom's Certificate: Open to Gold BHS members who must be at least 17 years and hold a minimum of the Horse Knowledge and Care sections of Stages 1 and 2. Holders are qualified to look after horses in general use under supervision.

BHS Intermediate Stable Manager (BHS IntSM): Open to Gold BHS members who must be at least 19 and hold a minimum of the Horse Knowledge and Care sections of Stages 1 and 2 and the Groom's Certificate. Holders are qualified to manage a small-to-medium yard without supervision.

BHS Stable Manager's Certificate (BHS SM): Open to Gold BHS members. Candidates must be at least 22 and hold the Intermediate Stable Manager's Certificate. Holders are qualified to run a large yard of horses, including those in competition at higher levels.

BA(Hons) Equine Sports Coaching: Offered in conjunction with University College Worcester, this degree incorporates the BHSI and/or FBHS certificates, plus additional modules, to obtain the degree. The aim is to produce high-quality coaches who can apply scientific training and coaching techniques to equestrian sport. Please contact the BHS for more details.

EQUESTRIAN TOURISM (B.E.T.):

In conjunction with the Trekking and Riding Societies of Scotland and Wales and the Association of Irish Riding Establishments, the BHS offers qualifications for:

Assistant Ride Leader: Must be 17 and hold the BHS Riding and Road Safety Certificate or S/NVQ Riding on the Road unit and a current Health & Safety First Aid at Work Certificate. An assistant ride leader may work FT or PT and is competent to take a ride of up to 2 hours' and assist a ride leader on longer rides.

Ride Leader: Must be 18 and hold the Assistant Ride Leader Certificate and a current Health & Safety First Aid at Work Certificate. A ride leader is able to take sole charge of first-time or more experienced riders and is also capable of taking charge of a centre for a temporary period not exceeding 1 month.

Holiday Riding Centre Manager: Must be over 22 and hold the Ride Leader Certificate *or* have operated a BHS, TRSS, WRTA or AIRE Centre for a minimum of 3 years. Holders are qualified to operate a riding holiday centre from both the practical and financial aspects. An expert to whom the others, including tourist organisations, can turn to for advice.

The Ride Leader and Holiday Riding Centre Manager Certificates are recognised by the FITE (Foundation Internationale de Tourisme Equestre).

S/NVQs: The Society is an awarding body for S/NVQs in the horse industry and currently awards the following:
Level One: Horse Care
Level Two: Horse Care
Level Three: Horse Care and Management with optional units at Levels 2 and 3 to include: breeding, exercising horses, schooling horses, driving, working with heavy horses, trekking, care of performance horses, assisting riders with special needs (Level 2 only), polo, breaking, competition groom, and coaching riders. These awards are available for those working with riding and working horses, and in studs.

Housing

THE CHARTERED INSTITUTE OF HOUSING

Octavia House
Westwood Way
Coventry
CV4 8JP
United Kingdom
Tel: 024 7685 1700
Fax: 024 7669 5110
Email: customer.services@cih.org
Website: www.cih.org

MEMBERSHIP:

Fellow (FCIH): Must have had **Corporate** Membership of the Institute for at least 7 years, and have completed at least 3 years' **Continuing Professional Development (CPD)** to be eligible. All Fellows have to complete an annual CPD programme. Fellowship denotes an individual who is a senior member of the housing profession.

Corporate Member (MCIH): Denotes that an individual is fully professionally qualified in housing. There are various routes to coporate membership contact the CIH for further details.
Affiliate: Available to anyone interested in housing matters and who is committed to improving housing practice.
Associate Member (ACIH): For those working in housing, but who are professionally qualified in another discipline. Entrance by interview.
Housing Practioner (Cert.CIH): Denotes that an individual has a CIH-recognised Housing Qualification (full list available on request) and is currently working in housing.
Student: Anyone who is currently undertaking or is eligible to undertake any housing qualification recognised by the Chartered Institute of Housing.

EXAMINATIONS:

Professional Qualifications: There are 2 routes through the Professional Qualification, non-graduate and graduate. Non-graduates complete a 2 year Stage 1 followed by a 2 year Stage 2. Graduates complete a 1 year Stage 1 and the 2 year Stage 2. The Professional Qualification is offered on a PT and FT basis at various centres throughout the country. Distance-learning versions of the courses are available through the CIH. An APEX programme of practical experence is also required.
Certificated Courses: The Chartered Institute of Housing offers a range of certificated courses at various centres throughout the UK. They are also available by distance learning.
Institute Recognised Courses: The Institute recognises a number of PT and FT courses which are available at various centres throughout the UK.
National/Scottish Vocational Qualifications (N/SVQ): N/SVQs Levels 2, 3 and 4 in Housing are currently on offer at a number of centres throughout the UK.

Hypnotherapy

BRITISH HYPNOTHERAPY ASSOCIATION

67 Upper Berkeley Street
London
W1H 7QX
United Kingdom
Tel: 020 7723 4443

Founded in 1958, the British Hypnotherapy Association is the leader in hypnotherapy. It's a therapist who has had at least 4 years of training in enabling people to understand and resolve their relationship difficulties or emotional problems. They are required to continue to maintain high standards of competence and ethics in their work. Their methods are shaped by their findings from the lifelong follow-up of results which they routinely do with their patients.

MEMBERSHIP:

Fellow (FBHA): May be elected from among members, who have had at least 10 years' experience as therapists, for important contributions to the advancement of psychotherapy or hypnotherapy from the viewpoint of the patients.
Honorary Member (HBHA): Someone who has made an outstanding contribution to hypnotherapy and has at least 7 years' experience as a therapist.
Full Member (MBHA): In addition to having completed the required training, has had at least 5 years' experience as a practitioner and has shown a satisfactory standard in the membership exam. Previously published work is accepted for the exam if it conforms to all the requirements.
Associate (ABHA): Someone who has completed adequate appropriate training in this work (see below).

EXAMINATION:

Full Membership Exam: In the form of a thesis; minimum length required 5000 words.

TRAINING:

Training to the standards required by the BHA is offered only by The Psychotherapy Centre. The minimum educational requirement is a university degree or equivalent. Candidates must be psychotherapy patients themselves with a practitioner recommended for this purpose by the Association before admission to the course, insight into oneself being essential for understanding and helping patients.
The course can be taken PT or FT – 4 years is the minimum length including the therapy. The aim of the course is to produce practitioners fully competent in the treatment of emotional problems, psychogenic disorders and relationship difficulties.
Note: In recent years there has been a rapidy increasing problem of people claiming, especially in hypnotherapy, qualifications or memberships which they don't have. It's advisable for anyone to check with us any claims as to qualifications in hypnotherapy.

Indexing

SOCIETY OF INDEXERS

Globe Centre
Penistone Road
Sheffield
S6 3AE
United Kingdom
Tel: 0114 281 3060
Fax: 0114 281 3061
Email: admin@socind.demon.co.uk
Website: www.socind.demon.co.uk

MEMBERSHIP:

Ordinary Membership: Open to all individuals and institutions concerned with indexing. To acquire recognition as qualified indexers, individual members may apply for admission to the Society's *Register of Indexers*. Each applicant's theoretical knowledge and practical technique and experience are scrutinised by assessors; if they are adjudged to conform with standards laid down by the Society, the applicant's admission to the Register is approved, and the member is designated a **Registered Indexer**.

TRAINING:

Society of Indexers 'Training in Indexing': Complete indexing course based on the principle of open learning and consisting of a set of 5 training manuals, tutorial support and tests. Successful completion of 5 formal tests will entitle a member of the Society to the status of Accredited Indexer. The course (but not the tests) may be taken by non-members. Accredited Indexers are encouraged to acquire the status of Registration.

Industrial Safety

BRITISH SAFETY COUNCIL

70 Chancellors Road
London
W6 9RS
United Kingdom
Tel: 020 8741 1231
Fax: 020 8741 4555
Email: mail@britsafe.org
Website: www.britishsafetycouncil.org

The British Safety Council is an internationally recognised organisation in the field of health, safety and the environment representing more than 12,000 companies covering the whole spectrum of commerce and industry. It conducts 30,000 delegate days of training a year and offers the following qualifications for those who are, or aspire to being, professional health, safety and environmental practitioners.

QUALIFICATIONS:

Diploma in Safety Management (DipSM): An examined international qualification, covering the key areas of competence in: Risk Assessment and Risk Management; Communications (at all levels); Occupational Health (including Workplace Wellness programmes); Total Loss Control Techniques (Case Studies); Developing a Safety Culture; Health and Safety Legislation (including EU-based regulations).
The exam comprises multi-choice questions, covering all aspects, and can be taken after successfully completing 5 distinct modules of training, together with 300 hours' additional study. An alternative, extended course of training is designed for overseas students.
Exams are conducted throughout the year at various centres, and Diploma holders can use the designatory letters **DipSM**. The Diploma is presented at prestigious London venues. The qualification is recognised by the HSE as appropriate for a competent person. The DipSM provides underpinning knowledge for the mandatory units for the NVQ in Occupational Health and Safety Practice.
The Diploma is accepted, with relevant experience, for admission to the International Institute of Risk and Safety Management as a full member, and allows delegates to use the designatory letters **MIIRSM**. Entry may also be granted by attaining NVQ Level 3 or 4 in OHSP No 3044.
Diploma in Environmental Management (DipEM): This is a three-part course covering: Regulatory Framework; Environmental Assessments and Audits; Emissions to Air, Water and Land; Waste Management and Minimisation; Environmental Monitoring; Treatment Systems, Introducing ISO 1400 series; Project Management. Holders are eligible for Associate Membership of the Institute of Environmental Management.
Certificate in Safety Management (CSM): An examined qualification for those who are coming into Occupational Health and Safety for the first time, managers and supervisors with safety responsibilities, and safety representatives.
The exam comprises a paper of multi-choice questions covering the fundamentals of Safety Management. The Certificate is accepted by the International Institute of Risk and Safety Management for Associate Members grade, and entitles the person to the designatory letters **AIIRSM**.
The Council is an approved NVQ centre.

THE INSTITUTION OF OCCUPATIONAL SAFETY AND HEALTH

The Grange
Highfield Drive
Wigston
Leicestershire
LE18 1NN
United Kingdom
Tel: 0116 257 3100
Fax: 0116 257 3101
Email: jacoba.siee@iosh.co.uk
Website: www.iosh.co.uk

CORPORATE MEMBERSHIP:

Fellow (FIOSH): Corporate Members may be elected to this grade if they have been a Corporate Member for a minimum of 5 years and have achieved eminence in the field of Safety and Health, attained a senior position in their work organisation, or carried out original academic or research work.
Member (MIOSH): Corporate Membership may be gained by a combination of relevant academic qualifications such as an accredited degree or diploma in Occupational Safety and Health and a minimum of 3 years' professional experience in the field of Occupational Safety and Health. Corporate Members with general health & safety responsibilities, as opposed to specialising in areas such as ergonomics, may apply to become a Registered Safety Practitioner (RSP).

NON-CORPORATE MEMBERSHIP:

Graduate: This grade is granted to persons who meet the academic but not the experience criteria for Corporate Membership.
Technician Safety Practitioner (TechSP): Technician level is open to personnel assisting more highly qualified OSH professionals, or dealing with routine matters in low-risk sectors. A TechSP must hold a recognised qualification such as Level 3 of the VQs for OHS Practice.
Affiliate: This grade is open to any other person with an interest in Health and Safety.

INTERNATIONAL INSTITUTE OF RISK AND SAFETY MANAGEMENT

70 Chancellors Road
London
W6 9RS
United Kingdom
Tel: 020 8600 5537
Fax: 020 8741 1349
Email: enquiries@iirsm.org
Website: www.iirsm.org

Professional body for Health and Safety practitioners. Comprehensive range of membership benefits include: designatory letters, free technical and legal helplines, *Health and Safety Manager's Newsletter*, *Safety Management Magazine*, certificate and membership card. A non-profit making charity for the advancement of accident prevention.
Fellow (FIIRSM): Awarded by the Board of Governors to persons who have submitted a successful Fellowship petition after 5 years of membership.
Member (MIIRSM): Open to holders of the British Safety Council Diploma in Safety Management, NVQ Level 3 in Occupational Health & Safety plus 3 years' experience, NVQ Level 4 in Occupational Health & Safety, Parts 1 & 2 of the NEBOSH Diploma or a Postgraduate Diploma in Health & Safety.
Associate (AIIRSM): Open to holders of the British Safety Council Certificate in Safety Management, NEBOSH Certificate or Part 1 of the NEBOSH Diploma.
Affiliate: Open to all individuals who have an interest in Health and Safety.
Student: Open to individuals who are studying for recognised Safety qualifications.

Insurance and Actuarial Work

ASSOCIATION OF AVERAGE ADJUSTERS

Secretariat: The Baltic Exchange
St Mary Axe
London
EC3A 8BH
United Kingdom
Tel: 020 7623 5501
Fax: 020 7369 1623
Email: aaa@balticexchange.com
Website: www.average-adjusters.com

MEMBERSHIP:

Fellow: Average adjuster who has qualified by passing all 6 modules of the Association's exams.
Associate: Someone working in an average adjuster's office or in another marine-related

field who has passed at least 3 modules of the Association's exams.

EXAMINATION:

The examination consists of 5 theoretical modules requiring written answers and one module requiring the candidate to prepare a practical adjustment.

THE CHARTERED INSTITUTE OF LOSS ADJUSTERS

Peninsular House
36 Monument Street
London
EC3R 8JL
United Kingdom
Tel: 020 7337 9960
Fax: 020 7929 3082
Email: info@cila.co.uk
Website: www.cila.co.uk

MEMBERSHIP:

Fellow (FCILA): Must have been an Associate for at least 5 years, and have been continuously in practice as a loss adjuster during this time and have fulfilled CPD requirements.
Associate (ACILA): A member who has passed the exams, is at least 25 and has been in practice for 5 years is eligible for election as an Associate.
Licentiate: A person who is elected, having passed the Institute's exams but who is not able to meet the age or experience requirements for Associateship.
Ordinary Member: Must be at least 18 and be in practice as an adjuster in a firm of loss adjusters.

THE INSTITUTE'S EXAMINATION:

The exam comprises 5 subjects and covers insurance law and claims procedure, report writing and the adjustment of various kinds of losses such as liability, property, burglary and third-party claims. It cannot be taken until ordinary members have completed a mimimum of 2 years in practice.

THE SOCIETY OF CLAIMS TECHNICIANS

Contact details as above. The Society was created in 1999 to provide an examination for anyone working in insurance claims and is affliated to The Chartered Institute of Loss Adjusters. There are 2 written exams and an additional requirement to satisfactorily complete an inter-personal skills course.
Completion of the exams leads to the award of Associate (ASCT). A further 2 years' experience leads to Fellowship (FSCT).

THE CHARTERED INSURANCE INSTITUTE

20 Aldermanbury
London
EC2V 7HY
United Kingdom
Tel: 020 8989 8464
Fax: 020 7726 0131
Email: customer.serv@cii.co.uk.
Website: http://www.cii.co.uk.

MEMBERSHIP:

Membership: Open to anyone employed or engaged in the insurance and financial services fields.

QUALIFICATIONS:

Fellowship (FCII): Open to Associates who complete an election programme.
Associateship (ACII): Recognised worldwide as the hallmark of a professional insurance education. It comprises 10 exam subjects based on published syllabuses, and is ideal for the career professional. Entry standards: minimum 2 A levels and 2 GCSEs or BTEC National Certificates or aged 25 and over. (NVQ Levels) Chartered titles – either Chartered Insurer or Chartered Insurance Practitioner or Chartered Insurance Broker – are available to all Fellows and Associates with five years' experience in the industry (not necessarily post qualification).
Certificate of Insurance Practice (CIP): Ideal for those who work at a technical level. Comprising 5 exam subjects, successful candidates are eligible to become members of the Society of Technicians in Insurance (MSTI) and are awarded 4 exemptions towards the Associateship. Entry standards: minimum 4 GCSEs or aged 21 and over. (NVQ Levels 3 and 4.)
Insurance Foundation Certificate (IFC): Provides a broad knowledge of insurance at a foundation level. There are no entry requirements. (NVQ Level 2.)
Foundation Insurance Test (FIT): An entry-level test, providing a basic understanding of general insurance. There are no entry requirements.
Advanced Financial Planning Certificate (AFPC): Demonstrates the attainment of a highly qualified level in the financial services field. Entry standards: the Financial Planning Certificate. Successful candidates are eligible to become members of the Society of Financial Advisers (MSFA), can proceed to Associateship and Fellowship of the Society of Financial Advisers (ASFA and FSFA designations) and are awarded 3 exemptions towards the Associateship (ACII).
Financial Planning Certificate (FPC): Designed for new or experienced financial

advisers and support staff. Meets regulatory requirements for those giving financial advice.

Financial Administration Foundation Certificate: Qualification for administration staff in life and pensions offices and for those who need to meet regulatory requirements for overseers. Comprises 2 exam subjects. There are no entry requirements.

Mortgage Advice Qualification (MAQ): In conjunction with the FPC demonstrates attainment of relevant knowledge required to give mortgage advice in accordance with the Council of Mortgage Lenders' Code. There are no entry requirements.

Certificate in IT for Insurance Practitioners: A stand-alone qualification developed and awarded jointly by the CII and the British Computer Society (BCS). Designed specifically to cover IT issues and responsibilities in the insurance industry. There are no entry requirement

THE FACULTY AND INSTITUTE OF ACTUARIES

Email: careers@actuaries.org.uk
Website: www.actuaries.org.uk

Faculty of Actuaries, Maclaurin House, 18 Dublin Street, Edinburgh EH1 3PP; tel: 0131 240 1300, fax: 0131 240 1313
Institute of Actuaries, Napier House, 4 Worcester Street, Oxford OX1 2AW; tel: 01865 268228, fax: 01865 268253

Actuaries are experts in assessing the financial impact of tomorrow's uncertain events. They enable financial decisions to be made with more confidence by analysing the past, modelling the future, assessing the risks involved, and communicating what the results mean in financial terms.

MEMBERSHIP:

The high regard in which the actuarial profession is held is earned through a good deal of effort and dedication. To become an actuary you must be a competent mathematician and be able to communicate effectively and clearly. There is a minimum entry requirement of grade B at A level, SCE higher grade, or equivalent.

Any degree discipline is acceptable, although most employers recruit graduates with good numerate degrees. Undergraduate degree courses in Actuarial Science and 1 year FT postgraduate diploma courses are available and may result in exemptions from some of the exams.

To qualify as an actuary you must pass the professional examinations. The earlier subjects provide a thorough understanding of the mathematical, statistical and financial techniques required in the later subjects and used in the workplace. The later subjects examine the 4 main areas of actuarial practice: investment, life insurance, general insurance and pensions. The Fellowship exam tests one practice area in greater depth.

QUALIFICATIONS:

Fellow of the Faculty of Actuaries (FFA): Any student of the Faculty who has completed the exams may be admitted as a Fellow.
Fellow of the Institute of Actuaries (FIA): Fellows of the Institute of Actuaries must have attained the age of 23 years, have passed all of the professional examinations and have also completed 3 years' practical actuarial work.
Associate of the Faculty of Actuaries (AFA): Any student of the Faculty who has completed all but the 400 series (Fellowship) subjects and who has completed a professionalism course.
Associate of the Institute of Actuaries (AIA): As for Associates of the Faculty of Actuaries but also can apply to those students who have passed all of the professional examinations but have not attained the age of 23 years of age or have not completed 3 years' relevant work experience.
Diploma in Actuarial Techniques: The joint Diploma in Actuarial Techniques is awarded to students of the Faculty and Institute of Actuaries who pass the relevant 100 series professional examinations.
Certificate in Finance and Investment: The joint Certificate in Finance and Investment is awarded to students of the Faculty and Institute of Actuaries who pass relevant professional examinations.

Journalism

THE CHARTERED INSTITUTE OF JOURNALISTS

2 Dock Offices
Surrey Quays Road
London
SE16 2XU
United Kingdom
Tel: 020 7252 1187
Fax: 020 7232 2302
Email: membershipservices@icj.co.uk

MEMBERSHIP:

Fellow (FCIJ): Elected by the Council from members who have given outstanding service.
Member (MCIJ): Must have been engaged in FT journalism for at least 3 years or 1 year if holding a recognised diploma or other qualification.

Student: Undergoing preparation for professional membership.

Affiliate: Engaged in the communication industry other than as a journalist, or as an occasional contributor to the media whose major income derives from sources other than journalism.

NATIONAL COUNCIL FOR THE TRAINING OF JOURNALISTS

Latton Bush Centre
Southern Way
Harlow
Essex
CM18 7BL
United Kingdom
Tel: 01279 430009
Fax: 01279 438008
Email: info@NCTJ.com
Website: www.NCTJ.com

JOURNALISM:

The National Council runs the offical training scheme for entrants to newspaper journalism. There are 2 ways of entering. One way is for the entrant to persuade a provincial editor to give him or her a 6 month trial and then permanent employment. During the first 2 years, training is given on and off the job. The other way is selection for the courses of preparation accredited by the National Council followed by permanent employment and during the first 18 months, training on the job. The educational requirements for these courses are at least 2 GCE A levels in England, 3 Highers in Scotland, including English, and at least 5 GCSE passes at Grade C or above, and 1 A and 5 GCSE passes, including English, in Northern Ireland. Direct entrants need to have at least 5 GCE O level or GCSE passes, including English, but many editors now require at least 1 A level. After at least 18 months in the industry, trainees take the National Certificate examination, the recognised professional exam. Panels of newspaper journalists take part and it includes oral and written exams in practical journalism. The **National Certificate** is awarded to successful candidates. The following colleges offer a 1 year FT pre-entry course before on-job training for the National Council's National Certificate: City College, Brighton and Hove; Crawley College; Darlington CT; East Surrey College; Gwent Tertiary College; Harlow College; Harrow College, Harrow; Liverpool Community College; North West Institute of F & H Education; Sheffield College; Southend College of A & T; Sutton Coldfield College; Warwickshire College; Wolverhampton College.

HND in Journalism Studies: May be taken at Cardonald College, Glasgow and Darlington College. A number of graduates attend a 1 year postgraduate journalism course at Cardiff University; University of Central Lancashire; or Strathclyde University/Glasgow Caledonian University (joint); De Montfort University, Leicester; University of Sheffield; Trinity & All Saints College, Leeds; University of Ulster, Belfast, before entry into the industry.

Graduate fast-track courses (18 or 20 weeks): Darlington College; East Surrey College; Harlow College; Highbury College, Portsmouth; Lambeth College, Vauxhall Centre; Liverpool Community College; Sheffield College.

Degree courses: Bournemouth University; Cumbria Institute of the Arts; Edgehill College, Ormskirk; University of Central Lancashire, Preston; University of Sheffield; Southampton Institute; Staffordshire University.

Day-release courses: Cardonald College; City of Liverpool Community College; Wolverhampton College.

The National Council also offers courses in magazine journalism. City College, Brighton and Hove offers a one-year, PT pre-entry course.

The following colleges offer postgraduate, fast-track courses (19 or 20 weeks): City College, Brighton and Hove; Harlow College; Liverpool Community College.

The NCTJ also offers distance-learning courses in newspaper and periodical journalism and sub-editing.

PHOTOGRAPHY:

The National Certificate in Photo Journalism of the National Council for the Training of Journalists: This test is taken by trainee press photographers after 2 years (18 months for pre-entry trainees) on-the-job experience on provincial newspapers. The educational qualifications for direct entry to press photography are at least 5 O levels or GCSESs including English in England and Wales with exceptions for industrial or course experience and 3 O grades including English in Scotland. Training is given on and off the job at special 12 week block-release courses.

The council has a 1 year FT pre-entry course in press photography for which you need 1 A level and 4 O or GCSE levels including English Language, or 2 Highers and 3 O grades including English for Scottish applicants.

Land and Property

THE COLLEGE OF ESTATE MANAGEMENT

Whiteknights
Reading
Berkshire
RG6 6AW
United Kingdom
Tel: 0118 986 1101
Fax: 0118 975 5344
Email: info@cem.ac.uk
Website: www.cem.ac.uk

COURSES:

The College of Estate Management offers a wide range of distance learning courses. Many of these courses meet the academic requirements of professional bodies such as The Royal Institution of Chartered Surveyors, the Chartered Institute of Building and The Architecture and Surveying Institute. Courses include the University of Reading's BSc in Estate Management, BSc in Quantity Surveying, BSc in Building Surveying, BSc in Construction Management, BSc in Property Management, MBA in Construction and Real Estate and MSc in Real Estate. In addition postgraduate diplomas in Arbitration, Facilities Management, Project Management, Building Conservation and Property Investment are also available. At technician level the College has introduced a Diploma in Surveying Practice. Most courses are taught by a combination of written instructional material supplemented by audio and videotapes, with assignments for completion by the student and assessment by tutors. All courses are now supported on-line through the College website. The majority of courses are also supplemented by short face-to-face teaching sessions at regional centres.

THE INSTITUTE OF REVENUES, RATING AND VALUATION

41 Doughty Street
London
WC1N 2LF
United Kingdom
Tel: 020 7831 3505
Fax: 020 7831 2048
Email: irrv.org.uk
Website: www.irrv.org.uk

The Institute offers professional and technical qualifications for all those whose professional work is concerned with Local Authority revenues and benefits, valuation for rating, property taxation and the appeals procedure. The Institute's qualifications are widely recognised throughout the profession.

CORPORATE MEMBERSHIP:

Corporate (IRRV): Corporate membership is granted by the Institute to those people who have passed the Institute's full professional exams with exemptions available to qualified members of certain other professional associations, including the Royal Institution of Chartered Surveyors and the Chartered Institute of Public Finance and Accountancy.

NON-CORPORATE MEMBERSHIP:

Technician: Available to persons who have passed the Institute's Technician exam or who have been exempted therefrom by possessing appropriate qualifications and practical experience.
Student: Open to those preparing for the Institute's exams.
Affiliate: Open to any person maintaining an interest in the work of the Institute, but cannot be used to imply a professional association with the Institute.

EXAMINATIONS:

The Institute conducts full professional exams at 3 levels. The exams conducted for Scottish candidates take account of differences in Scottish Law. The Institute also conducts Technician exams in revenues and housing benefits and has competence-based qualifications leading to Technical Membership.
Exemptions: May be granted from certain parts of the Institute's exams in respect of certain post A level qualifications, degrees and the exams of other professional associations.

ISVA – THE PROFESSIONAL SOCIETY FOR VALUERS AND AUCTIONEERS

3 Cadogan Gate
London
SW1X 0AS
United Kingdom
Tel: 020 7235 2282
Fax: 020 7235 4390
Email: educ.memb@isva.co.uk
Website: www.isva.co.uk

Fellow (FSVA): Must be at least 30, have passed ISVA's Units 5 and 6 examinations or equivalent thereto and have satisfied the Professional Assessment requirements. In addition applicants must have been in practice in the profession for at least 10 years or for at least 5 years as a principal or a manager and have been an Associate of ISVA for at least 2 years.
Associate (ASVA): Applicants must be at least 21, have passed ISVA's Units 5 and 6 examinations or equivalent thereto and have

satisfied the Professional Assessment requirements.

Student: Applicants must be at least 16 and should have obtained a standard of general education represented by 5 GCSE passes at Grade A, B or C, including English Language and Mathematics, 3 of which must have been passed at the same time. Intermediate and Advanced GNVQ accepted. For NVQ entry telephone for further information.

EXAMINATIONS:

Exams are held at Units 1–6 in the following divisions: General Practice; Agricultural Practice; Fine Arts and Chattels; Plant and Machinery. There is also a special entry route for non-cognate degree holders and those over the age of 30 with 10 or more years' experience in the profession. All students are required to complete the Professional Assessment as well as passing the exams. This is undertaken over a 2 year period of approved employment and comprises a journal and a pre-qualification assignment.

THE NATIONAL ASSOCIATION OF ESTATE AGENTS

Arbon House
21 Jury Street
Warwick
CV34 4EH
United Kingdom
Tel: 01926 496800
Fax: 01926 400953
Email: info@naea.co.uk
Website: www.naea.co.uk

MEMBERSHIP:

Open to application by practising Estate Agents. The minimum criteria for the main grades are: **Associate (ANAEA):** 21 years old and 3 years' experience in Estate Agency. Applicants must also pass an admission test.
Fellow (FNAEA): 25 years old, 5 years' experience in estate agency and the NAEA Certificate of Practice in Estate Agency, Certificate in Residential Lettings & Management or comparable qualification.
Other grades include Affiliate, Special Associate, Student, Honorary Member and Retired Member. Full details are available from the Head of the Membership Department.

QUALIFICATIONS:

The NAEA Certificate of Practice in Estate Agency: The highest available qualification in Estate Agency. It is open to both NAEA members and non-members. Successful candidates are entitled to use the designatory letters CPEA. Also available is the Certificate in Commercial and Business Transfer (CCBT), which is aimed at commercial agents.

The NAEA Certificate in Residential Lettings & Management: The highest available qualification in residential lettings and property management. It is open to NAEA members and non-members. Successful candidates are entitled to use the designatory letters CRLM.
Preparation courses for examination for both the CPEA and CRLM are studied via distance learning. An information pack is available from the NAEA Education & Training Department. The Association regularly organises a series of half- and full-day courses throughout the UK on a wide range of professional topics. In addition, the NAEA National Assessment Centre offers N/SVQ at Levels 2 and 3 in Residential Estate Agency and Residential Lettings and Property Management.

PROPERTY CONSULTANTS SOCIETY

107A Tarrant Street
Arundel
West Sussex
BN18 9DP
United Kingdom
Tel: 01903 883787
Fax: 01903 889590
Email: pcs@propco.freeserve.co.uk
Website: www.propco.freeserve.co.uk

The principal objects of the Society are to provide a central organisation for surveyors, architects, valuers, auctioneers, land and estate agents, master builders, and constructional engineers, who practise as consultants in their own branch of the profession and including members of the legal profession specialising in estate matters.

EXAMINATIONS: (not currently being held).

Fellow (FPCS): minimum age 27.
Associate (APCS): minimum age 21.
Entrance is judged on experience, training, etc.

THE ROYAL INSTITUTION OF CHARTERED SURVEYORS

RICS Contact Centre, Surveyor Court
Westwood Way
Coventry
CV4 8JE
United Kingdom
Tel: 0870 333 1600
Email: customerservice@rics.org.uk
Website: www.rics.org

MEMBERSHIP:

Fellow (FRICS): A Professional Associate of 5 years' standing may apply for transfer to the Fellowship. He or she will need to demonstrate career advancement as well as increased expertise and management responsibility. Contact Simon Bowen for further information.
Professional Member (MRICS): Member of the RICS having successfully undergone an extensive period of practical training coupled with degree-level education or an equivalent course of professional study in order to gain the qualification.
Technical Surveyor (TechRICS): Member of the RICS having successfully undergone an extensive period of practical training and holding a BTEC/SCOTVEC HNC/HND qualification.
Probationer: Member of the RICS having successfully completed a degree or equivalent course satisfying the academic requirement of the RICS.
Student: Member of the RICS currently studying for an RICS accredited qualification.

EDUCATION & TRAINING:

The majority of candidates join the Institution as a student whilst studying for, or on completion of, an approved degree or diploma course. Entrants must have attained the minimum standard of education for university matriculation. The majority of entrants to the profession qualify by undertaking a related FT, S, PT or distance-learning degree/diploma course accredited by the Institution. Entrants with an A level (or equivalent) may enrol on a related BTEC/SQA HNC/HND that will lead to qualification as a Technical Surveyor, or may then afford advanced entry to a relevant degree course. Graduates from non-surveying backgrounds may embark on FT, PT or distance-taught fast-track graduate conversion courses of 1 to 2 years' duration.
All candidates must also undergo a minimum period of 2 years' Professional Assessment comprising professional training and practical experience, and a professional interview.
The Royal Institution of Chartered Surveyors now incorporates the Society of Surveying Technicians, The Incorporated Society of Valuers and Auctioneers and Institute of Building Control.

Landscape Architecture

THE LANDSCAPE INSTITUTE

6–8 Barnard Mews
London
SW11 1QU
United Kingdom
Tel: 020 7350 5200
Fax: 020 7350 5201
Email: mail@l-i.org.uk
Website: www.l-i.org.uk

CORPORATE MEMBERS:

There are two grades of Corporate Membership of The Landscape Institute. The most senior grade is **Fellow (FLI)**, with the other grade being **Member (MLI)**. All corporate members must be educated to at least first degree level in Landscape Architecture, Landscape Management or Landscape Science, have postgraduate professional experience and have passed the Institute's Professional Practice Examination. Corporate members of the Institute are entitled to describe themselves as Chartered Landscape Architects.

NON-CORPORATE MEMBERS:

Associate: Associates have completed a recognised degree- or postgraduate-level course and are gaining professional experience before taking the Institute's Professional Practice Exam.
Student: Student members are studying a degree- or postgraduate-level course in Landscape Architecture at one of the universities with courses accredited by the Institute.

EXAMINATIONS:

The Institute's exam leading to Corporate Membership is the Professional Practice Exam. It consists of a written paper and an oral exam, in which the candidate's competence to act as a practising member of the profession is tested. Candidates must complete at least 2 years' relevant experience as an Associate member before taking this exam. Success in the Professional Practice Exam entitles candidates to apply for Corporate Membership.

Law

THE ASSOCIATION OF CHARTERED CERTIFIED ACCOUNTANTS

29 Lincoln's Inn Fields
London
WC2A 3EE
United Kingdom
Tel: 020 7396 5800
Fax: 020 7396 5858
Email: students@accaglobal.com
Website: www.accaglobal.com

Fellow (FCCA): Long-term Associate members (5 years minimum) advance to Fellowship automatically.

Associate (ACCA): Candidates must pass the ACCA's exams and obtain 3 years' approved financial experience, which can be in industry, commerce, public service or public practice.

The ACCA has been recognised and respected across the world for almost 100 years and currently has nearly 300,000 students and members in 160 countries. Whatever a student's background, the ACCA addresses their individual needs and goals in an ongoing partnership designed to last throughout their career.

Recognised as a professional body under UK companies and financial services legislation, the ACCA's role as a professional acountancy body is to train and regulate practising Chartered Certified Accountants. As such, the ACCA is responsible for ensuring its members and students are aware of changes in legislation and accounting standards.

NEW SYLLABUS:

The ACCA has launched a ground-breaking new syllabus which has transformed the way the profession will be trained in the future. The launch followed extensive consultation with leading employers, members, students and tuition providers worldwide. The new scheme places greater emphasis on corporate strategy, the design and management of business systems, risk assessment and strategic financial analysis, while retaining the core technical knowledge that the ACCA's research showed to be essential to the role of the modern financial professional.

QUALIFYING:

Students must complete the professional examinations (14 papers) and obtain a minimum of 3 years' relevant training. Study can be FT with training obtained later; or PT by day/evening class, open learning or home study whilst working full-time in relevant employment. Training can be obtained in any country and in any employment sector – industry, commerce, public practice or public service.

ENTRY LEVELS:

Minimum entry requirements are 2 A levels and 3 GCSEs, or their equivalent. All graduates from recognised universites can register and those with relevant degrees will be exempted from some examinations; some qualifications will qualify for up to 9 exemptions. Those who complete Parts 1 and 2 of the new scheme may also be eligible to apply for the award of a BSc (Hons) in Applied Accountancy from Oxford Brookes University.

Diploma in Financial Management (DipFM): The Diploma is a postgraduate qualification designed to equip managers with an understanding of how to compile, analyse and communicate financial information. The qualification is recognised for exemption from a number of MBA programmes.

Enrolment on the Diploma Register: Candidates must hold one of the following: a recognised degree, HND/C, NVQ Level 4 and/or membership of a non-accounting professional body. Candidates who do not hold the above may be admitted on the basis of experience if they are aged 23 or over and can provide an employer's reference to show their experience is relevant to the Diploma.

ACCA Accounting Technician qualification (CAT): This qualification was launched in August 1997 to enable candidates to qualify in accounting support roles. As there is no formal academic entry requirement, anyone can enrol, providing they are aged 16 or over. Some qualifications, such as A levels, HNC/Ds, RSA, Pitmans and LCCI qualifications will receive exemptions from some CAT examinations.

Mode of Application:
Contact the ACCA for a registration pack, or view vacancy information and register on-line on the ACCA website.

Application Deadline:
Register by 15 August for December examinations or 31 December for the following June examinations.

THE LAW SOCIETY OF SCOTLAND

26 Drumsheugh
Edinburgh
EH3 7YR
United Kingdom
Tel: 0131 226 7411
Fax: 0131 225 4243
Email: legaleduc@lawscot.org.uk
Website: www.lawscot.org.uk

The Law Society of Scotland is the Membership organisation of the Scottish Solicitors Profession. The Society promotes the interests of the profession and the interests of the public in relation to the profession. Services provided include post-qualifying legal education, administering courses and examinations for the Society of Law Accountants in Scotland (SOLAS), initial career advice, overseeing legal education in Scotland, monitoring traineeships and handling admissions to the profession.

MEMBERSHIP:

Membership is available only to those admitted as Scottish solicitors. Within this there are two levels. Non-Practising Members are those who do not currently hold a Practising Certificate but whose names remain on the Solicitors' Roll.

EXAMINATIONS:

The Society offers the following: Law Society professional examinations (for those qualifying through in-office training) and (from 2003) Test of Professional Competence. In addition, intending solicitors who are not qualifying through the Society's examinations must undertake an LLB degree at university. All intending solicitors also require the Diploma in Legal Practice and undertake a traineeship together with the Professional Competence course.

Leisure and Recreation Management

INSTITUTE OF GROUNDSMANSHIP

19–23 Church Street
The Agora, Wolverton
Milton Keynes
MK12 5LG
United Kingdom
Tel: 01908 312511
Fax: 01908 311140
Email: iog@iog.org
Website: www.iog.org

MEMBERSHIP:

Fellow: Must have 5 years' experience in the industry and hold the NDT in Turfculture.

Full Member: Must be a person over 18 employed in Groundsmanship or a related profession for at least 3 years. Others so employed can become **Professional Associate Members**, while anyone under 18 employed or training in Turfculture will be accepted as a **Junior Member**. Full time students are accepted free as **Student Members**.

Any Corporation concerned in any trade relating to and concerning the Grounds Management industry is eligible to be a **Corporate Member** of the Institute. Any club, college or organisation concerned in the promotion of sport or concerned in the promotion of any objects similar to the objects of the Institute is eligible to be an **Affiliate Member** of the Institute.

PROFESSIONAL EXAMINATIONS:

ND in the Science and Practice of Turfculture and Sports Ground Management (NDT): The exam is open to all employed in the profession of Groundsmanship who hold the Intermediate Diploma or equivalent. The exam consists of 3 parts: a number of written papers, a series of practical/oral tests and a dissertation.

Intermediate Diploma (NID): Follows a similar pattern to the NDT, without the dissertation, and is less demanding.

National Technical Certificate: Based on Amenity Horticulture NVQ/SVQ Level 2, Sports Turf Maintenance, and qualifies candidates for the Intermediate Diploma examination.

National Practical Certificate: The initial stage in the training and qualification of groundsmen.

INSTITUTE OF LEISURE AND AMENITY MANAGEMENT

ILAM House
Lower Basildon
Reading
Berkshire
RG8 9NE
United Kingdom
Tel: 01491 874800
Fax: 01491 874801
Email: info@ilam.co.uk.
Website: www.ilam.co.uk

MEMBERSHIP:

The ILAM was formed in 1983 by the amalgamation of four existing professional bodies. The Institute has a rapidly expanding membership and members' responsibilities include: leisure and sports centres, arts and entertainment complexes, parks, gardens and playgrounds,

museums and tourist attractions, countryside recreation, health and fitness clubs.
Member (MILAM): Those engaged in the Leisure industry in a position of responsibility.
Associate (AILAM): Someone working in the Leisure industry who does not fulfil the full membership requirements of the Institute.
Student: Someone engaged on a course or training scheme within Leisure Management.
Corporate Affiliate: Public bodies wishing to join the ILAM on an organisational basis.
Commercial Affiliate: Commercial companies wishing to join the ILAM on an organisational basis.

QUALIFICATIONS:

The new ILAM Professional Qualification Scheme was launched in August 2000. There are now 5 professional levels to the Scheme, as well as 2 technical qualifications.

Professional Qualifications

1. **ILAM First Award:** For those new to or with a junior position in the industry. Completion is by work-based projects.
2. **ILAM Certificate in Leisure Operations:** For candidates who have a basic working knowledge and understanding of the Leisure industry and who hold a junior supervisory position with a leisure organisation. Completion is by work-based projects.
3. **ILAM Certificate in Leisure Management:** For candidates who have a reasonable understanding of the Leisure industry and who hold a junior or supervisory management post with a minimum of 400 hours' relevant work experience. Completion is through a combination of exemptions, examinations and projects.
4. **ILAM Diploma in Leisure Management:** For candidates who can successfully demonstrate their managerial ability at a middle management level and who hold at least a middle management post and who aspire to senior management level. Completion is through a combination of exemptions, examinations and projects.
5. **ILAM Advanced Diploma in Leisure Management:** For candidates who can successfully demonstrate their managerial ability at a senior level and who hold a post at senior management level. Completion is through a combination of exemptions, examinations and projects.

To ensure that leisure managers are kept up to date, the ILAM offers a comprehensive programme of Continuing Professional Development courses and seminars. The Institute is also approved to train and assess in TDLB units for Assessors and Verifiers.

Technical Qualifications

5. **ILAM Certificate in Technical Operations (Operations & Maintenance of Swimming Pool Water Treatment & Plant).**
6. **National Aquatic Rescue Standards for Pool Lifeguards:** A lifesaving course run in association with the Swimming Teachers Association.

Both the above courses provide the underpinning knowledge that is required for the S/NVQ Operational Services (Level 2) and the material used is SPRITO approved.

INSTITUTE OF SPORT AND RECREATION MANAGEMENT (ISRM)

Giffard House
36–38 Sherrard Street
Melton Mowbray
Leicestershire
LE13 1XJ
United Kingdom
Tel: 01664 565531
Fax: 01664 501155
Email: ralphriley@isrm.co.uk
Website: www.isrm.co.uk

EXAMINATIONS:

Institute of Sport & Recreation Operations Certificate: A broad-based vocational training and accreditation programme which focuses on health and safety, effective customer care and the efficient technical operation of sport and recreation facilities. These courses deliver the underpinning knowledge required for S/NVQ Level 2.
ISRM Supervisory Management Certificate: Provides a national standard of training and accreditation for sport and recreation facility supervisors. These courses deliver the underpinning knowledge required for S/NVQ Level 3.
Institute of Sport & Recreation Management Certificate: A prestigious nationally recognised qualification relating to the management of sports halls, leisure centres, swimming pools and associated facilities. These courses deliver the underpinning knowledge required for S/NVQ Level 4.
ISRM Diploma: A higher-level exam for qualified ISRM members designed to provide sport and recreation facility managers with the knowledge and understanding to progress to senior management levels within the Sport and Recreation industry and/or manage major

facilities, and to give recognition to professionals qualified at this level.

Librarianship and Information Work

CILIP

7 Ridgmount Street
London
WC1E 7AE
United Kingdom
Tel: 020 7255 0500
Fax: 020 7255 0501
Email: info@cilip.org.uk
Website: www.cilip.org.uk

MEMBERSHIP:

Fellow (FLA): A fully qualified Chartered Member of The Library Association normally of at least 5 years' standing in the grade of Associate who has been elected by the Council to the Fellowship (the higher category of Chartered Membership) upon acceptance of evidence of continuing professional development and contribution to the profession.

Associate (ALA): A fully qualified Chartered Member of The Library Association, who is a graduate with the practical training and experience required by the Association, and has demonstrated professional competence through submission of an acceptable application based on his/her professional development since completing academic studies.

QUALIFYING EXAMINATION:

Before commencing the post-course practical training and experience required, candidates for Associateship must first successfully complete an accredited degree or postgraduate qualification (or equivalent) in Library and Information Studies. **Courses of Study accredited by the Library Association** are available at the following institutions: Robert Gordon's University; University of Wales, Aberystwyth; University of Central England in Birmingham; University of Brighton; University of Bristol; University of Strathclyde; Leeds Metropolitan University; Liverpool John Moores University; University of North London; Thames Valley University; University Coll London; City University; Loughborough University; Manchester Metropolitan University; University of Northumbria at Newcastle; University of Sheffield; Queen Margaret College, Edinburgh.

THE INSTITUTE OF INFORMATION SCIENTISTS

39–41 North Road
London
N7 9DP
United Kingdom
Tel: 020 7619 0624/0625
Fax: 020 7619 0627
Email: iis@dial.pipex.com
Website: www.iis.org.uk

MEMBERSHIP:

Fellowship: May be granted to Members who, after 10 years in information work, satisfy the Council that they have attained distinction by virtue of work in a senior position or of original work in the information field or have otherwise given distinguished service to the Institute. The Council may admit to **Honorary Fellowship** anyone of distinction.

Member: Admitted by Council and should comply with the following conditions: (a) being at least 25 years of age; (b) holding at least a degree granted by a British university, or a qualification accepted by Council as equivalent; and (c) either (i) holding a qualification approved by Council and having at least 2 years' approved experience in Information work, at least 1 of which must be subsequent to gaining the approved qualification, provided that Council may at its discretion require a greater amount of experience subsequent to gaining the approved qualification if that qualification is deemed to be equivalent to less than 3 years' experience in Information work, or (ii) having at least 5 years' approved experience in Information work, at least 4 of which must be subsequent to gaining the degree or equivalent.

Affiliate: Admitted by Council and should comply with the following conditions: (a) being a member of an association or institute or engaged in professional graduate-level work whose field of activity is deemed by Council to be relevant to that of the Institute; or (b) having the necessary academic qualifications and being employed in information work but lacking sufficient experience to qualify for admission as a Member or being under 25; or (c) having been or are being employed in Information work and attending an undergraduate course in a subject other than Information Science; or (d) having been or are being concerned directly with Information work in the course of one's employment or profession or studying information work but not qualifying for any other grade of membership.

Linguistics, Languages and Translation

THE GREEK INSTITUTE

34 Bush Hill Road
London
N21 2DS
United Kingdom
Tel: 020 8360 7968
Fax: 020 8360 7968

QUALIFICATIONS:

Diploma in Greek Translation: 3 papers of 3 hours each. Paper 1: **General Translation**. To translate 2 passages either from Greek into English or from English into Greek. Each passage to be about 750 words. Papers 2 & 3: **Specialised Translation**. To translate 2 passages in each paper either from Greek into English or from English into Greek. Each passage to be about 750 words. The passages will be of a specialised nature and will relate to *any* of the following areas: Humanities, Social Science, Tourism, Medicine, Science, Law or Business Studies. Dictionaries are allowed.
Candidates must satisfy the examiners in all 3 papers in order to pass. The standard of this examination is about the same as a first degree at a British university. Successful candidates may use the designation **DipGrTrans**.

Advanced Certificate: 2 papers of 3 hours each and an oral test of 20 minutes. Paper 1: Translations from and into Greek. Paper 2: Candidates will write essays in Greek on 3 different topics – (a) Modern Greek Literature (1 prescribed text); (b) Modern Greek History *or* History of Cyprus (20th Century); and (c) Geography and Tourism (on a specified region of Greece or Cyprus).
The standard of this examination is about the same as GCE A level Modern Greek.

EXAMINATIONS:

The Greek Institute conducts examinations for a **Preliminary Certificate** (1 paper of 2 hours and an oral test of 15 minutes at Elementary level), an **Intermediate Certificate** (1 paper 2« hours and an oral test of 20 minutes at GCSE level), and for the **Advanced Certificate** and the **Diploma in Greek Translation** (see above).
The Greek Institute Qualifications are included in the list of Vocational Qualifications approved by the Secretary of State for Education under section 3(1) and Schedule 2(A) to the Further and Higher Education Act 1992.
Successful candidates in the Diploma and the Advanced Certificate may be elected **Fellows** and **Associates** and may append the letters **FGI** or **AGI** respectively after their name.
Ordinary membership is open to anyone who is interested in Greece, Cyprus or in Modern Greek Studies.

THE INSTITUTE OF LINGUISTS

Saxon House
48 Southwark Street
London
SE1 1UN
United Kingdom
Tel: 020 7940 3100
Fax: 020 7940 3101
Email: info@iol.org.uk
Website: www.iol.org.uk

Fellow (FIL): Available only to those who have been Members for 3 years and attained a position of higher professional standing.

Member (MIL): The Institute admits applicants to membership on the basis of a degree in languages, or a degree with languages as a major component, an Institute qualifying exam such as the Diploma in Languages for International Communication or the Diploma in Translation. Applicants must have 3 years' experience in work requiring linguistic skills; 1 year must be prior to date of application. Membership (and Fellowship), if based on a full pass in the Diploma exam, is accepted by a number of Institutions as a degree equivalent.

Associate (AIL): The qualifying exams for this grade of membership are the Intermediate Diploma or equivalent.

Diploma in Translation (DipTransIoL): A post-graduate qualification in professional translation work. Some applicants for membership may be required to take an oral exam.

The minimum ages for entry into membership are: Fellow 25; Member 21; Associate 18. There are 2 unqualified grades.

Management

ASSOCIATION FOR PROJECT MANAGEMENT

Thornton House
150 West Wycombe Road
High Wycombe
Buckinghamshire
HP12 3AE
United Kingdom
Tel: 0845 458 1944
Fax: 01494 528937
Email: info@apm.org.uk
Website: www.apm.org.uk

MEMBERSHIP:

Fellow (FAPM): Someone who has met the requirements for the class of Member and has carried major responsibility in the field of project management for over 5 years.
Member (MAPM): Someone who practises, develops, teaches or uses the techniques of Project Management and who can demonstrate that they have the qualifications, experience and competence in project management required by the Association.
Associate: Someone involved in Project Management who has not gained the level of experience required for full Membership.
Student: Someone attending a recognised FT or PT Higher Education course. Maximum age for this grade is 30.

COMPANY MEMBERSHIP:

Higher Educational Institute: Available to universities, technical colleges and other academic bodies to provide an interface with the Association.
Corporate: Available to all companies or organisations who are, wholly or mainly, engaged in project-orientated activities from design through manufacturing and procurement to execution, or in providing services to industry and commerce, including professional firms.

EXAMINATIONS:

Certificated Project Manager (CPM): The qualification and title – Certificated Project Manager (CPM) – is available to Members and Fellows who pass a test of competence and have extensive experience as a Project Manager. This involves the successful completion of a 5000 word report on a project that the member has managed and attendance at an intensive professional interview. The status of Certificated Project Manager is recognised throughout Europe by the national project management organisations affiliated to the International Project Management Association (IPMA).
APMP Examination: This professional qualification recognises an individual's baseline knowledge and competent experience in project management. The written examination is in 2 parts: (a) multiple choice; and (b) particular questions whose answers demonstrate the candidate's knowledge and understanding of Project Management.

THE ASSOCIATION OF BUSINESS EXECUTIVES

William House
14 Worple Road
London
SW19 4DD
United Kingdom
Tel: 020 8879 1973
Fax: 020 8946 7153
Email: info@abeuk.com
Website: www.abeuk.com

The Association of Business Executives was founded in 1973 by a group of industrialists, educationalists and politicians as a non-profit-making organisation.
The object of the Association is the promotion and advancement of efficient administration and management in industry, commerce and the public service by the continued development of the study and practice of administration and management. The primary objective of the ABE is that students successfully completing its examinations will be more effective managers.
Membership is not restricted to UK residents and examinations are conducted in over 80 countries worldwide with over 25,000 students sitting examinations each year.

MEMBERSHIP:

Associate Membership (AMABE): Open to students who have sat and passed the Diploma exams of the Association.
Member (MABE) & Fellow (FABE): Students and Associate Members may advance to the grade of Member after acquiring 4 years' suitable executive experience or 2 years for holders of the ABE Advanced Diploma. Entry to Fellowship is open to suitably qualified persons who have made a significant contribution to the promotion of the Association at home and overseas.

Business Administration

EXAMINATIONS:

Certificate Level: No formal qualifications are required but applicants must demonstrate competence in the English Language by the attainment of 1 of the following: British Council – Intermediate Certificate in English/Upper

THE ASSOCIATION FOR PROJECT MANAGEMENT

150 West Wycombe Road, High Wycombe, Buckinghamshire HP12 3AE United Kingdom
Tel (UK): 0845 458 1944, Tel (International): +44 1494 440090, Fax: +44 (0)1494 528937,
email: info@apm.org.uk, website: www.apm.org.uk

The Association for Project Management (APM) is the UK's leading professional body in project management and the largest national organisation in the International Project Management Association (IPMA); APM's range of qualifications for project management professionals is thus recognised throughout the world by employers of project managers and project management practitioners.

APM's professional development framework includes qualifications for professionals at different levels of operation in project management, beginning at the foundation level with the APMP, a knowledge-based examination. This qualification covers the breadth of project management practices and gives candidates recognition for their knowledge and understanding of the fundamental principles of project management.

The APM Practitioner Qualification is a test of an individual's competence in project management practices which takes place over a two day assessment period. Candidates for this qualification will have a good working knowledge of practical project management so that they can demonstrate their capabilities.

APM also has an award for project managers with experience of complex projects. The Certificated Project Manager award involves a self-assessment activity, the auditing of that self-assessment, the completion of a 5000 word project report and a professional interview. Successful candidates are entered on to an International Register of Certificated Project Managers who are regarded as being among the highest qualified and most experienced project managers available.

In September 2003, APM will launch its Membership Qualification, which all those individuals aspiring to full Membership of the Association will be required to pass. Details of this award will be available from Summer 2003.

Continuing Professional Development is at the heart of the APM's professional development activities and services. All members of APM are expected to maintain their knowledge base and competence to an acceptable level.

The Association provides members with a wide and diverse range of development opportunities through its Branch programmes, Specific Interest Group programmes and through its accreditation of training and development and education providers and their learning materials.

APM also offers qualifications in specific aspects of project management through its single-subject certificates. For example, APM now offers a Foundation Certificate and Practitioner Certificate in Risk Management as well as a Foundation Certificate in Contracts and Procurement. More are planned.

APM's qualifications are widely available. Details of how to find courses to support study towards the APMP or the single-subject certificates are available on the APM website www.apm.org.uk or by telephoning 0845 458 1944 or +44 1494 440090 if outside the UK.

Advanced Certificate in English; LCCI – English for Business (EFB) 1st and 2nd Level; Pitman/City & Guilds – English for Speakers of Other Languages (ESOL)/English for Business and Communication.

Syllabus: Introduction to Business, Introduction to Quantitative Methods, Introduction to Accounting, Introduction to Business Communication.

Diploma Level: Applicants must have attained 1 of the following entry requirements: ABE Certificate; 2 GCE A levels plus 4 GCSE passes at Grade A, B or C, 2 of which must be English and Maths. Such overseas qualifications which follow University of London guidelines may be accepted by the Registrar as being equivalent to the above. In addition the ABE welcomes applications for Student Membership from intending Diploma candidates who, although not holding a formal qualification, have been in appropriate employment for at least 2 years. A reference letter from employer(s) must accompany all such applications. The decision of the Council as to the suitability of the candidate shall be final.

Syllabus: Part 1: Economics, Organisational Behaviour, Accounting, Business Communication. **Part 2:** The compulsory papers are: Marketing, Quantitative Methods, Management Accounting, Human Resource Management. Students must also pass 1 of the following options: Principles of Business Law, System Analysis.

Advanced Diploma in Business Administration: Applicants must have attained 1 of the following qualifications: ABE Diploma; a recognised degree; other recognised qualifications of approved Overseas institutions of Higher Education.

Syllabus: The 3 compulsory papers are: Corporate Strategy, Management Organisation, International Business. Students must also sit 2 of the following options: Strategic Marketing, Corporate Finance, Strategic Human Resource Management, Managing the Information Resource.

Business Information System

EXAMINATIONS:

Certificate Level: The entry requirements are the same as for the Certificate Level in Business Administration (see above).
Syllabus: Introduction to the World of Computers, IT Applications & Skills, Introduction to Accounting and Introduction to Business.
Diploma Level: The entry requirements are the same as for the Diploma Level in Business Administration (see above).
Syllabus: Part 1: The 3 compulsory papers are: Computer Applications in Business & Finance, Computer Fundamentals, Business Communication. Students must also sit 1 of the following subjects: Management Organisations, or Accounting. 1. **Part 2:** The 4 compulsory papers are: Networks & Distributed Systems, Principles of Programming, Quantitative Methods, Systems Analysis. Students must also sit 1 of the following subjects: Management 2, Marketing, Management Accounting.
Advanced Diploma: The entry requirements are the same as for the Advanced Diploma Level in Business Administration (see above).
Syllabus: The 4 compulsory papers are: Contemporary Application Development Methods, Internet Systems Development, Managing Systems Change, Relational Database Applications in Business. Students must also sit 1 of the following subjects: Strategic Management, Financial Management.

Travel, Tourism & Hospitality

EXAMINATIONS:

Certificate Level: The entry requirements are the same as for the Certificate Level in Business Administration (see above).
Syllabus: Introduction to Business Communication, Introduction to Accounting, Introduction to Business, Introduction to Travel, Tourism & Hospitality.
Diploma Level: The entry requirements are the same as for the Diploma Level in Business Administration (see above).
Syllabus: Part 1: Economics, Organisational Behaviour, Accounting, Travel, Tourism & Hospitality. **Part 2:** Principles of Marketing, Travel, Tourism & Hospitality Operations Management, Human Resource Management. Plus 2 options from: Management Accounting, Principles of Business Law, Systems Analysis.
Advanced Diploma: The entry requirements are the same as for the Advanced Diploma Level in Business Administration (see above).
Syllabus: 5 subjects to be passed: Corporate Strategy, International Travel, Tourism & Hospitality, Tourism & the Environment. Plus 2 options from: Management Organisation, International Business, Strategic Marketing, Strategic HRM, Managing the Information Resource.

EXEMPTIONS:

Holders of the ABE Diploma exams can obtain exemptions from many professional bodies.

POSTGRADUATE OPPORTUNITIES:

Successful completion of the ABE Advanced Diploma will qualify students for entry into many MBA and other postgraduate programmes in the UK and overseas. Students are, however, advised that most institutions offering postgraduate qualifications will expect entrants to satisfy their other admission criteria, ie to pass the GMAT test and/or TOEFL and to provide evidence of experience in industry or commerce. Many universities will accept holders of the Advanced Diploma who do not have the requisite industrial experience onto the final year of the bachelor degrees.

BUSINESS MANAGEMENT ASSOCIATION

Admin Office
50 Burnhill Road
Beckenham
Kent
BR3 3LA
United Kingdom
Tel: 020 8663 3577
Fax: 020 8663 3212
Email: peter@wadetrade.com

The Association aims to provide a professional body of business managers for the promotion and exchange of management skills, knowledge and business planning techniques, specialising in the small business sector.

MEMBERSHIP:

Fellow (FBMA): Candidates must have at least 5 years' managerial experience and must have passed the Final Exam of the Association. Exemption conditions as per Membership Grade apply to this category.
Member (MBMA): Candidates must have at least 3 years' managerial experience and must have passed the Final Exam of the Association. Exemption from the Final Exam is granted to candidates who are members of approved professional organisations, or who have passed equivalent exams.
Associate (ABMA): Candidates must have at least 1 year's managerial experience and must hold a qualification considered by the membership committee to warrant election to this grade.
Affiliate (Aff.BMA): Candidates must be either following a course of study in pursuit of an award of the Association or alternatively studying for an equivalent award of another organisation.

EXAMINATIONS:

Business Management Association Diploma in Business Management (DipBMA): Papers in (1) Accounting & Finance; (2) Business Law; (3) Business Administration & Management; (4) Sales & Marketing.

Certified Doctor of Business Administration (CDBA): Candidates must have been awarded a DBA by an organisation recognised by the Membership Committee as being of a sufficiently high standard.
Certified Master of Business Administration (CMBA): Candidates must have been awarded an MBA by an organisation recognised by the Membership Committee as being of a sufficiently high standard.
Certificates and Diplomas are also awarded in International Trade and Independent Consultancy.
Exemption from the qualifying exams may be granted to mature candidates with extensive senior management experience.

CHARTERED MANAGEMENT INSTITUTE

Membership Department
Management House
Cottingham Road
Corby
Northamptonshire
NN17 1TT
United Kingdom
Tel: 01536 207307
Fax: 01536 201651
Email: member@inst.mgt.org.uk
Website: www.inst.mgt.org.uk

The Institute of Management promotes the art and science of Management by: (a) encouraging and supporting the lifelong development of managers; (b) raising the level of competence and qualification of management; (c) initiating, developing, evaluating and disseminating management thinking, tools, techniques and practices; and (d) influencing policy makers and opinion formers on management issues.

MEMBERSHIP:

The membership application process focuses on providing the correct level of recognition for individuals, appraising two main elements: academic or vocational qualifications and experience as a practising manager.
Student: For anyone who is studying, FT or PT, towards a qualification in management or business.
Associate (AIMgt): For managers with a recognised management qualification but with limited management experience.
Member (MIMgt): For managers with a degree-level management qualification and appropriate management experience at an operational level.
Fellow (FIMgt): For managers with a degree-level management qualification including a strategic component and appropriate experience at a strategic level.

CHARTERED MANAGEMENT INSTITUTE

Chartered Management Institute, Management House, Cottingham Road,
Corby, Northants NN17 1TT
Telephone: 01536 207373, Fax: 01536 207384,
email: cmd.customerservice@managers.org.uk, website: www.managers.org.uk

As the champion of management, the Chartered Management Institute shapes and supports the managers of tomorrow. By sharing intelligent insights and setting standards in management development, the Institute helps to deliver results in a dynamic world.

The Institute's Centre for Management Development offers an integrated learning programme, which leads to professional, academic and vocational qualifications. The various combinations and starting points will depend on the level and experience of participants and on the organisation requirements.

Many organisations use these programmes to improve organisational performance through the development of their management teams. At the same time they motivate managers by reinforcing commitment to their development and offering them a chance to achieve nationally recognised qualifications. They are also an ideal way of implementing a career progression or succession planning framework.

Breadth and depth of support

Undertaking a qualification programme requires a significant investment in time and effort. Therefore support is important to help ensure continued motivation and success. Each individual registered on the programme becomes a student member of the Chartered Management Institute at no additional cost.

Range of programmes available:

- Master of Business Administration (MBA)*
- Diploma in Management Studies (DMS)*
- The Institute's – Diploma in Management
- Certificate in Management*
- The Institute's – Certificate in Management
- NVQ Levels 3–5 in Management
- Certificate in Supervisory Management
  *Validated by the Open University

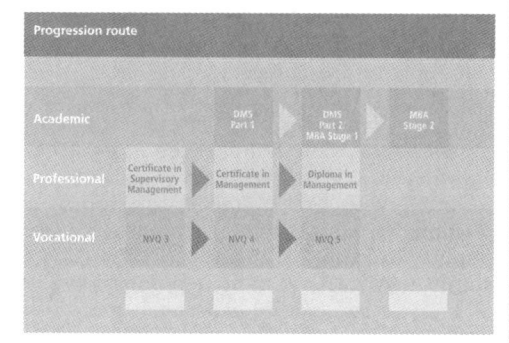

Open programme option

Individuals can attend 'open programmes' with participants from other organisations. This option is suitable for organisations with a small number of managers or those with managers that particularly require interactive learning and networking with external managers.

Tailored option

A particular benefit of running a tailored programme for a group of your team leaders or managers is the close link to organisational objectives. The programme can be specifically designed to meet your organisational needs whilst offering a flexible approach, benchmarked against national standards.

Throughout the programme participants are assessed on work-based assignments and projects, ensuring that the learning is relevant and contributing to the overall success of the organisation.

For individuals who have an interest in management and who want access to limited member benefits but don't yet have the qualifications or experience to be eligible for membership, there is the opportunity to join as an **Affiliate**.

Further details can be provided by phoning the Membership Operations number.

INSTITUTE OF ADMINISTRATIVE MANAGEMENT

16 Park Crescent
London
W1B 1BA
United Kingdom
Tel: 0207 612 7099
Fax: 0207 612 7094
Email: info@instam.org
Website: www.instam.org

The Institute of Administrative Management is the only organisation in the UK specialising in the promotion of Administrative Management in the fields of industry and commerce, from the large multinational to the small, independent firm, central and local government, the armed forces, public utilities and nationalised industries.

MEMBERSHIP:

Fellow (FInstAM): To qualify for election as a Fellow the applicant must either have been a member of the IAM for at least 5 years, be at least 30 years old and occupy a senior post or meet other criteria as laid down by the Admissions Committee.

Member (MInstAM): Applicants should be over 28 years (exceptionally 26), have at least 5 years' Administrative Management experience and meet the criteria laid down by the Admissions Committee. Alternatively, the applicant must have passed the Institute's Advanced Diploma exam. Members are entitled to use the letters MInstAM; those who have passed the Advanced Diploma are entitled to use the letters MInstAM(AdvDip).

Associate (AInstAM): Associate Members of the IAM are entitled to use the designatory letters AInstAM if they are 25 or over and have at least 2 years' Administrative Management experience. Alternatively, if they have passed the Diploma exam they can use the letters AInstAM(Dip).

Affiliate: In order to qualify for Affiliate Membership to enter for the Institute's Advanced Diploma exams, an applicant must hold one of the following qualifications or a similar level qualification: HNC/D, UK degree, NEBS Management Diploma, N/SVQ Level 4 in Management or Administration.

Student: In order to qualify for Student registration to enter for the Institute's Diploma exams, a minimum of 4 GCE O level subjects or GCSE subjects are required, one of which must be English, as well as 1 pass at A level. Approved equivalent qualifications will be accepted. Students who do not meet these criteria can enter for the Certificate only (as will a candidate who has had at least 3 years' relevant work experience).

Corporate Partner: Company Membership of the IAM is open to all organisations. Please apply to Institute for further information.

EXAMINATIONS:

Certificate in Administrative Management: This is an open access route to the IAM's qualifications, and consists of 3 modules (which are the first 3 modules of the Diploma).

Diploma in Administrative Management: The Diploma is a 1 year PT programme. It consists of 6 modules and a Case Study or Work Project Report. The titles of the individual modules are: Business Administration; Systems & Activities; The Individual and the Organisation; Human Resources; Effective Management; Management Information; plus the Case Study or Work Project Report. To obtain the Diploma it is necessary to successfully complete 7 modules. To obtain the Certificate it is necessary to pass the first 3 exams only.

Advanced Diploma in Administrative Management: This is a 2 year PT programme. The syllabus consists of 4 compulsory modules, 2 optional modules (from a choice of 5) and a Case Study or Work Project Report. The titles of the core modules are: Managing Contemporary Issues; Managing Financial Resources; Managing People and Managing Processes. The optional modules are: Managing Facilities; Managing Marketing; Managing Information – Analysis and Presentation; Managing Training and Development; Managing Information and Technology.

THE INSTITUTE OF COMMERCIAL MANAGEMENT

The Fusee
20a Bargates
Christchurch
Dorset
BH23 1QL
United Kingdom
Tel: 01202 490555
Fax: 01202 490666
Email: info@icm.ac.uk
Website: www.icm.ac.uk

The Institute is an acknowledged specialist in the design and development of progressive and multifunctional programmes of study for use by universities, business schools, colleges, International Development and government agencies.

As a recognised international examining board for those undertaking professional business and management studies, the Institute also examines and certifies candidates to an internationally consistent standard.

Working with education providers worldwide, the ICM offers examinations and certification in the following areas: Accounting, Banking and Finance; Business and Management Studies; Communication Studies; Computer Studies; Hospitality Management; Information Technology; International Trade; Languages; Legal Studies; Marketing Management; Public Relations; Purchasing and Supply Management; Retail and Distribution Management; Safety Management; Sales Management and Marketing; Security Management; Sports and Leisure Management; Travel and Tourism Management.

Recognition of ICM Awards: Subject to status, students holding ICM Diploma, Advanced Diploma and Graduate Diploma level qualifications are accepted onto undergraduate and postgraduate degree programmes offered by institutions in the EU, Eastern Europe, North America, the Middle East, the Far East, SE Asia, sub-Saharan Africa and Australasia. The Institute's awards are also recognised by the majority of the world's leading professional examining boards for either subject or registration purposes.

ICM Vocational Education Awards: ICM programmes are designed to address a wide variety of personal development and training needs. Unless a candidate undertakes a single-subject examination, all ICM programmes are multi-subject and candidates are required to undertake formal and externally set and marked examinations in all subjects within any programme.

Certificate Level Programmes: These are introductory and foundation programmes designed for school leavers and adults with few or no formal academic qualifications (3 to 6 months FT/9 months PT).

Diploma Level Programmes: Designed for business students and working adults (1 to 2 years FT/2 to 3 years PT). Most Diploma level programmes offer study equivalent to the first year of a degree, and relevant ICM Diploma awards are accepted by institutions of HE for degree entry purposes.

Advanced Diploma Programmes: Designed for business students, supervisors, managers and mature working adults with existing business qualifications (1 year FT/2 years PT). Offering learning equivalent to 2 years of undergraduate study, most Advanced Diploma programmes are taken as an end in themselves, but can also be used for entry at appropriate level to first degree studies.

Graduate Diploma Programmes: Designed for practising managers and business students, these are 1 year postgraduate courses (some exemptions depending on experience) which, subject to status and exam grades, qualify the holder for entry onto a wide range of Masters programmes.

INSTITUTE OF DIRECTORS

116 Pall Mall
London
SW1Y 5ED
United Kingdom
Tel: 020 7839 1233
Fax: 020 7930 1949
Website: www.iod.co.uk

The IoD is a chartered institute, whose 50,000 members form a unique and influential global network spanning the whole spectrum of business leadership. The Institute's principal objectives are to advance the interests of its members as company directors, to provide business facilities and services of all kinds for these members, and to help directors enhance their professional competence.

MEMBERSHIP:

Fellow (FInstD): Open to IoD members of 1 year's standing who have been: (a) a director for a minimum of 5 years, with 10 years' business experience, who hold the IoD Diploma in Company Direction or equivalent; or (b) a director for a minimum of 10 years.

Member (MInstD): Open to: (a) directors of 1 year's standing, with 5 years' business experience who have attended the IoD's foundation course covering the role and responsibilities of directors and the board; or (b) directors of 3 years' standing, with 7 years' business experience.

Associate Member: Open to directors waiting to qualify for Member grade; partners in professional practice and those with professional qualifications working in industry or commerce; sole proprietors; senior executives.

TRAINING:

The IoD's Director Development department is the premier specialist provider of director training services, with a reputation for delivering relevant, practical learning experiences. It is uniquely concerned with the development needs of company directors whatever their experience, company size or type of business; whether or not they are IoD members. The learning approach draws upon and enhances

INSTITUTE OF DIRECTORS

116 Pall Mall, London SW1Y 5ED
Tel: 020 7766 2601, email: chartered.director@iod.com,
website: www.iod.com/chartered

Chartered Director

The IoD is the leading advocate of company direction. It offers a unique range of products and services, designed by directors for directors, providing the training and skills needed to achieve business excellence. Chartered Director, the world's first professional qualification for directors, was launched by the IoD in June 1999.

Chartered Directors demonstrate the expertise and integrity needed to meet the challenges of business today and to succeed. They are professionals who guide their organisations, whether in the private or public sector, to operate on the highest strategic level.

Succeed as an Executive Director or Non-Executive Director

The leaders of many organisations are now embracing Chartered Director for all their executive directors and non-executive directors. Evidence shows that organisations with Chartered Directors gain advantage. For others it can aid collective understanding of the key issues. For those seeking a new position or wishing to step into a non-executive post there is no better mark of ability.

Chartered Director is a unique designation. It is available only to experienced directors who have demonstrated the requisite knowledge and conduct to act in this professional capacity. The IoD is working with government, regulators, executive search agencies, major organisations, and the public sector to promote its value.

Many Chartered Directors are already chartered professionals in their own practice fields. They all recognise that their vocational training has lead them to a board or equivalent position but that Chartered Director is the only designation that recognises and rewards their capabilities as a director.

How to qualify

There are several options as to how you can embark on the Chartered Director programme.

The first stage is to pass the examination in Company Direction. The exam assesses the seven courses of the IoD Company Direction programme. You may register for the exam without undertaking any study and to help you with this decision the IoD has an interactive practice exam at www.iod.com/practiceexam

Alternatively choose the whole programme and with the exam you may also gain a Diploma in Company Direction.

If you are successful in completing all the steps towards becoming a Chartered Director and sign the IoD's code of conduct, you will join the growing number of professional directors able to use the designation C Dir.

For further information on Chartered Director:

Email: chartered.director@iod.com
Tel: 020 7766 2601
Web site: www.iod.com/chartered
IoD
116 Pall Mall
London
SW1Y 5ED

directors' knowledge, skills and understanding, and focuses on helping them to improve business performance.

The unique directors' programme, the **IoD Company Direction Programme**, covers the essentials of directing a successful modern company. A certificate of Completion is provided for attending the entire programme; however, those who wish to achieve a recognised qualification can undertake an assessment, successful completion of which leads to the award of the prestigious **IoD Diploma in Company Direction**. The Diploma is also a major step towards becoming a **Chartered Director**, the new professional status launched by the IoD in 1999. It is offered at the IoD in London and 7 regional UK centres: Durham, Edinburgh, Leeds/Wakefield, Loughborough, Salford, Stirling, Ulster and Wolverhampton. There is also a concise programme which equips newly appointed and prospective directors with the knowledge and confidence to fulfil their new appointment effectively.

The IoD also provides an extensive range of business and boardroom publications, and runs conferences on topical issues of interest to directors.

INSTITUTE OF EXECUTIVES AND MANAGERS

Abbey Lakes Hall
Orrell
Wigan
Lancashire
WN5 8QZ
United Kingdom
Tel: 01695 622226
Fax: 01695 627199

The Institute was originally founded over 30 years ago to provide an organisation international in dimension for executives and managers in all vocations.

MEMBERSHIP:

Fellow (FIEM): Candidates must: (a) already be a Member of the Institute; (b) be not less than 30 years of age; *or* (c) already be an Associate of the Institute; (d) be not less than 35 years of age.
Member (MIEM): Candidates must: (a) already be a Graduate of the Institute; (b) be not less than 25 years of age; (c) hold the Institute's Diploma in Executive Management.
Graduate (GIEM): Candidates must: (a) be an Associate or Licentiate of the Institute; (b) be not less than 21 years of age; (c) hold the Institute's Certificate in Executive Management.
Associate (AIEM): Candidates must: (a) be a Licentiate of the Institute; (b) be not less than 25 years of age; (c) hold such academic qualifications and have such practical experience as the Council of the Institute considers appropriate.
Licentiate (LIEM): Candidates must: (a) be a Student of the Institute; (b) be not less than 21 years of age; (c) hold such academic qualifications and have such practical experience as the Council of the Institute considers appropriate.
Student: Candidates must not be less than 16 years of age and hold such academic qualifications and have such practical experience as the Council of the Institute considers appropriate.

EXAMINATIONS:

Diploma in Executive Management (DEM): A comprehensive distance-learning study programme, available direct from the Institute and through certain accredited universities and colleges. Taking the form of modular study packages, audio cassette programmes and video cassette programmes, these cover a wide range of topics including Finance for Non-Financial Managers and Marketing, etc. The Diploma is an aggregation of subjects, each one carrying a certain number of credits. To be awarded the Diploma candidates need to have aggregated 6 credits. Individual subjects carry a certificate of completion and an indication of the credits earned towards the Diploma. Candidates for the Diploma Programme must hold the Certificate in Executive Management, or similar qualifications which in view of the Council of the Institute would equate to 3 credits on the Certificate scale.
Certificate in Executive Management (CEM): A comprehensive distance-learning study programme, available direct from the Institute and through certain accredited universities and colleges. Taking the form of modular study packages, audio cassette programmes and video cassette programmes, these cover a wide range of topics including Appreciation of Accounting for Non-Financial Managers, Personnel Interviewing and Selection, etc. The Certificate is an aggregation of subjects, each one carrying a certain number of credits. To be awarded the Certificate candidates need to have aggregated 3 credits. Individual subjects carry a certificate of completion and an indication of the credits earned towards the Certificate.

BENEFITS:

Designation: All grades of members, except Students, may use the designation 'Management Executive'. Certificate and Diploma holders need not necessarily be members of the Institute.
Publications: Members receive a regular copy of the Institute's magazine *Management*

Executive, a copy of the Institute's 'Budget Summary' and annually the Institute's diary. All members receive a free subscription to *International Management Focus*.
Group Membership: The Institute has negotiated 'Group Membership Benefits' for car hire, hotels, travel, etc.
Social: The Institute offers a full and active social programme.
Employment: The Institute gives every support to all members seeking employment and those wishing to have vacancies filled. Any members seeking employment will be placed, if they wish, on the Institute's employment register, and allowed to advertise in situations wanted free of charge in the Institute's magazine. Any members or their employers wishing to fill vacancies can advertise situations vacant in the Institute's magazine at greatly reduced rates.

INSTITUTE OF LEADERSHIP & MANAGEMENT

Stowe House
Netherstowe
Lichfield
Staffordshire
WS13 6TJ
United Kingdom
Tel: 01543 251346
Fax: 01543 415804
Email: mes@ismstowe.demon.co.uk
Website: www.ismstowe.com

The ISM has over 20,000 corporate members drawn from supervisors and managers in all sections of the economy. A member may be allocated to one of four grades:
Corporate Membership is allocated to:
Fellowship (FISM): Awarded to those members who have completed a suitable course of study approved by the Governing Body and have attained a management position involving a higher degree of responsibility for man-management than that required for Corporate Member.
Member (MISM): Must normally have had 5 years' experience in supervision, although exceptions are made for those whose appointments involve higher levels of responsibility or qualifications.
Associate Member (AMISM): Awarded to anyone in a supervisory post who has successfully completed the Institute's Certificate or a course of similar standard in Management.
Non-corporate membership is allocated to:
Affiliate: Awarded to anyone who has completed the ISM introductory award in Supervision.

TRAINING AND EDUCATION:
The ISM currently accredits over 500 centres to run its traditional and competence-based (NVQ) courses. Its traditional courses include:
Introductory Award: This gives candidates an outline of the work and skills of a supervisor. It is suitable for newly appointed supervisors or those aspiring to this level of Management (40–50 hours).
Certificate in Management: The main award of the Institute which seeks to impart the knowledge and skills which the first-line manager needs to broaden his/her understanding of Management. The programme is assessed through work-based assignments (including a mandatory project) and an oral presentation (180 hours, provides the underpinning knowledge for NVQ Level 4).
Diploma in Management: This seeks to apply the skills and knowledge acquired on the Certificate course to middle management requirements (180 hours, provides the underpinning knowledge for NVQ Level 5).
S/NVQ Awards: The Institute is also an awarding body for S/NVQ Level 3 and NVQ Levels 4 and 5 in Management, S/NVQ Level 3 in Customer Service, NVQ Level 2 in Customer Service and NVQ Level 3 in Training and Development.
Award for First Line Managers: For people in post who want a more detailed course on the principles of Management (120 hours, provides the underpinning knowledge for NVQ Level 3).
Consolidation Course in Management: For experienced managers who have had no formal training, but would like to consolidate their acquired knowledge with appropriate theoretical training (108 hours).
Managing Customer Care Award: A stand-alone qualification of 44 hours. It provides the underpinning knowledge for NVQ Level 3 (Customer Service).
Certificate in Training Management: A stand-alone qualification of 108 hours. It provides the underpinning knowledge for NVQ Level 3 (Training and Development).
Quality Assured Awards: Aspire and Insignia: provide accreditation for tailored programmes having Management or Leadership content.
World Class Awards: A family of awards based on the 4 pillars: occupational competence, managing people, managing processes and developing people.
Learning Together: A flexible, continuing professional development tool for groups and individuals.

INSTITUTE OF MANAGEMENT CONSULTANCY

3rd Floor
17–18 Hayward's Place
London
EC1R 0EQ
United Kingdom
Tel: 020 7566 5220
Fax: 020 7566 5230
Email: consult@imc.co.uk.
Website: www.imc.co.uk

The Institute of Management Consultancy (IMC) is the professional body that sets and maintains high standards of quality, independence, objectivity and integrity for Certified Management Consultants (CMC) in the UK. It also provides the opportunity to advance to the status of Fellow grade Certified Management Consultant (FCMC).

MEMBERSHIP:

Affiliate Membership: Offered to all individuals and organisations who are interested in Management Consultancy.

Associate Membership (AIMC): An Associate is a Management Consultant, or a potential Management Consultant, who has chosen to work towards the CMC qualification and has agreed to abide by the IMC Code of Conduct. The applicant must provide evidence of 1 of the following: at least 1 year's experience as a Management Consultant; at least 5 years' experience in management or a functional specialism; an MA in Management Consultancy or an MBA with a management consultancy module or an MBA plus an appropriate short course for management consultancy core skills; current work as a consultant within an IMC Certified Practice. Associates are entitled to use the designation AIMC after completing one year of CPD.

QUALIFICATIONS:

Gaining the Certified Management Consultant (CMC) qualification: A CMC is a Management Consultant who has demonstrated competence and understanding in a range of consultancy situations against an agreed standard, and has signed up to the IMC Code of Conduct. The assessment process requires the applicant to collect evidence of competence, experience, education and training. It is therefore necessary to have quality experience as a Management Consultant before applying to become a CMC. Candidates are unlikely to be successful if they have less than 3 years' experience. The assessment process includes: submission of a professional record to demonstrate competence against IMC standards; an assignment study which is a detailed description, critique and reflection on a real consultancy project that considers the successes and difficulties encountered; an hour-long interview; and a CV, application form and 3 references. Qualified members are entitled to use the CMC designatory letters and logo.

Fellow grade Certified Management Consultant (FCMC): This is a Management Consultant of some seniority who has demonstrated substantial additional experience and continuing professional development beyond that required to become a CMC, and continues to abide by the IMC Code of Conduct. This level of membership recognises competence at a strategic level gained over a period of not less than 5 years FT after becoming a CMC. Individuals cannot join directly at Fellow level.

INSTITUTE OF MANAGEMENT SERVICES

1 Cecil Court
London Road
Enfield
Middlesex
EN2 6DD
United Kingdom
Tel: 020 8366 1261
Fax: 020 8367 8149
Email: ims@imgtserv.co.uk
Website: www.ims-productivity.com

MEMBERSHIP:

Corporate Membership: There are 2 levels, Fellow and Member. Entry is based upon a combination of experience and qualifications, although both grades are open to experienced personnel holding a position of responsibility, irrespective of qualifications.

Non-Corporate Membership: There are 2 levels, Affiliate and Associate. Associate grade requires both experience and the Institute's Certificate. Affiliate grade is the equivalent of student, and open to those already engaged in, or having an interest in, management services.

EXAMINATIONS:

The Certificate is designed to qualify for Associate grade and requires candidates to take 5 vocational-based tests. These range across the spectrum of Methods, Investigations and Study to Work Measurement and Change Management. The Diploma requires a generic management qualification at Higher National level plus successful completion of the IMS Project Management based Diploma course (assignments). There is a reserved grade of MMS(Dip) for members holding the Diploma and Certificate.

THE INSTITUTE OF MANAGEMENT SPECIALISTS

Head Office
Warwick Corner
42 Warwick Road
Kenilworth
Warwickshire
CV8 1HE
United Kingdom
Tel: 01926 855498
Fax: 01926 513100

THE INSTITUTE OF MANAGEMENT SPECIALISTS MEMBERSHIP DIPLOMA:

Companion (CompIMS): Must have been Fellow grade.

Fellow (FIMS) Level 5: Must hold a university degree or membership of a professional institute, plus an appropriate number of years' experience at top level as a professional management specialist or as a specialist involved in modern management and technology linked to one or more of the following disciplines: commerce, industry, computing, information technology, management services, finance, marketing, engineering, science, administration, manufacturing, training, or proven associated disciplines.

Member (MIMS) NVQ Level 4: Must hold one of the following: DBA, DMS, HND/HNC, BTEC, SQA, C&G, NEBSM or similar/equivalent awards, plus appropriate experience in one or more of the disciplines as under Fellow.

Associate (AMIMS) NVQ Level 3: Must hold CMS, HNC, BTEC, SQA, C&G, NEBSM or similar/equivalent awards, plus appropriate experience in one or more of the disciplines as under Fellow.

Student (StudIMS) NVQ Level 1: Must be at least 16 years of age and hold 4/5 O levels, GCSEs, CFSs; 4 passes are acceptable with appropriate experience. Alternatively acceptable are a Foundation Course, First Year Certificate or Diploma, or a specialised short course with work or office experience.

THE INSTITUTE OF MANAGEMENT SPECIALISTS CERTIFICATE AND DIPLOMA OF MERIT:

The Institute's exam structure consists of its Certificate and Diploma of Merit. Success in the exams plus practical experience at an appropriate level of responsibility are requisites for membership.

Exemption from these exams is allowed for those who hold appropriate PHd, MBA or university, BTEC, SQA, C&G or equivalent awards. Exemption is also allowed for those who hold membership of professional bodies whose standards of entry to membership are not less than those of the Institute. In all cases applicants must have the necessary experience at an appropriate level of responsibility.

The Institute conducts its own flexible open-learning course (home study) leading to exams for the Institute's Certificate and Diploma of Merit. The Certificate of Merit course is open to Student members holding 4 GCSEs, O levels or CFSs at grades A or B, including English, Mathematics, and a Science subject. Minimum age 16.

The Diploma of Merit course is open to members holding the Certificate of Merit of the Institute or similar qualifications acceptable to the Management Educational & Examinations Board of the Institute. The IMS also operates distance-learning courses, details of which are available from Head Office.

THE INSTITUTE OF PROFESSIONAL MANAGERS AND ADMINISTRATORS

La Dependance
Route de Vinchelez
Jersey
JE3 2DA
United Kingdom
Tel: 01534 485500
Fax: 01534 485500
Email: success@cpmtraining.com

MEMBERSHIP:

Membership is international.

Fellow (FInstPM): Open to those holding a top managerial or administrative post in commerce, industry or government, and to those who have made an outstanding contribution to management *in their own country or internationally*, and to those who have been professionally involved in the training of managers.

Member (MInstPM): Open to those holding middle/senior management or administration positions, and to those holding management qualifications recognised by the Institute who have also had adequate practical experience.

Associate Member (AInstPM): Open to those holding junior management, administration or supervisory posts, and to those who have undertaken courses on management or administration recognised by the Institute. Transfer to full membership is possible via an Advanced Certificate Examination.

EXAMINATIONS:

Diploma and Higher Diploma Certificates: A wide range of managerial, business and administrative Training Programmes and examinations are available through the Institute's associate college.

Advanced Certificates: 4 Advanced Certificates are available. Only Members are eligible to sit these examinations: (1) Management, Administration and Human Resources; (2) Business Studies; (3) Financial Bookkeeping and Accounting; (4) Tourism, Hotel and Hospitality Management.

INSTITUTE OF VALUE MANAGEMENT
1–3 Birdcage Walk
Westminster
London
SW1H 9JJ
United Kingdom
Tel: 0870 9020905
Email: ivmsecr@aol.com
Website: www.ivm.org.uk

The Institute aims to establish Value Management as a process for achieving value in every sector of the economy and to provide support in the innovative use of Value Management techniques.

MEMBERSHIP:

Corporate Membership: Open to any company or organisation practising or promoting Value techniques. Each corporate member may nominate up to 10 members of their organisation as representatives to the Institute. A member nominated by a corporate body can hold executive office and has full voting rights.
Ordinary Membership: Open to any professional person who has an interest in and can demonstrate an involvement in practising Value techniques.
Student Membership: Open to students who have an interest in Value Management and who are registered FT students possessing a valid student card.
Fellow: Awarded to a member as a special honour for outstanding contribution to the field of Value Management.

CERTIFICATION & ROLL OF PRACTITIONERS:

Certificate and Training: The Institute has worked closely with the Commission of the European Communities to establish a European Training System and Certification Procedure.
Roll of Practitioners: The Institute maintains an authorised list of Value Practitioners who are members of the Institute.
It launched its European Training and Certification System in 1998. This European Commission funded initiative offers, through the IVM's Certification Board, certification in the following categories: **Certifcated Value Analyst(CVA); Professional in Value Management (PVM); Certificated Value Manager (CVM); Trainer in Value Management (TVM)**. The Certification Board also approves basic and advanced courses in Value Management that have been designed by Trainers in Value Management. The Institute provides a list of trainers.

THE INTERNATIONAL PROFESSIONAL MANAGERS ASSOCIATION
Kester House
159–163 Clapham High Street
London
SW4 7SS
United Kingdom
Tel: 020 7720 4414
Fax: 01622 755149
Email: registrar@ipma.co.uk
Website: www.ipma.co.uk

The Association provides students who wish to pursue a career in management, marketing or computing (IT) with an examination scheme that is relevant to the needs of employers in both the public and private sectors.
The examinations comprise a Diploma, Advanced Diploma and a Graduate Diploma for each of the disciplines in Management, Marketing and Information Technology.
Subject to the status of the individual, students awarded the IPMA Diploma, Advanced Diploma and Graduate Diploma are accepted by a number of universities in the UK, USA, Australia and New Zealand.
With local branches, students and members have access to various activities and opportunities to meet practising managers.
Members and students of the Association have access, through the Internet, to an e-library for their study and research.
The Diploma in Management: A 1 year programme of study. The Diploma consists of 8 subjects: Accounting and Finance, Behavioural Studies, Business Law, Business Organisation and IT, Business Economics, Management Skills, Marketing, and Business Statistics.
The Advanced Diploma in Management: A 1 year programme of study. The Advanced Diploma consists of 6 subjects: Advanced Company Law, Financial Resource Management, Human Resources Management, General Management, Advanced Quantitative Methods, and Corporate Environment.
The Graduate Diploma in Management: A 1 year programme of study. The Graduate Diploma consists of 7 subjects: Strategic Management, Organisational Behaviour, Corporate Financial Management, Information Systems Management, Organisational Development

and Change, International Business Management, and a Case Study.

The Diploma in Marketing: A 1 year programme of study. The subjects are similar to the Diploma in Management.

The Advance Diploma in Marketing: A 1 year programme of study. The Advanced Diploma consists of 6 subjects: Advanced Quantitative Methods, Corporate Environment, Financial Resource Management, Human Resources Management, Advanced Marketing Communication, and Advanced Marketing Management.

The Graduate Diploma in Marketing: A 1 year programme of study. The Graduate Diploma is similar to the Graduate Diploma in Management.

The Diploma in Computing and IT: A 1 year programme of study. The Diploma consists of 6 subjects: Practical Spreadsheets, Practical Database, Practical Word Processing, Introduction to Information Technology, Practical Desktop Publishing and Presentation, and Introduction to Programming.

The Advanced Diploma in Computing and IT: A 1 year programme of study. The Advanced Diploma consists of 6 subjects: Advanced Spreadsheets, Advanced Database Management, Networking and the Internet, Systems Analysis and Design, Advanced Programming, and Management Information Systems.

The Graduate Diploma in Computing and IT: A 1 year programme of study.

The Graduate Diploma comprises 6 subjects: Software Engineering, Strategic Business Management, e-commerce marketing, Technology, Internet Application Development, and a Project.

PROFESSIONAL BUSINESS AND TECHNICAL MANAGEMENT

Head Office
Warwick Corner
42 Warwick Road
Kenilworth
Warwickshire
CV8 1HE
United Kingdom
Tel: 01926 855498
Fax: 01926 513100

MEMBERSHIP:

Companion (CProfBTM)
Fellow (FProfBTM): Must have Fellow grade. Must hold a university degree, HND or membership of a professional institute, plus an appropriate number of years' experience at top level in professional business management, professional technical management or modern technology and systems. Involving fields of activity linked to one or more of the following disciplines: business, administration, commerce, industry, computing, technology, engineering, information technology, science, marketing, finance, training, accounting, or proven associated disciplines.

Full Member (MProfBTM) NVQ Level 4: Must hold DBA, DMS, HNC, OND, BTEC, SQA, C&G, NEBSM or similar/equivalent awards, plus appropriate experience in one or more of the disciplines as under Fellow.

Associate Member (AMProfBTM) NVQ Level 3: Must hold CMS, ONC, BTEC, SQA, C&G, NEBSM or similar/equivalent awards, plus appropriate experience in one or more of the disciplines as under Fellow.

Student Member (StudProfBTM) NVQ Level 1: Must be at least 16 years of age and hold 4/5 O levels, GCSEs, CFSs; 4 passes are acceptable with appropriate experience. Alternatives are a Foundation Course, First Year Certificate or Diploma, or a specialised short course with work or office experience.

EXAMINATIONS:

PBTM's exam structure consists of its own Certificate and Diploma of Merit. Success in the exams plus practical experience at an appropriate level of responsibility are requisites for membership.

Exemption from these exams is allowed to those who hold appropriate university, BTEC, SQA, C&G or equivalent awards, and also to those who hold membership of a professional body whose standards of entry to membership are not less than those of the PBTM. In all cases applicants must have the necessary experience at an appropriate level of responsibility.

The PBTM conducts its own **flexible, open-learning courses** (home study) leading to exams for the PBTM Certificate and Diploma of Merit. The Certificate of Merit course is open to Student Members holding 4 O levels grades A or B, including English, Mathematics and a Science subject. Minimum age 16.

The Diploma of Merit course is open to members holding the Certificate of Merit of PBTM or similar qualifications acceptable to the Management Education & Examinations Board of Professional Business and Technical Management. Also, in addition to the above, the PBTM operates 5 distance learning courses, details of which are available from Head Office.

THE SOCIETY OF BUSINESS PRACTITIONERS

PO Box 11
Sandbach
Cheshire
CW11 3GE
United Kingdom
Tel: 01270 526339
Fax: 01270 526339
Website: www.mamsasbp.com

MEMBERSHIP:

Fellow (FSBP): Elected on the basis of a high level of achievement in Business Practice and/or a significantly important contribution to Business Education/Practice.

Certified Professional Manager (CPM): Senior membership open to business practitioners who have the SBP Postgraduate Diploma in Business Administration (or its equivalent) and who satisfy other requirements.

Member (MSBP): Elected after obtaining the SBP Advanced Diploma in Business Administration and additional diplomas (or equivalent), and having satisfied other requirements.

EXAMINATIONS:

The Society conducts bi-annual exams, internationally, for all its qualifications. Preparatory tuition is offered internationally at approved centres. Exam reciprocal exemption agreements are in force with other professional institutes and for entrance to BBA and MBA degrees at selected universities.

Diploma in Business Administration: Entry requirements: minimum age 18. Must be a registered student and have at least 1 of the following: (a) 4 GCSEs at grade C, or higher, 1 of which must be English Language, plus 2 A levels; (b) BTEC Cert or Dip in Business & Finance; (c) Matric or entrance exams of a recognised university; (d) LCCI Stage I (Intermediate) exams or RSA exams at Stage III; (e) an equivalent qualification from a recognised professional institute or educational establishment; (f) mature students may enter on the basis of general educational qualifications and an acceptable level of business experience.

Diploma in Marketing Management: Same entry requirements as for Diploma in Business Administration.

Advanced Diploma in Business Administration: Entry requirements: must have SBP Diploma in Business Administration (or equivalent) and meet its entry conditions.

Advanced Diploma in Marketing Management: Same entry requirements as for Advanced Diploma in Business Administration.

Postgraduate Diploma in Business Administration: Entry requirements: must have SBP Advanced Diploma in Business Administration (or equivalent) and/or a recognised degree in a relevant subject.

Postgraduate Diploma in International Marketing: Same entry requirements as for Postgraduate Diploma in Business Administration.

Manufacturing

THE INSTITUTE OF MANUFACTURING

Head Office
Warwick Corner
42 Warwick Road
Kenilworth
Warwickshire
CV8 1HE
United Kingdom
Tel: 01926 855498
Fax: 01926 513100

THE INSTITUTE OF MANUFACTURING MEMBERSHIP DIPLOMA:

Companion (CompIManf): Must have Fellow grade.

Fellow (FIManf) Level 5: Must hold a university degree or membership of a professional institute, plus have an appropriate number of years' experience at top level in professional manufacturing, manufacturing management, or modern and advanced manufacturing technology and systems involving fields of activity linked to these disciplines, including: industry, commerce, computing, science, engineering, information technology, production, administration, marketing, finance, training, safety, and quality.

Full Member (MIManf) NVQ Level 4: Must hold one of the following: DBA, DMS, HND/HNC, BTEC, SCOTVEC, C&G, NEBSM or similar/equivalent awards, plus appropriate experience in one or more of the disciplines as under Fellow.

Associate Member (AMIManf) NVQ Level 3: Must hold CMS, BTEC, SCOTVEC, C&G, NEBSM or similar/equivalent awards, plus appropriate experience in one or more of the disciplines as under Fellow.

Student Member (StudIManf) HVQ Level 1: Must be at least 16 and hold 4/5 O levels, GCSEs, CFSs; 4 passes are acceptable with appropriate experience. Alternatives are a Foundation Course, First Year Certificate or Diploma, or a specialised short course with work or office experience.

THE INSTITUTE OF MANUFACTURING CERTIFICATE AND DIPLOMA OF MERIT:

The Institute's exam structure consists of its Certificate and Diploma of Merit. Success in the exams plus practical experience at an appropriate level of responsibility are requisites of membership.

Exemption from these exams is allowed to those who hold Phd, MBA, university degree, BTEC, SCOTVEC, C&G or equivalent awards. Exemption is also granted to those who hold membership of professional bodies whose standards of entry to membership are not lower than those of the Institute. In all cases applicants must have the necessary experience at an appropriate level of responsibility.

The Institute conducts its own flexible, open-learning (home study) courses leading to exams for the Institute's Certificate and Diploma of Merit. Entry standards: the Certificate of Merit Course is open to Student Members holding 4 GCSEs or O levels grades A or B, including English, Mathematics and a Science subject. Minimum age 16.

The Diploma of Merit course is open to members holding the Certificate of Merit of the Institute or similar qualifications acceptable to the Management Education & Examinations Board of the Institute. Also, in addition to the above, the Institute operates 12 distance-learning courses, futher information about which is available from the Head Office.

Marine Engineering

THE INSTITUTE OF MARINE ENGINEERING, SCIENCE AND TECHNOLOGY

80 Coleman Street
London
EC2R 5BJ
United Kingdom
Tel: 020 7382 2600
Fax: 020 7382 2670
Email: membership@imarest.org
Website: www.imarest.org

MEMBERSHIP:

Every candidate for admission to any category of membership is required to complete and sign the Institute's application form. There are 7 categories of member, the detailed requirements for these categories are set out below.

Fellow (FIMarEST): A candidate should be at least 35 years of age at the time of application and:

(a) be a Member or qualify for the category of Member and have a level of competence and commitment acquired through extended experience and CPD involving superior responsibility for at least 5 years engaged in the execution of important work in a marine-related profession; *or*

(b) be an Associate Member or qualify for the category of Associate Member and have a level of competence and commitment acquired through extended experience and CPD involving superior responsibility for at least 5 years engaged in the execution of important work in a marine-related profession; *or*

(c) be an Associate or qualify for the category of Associate and have a level of competence and commitment acquired through extended experience and CPD involving superior responsibility for at least 5 years engaged in the execution of important work in a marine-related profession; *or*

(d) have attained a position of such professional eminence in Marine Engineering, Science or Technology as to qualify for admission to the category of Fellow.

Member (MIMarEST): A candidate should be at least 25 years of age at the time of application and:

(a) be a Graduate member or qualify for the category of Graduate member and have demonstrated a level of competence and commitment acquired through a structured programme of Initial Professional Development (IPD) involving responsibility engaged in the design, management or execution of important work in a marine-related profession; *or*

(b) be an Associate Member or qualify for the category of Associate Member and have a level of competence and commitment acquired through extended experience, management or execution of important work in a marine-related profession; *or*

(c) be an Associate or qualify for the category of Associate and have a level of competence and commitment acquired through enhanced and extended experience, experiential learning and CPD involving increased responsibility engaged in the design, management or execution of important work in a marine-related profession; *or*

(d) be at least 35 years of age and have attained, over a period of 15 years, a position of such experience in their profession by their contribution to Marine Engineering, Science and Technology or other marine-related discipline as to qualify for admission to the category of Member.

Associate Member (AMIMarEST): A candidate should be at least 35 years of age at the time of application and:

(a) be a Graduate member or qualify for the category of Graduate member and have demonstrated a level of competence and commitment acquired through a structured programme of Initial Professional Development (IPD) involving responsibility engaged in the design, management or execution of important work in a marine related profession. **or**
(b) be an Associate or qualify for the category of Associate and have a level of competence and commitment acquired through extended experience, experimental learning and CPD involving increased responsibility engaged in the design, management or execution or important work in the marine related profession. **or**
(c) be at least 35 years of age and have attained, over a period of 15 years, a position of such experience in their profession by their contribution to marine engineering, science and technology or other marine related discipline as to qualify for admission to the category of Associate Member.

Associate (AIMarEST): A candidate should be at least 21 years of age at the time of application and either

(a) be a Graduate member or qualify for the category Graduate member and have demonstrated a level of competence and commitment acquired through a structured programme of Initial Professional Development (IPD) involving responsibility engaged in the design, management or execution or important work in a marine related profession. **or**
(b) be at least 35 years of age and have attained, over a period of 15 years, a position of such experience in their profession by their contribution to marine engineering, science and technology or other marine related discipline as to qualify for admission to the category of Associate.

Graduate (GIMarEST): A candidate should be at least 21 years of age at the time of application and

(a) have completed a programme of further or higher education accredited or recognised by IMarEST. **and**
(b) be in the process of completing a structured programme of Initial Professional Development (IPD). The IPD should be approved by the IMarEST and will satisfy the requirements laid down by the IMarEST for transfer to any category of corporate member within 10 years following election/transfer to the category of Graduate.

Student (SIMarEST): Student members shall be enrolled on a programme of further or higher education accredited or recognised by the IMarEST.

Affiliate: A candidate shall either:

(a) be persons who have an interest in or may contribute to the activities of the institute; **or**
(b) be persons who in the opinion of the IMarEST can contribute to or wish to have access to the technical services of the Institute and are resident in a recognised overseas territory and who are also members of a professional society with which the Institute has reciprocal arrangements.

Marketing and Sales

THE CHARTERED INSTITUTE OF MARKETING

Moor Hall
Cookham
Maidenhead
Berkshire
SL6 9QH
United Kingdom
Tel: 01628 427120
Fax: 01628 427158
Email: education@cim.co.uk
Website: www.cim.co.uk

MEMBERSHIP:

All grades are awarded following an assessment during which account is taken of the candidate's academic/vocational qualifications and marketing resource management experience.

Member (MCIM): A person who holds a recognised university degree in marketing, CIM Postgraduate Diploma or equivalent diploma, or Chartered Professional Body admission exam or NVQ Level 5 in marketing; at least 3 years' experience in marketing, including 1 year's experience in marketing resource management.

Fellow (FCIM): A person who has the academic qualifications required for a Member and a proven record of expertise, experience and success, holding a role such as Chief Exec, Exec Director, Senior Marketing Exec, Prof of Marketing or Senior Academic for at least 5 years.

EXAMINATIONS:

The 3-tiered syllabus comprises the **Postgraduate Diploma in Marketing, Advanced Certificate in Marketing** and **Certificate in Marketing**. Available at over 300 study centres world-wide and through DL or intensive study, each qualification is in June and December.

The **Postgraduate Diploma in Marketing, Advanced Certificate** and **Certificate in Marketing** embrace the marketing concept and reflect the key knowledge and skills required by professional marketing and sales practitioners. Emphasis is on the practical application of marketing theory, problem solving and marketing planning from a fundamental level to a more strategic focus at Diploma level.

The **Postgraduate Diploma in Marketing (DipM)** is internationally recognised and with the relevant experience gives eligibility for full membership of the CIM and Chartered Marketer Status. The Open University validation service have awarded the CIM Diploma 70 Master points. Modules include Integrated Marketing Communications Strategy, International Marketing Strategy and a Strategic Marketing Management Section comprising Planning & Control and Analysis & Decision (case study).

Student registration forms, study centre lists and further information regarding exemptions and entry points may be obtained from: *The Education Dept*, tel: 01628 427120, fax: 01628 427158, e-mail: education@cim.co.uk.

THE INSTITUTE OF SALES AND MARKETING MANAGEMENT

Romeland House
Romeland Hill
St Albans
Hertfordshire
AL3 4ET
United Kingdom
Tel: 01727 812500
Fax: 01727 812525
Email: sales@ismm.co.uk

The Institute of Sales and Marketing Management offers a suite of 4 professional qualifications in Sales and Marketing Management. The qualifications are accredited by the Qualifications and Curriculum Authority, the body set up by the government to regulate vocational qualifications. Subsequent to the QCA accreditation, the qualification titles and standing have been upgraded and now lead to the following qualifications:

Level 2: Certificate in Sales and Marketing
Level 3: Advanced Certificate in Sales and Marketing
Level 4: Diploma in Sales and Management
Level 4: Diploma in Key Account Management

The programme is available through colleges of FE, approved private training centres and in-company training departments, and as a distance-learning course through RRC Business Training.

Membership of the ISMM is awarded on the basis of achieving these qualifications or in recognition of a proven track record in sales and marketing management.

MANAGING & MARKETING SALES ASSOCIATION EXAMINATION BOARD

PO Box 11
Sandbach
Cheshire
CW11 3GE
United Kingdom
Tel: 01270 526 339
Fax: 01270 526 339
Email: info@mamsasbp.com
Website: www.mamsasbp.com

MEMBERSHIP:

Student Member: Registered for 2 years to undertake the MAMSA exams.
Graduate Member: Annual membership of holders of MAMSA qualifications (Grad-MAMSA).
Professional Member and Fellow: Annual Membership.

EXAMINATIONS:

Intermediate Diploma in Selling: Entry requirements: minimum age 18 years.
Standard Diploma in Salesmanship: Entry requirements: as above *or* 5 GCSEs at grade C or above *or* 20 years old with 2 years' approved employment.
Certificate in Sales Marketing: Entry requirements: as for Salesmanship.
Higher Diploma in Sales Marketing: Entry requirements: as for Salesmanship.
Advanced Diploma in Sales Management: Entry requirements: 5 GCSEs at grade C or above and 1 A level, including English and a branch of Mathematics *or* BTEC ONC Business Award *or* 3 years' experience in Selling and Marketing.
Certificate/Diploma in Marketing Strategy & Management: Entry requirements: as for Sales Management.
Diploma in Business Administration & Practices: Entry requirements: as for Sales Management.
Advanced Diploma in the Practice of Business Management: Entry requirements: as for Sales Management.
Certificate in Quality Services
Diploma in Supervisory Skills: Distance-learning courses available for all diplomas and for in-company groups.

THE SOCIETY OF SALES AND MARKETING

40 Archdale Road
East Dulwich
London
SE22 9HJ
United Kingdom
Tel: 020 8693 0555
Fax: 020 8693 0555
Email: ssam@totalise.co.uk

EXAMINATIONS:

The Society is the only professional body which awards specialist certificates and diplomas in all the four major divisions of selling, namely: Selling & Sales Management, Marketing, Retail Management and International Trade. The examinations are held twice a year (in May and November). The subjects for the Certificate in Selling & Sales Management, Certificate in Marketing, Certificate in Retail Management and Certificate in International Trade are: (a) Business Communications; (b) Accounting & Finance. The subjects for the Advanced Certificate in Selling & Sales Management, Advanced Certificate in Marketing, Advanced Certificate in Retail Management and Advanced Certificate in International Trade are: (c) Selling & Sales Management; (d) Marketing; (e) Principles of Selling; (f) Principles of Management; (g) Retail Management; (h) International Trade & Payments. The subjects for the Diploma in Selling & Sales Management, Diploma in Marketing, Diploma in Retail Management and Diploma in International Trade are: (i) Consumer Affairs; (j) Management Information Systems; (k) Export Practice; (l) Elements of Export Law. A dissertation on a relevant topic is essential for the Advanced Diploma in Selling & Sales Management, Advanced Diploma in Marketing, Advanced Diploma in Retail Management and Advanced Diploma in International Trade. N/SVQ candidates may apply for exemptions or membership according to age, qualifications and experience.

MEMBERSHIP:

Registered students are eligible to take the Society's professional exams. They must be over 18. Registration expires after 3 years, and it is renewable.
Fellow (FSSAM): Candidates must have been Associate Members for at least 2 years, and be engaged in selling, retailing, marketing or international trade, or hold a position of responsibility; or must have been a lecturer in sales and related subjects for at least 2 years.
Associate (ASSAM): Candidates must have passed the Society's professional exams or been exempted from them, and be engaged in selling, sales management, retailing, marketing or international trade, or hold a position of responsibility; or must have been a lecturer in sales and related subjects for at least 2 years.
Graduate (GSSAM): Candidates must have been recommended by their employers as fit and proper persons to benefit from membership, or must have shown proof of outstanding selling abilities, eg agents of mail-order firms.

Martial Arts

THE SOCIETY OF MARTIAL ARTS/COLLEGE OF HIGHER EDUCATION OF MARTIAL ARTS

PO Box 34
Manchester
M9 8DN
United Kingdom
Tel: 0161 702 1660
Fax: 0161 702 1660
Email: registrar@societyofmartialarts.co.uk or principal@chema.co.uk
Website: www.societyofmartialarts.co.uk or www.chema.co.uk

The Society offers appropriate membership grades to practitioners of martial arts. The College offers graduateship qualifications through distance learning and exams, and arranges postgraduate studies in martial arts for qualified students through universities. Exemptions are granted to those with relevant degree or postgraduate qualifications in sports science or martial arts.

MEMBERSHIP:

Student Member: This class of membership is open to anyone undergoing an approved FT or PT education in martial arts.
Graduate Member (GradSMA): This class of membership is open to martial artists who have completed the Graduateship exam offered by the Society or an approved degree course qualification with a black belt or equivalent grade in martial arts.
Full Member (MSMA): Open to Graduate Members with relevant experience. Some practitioners with many years' experience may be able to join directly as a Full Member, provided they complete a thesis in martial arts research.
Fellow Member (FSMA): In general candidates must have relevant experience. Some candidates with many years' experience and who have made an exceptional contribution to the field of martial arts may be elected to this class of membership directly.

Affiliate Member: This is available to organisations promoting martial arts.

GRADUATESHIP IN MARTIAL ARTS (GradMA):

Through the College of Higher Education of Martial Arts.
Entry requirements: At least C grades at GCSE in English, Maths and Science. Candidates over 25 years may enrol as mature students. All candidates without formal qualifications must attend an interview.
Part 1: Candidates must be competent practitioners of any form of martial arts; exemptions are allowed only to those who are holders of a black belt (1st Dan) or equivalent qualification in martial arts.
Part 2: Students are normally expected to have completed Part 1 before continuing with the programme. The subjects offered for study in Part 2 carry a total of 360 credits (3 years).
First-year core subjects (total 120 credits): Introduction to Sports Science; Human (Functional) Anatomy; Human Physiology; Introduction to Coaching Science; History of Martial Arts; Philosophy (Metaphysics, Epistemology, Aesthetics and Ethics); Sports Sociology; one optional subject to be chosen by the student from any department at an accredited university.
Second-year core subjects (total 120 credits): Exercise Physiology; Biomechanics; Acquisition of Martial Arts Motor Skills; Law and Martial Arts; Research Methods; Statistics; Sports Pedagogy; one optional subject to be chosen by the student from any department at an accredited university.
Third-year core subjects (total 120 credits): Pediatric Exercise Science; Assessing and Evaluating Martial Arts Skills; Sports Nutrition; Sports Psychology; Epidemiology of Martial Arts injuries. Research project (total 40 credits).
Assessment: Subjects studied in years 1 to 3 are assessed by either 3 written assignments (25%), or 1 review paper (50%). In both cases, a 3 hour unseen paper makes up the balance of the total marks. The research dissertation is usually a written presentation of *c.*10,000 words followed by a viva voce. The pass mark for all papers is 50%.

MATURE STUDENTS' ROUTE TO GRADUATESHIP IN MARTIAL ARTS (MMA):

This route is by 1 year's FT research. Candidates submit a thesis of 30,000 words followed by a viva voce and 1 publication. [Can be studied together for a BPhil from Knightsbridge University, Denmark.]

MASTERSHIP IN MARTIAL ARTS (MMA):

Students with a degree in martial arts carry out advanced research for 1 year and submit a thesis of 40,000 words followed by a viva voce and 2 publications. [Can be studied together for a MPhil from Knightsbridge University, Denmark, and a PhD.]

ACCESS TO MARTIAL ARTS AND EXERCISE SCIENCE:

For those who are over 21 years, without formal qualifications to enter undergraduate studies, this course provides entry.

TEACHING ADULTS ADVANCE CERTIFICATE (PHYSICAL EDUCATION) (MARTIAL ARTS SPECIAL):

This qualification provides an opportunity to gain a recognised teaching qualification at Level 3.

ACCESS TO INTELLIGENCE, SECURITY AND TERRORISM STUDIES:

For those who are over 21 years without formal qualifications.

Massage and Allied Therapies

INTERNATIONAL COUNCIL OF HOLISTIC THERAPISTS

3rd Floor, Eastleigh House
Upper Market Street
Eastleigh
SO51 9FD
United Kingdom
Tel: 023 8048 8900
Fax: 023 8048 8970
Website: www.fht.org.uk

This professional association supports therapists in Holistic Therapies, including Aromatherapy, Reflexology, Indian Head Massage, Body Massage, and many more. Membership is only open to those qualified through awarding bodies such as the IIHHT, VTCT, S/NVQ, BTEC and City & Guilds. Exemptions from these qualification requirements are granted only for those who have other acceptable qualifications and experience.

LCSP REGISTER OF REMEDIAL MASSEURS AND MANIPULATIVE THERAPISTS

330 Lytham Road
Blackpool
FY4 1DW
United Kingdom
Tel: 01253 408443
Fax: 01253 401329
Email: admin.lcsp@ic24.net
Website: www.lcsp.uk.com

MEMBERSHIP:

Full Membership: Open to those persons who have passed the written and practical sections of the qualifying exam and who have not less than 3 years' FT practical experience in the profession. Such membership carries the designating letters LCSP(Phys), LCSP(Chir) or LCSP(BTh) according to whether the member is approved by the Council as a practitioner in remedial massage and manipulative therapy, chiropody, or health and beauty therapy.
Associate Membership (LSCP (Assoc)): Open to those persons who have passed the written and practical section of the qualifying exam, and who have less than 3 years' FT practical experience in the profession.
Fellowship (FLCSP): Conferred on members who have given distinguished service to the profession or Register.
Honorary Membership: May be conferred by the Council on outside persons who are genuinely associated with the profession and work of the Register.
Student Membership: Open to bona fide registered students of the profession.

EDUCATION AND EXAMINATION:

The Register recognises the Northern Institute of Massage (NIM) as its official training establishment, but may also approve of such other sources of training or apprenticeship submitted by an applicant for membership at the discretion of the Council.
Students who have successfully completed the tuition course of the NIM may apply to take their final qualifying exam for the Diploma of the NIM under the auspices of the Register, such exam also qualifying the successful candidate for Membership of the Register. The Exam consists of 2 written papers and a practical exam.
Exemptions from the written exam may be granted on a subject-for-subject basis to holders of certain qualifications recognised by the Register, eg qualified nurses, medical auxiliaries, etc.
Exemptions from the practical exam can only be granted in special circumstances where the applicant is known to be an established practitioner of the profession, and such applicants for admission will, in every case, be required to attend for interview before the Council of the Register.

THE NORTHERN INSTITUTE OF MASSAGE

14–16 St Mary's Place
Bury
Lancashire
BL9 0DZ
United Kingdom
Tel: 0161 7971800
Email: information@nim56.co.uk
Website: www.nim56.co.uk

The College offers PT and home-study extension courses in Remedial Massage, Manipulative Therapy and allied subjects. Official training establishment to the London and Counties Society of Physiologists. The College is accredited by the Open and Distance Learning Quality Council, and is a Member of the Association of British Correspondence Colleges.

EXAMINATIONS:

Diploma in Remedial Massage: Leading to LCSP(Assoc) qualification.
Higher Grade Diplomas in Advanced Remedial Massage and Manipulative Therapy: Subsequent to satisfactory completion of postgraduate training in Advanced Massage, Electro-therapy and Manipulative Therapy.

Materials

THE INSTITUTE OF MATERIALS

1 Carlton House Terrace
London
SW1Y 5DB
United Kingdom
Tel: 020 7451 7300
Fax: 020 7839 4534
Email: membership@materials.org.uk
Website: www.materials.org.uk

The Institute of Materials was formed on 1 January 1992 following an earlier amalgamation of The Metals Society and The Institute of Metallurgists. The Institute of Metallurgical Technicians was incorporated into the latter in 1984. The Institute also amalgamated with The Plastics and Rubber Institute and the Institute of Ceramics on 1 January 1993.

MEMBERSHIP:

Fellow (FIM): A person with an outstanding reputation in the field of Materials.

Professional Member (MIM): A person with proven technical competence in the field of Materials, innovative by character and capable of developing the science and technology of Materials.

Member: A person who is not a Materials Scientist or Technologist but has a general interest in the profession and who may be expected to be a professional engineer in the field of Metallurgy, Materials, Polymers or Ceramics, or a scientist of a closely allied discipline.

Associate (AMIM): Incorporated Engineer: A person typically with an HNC/HND qualification who understands and can apply existing technology but is not necessarily of an innovative character.

Technician: A person capable of following prescribed routines which are dictated by a professional member or incorporated engineer.

Student: This grade of membership is open to persons pursuing a first qualification in the field of Materials.

Affiliate: Those generally interested in Materials but who would not necessarily qualify for the grades previously mentioned.

As a nominated body of the Engineering Council, the Institute is also empowered to nominate members in relevant grades to the Engineering Technician, Incorporated Engineer and Chartered Engineering sections of their Register.

Mathematics

EDINBURGH MATHEMATICAL SOCIETY

JCMB, Kings Building
Mayfield Road
Edinburgh
EH9 3JZ
United Kingdom
Tel: 0131 650 5040
Fax: 0131 650 6553
Email: edmathsoc@maths.ed.ac.uk
Website: www.maths.ed.ac.uk

The Edinburgh Mathematical Society is the principal mathematical society for the university community in Scotland. Its membership is drawn from all Scottish universities and other educational institutions as well as mathematicians in industry and commerce. The society organises a variety of events intended to appeal to a wide range of its members. These include: about 8 ordinary meetings each year, where a senior mathematician delivers a talk; occasional joint meetings with other mathematical societies; publication of research papers in its journal, the *Proceedings*; and support of a variety of mathematical activities through its various funds.

MEMBERSHIP

Membership is open to all who are interested in this field. Prospective members are nominated at a meeting of the society and elected at the following meeting. Membership is either *Ordinary* or *Reciprocal* (this gives membership at a reduced rate to those already belonging to certain other mathematical societies). Member may obtain *Proceedings* at a reduced rate.

THE INSTITUTE OF MATHEMATICS AND ITS APPLICATIONS

Catherine Richards House
16 Nelson Street
Southend-on-Sea
Essex
SS1 1EF
United Kingdom
Tel: 01702 354020
Fax: 01702 354111
Email: post@ima.org.uk
Website: www.ima.org.uk

MEMBERSHIP:

Fellow (CMath FIMA): Corporate Membership with Chartered Status. Fellows have demonstrated seniority or distinction in professional activities involving mathematics. As a guide, the minimum period after which an Honours Mathematics graduate might qualify is 7 years for mathematics in research or 10 years for those using or applying mathematics.

Member (CMath MIMA): Corporate Membership with Chartered Status. Members have an appropriate degree, a minimum period of 4 years' postgraduate training and experience, and a position of responsibility involving the application of mathematical knowledge or training in mathematics.

Associate Fellow (AFIMA): Corporate Membership. This grade is still in existence but was closed to further admissions in December 1997.

Graduate (GIMA): Grade leading to Chartered Status. Graduates hold an Honours degree in Mathematics or have obtained an Honours degree in a related subject and are participating in training or work experience in which mathematical knowledge of a similar level is attained.

Licentiate: Grade leading to Chartered Status. Licentiates hold an ordinary degree or pass degree or HND in Mathematics or a degree

where mathematics is only a subsidiary component. A more extensive period of postgraduate training and experience are required to meet Chartered Status requirements.
Student: Grade leading to Chartered Status. Students are undertaking a course of study which will lead to a qualification that meets Graduate or Licentiate Member requirements.
Companion: Grade for non-professional members. No academic requirements are required for entry into this grade.

THE MATHEMATICAL ASSOCIATION

259 London Road
Leicester
LE2 3BE
United Kingdom
Tel: 0116 221 0013
Fax: 0116 212 2835
Email: office@m-a.org.uk
Website: www.m-a.org.uk

The Mathematical Association offers professional development for mathematics teachers in the form of journals, talks, conferences and courses. Courses leading to the award of transferable accreditation towards a Masters in Education degree are offered by the Association. Training in the use of graphic calculators in the teaching of mathematics is also offered through the T3 training programme.

Mechanical Engineering

THE INSTITUTION OF MECHANICAL ENGINEERS

1 Birdcage Walk
Westminster
London
SW1H 9JJ
United Kingdom
Tel: 020 7222 7899
Fax: 020 7222 4557

Honorary Fellow (HonFIMechE): Persons of distinguished scientific attainment, distinction in Engineering, or eminence who has given distinguished service to the Institution.
Fellow (FIMechE): Established mechanical engineer who, in addition to meeting the requirements for Member, holds a post of greater responsibility. Fellows are entitled to register as Chartered Engineers.
Member (MIMechE): Established mechanical engineer who, in addition to the requirements for Associate Member, has completed a period of responsible professional practice. Members are entitled to register as Chartered Engineers.

Associate Member (AMIMechE): A person who has satisfied the practical and professional training requirements, and meets the academic requirements either partially or in full (minimum Honours degree or equivalent).
Graduate: Usually a person with a Mechanical Engineering or other acceptable degree.
Student: A person following an appropriate Engineering course at degree level or a pre-academic year of practical training.
In addition, there are 2 classes for persons who do not aspire to full qualification as Chartered Engineers:
Associate: A person engaged or interested in Mechanical Engineering.
Companion: A person occupying a distinguished position in a related profession or who has rendered important services to Mechanical Engineering.
The academic standard for Membership is an accredited degree in Mechanical, Electro-mechanical, Manufacturing Systems or a similar Engineering field. A list of accredited courses is available on enquiry from the Bury St Edmunds Office of the Institution (Karen Borley, Northgate Avenue, Bury St Edmunds, Suffolk IP32 6BN; tel 01284 763277, fax 01284 704006).

Medical Herbalism

THE NATIONAL INSTITUTE OF MEDICAL HERBALISTS

56 Longbrook Street
Exeter
Devon
EX4 6AH
United Kingdom
Tel: 01392 426022
Fax: 01392 498963
Email: nimh@ukexeter.freeserve.co.uk
Website: www.nimh.org.uk

MEMBERSHIP:

Fellow (FNIMH): Fellowship of the Institute may be offered to a member who has rendered conspicuous service to the Institute and who has been in active membership for more than 10 years.
Member (MNIMH): Those who have successfully completed the training and passed all exams are eligible to apply for membership of Institute.

TRAINING:

The School of Phytotherapy, Bucksteep Manor, Bodle Street Green, Hailsham, East Sussex, runs a 5 year tutorial course with intensive theory and practical work. There is also a FT course at the School. Middlesex University, the Scottish School of Herbal Medicine, University of Central Lancashire and University of Westminster run a 4 year BSc (Hons) degree course in Herbal Medicine and Napier University (Edinburgh)

Medical Secretaries

ASSOCIATION OF MEDICAL SECRETARIES, PRACTICE MANAGERS, ADMINISTRATORS AND RECEPTIONISTS

Tavistock House North
Tavistock Square
London
WC1H 9LN
United Kingdom
Tel: 020 7387 6005
Fax: 020 7388 2648
Email: info@amspas.co.uk
Website: www.amspar.co.uk

MEMBERSHIP:

Fellow (FAMS): May be conferred in recognition of services to the Association.
Member (MAMS): Open to (a) holders of the Association's Diploma in Medical Secretarial Studies; (b) holders of the Diploma or Certificate in Practice Management upon qualifying; and (c) holders of the Diploma in Health Services Reception, or following 10 years' relevant experience in a health care environment.
Associate Member (AAMS): Holder of the Association Certificate in General Practice Reception/Hospital Reception, Certificate in Medical Terminology or Certificate in Medical Secretarial Studies or qualification by five years' relevant experience in the Health Care environment.
Affiliate (AMS (AFF)): Affiliateship is open to any person currently working in the medical field for under 5 years.

DIPLOMAS AND CERTIFICATES:

Advanced Diploma for Medical Secretaries: FT/PT course normally over 12 months, open to school leavers, mature students and those already in post.
Intermediate Diploma in Medical Reception: FT/PT course for school leavers, mature students and those already working in a health care environment.
Diploma in Practice Management: PT course normally 12–18 months, suitable for those working within general practice in a management or administrative role and those with at least 3 years' relevant experience.
Certificate in Medical Terminology
AMSPAR General Practice Reception Programme
AMSPAR Hospital Reception Programme
AMSPAR is a registered awarding body approved by the Qualifications and Curriculum Authority.

Medicine

BRITISH INSTITUTE OF MUSCULOSKELETAL MEDICINE

34 The Avenue
Watford
Herts
WD17 4AH
United Kingdom
Tel: 01923 220999
Fax: 01923 249087
Email: bimm@compuserve.com
Website: www.bimm.org.uk

There are currently 380 Members in the Institute, and Membership is open to registered doctors in the UK who have an interest in musculoskeletal medicine and experience in 1 or more of the following branches of medicine: orthopaedics, rheumatology, sports medicine and osteopathy. Courses are run several times a year and there is a Diploma in Musculoskeletal Medicine from the Society of Apothecaries of London and a MSc course in association with the London College of Osteopathy and University College London. The Institute is affiliated to the International Federation of Manual Medicine (FIMM).

BRITISH MEDICAL ASSOCIATION (BMA)

BMA House
Tavistock Square
London
WC1H 9UP
United Kingdom
Tel: 020 7387 4499
Fax: 020 7388 6400
Email: info.web@bma.org.uk
Website: www.bma.org.uk

The BMA is a voluntary professional association for doctors as well as a scientific and educational body and publishing house.

MEMBERSHIP

Registered Medical Practitioners and Medical Students are eligible for membership.

THE ROYAL COLLEGE OF ANAESTHETISTS

48–49 Russell Square
London
WC1B 4JY
United Kingdom
Tel: 020 7908 7314
Fax: 020 7636 8280
Email: exams@rcoa.ac.uk
Website: www.rcoa.ac.uk

Fellowship of the Royal College of Anaesthetists (FRCA): The Fellowship examination consists of 2 parts, Primary and Final. Entry to the Primary FRCA examination is conditional upon the candidate having undertaken at least 12 months of approved anaesthetic training in the UK or Republic of Ireland. Entry to the Final FRCA exam requires a minimum of 30 months of anaesthetic training, of which at least 18 months must be in approved posts in the UK or Republic of Ireland.
Exemption from the Primary FRCA exam may be granted to holders of certain overseas qualifications.
Further details can be obtained from the College.

THE ROYAL COLLEGE OF GENERAL PRACTITIONERS

14 Princes Gate
Hyde Park
London
SW7 1PU
United Kingdom
Tel: 020 7581 3232
Fax: 020 7225 3047
Email: info@rcgp.org.uk
Website: www.rcgp.org.uk

The aims of the College are to encourage, foster and maintain the highest possible standards in general medical practice. Entry to the College is by exam or assessment; the grade of **Associate** is intended for general practitioners who have not yet gained the necessary experience to take the exam and for those in general practice or other branches of medicine who support the aims of the College but who do not wish, or are not eligible, to become members.
Fellow (FRCGP): There are 2 forms of Fellowship for members of the College: Fellowship by nomination is for members who have made a significant contribution either to the science or practice of medicine or to the aims of the College; Fellowship by assessment is open to all members of the College of 5 years' continuous standing.
Member (MRCGP): Candidates must be fully registered medical practitioners who have passed the membership exam and completed vocational training or completed Membership by Assessment of Performance (see below).
Exam: The examination consists of 4 modules, 2 written papers, an assessment of consulting skills and an oral examination. The modules may be taken at different times but must be passed within 3 years of application to complete the examination.
Eligibility: You must be eligible to be an independent practitioner of general practice or undergoing vocational training with this in view.
Membership by Assessment of Performance (MAP): This is an alternative route to College membership other than taking the exam. General Practitioners who have been in independent practice in the UK for at least 5 years may elect to be assessed on evidence of good quality practice. This has 3 components: a portfolio of evidence that the College's assessment criteria have been met; evidence of consulting skills; and an evaluation following a practice visit.

THE ROYAL COLLEGE OF OBSTETRICIANS AND GYNAECOLOGISTS

27 Sussex Place
Regent's Park
London
NW1 4RG
United Kingdom
Tel: 020 7772 6200
Fax: 020 7723 0575
Email: coll.sec@rcog.org.uk
Website: www.rcog.org.uk

MEMBERSHIP:

Fellow (FRCOG): Members who have been judged by the Council to have advanced the science and/or practice of Obstetrics and Gynaecology or have attained such a position in the medical profession or in other fields as to merit promotion to Fellowship.
Member (MRCOG): Registered medical practitioners who have passed the Membership exam.

EXAMINATIONS:

Part 1 Membership: 2 multiple-choice question papers covering basic sciences.
Part 2 Membership: 2 essay papers plus 1 multiple-choice question paper in Obsterics and Gynaecology, and an oral exam. Candidates must obtain a pass mark in the written section in order to progress to the oral.
Training: Candidates must complete the following periods of post-registration training for the Part 2 exam: (a) **Obstetrics:** 12 months' recognised appointment; (b) **Gynaecology:** 12

months' recognised appointment. Candidates whose Part 2 training forms and certificates reach the College after 1 September 2002 will be required to complete 4 years in recognised posts in obstetrics and gynaecology.

Diploma (DRCOG): Candidates must have permanent British or Irish registration or be eligible for it and have complied with the following requirement: **Obstetrics/Gynaecology:** 6 consecutive months' residence in a combined appointment recognised by the College for the exam.

The Exam: Covers obstetrics, including family planning, cytology, postnatal care of mother and child and the disabilities which may arise from childbirth and those aspects of gynaecology necessary to the practice of a general practitioner, including cervical cytology. It consists of a multiple-choice question paper and an objective structured clinical exam (OSCE).

THE ROYAL COLLEGE OF PATHOLOGISTS

2 Carlton House Terrace
London
SW1Y 5AF
United Kingdom
Tel: 020 7451 6700
Fax: 020 7451 6701
Email: info@rcpath.org
Website: www.rcpath.org.

Examinations Dept Tel: 020 7451 6757

MEMBERSHIP:

Fellowship: Members of at least 8 years' standing may be considered for election to Fellowship.

Membership: Persons must hold an approved medical or science degree or equivalent, or an approved dental or veterinary qualification. Admission may be gained by exam or submission of published works.

EXAMINATIONS:

Training programmes are approved for all Pathology specialities and subspecialities. The exact examination arrangements vary for each speciality but they all involve a Part 1 and a Part 2 which include *inter alia* written, practical and oral components. In addition, the College offers a **Diploma in Dermatopathology, Diploma in Forensic Pathology** and a **Diploma in Cytopathology**.

Further details may be obtained from the Exams Department at the above address.

THE ROYAL COLLEGE OF PHYSICIANS OF LONDON

11 St Andrews Place
Regent's Park
London
NW1 4LE
United Kingdom
Tel: 020 7935 1174
Fax: 020 7224 2032
Email: Linda.Cuthbertson@rcplondon.ac.uk
Website: www.rcplondon.ac.uk

MEMBERSHIP:

Fellow (FRCP): Elected from among Members of the Royal College of Physicians of London and Members of the Royal Colleges of Physicians of the UK of at least 4 years' standing and distinction, and from among other distinguished persons holding medical qualifications. Provisions exist to elect non-members and persons without medical qualifications, but only in exceptional circumstances.

Member (MRCP): Elected from among distinguished persons holding medical qualifications. There is also an honorary category for persons who are not medically qualified.

Membership (MRCP(UK)): See under Examinations below.

EXAMINATIONS:

Membership (MRCP(UK)): Candidates in General Medicine may enter through any of the 3 UK Colleges of Physicians. **Part 1:** Consists of a multiple-choice question paper. **Part 2:** A full copy of the regulations may be obtained from the address above. The College also offers a **Diploma in Geriatric Medicine**, and a **Diploma in Tropical Medicine and Hygiene.**

Part 2 Consists of A Written Examination that candidates must pass before proceeding to a Clinical Examination. A pass in the Written Examination affords up to 3 attempts at the Clinical Examination. The Clinical Examination is called PACES – the Practical Assessment of Clinical Examination Skills. This is a standardised and objective assessment of clinical examination skills and ability to elicit a history and communicate with patients.

MEMBERSHIP OF THE ROYAL COLLEGES OF PHYSICIANS:

Membership (MRCP(UK)): Candidates for the Exam for Membership of the Royal Colleges of Physicians of the UK may enter through the Royal College of Physicians of Edinburgh or the Royal College of Physicians and Surgeons of Glasgow or the Royal College of Physicians of London. Candidates for Part 1 must have been qualified as medical practitioners for at least 18 months. Part 1 consists of a multiple-choice question paper and may be taken in General Medicine or Paediatrics. Candidates may apply for exemption from this if they are holders of specified Fellowships, Memberships or Postgraduate Diplomas, listed in the regulations. To enter the Part 2 Written Examination, candidates need to pass Part 1 or hold the relevant exempting qualification. Before being admitted to Part 2 Clinical Examination (PACES), candidates must have completed a period of training lasting 18 months after full registration with the General Medical Council (ie 2.5 years after graduation in Medicine). Of this period, not less than 12 months should have been spent in post involving the admission and hospital care of acutely ill medical patients (18 months for candidates not fully registered with the General Medical Council). The Part 2 Exam consists of (a) a written test in 3 sections; (b) an oral test; (c) a clinical test and candidates have the choice of being examined in either General Medicine or Paediatrics. Part 2 must be completed within 7 years of success at Part 1

THE ROYAL COLLEGE OF PSYCHIATRISTS

17 Belgrave Square
London
SW1X 8PG
United Kingdom
Tel: 020 7235 2351/5
Fax: 020 7245 1231
Email: adean@rcpsych.ac.uk
Website: www.rcpsych.ac.uk

MEMBERSHIP:

Fellow (FRCPsych): Open, by election, to Members of not less than 5 years' seniority, on the nomination of 2 Fellows. Particular attention is paid to qualifications and professional standing, to appointments held, and to contributions to research and to the literature and the practice of psychiatry.
Member (MRCPsych): Candidates must be registered with the GMC and have undergone approved training for at least $2\frac{1}{2}$ years. They must pass both parts of the MRCPsych exam. The College has recently introduced a further means by which doctors who meet certain strict criteria can gain membership of the College without examinations under Bye law III 2 (ii). The College also has **Honorary Fellows, Inceptors, Corresponding Fellows, New Associates** and **Affiliates**.

Metallurgy

INSTITUTE OF CORROSION

Corrosion House
Vimy Court
Vimy Road
Leighton Buzzard
Bedfordshire
LU7 1FG
United Kingdom
Tel: 01525 851771
Fax: 01525 376690
Email: admin@icorr.demon.co.uk
Website: www.icorr.org

Fellows (FICorr): Candidates must be 35 or over and have an established reputation as a corrosion scientist or corrosion technologist. They should have made a notable contribution to the understanding or practice of corrosion prevention and control and/or have rendered special services to the Institute.
Professional Members (MICorr): Candidates must be 25 or over and be able to demonstrate knowledge and experience in the field of corrosion science and technology. Normally an academic qualification at degree standard or equivalent is needed, although occasionally this requirement may be waived.
Technican (TechICorr): Candidates must be 25 or over, have some academic knowledge (eg have passed the Institute's Fundamentals of Corrosion Course*) and be actively and practically involved in the practice of corrosion science and corrosion technology.
Ordinary Members: Ordinary members must indicate that they have an interest in the practice of corrosion science and corrosion technology.
Student Members: Students must be 18 or over and be studying corrosion science or corrosion technology or related subjects. Students must apply for transfer to other grades of membership within 6 months of ceasing to be a student or within 6 years of first becoming a Student Member.
Note: *Details of current courses available from the Institute.

THE INSTITUTE OF METAL FINISHING

Exeter House
48 Holloway Head
Birmingham
B1 1NQ
United Kingdom
Tel: 0121 622 7387
Fax: 0121 666 6316

Fellow (FIMF): Must usually be at least 35, have an established and mature reputation in the field of Metal Finishing and have made a marked contribution to the science or practice of Metal Finishing.

Member (MIMF): Must be experienced in Metal Finishing *or* hold an appropriate postgraduate qualification and have 1 year's approved experience, *or* be usually not less than 35 and have been engaged in Metal Finishing for at least 15 years, of which a large part has been spent in an important position of responsibility, *or* be 30 or over, have been engaged in metal finishing for at least 10 years and have been a Licentiate for a minimum of 5 years.

Licentiate (LIMF): Must have adequate practical experience in Metal Finishing and either have possession of the Advanced Technicians Diploma in Metal Finishing together with an approved industrial project, or have passed an exempting exam (such as an approved HND or HNC in Chemistry, Metallurgy or Engineering subjects, together with a pass in an approved supplementary course in a Metal Finishing Technology and a suitable project).

EXAMINATIONS:

An examination for the Institute Foundation Certificate is held for candidates completing an introductory course.

Technician's Certificate in Metal Finishing: Consists of two modules: General Principles, a broad introduction to finishing processes, and Plating Practice. No academic qualifications are required.

Advanced Technician's Certificate in Metal Finishing: Follows on from the Technician's Certificate and consists of modules in Electrochemistry, Materials Science, Surface Coating, and Process Management.

Advanced Technician's Diploma in Metal Finishing: Awarded to those who complete a suitable project post the Advanced Certificate level.

Technical Courses: The IMF provides Training routes for the Surface Engineering and Coatings industry, to Foundation, Ordinary and Advanced Certificate, Diploma and Licentiatship level of the Institute's qualifications. Taught courses for Foundation and Ordinary certificates are offered through the IMF's Midland and London Branches as well as by a number of Independent centres. Alternatively, Distance Learning routes, based on the Open Tech System, are offered for Ordinary and Advanced Certificates as well as the Diploma and Licentiate levels. At present, 4 modules cover a range from General Principles (MFI) to Process Management (MF4), covering Plating Practice (MF2), Electrochemistry (MF3a), Materials Science (MF3b) and Surface Coating (MF3c).

CPD: Through Branch and Group Meetings, Conferences, Special Courses and Symposiums the IMF offers opportunity for continuous professional development for anyone working in the Surface Engineering and Coatings field. Procedures are in hand for linking the CPD portfolio for part recognition for the Institute's formal qualifications. Information on all these courses can be obtained from the above address.

Microscopy

THE ROYAL MICROSCOPICAL SOCIETY

37–38 St Clements
Oxford
OX4 1AJ
United Kingdom
Tel: 01865 248768
Fax: 01865 791237
Email: info@rms.org.uk
Website: www.rms.org.uk

MEMBERSHIP:

Fellow: Any person over 21 who has a genuine interest in Microscopy.

Corporate Member: This category of membership is specially intended to enable scientists from overseas and members of colleges and schools to attend the Society's meetings and courses. It is possible for academic, research and manufacturing organisations, and schools with well-developed science departments to join the Society so that their staff and pupils may attend meetings at reduced rates and receive the Society's publications.

Junior Member: Any person whose work or study involves the use of the microscope and who is between 16 and 25.

Standard of the Diploma (DipRMS):

1. The Diploma is awarded to Fellows of the Society for work at postgraduate level in the field of microscopy or cytometry. To qualify for the Diploma, a Fellow shall have a relevant qualification and/or practical experience in microscopy or cytometry, shall have attended

courses approved by the Society, submitted a thesis and passed an oral examination. As an alternative to attendance at courses and submission of a thesis, a candidate may submit examinable evidence of an acceptable degree of competence in microscopy or cytometry (e.g. published work, patented instrumentation). The oral examination is obligatory. Successful Candidates shall be entitled to use the style DipRMS.

Qualifications for Registration

2. The Candidate shall:
a. be a paid up Fellow of the Royal Microscopical Society;
b. be engaged in work in which microscopy or cytometry plays an important part;
c. (i) be a science or medical graduate of a recognised university, with at least 3 years' practical experience in microscopy or cytometry; *or*
   (ii) hold a qualification approved by the Society and have at least 5 years' practical experience in microscopy or cytometry; *or*
   (iii) have at least 7 years' practical experience and a suitable recommendation from the head of the Candidate's institution.

Note: The length of experience under Regulation 2c is to be calculated at the date of application for the Diploma, at the end of the study period.

Qualification in the Technology of Microscopy (TechRMS)

Standard of the Award:
1. This qualification is of particular interest to those engaged in practical microscopy or cytometry, who seek a professional qualification. The qualification parallels graduate awards. The TechRMS qualification will be awarded after the following requirements have been met: the completion of appropriate training, which will be examined formally, the submission of a practical work project, and a short oral examination. The oral examination is obligatory. Successful Candidates shall be entitled to use the style TechRMS.

Qualifications for Registration

2. The Candidate shall:
a. be a paid up Student member or a Fellow of the Royal Microscopical Society;
b. be engaged in work in which microscopy or cytometry plays an important part.

Mining Engineering

INSTITUTE OF EXPLOSIVES ENGINEERS

Centenary Business Centre
Hammond Close
Attleborough Fields
Nuneaton
Warwickshire
CV11 6RY
United Kingdom
Tel: 024 7635 0846
Fax: 024 7635 0831
Email: info@iexpe.org
Website: www.iexpe.org

CORPORATE AND NON-CORPORATE MEMBERS:

Fellow (FIExpE): Members of the Institute who are over 35, have had at least 15 years' experience in pursuits connected with explosives engineering, and are, to the satisfaction of Council, either: (a) recognised by others, in their own specialist field, as a leading authority by having planned, negotiated, organised and supervised work of a sufficiently complex nature and responsibility; or (b) recognised by scientific and academic bodies as a research leader or technical innovator in their chosen field; or (c) a regular, authoritative contributor to scientific or technical papers on explosives-related sciences, engineering or related topics; or (d) known to have contributed greatly to the improvement in safety practices and standards within the explosives industry.

Honorary Fellow (HonFIExpE): The status of Honorary Fellow may be accorded to someone who is, to the satisfaction of Council, worthy. Honorary Fellows shall be either distinguished persons, who from their position have been or are enabled to render assistance to the Institute, or persons eminent for science and experience in pursuits connected with Explosives Engineering, whether or not currently engaged in the practice of that profession.

Member (MIExpE): The status of Member shall be accorded by the Council to candidates over 23 who have: (a) passed or been exempted from the appropriate examinations stipulated by the Council; (b) have either (i) been trained and become qualified for, and shall have held for at least 3 years, a responsible post engaged in Explosives Engineering or equivalent technical explosives management duties; or (ii) have been trained and become qualified as Ammunition Technical Officers or Ammunition Technicians Class I in the Army, or their equivalents in the British or appropriate foreign armed services; and (c) have been approved for admission by an Individual

Membership Committee comprising 3 members of Council none of whom shall be elected representatives of Company Members; or, exceptionally, (d) do not hold adequate academic and/or professional qualifications which would permit exemption from the Institute examinations, but are applying for membership without examination and can demonstrate their competence by submitting a thesis of 5000 words in length, supported by diagrams, graphs and photographs on a topic related to explosives technology. The candidate, where appropriate, in the last category shall be interviewed by an examining board appointed for the purpose and this board shall ascertain whether the applicant has knowledge adequate to have completed the thesis by his own original work and shall report its findings to the Membership Committee.

Associate (AIExpE): The status of Associate shall be granted by the Council to candidates not less than 23 years old who shall have: (a) either (i) been trained and become qualified to hold a responsible post as a skilled operative in such pursuits as explosives development, manufacture or use; or (ii) been trained and become qualified as a serviceman or related civilian whose duties involve the handling and use of military explosives and associated munitions, but whose expertise does not equate to the standards; or (b) reached a responsible position and gained adequate experience, but who have not yet sat or been exempted from the examinations for full membership status; and (c) attended for interview by members of Council, if so required.

Student: The status of Student shall be granted by the Council to candidates of at least 18 years of age who are either following a course of study or otherwise learning a trade which requires knowledge of the science and/or practice of explosives technology. Students are not entitled to use any designatory letters after their name.

Company Membership: The status of Company Member may be accorded to any company, firm or sole trader engaged in the development and/or manufacture of explosives or associated munitions or in the use of explosives in mining, tunnelling, quarrying, demolition, excavation, underwater or offshore work, or other appropriate commercial or government enterprise, as approved by the Council. Admission to Company Membership shall be granted provided that suitable applicants are proposed by one Company Member or Council Member, and seconded by another Company Member or Council Member, and approved by the Council. These provisions of Company Membership shall apply to British and appropriate foreign enterprises.

Company Affiliate: Any company, firm or sole trader shall be admissible as a Company Affiliate provided that the applicant satisfies Council that it has an appropriate interest in explosives technology.

THE INSTITUTE OF QUARRYING

7 Regent Street
Nottingham
Nottinghamshire
NG1 5BS
United Kingdom
Tel: 0115 9411315
Fax: 0115 9484035
Email: mail@quarrying.org
Website: www.quarrying.org

CORPORATE MEMBERSHIP:

Fellow (FIQ): Must: (a) be employed in the industry; (b) be at least 33 years of age; (c) have met the Membership requirements (see below); and (d) have had at least 7 years' experience in the industry, including 4 years in a position of senior managerial charge.

Member (MIQ): Must: (a) be employed in the industry; (b) be at least 23 years of age; (c) have passed the Professional Examination of the Institute or possess an exempting qualification; and (d) have completed a period of training and experience in the industry, of which not less than 3 years was in a position of responsible charge.

NON-CORPORATE MEMBERSHIP:

Associate: Must: (a) have reached the age of 21 and have passed the Professional Examination of the Institute; *or* (b) have reached the age of 21, have obtained an approved technical or administrative qualification and have at least 1 year's experience in the industry; *or* (c) have reached the age of 21 and have 3 years' experience in the industry.

Note: Mature candidates' rights are available to Associates over 38 who have 10 years' experience in the industry, including 5 years in a position of managerial charge. The applicant can qualify for the Corporate grades of Fellow or Member through the preparation of a thesis or by passing the Quarrying Operations and Safety and Legislation papers of the Institute's Professional Examination.

Student: Must: (a) be at least 16 years of age and normally not more than 21 (unless extended at the discretion of the Council); and (b) be engaged in a FT course of study or training relating to the industry.

EXAMINATIONS:
The **Professional Exam** is at HNC level. Qualifications in Quarrying at HNC level or above give complete exemption. Qualifications in Engineering at HNC level or above give partial exemption. An Assisted Private Study Scheme for the **Professional Exam** is available at Doncaster College. Special exemptions may be granted to 'mature students' who are over 38 with 10 years in the industry.

THE INSTITUTION OF MINING AND METALLURGY

Danum House
South Parade
Doncaster
DN1 2DY
United Kingdom
Tel: 01302 320486
Fax: 01302 380900
Email: hq@imm.org.uk
Website: www.imm.org.uk

Honorary Fellow (HonFIMM): Elected by the Institution's Council from among existing Fellows in recognition of their distinguished attainments and contribution to the advancement of the Minerals industry and associated branches of technology.
Companion: A person who is not eligible for Corporate membership and is elected by the Institution's Council in recognition of their distinguished achievements in, or contribution to, the international minerals industry. They must be at least 30 at the time of their election and must be able to satisfy the Council as to their fitness and propriety for this class of membership.
Fellow (FIMM): Must be at least 30 and have been a Member, or have satisfied the conditions for admission as a Member. They should have had at least 5 years' experience in responsible charge of important operations, or as a consultant or holder of an important academic or research post in a relevant subject.
Member (MIMM): Must be at least 25 and, having satisfied the appropriate academic requirements, should also have had at least 2 years of practical training followed by a minimum 2 years of responsible work in the Minerals industry.
Associate Member (AMIMM): Must be at least 23 and, having satisfied the appropriate academic requirements, should have at least 2 years of approved training and be in a position of responsibility at the time of their application.
Technician Member: Must be not less than 21 and, lacking the academic standard for Corporate or Associate membership, should nevertheless have passed such examinations as the Institution's Council may prescribe from time to time. They must also have undergone such appropriate training and obtained such professional experience, again, as the Council may prescribe.
Affiliate: Must be not less than 24 and, lacking academic qualifications for the previously mentioned classes of membership, must be engaged professionally in the Minerals industry.
Graduate: Must be not less than 20 and have satisfied the exam requirements of the Council and be engaged in professional training or work in the Minerals industry.
Student: Must be not less than 18 and being educated or trained for the profession of environmental engineering, mining, metallurgy, mineral technology, geology, geotechnical engineering, or petroleum engineering.

Museum and Related Work

THE MUSEUMS ASSOCIATION

42 Clerkenwell Close
London
EC1R 0PA
United Kingdom
Tel: 020 7608 2933
Fax: 020 7250 1929
Email: info@museumsassociation.org
Website: www.museumsassociation.org

MEMBERSHIP:
Fellowship of the Museums Association (FMA): Open to individual Members of the Association who have held the Associateship of the Association (AMA) for at least 5 years, or are able to demonstrate an equivalent level of attainment. Fellowship conditions are: demonstrating a high level of professionl experience, development and contribution in any area of museum work; undertaking at least 2 years' Continuing Professional Development (CPD); and attendance at a Fellowship appraisal.
Associateship of the Museums Association (AMA): Replaced **Museums Diploma** in 1996. Associate Membership is open to all those who work for or in museums. Routes include the registration of HE qualifications/NVQs/SVQs; set periods of experience; 10 days' Continuing Professional Development (CPD) over 2 years; and a structured professional review. Further details and an introductory leaflet are available from the Professional Development Manager at the Museums Association.

Music

THE INCORPORATED SOCIETY OF MUSICIANS
10 Stratford Place
London
WIC 1AA
United Kingdom
Tel: 020 7629 4413
Fax: 020 7408 1538
Email: membership@ism.org
Website: www.ism.org

Chief Executive: Neil Hoyle

MEMBERSHIP:
Full Member: A professional musician, normally holding recognised qualifications or equivalent skills, who is elected to the Society. He/she receives a fully comprehensive package of services, and is entitled to stand for office and vote. There are about 4,600 Full Members.
Associate Member: Usually an amateur or music lover, though professionals can apply for this category if they wish. He/she receives a limited package of benefits and rights. There are about 300 Associate Members.
Student Member: Must be engaged in study for a recognised professional musical qualification. He/she receives a limited package of benefits and rights, geared to young musicians' needs. There are about 120 Student Members.
Corporate Member: A business, organisation, college or school that wishes to support the Society and its work. It is entitled to benefits such as major discounts on advertising, and has a special representative on the Society's Council. There are about 150 Corporate Members.

EXAMINATIONS:
The ISM is a professional association. It does not conduct exams, though it publishes registers of specialists among its members – performers and composers, musicians in education and private teachers – who have, in the Society's view, attained certain minimum levels of professional merit.

Musical Instrument Technology

THE INCORPORATED SOCIETY OF ORGAN BUILDERS
Secretary, D M van Heck
Freepost
Liverpool
L3 3AB

Fellow (FISOB): A person shall only be admitted as a Fellow if he/she holds a position of authority in the craft of Organ Building and has been an Associate Member for not less than 5 years; or has had recognised training in the craft of Organ Building and 15 years' practical experience (excluding the period of recognised training), and has both passed such exam or exams (if any) as the Council may require.
Associate Member (AISOB): A person shall only be admitted as an Associate Member if he/she has been an Ordinary Member of the Society for not less than 5 years; or has had recognised training in the craft and 10 years' practical experience in such craft (excluding a period of recognised training); and has both passed such exam or exams (if any) as the Council may determine.
Ordinary Member (MISOB): A person shall only be admitted as an Ordinary Member if he/she has had recognised training in the craft of Organ Building and has had 5 years' experience (excluding a period of recognised training) in the craft; and is sponsored by 2 Members of the Society (other than Students), and holds a recognised Certificate of Competence in the craft of Organ Building or has passed such exam or exams as the Council may determine.
Student Member: A person shall only be admitted as a Student Member if he/she is undergoing recognised training in the craft of Organ Building; or has entered upon but not completed 5 years' practical experience (excluding a period of recognised training) in such craft; and is sponsored by a Fellow, Counsellor, Associate or Ordinary Member of the Society.
Counsellor (CISOB): A person shall only be admitted as a Counsellor if (though failing to qualify as a Student, Ordinary Member, Associate Member or Fellow of the Society) he/she holds or has held a position of responsibility in the craft of Organ Building for more than 10 years and is both sponsored by 2 Members and accepted by the Council.

PIANOFORTE TUNERS' ASSOCIATION

10 Reculver Road
Herne Bay
Kent
CT6 6LD
United Kingdom
Tel: 01227 368808
Fax: 01227 368808
Website: www.pianotuner.org.uk

MEMBERSHIP:

Membership: A candidate must: (a) *either* (i) have trained as a Pianoforte Tuner Technician or Maker in a reputable factory or workshop for not less than 3 years, or have completed an approved course in Pianoforte Tuning or Technical Studies at a recognised college and have gained the proficiency certificate, and have subsequently earned his/her living as a Pianoforte Tuner, Technician or Maker for a period (at least 2 years), which combined with the training period is at least 5 years, *or* (ii) have earned his/her living as a Pianoforte Tuner, Technician or Maker for at least 7 years; and (b) at the time of application be engaged FT in the Piano industry; and (c) *either* (i) pass a test of tuning and elementary repairs plus an oral test of knowledge of the tuning, construction and repair of pianos, *or*, if applying for Technician Membership, (ii) pass an assessment of practical ability in a specialist field of piano technology.
Associateship: May be granted by the Executive Council to any applicant who must: (a) *either* (i) have trained as a Pianoforte Tuner, Technician or Factory Operative in a reputable factory for not less than 3 years or have gained an approved course from a recognised College, *or* (ii) be a member of another tuners' association and satisy the Executive Council that his/her tuning proficiency can be shown to be of a satisfactory standard, or have earned a living as a Pianoforte Tuner for at least 7 years; and (b) at the time of application, currently be engaged in the piano industry.
Student: Someone who is receiving instruction in a training establishment or workshops acceptable to the PTA, or who has received instruction as above and gained the necessary proficiency certificate, may be registered as a PTA Student and may attend all PTA General Meetings on a non-voting basis. He/she may not publicly advertise their Registration and may not use the PTA name or emblem.
Patron: Any person may become a Patron of the PTA upon payment of an annual subscription. He/she will be invited to all General Meetings on a non-voting basis, but may not publicly advertise their PTA connection or use the PTA name or emblem for the purpose of business.

Naval Architecture

THE ROYAL INSTITUTION OF NAVAL ARCHITECTS

10 Upper Belgrave Street
London
SW1X 8BQ
United Kingdom
Tel: 020 7235 4622
Fax: 020 7259 5912
Email: membership@rina.org.uk

MEMBERSHIP:

Membership of The Royal Institution of Naval Architects is international, reflecting the global nature of Naval Architecture and the maritime industry, and provides access to the wide range of benefits and services which the RINA is able to offer. There are 7 grades of membership to suit all those involved or interested in Naval Architecture and maritime technology, whether in a technical capacity or in non-technical occupations. The grades of membership reflect the levels of education, training, experience and professional responsibility achieved.
Fellow (FRINA): Persons who have held a position of superior professional responsibility in the fields of naval architecture and maritime engineering.
Member (MRINA): Persons who are primarily concerned with the progress of maritime technology through innovation, creativity and change, the development and use of new technologies, the promotion and use of advanced design and production methods, and the pioneering of new engineering services and management techniques in the fields of naval architecture and maritime technology.
Associate Member: Persons who are primarily concerned with the management of existing technology at peak efficiency, in the fields of naval architecture and maritime technology, with managerial responsibility as leaders of teams or with individual responsibility at a high level.
Associate: Persons who are primarily concerned with the application of proven engineering techniques to the solution of practical problems in the fields of naval architecture and maritime technology.
Graduate Member: Persons who have gained the academic qualification and are undertaking the training required for the grade of Member, Associate Member or Associate.

Student Member: Persons who have achieved or are studying to achieve the academic qualification required for Graduate Member.
Companion: Persons who are interested or involved in naval architecture and maritime enginering, but whose professional qualifications and experience are in other fields.

Further information on the requirements for membership and advice on application may be obtained from the Membership Department at the above address.

Navigation, Seamanship and Marine Qualifications

THE NAUTICAL INSTITUTE
202 Lambeth Road
London
SE1 7LQ
United Kingdom
Tel: 020 7928 1351
Fax: 020 7401 2817
Email: sec@nautinst.org
Website: www.nautinst.org www.nauticalcampus.org

MEMBERSHIP:

Member (MNI): To be elected a Member the candidate must satisfy Council as to his/her professional qualifications and that he/she:
1. Is at least 24 years old, and
2. Holds a STCW '78/'95 Certificate of Competency as Master with no limitations concerning vessel size or trading area; *or*
3. Holds an equivalent pre-STCW '78/'95 Certificate of Competency issued by an approved maritime administration on the basis of examination; *or*
4. Holds Ocean-going Ship Command qualifications from a naval (military) administration; *or*
5. Holds a First Class Licence issued by a recognised pilotage authority and 3 years' experience as a First Class Pilot; *or*
6. Is an officer qualified as an Associate Member on the basis of holding a STCW '78/'95 Certificate of Competency as Master of vessels of 500 gt or more and no trading area limits with 5 years in command of sophisticated ships*; *or*
7. Is an officer qualified as an Associate Member on the basis of holding a STCW '78/'95 Certificate of Competency as Master of vessels of 500 gt or more with trading area limits who has been in command of ships of more than 3000 gt for over 5 years*; *or*
8. Is an officer qualified as an Associate Member who holds an approved Maritime Studies degree from a recognised university and has 5 years' relevant experience in the maritime industry since graduation**; *or*
9. Holds other qualifications approved by Council for membership.

Associate Member (AMNI)
To be elected as an Associate Member the candidate must satisfy Council as to his/her professional qualifications and that he/she:
1. Is at least 21 years old, and
2. Holds a STCW '78/'95 Certificate of Competency as Master with tonnage and/or trading area limitations; *or*
3. Holds a STCW '78/'95 Certificate of Competency as Chief Mate; *or*
4. Holds a STCW '78/'95 Certificate of Competency as Officer in charge of a navigational watch with no trading area limitations; *or*
5. Holds an equivalent pre-STCW '78/'95 Certificate of Competency on the basis of examination; *or*
6. Holds a naval (military) Bridge Watchkeeping Certificate and Ocean Navigation Certificate; *or*
7. Holds other qualifications approved by Council for this purpose.

Associate
To be elected an Associate the candidate must satisfy Council as to his/her professional qualifications and that he/she:
1. Is at least 18 years old, and
2. Holds a STCW '78/'95 Certificate of Competency as Officer in charge of a navigational watch with trading area limitations; *or*
3. Holds an equivalent pre-STCW '78/'95 Certificate of Competency on the basis of examination; *or*
4. Holds a naval (military) Bridge Watchkeeping Certificate; *or*
5. Holds other qualifications approved by Council for this purpose.

Companion
A non-voting category of membership for any person, such as a naval architect, marine engineer, lawyer, or yachtsman, not being a qualified member of the Nautical Profession, who satisfies Council that his/her association with the Institute will promote the general advancement or application of nautical science.

Student
Must be at least 16 years of age and undertaking a course of training or education approved by Council. Duration of student membership is limited to 3 years and the

student must intend to become an Associate Member or Companion of the Institute on completion of his/her course of study.

Notwithstanding the criteria set out above, Council reserves the right in the maintenance of professional standards to consider all applications for membership on their merits and its decision shall be final.

* Officers joining under the criteria relating to command must include photocopies of their Certificate of Competency and Discharge Book entries to verify their sea time, rank and ship size.

** Graduates must supply written evidence of their employment and a copy of their degree.

EXAMINATIONS:

The Harbour Master Certificate
The Nautical Surveyors Certificate
The Dynamic Positioning Operator Certificate
The Command Diploma
Pilotage Certificate
Management Diploma
Square Rig Sailing Ship Certificate
Nautical Education and Training Diploma

THE ROYAL INSTITUTE OF NAVIGATION

1 Kensington Gore
London
SW7 2AT
United Kingdom
Tel: 020 7591 3130
Fax: 020 7591 3131
Email: info@rin.org.uk
Website: www.rin.org.uk

MEMBERSHIP:

Honorary Fellow (HonFRIN): Distinguished person on whom the Institute wishes to confer an honorary distinction.
Fellow (FRIN): Must have been a Member for at least 3 years, holding certain qualifications, which include having made a contribution of value to Navigation.
Member (MRIN): Must be not less than 21 and must satisfy the Institute of their interest in Navigation.
Student Member: Must be under 25 and be studying at a recognised school or university with a view to making Navigation or an allied interest their career.
Corporate Member: A company, school, university, government department or similar organisation at home or abroad that is directly or indirectly interested in the science of Navigation.
Associate: Someone wishing to join a special interest group and who feels that full membership is inappropriate.
Junior Associate: Someone 18 or under with an interest in navigation.

Non-destructive Testing

THE BRITISH INSTITUTE OF NON-DESTRUCTIVE TESTING

1 Spencer Parade
Northampton
NN1 5AA
United Kingdom
Tel: 01604 630124
Fax: 01604 231489
Email: info@bindt.org
Website: www.bindt.org

MEMBERSHIP:

Honorary Fellow (HonFInstNDT): A distinguished person intimately concerned with Non-Destructive Testing or a science allied to it whom the Institute especially wishes to honour.
Honorary Member (HonMInstNDT): Any person whom the Institute wishes to honour is eligible for Honorary Membership.
Fellow (FInstNDT): Members of not less than 5 years' standing who have reached the age of 35 may be elected to Fellowship. The academic qualifications for Fellow are at degree level.
Member (MInstNDT): Persons who have reached 23 and have 5 years' Non-Destructive Testing experience and hold a position of responsibility may be elected to Membership. The academic qualifications for Membership are at HNC level or NDT Certification at Level 3.
Graduate Member (GradInstNDT): Persons who have reached 21 and have 3 years' experience in Non-Destructive Testing and a high degree of competence in any specific NDT method may be elected to Graduate Membership. The academic qualifications for Graduate Membership are at ONC level or NDT Certification at Level 2.
Practitioner Member (PInstNDT): Persons who have Level 1 Certification in NDT or academic qualifications at City & Guilds Part 2 Craft Level or equivalent, plus 3 years combined approved training and experience in NDT.
Corporate Member: A Member eligible for registration as Chartered Engineer, Incorporated Engineer or Engineering Technician as appropriate to educational qualifications, NDT training, experience and age. Chartered Engineers and Incorporated Engineers can be registered in Europe with FEANI.

Student Member: Students of science, engineering, metallurgy or allied subjects and/or trainees or assistants engaged in the practice of Non-Destructive Testing may be granted Student Membership. They receive a free Log-Book.

The Institute also has **Subscribers, Licentiates, Companions** and **Associates** (firms and other organisations).

QUALIFICATIONS:

Personnel Certification in Non-destructive Testing: PCN is an accredited independent certification body, complying with the criteria of European Standard EN 45013. PCN is part of the Certification Services Division of the British Institute of Non-Destructive Testing.

Nuclear Engineering

THE INSTITUTION OF NUCLEAR ENGINEERS

Allan House
1 Penerley Road
London
SE6 2LQ
United Kingdom
Tel: 020 8698 1500
Fax: 020 8695 6409
Email: inuce@lineone.net
Website: www.inuce.org.uk

CORPORATE MEMBERSHIP:

Fellow: Must be a Nuclear Engineer or scientist who satisfies the requirements for Member and who has established a superior professional reputation by holding, normally for at least 5 years, an important position of responsibility in the Nuclear field. They will normally be over 35. The usual route to Fellowship is by transfer from the class of Member.

Member: Must be an engineer or scientist who holds an approved degree or has passed the Engineering Council Exam Parts I and II or has equivalent qualifications; they must have undergone structured training or experience in lieu, have had practical experience over a period amounting to at least 3 years, have attained a position of professional responsibility in the Nuclear field and be at least 25.

Applicants accepted for corporate membership will normally be eligible for registration with the Engineering Council as Chartered Engineers.

NON-CORPORATE MEMBERSHIP:

Graduate Member: Candidates should normally be at least 21. The requirements are an approved degree in engineering or natural sciences or pass in EC Exam Parts I and II or equivalent approved qualifications; candidates must also be engaged in professional work or training in the Nuclear field.

Note: The Institution does not at present hold Graduate exams.

Associate Member: Candidates must be 23 or over and have reached a satisfactory standard of technical competence in the Nuclear field. The requirements are BTEC, HNC or HND in an appropriate subject at an approved institution or the possession of certain other approved qualifications, together with 5 years' engineering experience, of which 2 years must have been devoted to practical training and 3 years must have been in the Nuclear field. Applicants accepted for this class of membership will normally be eligible for registration with the Engineering Council as Incorporated Engineers.

Associate: This class is open to persons who are not qualified for Corporate Membership but who show a keen interest in Nuclear matters and would usually hold a position of some responsibility. They should be at least 30.

Technician Member: The requirements for this class of membership are a minimum of 3 years' engineering experience, of which at least 2 years must have been devoted to approved practical training in the Nuclear field, and that the applicant has attained the age of 21 years. An engineering education to the standard of a BTEC or SCOTVEC National Certificate in an acceptable subject is required; older qualifications, eg an Ordinary National Certificate, or a City & Guilds of London Institute (CGLI) Part II Final Technicians Certificate or the CGLI Radiation Safety Practice Stage II Certificate are also acceptable. In future, as NVQs at the appropriate level become available, these too will be acceptable.

The requirements for training and experience are: (a) a recognised apprenticeship lasting not less than 3 years in mechanical maintenance or fitting, electrical maintenance or fitting, instrumentation maintenance or fitting, or other relevant discipline. In addition, the candidate must have received training in safety and quality assurance appropriate to work in the Nuclear field and have worked in the Nuclear industry for at least 2 years, *or* (b) a systematic course of training designed to ensure that the candidate has a comprehensive knowledge of the techniques required to work in a specialist field, installing, maintaining, repairing, commissioning, building or operating equipment in the Nuclear industry. The candidate should be able to demonstrate a thorough understanding of the standards, quality assurance and safety of the work and to have worked in the industry for not less than 2 years.

All applicants for Technician grade, and for registration with the Engineering Council as EngTech are required to provide a short personal statement about their career to date, outlining what work experience they have received, what work-related training they have attended and what responsibilities they hold. This brief CV should be similar to that for a job application and should not exceed one A4 page. For those who lack the academic qualifications stipulated, there is a mature candidate route to Technician Membership. Further details are available from the Institution.

The Institution also elects Radiological, Medical and Student members.

Occupational Therapy

THE COLLEGE OF OCCUPATIONAL THERAPISTS

106–114 Borough High Street
Southwark
London
SE1 1LB
United Kingdom
Tel: 020 7357 6480
Fax: 020 7450 2299
Website: www.cot.co.uk

A BSc degree in Occupational Therapy (normally with Hons) is awarded to students who have successfully completed a prescribed course of education. FT or PT courses leading to the degree qualification are $3\frac{3}{4}$ year long: 2 year accelerated courses are available for graduates with a relevant degree; 4 year PT courses are available to people with experience of working in Occupational Therapy. Some of the following subjects are studied during the course: the principles and practice of occupational therapy; biological, behavioural and medical sciences; communication and management; therapeutic use of activity.

Additionally, students must usually have completed at least 1000 hours of fieldwork placement before qualifying in order to be eligible for state registration. The minimum entry qualifications are: students must have reached the age of 18 (17 in Scotland) and have obtained 5 GCE/GCSE subjects of which 2 must be at A level, or 6 SCE subjects of which 3 must be at H grade, or an equivalent as recognised by Higher Education, eg a BTEC National Diploma or a validated Access Course. Mature candidates are welcome to apply, but are expected to show evidence of and attainment in a course of recent academic study to A level standard (or its equivalent). Contact individual schools for their specific entry requirements. The British Association of Occupational Therapists has around 22,000 members.

Opticians (Dispensing)

THE ASSOCIATION OF BRITISH DISPENSING OPTICIANS

A.B.D.O. College of Education
Godmersham Park Mansion
Godmersham
Kent
CT4 7DT
United Kingdom
Tel: 01227 738829
Fax: 01227 773900
Email: education1@abdo.org.uk
Website: www.abdo.org.uk

Fellowship (FBDO): This can be taken after: (a) a 2 year FT course, with 1 year of approved practical experience following the Final exam; (b) 3 years' practical experience in employment supplemented by PT classes at a technical college or by a correspondence course; (c) a 3 year FT BSc(Hons) in Optical Management offered at Anglia Polytechnic University or a BSc in Opthalmic Dispensing with Management at Bradford and also a BSc in Ophthalmic Dispensing via Glasgow Caledonian University.

Entry requirements are 5 GCSEs grades A–C including Maths or Science and English, plus 2 A levels for those considering a degree.

The Fellowship Exam: Minimum entry requirements for all systems of training are: 5 GCSE passes: Maths, English, another science-based subject and 2 further (optional) subjects (ie A, B or C grade passes) which include English, Maths or Physics. Candidates must be at least 17 at the date of the preliminary exam. The exam is in 2 parts – Part One and Final Dispensing. Both have practical and theoretical sections and the subjects include Light, Prisms and Lenses; Ocular Anatomy and Physiology; General and Visual Optical Principles; Practical Work on Lenses and Frames including Fitting.

OTHER AWARDS:

Diploma of Honours Fellowship (FBDO(Hons)): Granted to students who pass the Final Dispensing and also an exam in 1 of: Contact Lens Practice; Geometric Optics of Ophthalmic Lenses; and Low Visual Acuity. Those who obtain the Fellowship Diploma and the Diploma in Contact Lens Practice are entitled to style themselves FBDO(Hons)CL.

Diploma in Contact Lens Practice (CLABDO): Can be taken by members who have not passed the Fellowship exam. Candidates must normally hold the qualifying diploma of a recognised optical body. The exam is theoretical and practical; it covers: Anatomy; Pathology of the Eye and the Adnexa; Physiology; Optics; Indications for Use of Contact Lenses and Clinical Procedure. The practical exam is taken in 2 parts. The second part requires submission of case histories of a prescribed number of patients and deals with advanced aftercare.

Diploma in Geometric Optics of Ophthalmic Lenses: Open only to those who have passed the Final Theoretical Dispensing exam. If the student has passed the Full Dispensing exam, the addition of this Diploma qualifies him/her for Honours Fellowship. The exam covers advanced general optical principles and the study of various types of complex lenses.

Diploma in Low Visual Acuity: Open only to qualified opticians who wish to enhance their knowledge of the dispensing of low-vision aids.

Orthoptics

BRITISH ORTHOPTIC SOCIETY

Tavistock House North
Tavistock Square
London
WC1H 9HX
United Kingdom
Tel: 020 7387 7992
Fax: 020 7383 2584
Email: bos@orthoptics.org.uk
Website: www.orthoptics.org.uk

MEMBERSHIP:
Members are qualified orthoptists who hold the Diploma of the British Orthoptic Society (DBO) or a degree in Orthoptics. Student Members are those working to qualify as orthoptists.

EXAMINATIONS:
Degrees in Orthoptics are offered by Liverpool University and Sheffield University. Entry requirements are normally 3 A levels or Scottish Highers. Preference is given to candidates with a Science subject. The courses incorporate both theory and clinical teaching and include in-depth study of orthoptics, optics, anatomy and physiology. Other areas such as applied sciences, statistics and research methodology are also covered.

Post-registration degrees are available to orthoptists who hold the DBO. These are offered by the University of Sheffield.

Osteopathy and Naturopathy

THE GENERAL COUNCIL AND REGISTER OF NATUROPATHS

Goswell House
2 Goswell Road
Street
Somerset
BA16 0JG
United Kingdom
Tel: 01458 840072
Fax: 01458 840075
Email: admin@neuropathy.org.uk
Website: www.neuropathy.org.uk

The Association maintains Registers of Naturopaths who have satisfied the Board of Examiners and the Executive Council. Most entrants are graduates of the British College of Naturopathy and Osteopathy where the course comprises 4 years' FT training in the principles and clinical practice of naturopathic and osteopathic medicine. The course is as follows: Basic Sciences: Biology, Anatomy and Physiology; Principles of Natural Therapeutics. The course orientation stresses the importance of the environment as a determining factor in the expression of the living process. Clinical Sciences; General Clinical Procedures; Naturopathic Procedures; Clinical Practice; Application of Naturopathic and Osteopathic Procedures in Clinical Practice.

The College has been recognised by a number of LEAs for major County and FE Awards to applicants possessing the College Education or entry qualifications. Successful graduates are awarded a Diploma in Naturopathy (ND) and a BSc(Hons) degree in Osteopathic Medicine.

THE LONDON SCHOOL OF OSTEOPATHY

First Floor
56–60 Nelson Street
London
E1 2DE
United Kingdom
Tel: 020 7265 9333
Fax: 020 7265 8877
Email: lso@mcmail.com

The London School of Osteopathy is based in Whitechapel and offers a 5 year modified attendance programme in the principles and clinical practice of Osteopathy. Practical tuition is given throughout the 5 years and students gain their clinical experience under supervision in the Schools' Outpatient Clinic situated on the premises.

The minimum requirements are passes in 2 subjects at GCE A level (science subjects are preferred) supported by GCSE passes at grade C or above in 3 other subjects (including Maths and English). Mature students are particularly welcomed and may present APEL credits for previous relevant learning experiences. Students successfully completing the course are awarded a BSc(Hons) Osteopathy.

The LSO has gained 'Recognised Qualification' status after a successful accreditation process by the General Osteopathic Council. This enables LSO graduates to be automatically entered onto the professional register.

Packaging

THE INSTITUTE OF PACKAGING

Sysonby Lodge
Nottingham Road
Melton Mowbray
Leicestershire
LE13 0NU
United Kingdom
Tel: 01664 500055
Fax: 01664 564164
Email: info@iop.co.uk
Website: www.iop.co.uk

The Institute of Packaging is the awarding body for packaging qualifications and the professional membership organisation of the Packaging industry.

MEMBERSHIP:

Fellow (FInstPkg): Usually over 35 years of age; have been a Member for 5 years; have held a responsible executive, administrative or similar position in the profession of Packaging for at least 10 years; can produce evidence of their contribution to the art and/or science of Packaging; and have 3 referees (all of whom must be Members and at least 1 of whom must be a Fellow) sponsoring their application. The Council may confer the grade of Fellow upon any Member of the Institute in recognition of outstanding service to the Institute where the Certificate of Merit is deemed inappropriate, or any person of eminence in the practice of packaging technology, management, administration or related disciplines.

Diploma Member (MInstPkg(Dip)): Must have passed all parts of the Institute's membership qualifying exam (see below).

Member (MInstPkg): Must have held, and continue to hold, a responsible position in Packaging for a period of 5 years, and have provided evidence satisfactory to the Council that either their knowledge of Packaging in general or their profound knowledge of a specific area of Packaging is compatible with the status of Membership as attained by passing the qualifying exam.

Associate (AInstPkg): Must work (or be seeking work) in Packaging or a related industry and whilst not currently qualified for Member status is considered capable of furthering the objectives of the Institute, or is studying for the Diploma.

Student Member: A junior grade of membership only for those studying Packaging FT at a university or college of further education or higher education.

EXAMINATIONS:

The Diploma in Packaging Technology: Awarded to those who successfully pass all 3 parts of the exam. These are:

Part 1: Successfully complete a series of continuous assessment objective tests on the fundamentals of Packaging as part of the chosen study method and gain a credit exemption, or sit a written paper (Paper 1).

Part 2: Successfully complete 2 more written papers – Paper 2: Packaging materials forms and components; and Paper 3: Packaging design, development and production.

Part 3: Complete a 10,000 word dissertation within 6 months of successfully passing Part 2. The Diploma is equivalent to an HND/NVQ Level 4, is university CATS accredited and is accepted by Brunel and Loughborough Universities for entrance to the MSc in Packaging Technology.

Training: Short technical courses at the Packaging School in Melton Mowbray; intensive pre-exam courses at other venues; IOP supported PT courses for the Diploma at various venues and a comprehensive open-learning course and distance-learning provision for those unable to attend scheduled courses.

Pension Management

THE PENSIONS MANAGEMENT INSTITUTE
PMI House
4–10 Artillery Lane
London
E1 7LS
United Kingdom
Tel: 020 7247 1452
Fax: 020 7375 0603
Email: education@pensions-pmi.org.uk
Website: www.pensions-pmi.org.uk

MEMBERSHIP:

Fellow (FPMI): Applicants must already be an Associate and have at least 8 years' relevant practical experience and fulfil CPD requirements.
Associate (APMI): Applicants will have successfully completed the Institute's exams and have had a period of not less than 3 years' relevant practical experience.
Student: Applicants must be at least 18 and possess: (a) at least 2 GCE A levels and 3 GCSEs, the latter to include English Language and Mathematics; or (b) an ONC in Business Studies; or (c) a BTEC NC; or (d) any other public exam or experience which in the opinion of the Council is equivalent. Possession of the Qualification in Pensions Administration (QPA) is an entry for studentship for the Pensions Management Institute, but does not entitle the holder to be exempt from any of the Institute's exams.

EXAMINATIONS:

The Institute's exams cover the whole range of knowledge and experience required in relation to the operation, management and administration of pension funds, schemes and arrangements of all kinds. The examinations comprise 10 papers; students must pass 9, choosing 2 from subjects G, H, and I: (A) Introduction to Retirement Provision; (B) Taxation; (C) Pension Arrangements; (D) Law and Constitution; (E) Design and Administration; (F) Financing and Investment; (G) Total Remuneration; (H) Management; (I) International; (J) Communication. The Pensions Management Institute is also the awarding body for 2 qualifications, each of which is an NVQ and an SVQ. One, the **Qualification in Pensions Administration (QPA)**, is at Level 4; the other, the **Qualification in Public Sector Pensions Administration**, is at Level 3. Both are standards-based qualifications where the industry itself has defined the tasks of a pensions administrator and identified the criteria that must be satisfied if tasks are to be performed to standard.

There are no entry requirements for either qualification. The Level 4 N/SVQ is for all pensions administrators, regardless of sector. It comprises 9 units, assessed by case study examinations and by work-based assessments. The Level 3 N/SVQ is for all administrators of public sector schemes. It comprises 10 units, all of which are assessed in the workplace.

The Institute also offers a **Certificate of Essential Pensions Knowledge** for trustees of occupational pensions schemes. A specialist **Diploma in International Employee Benefits** was introduced in 1996.

Personnel Management

CHARTERED INSTITUTE OF PERSONNEL AND DEVELOPMENT
CIPD House
35 Camp Road
London
SW19 4UX
United Kingdom
Tel: 020 8971 9000
Fax: 020 8263 3333
Email: cipd@cipd.co.uk
Website: www.cipd.co.uk

FULL GRADES OF MEMBERSHIP:

Fellow (FCIPD): An applicant for Fellowship must be a Member of the Institute, have worked in Personnel and Development or one of its specialisms at a professional level for at least 10 years or are currently operating at a strategic level and have undertaken appropriate CPD (continuing professional development).
Member (MCIPD): An applicant for full Membership must be a Graduate of the Institute, have performed executive and/or advisory duties in Personnel and Development or one of its specialisms for at least 3 years, and have undertaken appropriate CPD.

OTHER GRADES OF MEMEBERSHIP:

Graduate (Graduate CIPD): Obtained by meeting the Institute's professional standards in 4 fields: Core Management, People Management and Development, a range of generalist or specialist electives, and a Management Report and CPD.
Licentiate (Licentiate CIPD): Obtained by meeting the Institute's professional standards in any 1, 2 or 3 of the above fields.
Associate (Associate CIPD): Obtained by gaining 1 of the Institute's Certificate-level

CHARTERED INSTITUTE OF PERSONNEL AND DEVELOPMENT

CIPD House, Camp Road, London SW19 4UX
Tel: 020 8971 9000, fax: 020 8263 3333, email: cipd@cipd.co.uk, website: www.cipd.co.uk

We are the leading professional body for all those concerned with the management and development of people. We currently have over 116,000 members across the UK and Ireland. Our membership is highly respected and widely accepted by employers as a requirement of practice. Being a member will ensure that you get the recognition you deserve, keeping you ahead of your peers.

We have various grades of membership, which are determined by qualifications and attained experience. Our qualifications are designed to suit everyone from those with little or no experience to those in more senior positions. They include:

Support-level qualifications

Certificate in Personnel Practice (CPP)
Designed to introduce you to the wide range of practical skills required by those in personnel. Leads to Associate Membership of the Institute.

Certificate in Training Practice (CTP)
Will provide you with your first step to a successful career in training and welcome you to the Institute as an Associate Member.

Certificate in Recruitment and Selection (CRS)
Takes a skills based approach and provides practical and authoritative guidance on best practice set in the context of today's challenging workplace issues. Leads to Associate membership of the Institute.

Practitioner-level qualifications

Professional Development Scheme (PDS)
A postgraduate-level qualification that is designed to provide you with the knowledge, understanding and confidence that you require in the vital fields of personnel and development. Successful completion can lead to Graduate membership of the Institute, which is the first step towards achieving full membership.

Choose how to study
All our professional qualifications are offered at accredited/approved universities or colleges throughout the UK and Ireland. You can choose to study full time, part time or through flexible learning (PDS students only).

When you start your studies you will join us as a studying Affiliate, which will give you access to all our member benefits and services which you'll find invaluable when studying for your CIPD qualification.

Qualification leads to recognition
As you progress through each qualification stage, you will move closer to gaining full membership. This will not only enhance your career prospects but it will also give you greater recognition, within the profession, your company and among your peers.

Getting started and getting ahead
To enrol on one of our qualifications you will need to contact your local university or college. Visit our website at www.cipd.co.uk for the latest centre listing. Alternatively you can give us a call on 020 8263 3699 or send us an e-mail at profed@cipd.co.uk

qualifications, in Personnel Practice, Training Practice or Recruitment and Selection.

Affiliateship: Affiliateship is available to anyone and is particularly useful to those working in Personnel Development or one of its specialisms, those engaged in executive, advisory, teaching or research duties, and those in a profession or occupation where knowledge of the principles of Personnel and Development is desirable. Affiliateship offers the Institute's services, but does not confer any professional qualification or status. Discounted sub-grades are available for those engaged on a study or assessment programme leading to an CIPD qualification and/or membership.

PROFESSIONAL DEVELOPMENT SCHEME:

This incorporates 4 elements: Core Management, People Management and Development, a range of electives, of which 4 must be chosen, and a Management Report and CPD. The Institute also offers a Certificate in Personnel Practice, a Certificate in Training Practice and a Certificate in Recruitment and Selection, which are lower-level skills-based qualifications.

For further information on qualifications and assessments please contact the Membership Development or Professional Education departments at CIPD House.

Pharmacy

THE COLLEGE OF PHARMACY PRACTICE

University of Warwick Science Park
Barclays Venture Centre
Sir William Lyons Road
Coventry
CV4 7EZ
United Kingdom
Tel: 024 7669 2400
Fax: 024 7669 3069
Email: cpp@collpharm.org.uk
Website: www.collpharm.org.uk

The College of Pharmacy Practice is an organisation of pharmacists who share the aim of promoting and maintaining a high standard of Pharmacy Practice. Its mission is to promote professional and personal development through education, examination, practice and research, benefiting patients and healthcare provision.

All UK registered pharmacists are eligible to join the College as Associates (ACPP), and may proceed to full Membership (MCPP) by examination, or by practice, through the use of the College Continuing Professional Development Portfolio. Members may go on to achieve the Advanced Award and Fellowship of the College (FCPP).

In 2001, the College launched a Faculty structure to recognise and promote a high level of practice in specialist fields. The Faculty of Prescribing Medicines Management has been established and plans to launch the Faculty of Neonatal and Paediatric Pharmacy are well advanced. Others will follow in due course.

THE PHARMACEUTICAL SOCIETY OF NORTHERN IRELAND

73 University Street
Belfast
BT7 1HL
United Kingdom
Tel: 028 9032 6927
Fax: 028 9043 9919
Email: chief.executive@psni.org.uk

MEMBERSHIP:

Member (MPS): One whose name is included in the Register of Pharmaceutical Chemists for Northern Ireland.

Student: One who has satisfied the regulations for admission to: (a) a first degree course in Pharmaceutics of a university or institution of similar academic status in Northern Ireland; or (b) a university or other institution in GB awarding a degree recognised by the Royal Pharmaceutical Society of GB, and being so registered.

Candidates wishing to become registered as a Pharmaceutical Chemist must hold a degree of a UK university obtained under conditions approved by the Council of the Society. A graduate must undergo a 1 year period of practical training under the supervision of a registered pharmaceutical chemist and pass the registration exam set by the Society.

THE ROYAL PHARMACEUTICAL SOCIETY OF GREAT BRITAIN

1 Lambeth High Street
London
SE1 7JN
United Kingdom
Tel: 020 7735 9141
Fax: 020 7735 7629
Email: enquiries@rpsgb.org.uk
Website: www.rpsgb.org.uk

36 York Place, Edinburgh EH1 3HU; tel: 0131 556 4386, email: 101561.2226@compuserve.com

MEMBERSHIP:

Fellow (FRPharmS): Elected for distinguished service within the profession.

Member (MRPharmS): Membership of the Society is available only to those who have a degree in Pharmacy, have satisfactorily completed a 1 year period of pre-registration training in a pharmacy and passed the Royal Pharmaceutical Society's registration exam. Both the pharmacy and the tutor appointed to supervise the graduate must be approved by the Royal Pharmaceutical Society. Candidates may then apply to the Royal Pharmaceutical Society for admission to the Register of Pharmaceutical Chemists.

Photography

ASSOCIATION OF PHOTOGRAPHERS (AOP)

81 Leonard Street
London
EC2A 4QS
United Kingdom
Tel: 020 7739 6669
Fax: 020 7739 8707
Email: general@aophoto.co.uk
Website: www.aophoto.co.uk

The Association of Photographers (AOP) was founded in 1968 to promote the highest standards of work and practice throughout the industry and to protect and improve the rights of all professional photographers based in the UK. AOP's international membership currently comprises 1800 professional photographers and photographic assistants in advertising, editorial and fashion photography.

MEMBERSHIP:
The Association of Photographers has various levels of membership to suit photographers at different stages of their career:
Full Membership: This level is designed for practising professional photographers who have been working for over 2 years.
Assistant Membership: Assistant Membership is open to both full-time and freelance assistants. To apply, you need to provide satisfactory references from photographers worked for, preferably AOP members.
Graduate Membership: This is available to graduate photographers.
For all categories of membership, applicants will be required to submit the names of 2 Association members who can act as proposer and seconder, except in the case of an assistant who will need to supply three names if they are freelance or one if they are working full time.

BRITISH INSTITUTE OF PROFESSIONAL PHOTOGRAPHY

Fox Talbot House
2 Amwell End
Ware
Hertfordshire
SG12 9HN
United Kingdom
Tel: 01920 464011
Fax: 01920 487056
Email: bipp@compuserve.com
Website: www.bipp.com

MEMBERSHIP:
Honorary Fellow (HonFBIPP): Elected from among distinguished professional photographers.
Fellow (FBIPP): This is awarded for distinguished ability in professional photography. A Fellow may describe himself as an 'Incorporated Photographer' or 'Incorporated Photographic Technician'.
Associate (ABIPP): Must either have passed approved exams in photography with an appropriate period of experience, or submit a thesis on an approved photographic subject or examples of work. Associates may describe themselves as 'Incorporated Photographers' or 'Incorporated Photographic Technicians'.
Licentiate (LBIPP): Must be at least 18 and have passed approved exams in photography or can submit evidence of their photographic or technical ability. Licentiates may describe themselves as 'Incorporated Photographers' or 'Incorporated Photographic Technicians'.
Graduate: One who has successfully completed a recognised course in photography and is engaged in professional photography, but is not yet qualified, either by age, or experience, to take up corporate membership.
Student: Available for those pursuing a course in photography at an educational establishment.
Affiliate: Open to persons who have a professional interest in photography, but because of age or other limitations have not yet qualified, or may be unable to qualify, for corporate membership.

EXAMINATION:
Licentiateship may be awarded to candidates who have successfully completed a course, recognised by the BIPP, leading to a degree, HND or HNC. Following 2 years' relevant experience at the appropriate level, such candidates may apply for Associateship.
Candidates with a degree, HND or HNC in any subject from an educational establishment in the UK, and who have been employed at the appropriate level in professional photography,

imaging or photo technology for a minimum of 2 years, may apply for the Licentiateship. Applications for Associateship may be made immediately by candidates who have successfully completed the **BIPP Professional Qualifying Exam**.

MASTER PHOTOGRAPHERS ASSOCIATION

Hallmark House
1 Chancery Lane
Darlington
Co Durham
DL1 5QP
United Kingdom
Tel: 01325 356555
Fax: 01325 357813
Email: generalenquiries@mpauk.com

The Master Photographers Association is now the UK's only fully qualified organisation for practising FT professional photographers. There is a comprehensive range of free benefits including business building promotions, legal support, business and promotional stationery, friendly and informative regional meetings and trade magazine offered by the Association.

Members may apply for qualification through submission of prints on 3 levels:

Licentiate (LMPA): Shows evidence of competence and ability to create merchantable-quality photography.

Associate (AMPA): Given in recognition of excellence in technique and/or creative interpretation.

Fellowship (FMPA): The highest award given in recognition of absolute excellence.

The Qualifications Panel meets 4 times a year in respect of Licentiate submissions and once a year for Associate and Fellowship submissions. There is also a separate Video category for this specialised field.

QUALIFICATIONS

Diploma In Photographic Practice: Open to all Members of the Association. It covers a wide range of photographic and business skills, with the emphasis on upgrading existing business practices and the provision of underpinning knowledge in the modern business world.

THE ROYAL PHOTOGRAPHIC SOCIETY

The Octagon
Milsom Street
Bath
BA1 1DN
United Kingdom
Tel: 01225 462841
Fax: 01225 448688
Email: rps@rps.org/carol@rps.org
Website: www.rps.org

MEMBERSHIP AND DISTINCTIONS:

Honorary Fellow (HonFRPS): Elected by the Council. Distinguished persons who, from their position or attainments, are intimately connected with the science or art of photography, its practice and applications.

Honorary Member: One who has rendered distinguished service to the Society or to photography.

Fellow (FRPS): Associates may apply for Fellowship by submitting photographic work. Fellowship is granted in various categories and a candidate may be admitted in 1 or more categories. Outstanding ability and individuality or originality are required of applicants for this award.

The categories are: Applied and Professional; Film and Video; Nature; Research & Development; Printing; Science; Slide–Sound Sequences; Visual Art; Contemporary; Documentary and Visual Journalism; Travel. There is also a direct application route to the Fellowship for those with a photographic reputation at the highest level, based on CV/referees and photographic achievements such as exhibitions, publications, awards, etc.

Associate (ARPS): Licentiates, Members and non-members may apply for Associateship by submitting photographic work in 1 or more of the categories listed under Fellowship above. Associateship may be granted in more than 1 category. The award is granted in recognition of photography of good technical standard and aspects such as choice and treatment of subject and presentation are taken into account. Certain courses are also recognised, eg degree.

Licentiate (LRPS): The Licentiateship may be granted to any Member or non-member who satisfies the Council of their competence and ability in still photography, film and video or slide–sound sequences; or upon evidence of passing a recognised course in photography. Reciprocal arrangements also exist with other organisations, eg the MPA and BIPP for both LRPS and ARPS.

Ordinary Member: Membership is open to anyone interested in photography, amateur or professional.

QUALIFICATIONS:

The RPS Imaging Scientist Qualifications provide a structure leading to professional qualifications for engineers, scientists and technologists whose professional activities are concerned with quantitative or mechanistic aspects of imaging systems or their application. Successful candidates automatically qualify for the appropriate level of Society Distinction.

Qualified Imaging Scientist (QIS): For those with academic qualifications below degree level (LRPS).
Graduate Imaging Scientist (GIS): For those with a first degree (ARPS).
Accredited Imaging Scientist (AIS): For those with postgraduate experience as Imaging Scientists (ARPS).
Accredited Senior Imaging Scientist (ASIS): The senior professional qualification for established scientists (FRPS).

Physics

THE INSTITUTE OF PHYSICS

76 Portland Place
London
W1B 1NT
United Kingdom
Tel: 020 7470 4800
Fax: 020 7470 4848
Email: physics@iop.org
Website: www.iop.org

MEMBERSHIP:
(http://physics.iop.org/IOP/Member/category.html)

Chartered Physicist (CPhys): Available to Members and Fellows who can demonstrate a high level of competence and professionalism in the practice of Pure or Applied Physics.
Fellowship (FInstP): For candidates who have made an outstanding contribution in Physics or a related field. Requirements: age at least 30, completed at least 7 years' responsible work in physics or its applications, or at least 10 years' experience in responsible work demanding a knowledge of physics.
Member (MInstP): Requirements: age at least 24, Physics degree or degree qualifications in an acceptable related discipline and evidence of at least 3 years' post-graduation experience. Appropriate experience can sometimes be accepted in lieu of academic qualifications.
Associate Member (AMInstP): Requirements: age at least 20, an academic qualification acceptable for MInstP.

Studentship: age at least 16. Open to those following an appropriate course of study in Physics or a related discipline.

Physiotherapy

THE CHARTERED SOCIETY OF PHYSIOTHERAPY

14 Bedford Row
London
WC1R 4ED
United Kingdom
Tel: 020 7306 6666
Fax: 020 7306 6611
Email: education@csphysio.org.uk
Website: www.csp.org.uk

MEMBERSHIP:

Fellow (FCSP): Member who makes an exceptional contribution to the advancement of the profession.
Member (MCSP): Must have successfully completed an approved 3 year or 4 year Honours degree leading to eligibility for membership of the Chartered Society of Physiotherapy and for state registration by the Physiotherapists Board at the Council for Professions Supplementary to Medicine.

TRAINING REQUIREMENTS:

Candidates for entry to training must have GCSE or SCE O level passes in a *minimum* of 5 subjects including English and 2 sciences, and at least 3 passes at A level grade C or above, or 4 at H grade, 1 of which should be a Biological Science. Equivalent qualifications such as BTEC, Science or Health Studies GNVQ Level 3 may be acceptable.
There are 30 institutions offering programmes leading to state registration/memberhip of the Chartered Society of Physiotherapy.

Plant Engineering

THE INSTITUTION OF PLANT ENGINEERS
77 Great Peter Street
Westminster
London
SW1P 2EZ
United Kingdom
Tel: 020 7233 2855
Fax: 020 7233 2604
Email: mail@iplante.org.uk
Website: www.iplante.org.uk

CORPORATE MEMBERSHIP:
Fellow (FIPlantE): Applicants must be 25 or over, have academic qualifications at university MEng degree level in Engineering or equivalent, and have had at least 6 years' combined training and experience and responsibility in senior Plant Engineering positions. Alternatively, applicants can be of mature age and submit an acceptable written paper. Both these routes are eligible for consideration for CEng registration. The third route to Fellow is for those over 35 who do not require CEng registration.
Member (MIPlantE): Applicants must be 23 or over, have obtained a pass degree or HNC/HND in an engineering discipline, plus a Matching Section, have had 4 years' combined training and experience and 2 years in responsible appointments. Alternatively, applicants can be over 35, have had 15 years' combined training and experience and 2 years in responsible positions, and submit an acceptable written paper. Both these routes are eligible for IEng registration. The third route to Member is for those over 26 who do not require IEng registration.

NON-CORPORATE MEMBERSHIP:
Associate Member (AMIPlantE): Applicants must be 21 or over, have had 4 years' combined training and experience and have obtained a BTEC/SCOTVEC NC/ND in an engineering discipline or ONC/OND or C&G Part II in an EngC approved subject. This grade is eligible for EngTech registration.
Graduate Member: Applicants must be over 18 and have obtained the BTEC/SCOTVEC NC/ND or HNC/HND or degree in an EngC approved subjects and be engaged on an EngC approved system of training and experience.
Student Member: Applicants must be over 16 and be studying an approved course of engineering.
The Institution is associated with the EngC and can register certain grades of membership as CEng, IEng or EngTech.

Plastics and Rubber

SCHOOL OF POLYMER TECHNOLOGY
The University of North London
166–220 Holloway Road
London
N7 8DB
United Kingdom
Tel: 020 7753 5128
Fax: 020 7753 5081
Email: polymers@unl.ac.uk
Website: www.unl.ac.uk/spt

QUALIFICATIONS:
National Certificate (Polymer Technology): Obtained on successful conclusion of a 1 year FT or 2 year PT course. The course is also available through distance learning. Candidates must hold GCE O level or GCSE passes (grades A, B or C) in English, Mathematics and a Science subject and 1 other, or an equivalent qualification. People working in the Polymer industry are encouraged to join the cause.
BSc(Hons) Polymers and with a number of subjects including Computing, Chemistry and Business: Awarded after a 3 year FT or 4 year S course.
Entry requirement for BSc courses is 5 GCSE passes, including Mathematics, and 2 A level passes, including a physical science or engineering subject; or a BTEC NC/ND with merit grades in 3 appropriate Level III units.
BEng (Hons) Polymer Engineering: Awarded after a 3 year FT or 4 year S course. PT mode available. Direct entry into Part 2 possible for FT or PT mode with entry requirement of HNC/HND in relevant subject.
MSc Polymer Science and Engineering: Awarded after a 1 year FT or 2 year PT course to holders of a Science Honours degree, or equivalent. February and September start.
MSc Manufacture and Design for Polymer Products: Awarded after 3 year PT course. Open to holders of science or engineering degrees and those with relevant industrial experience. The course is in collaboration with the Open University and is studied by a combination of short courses and distance learning. The course is part of the EPSRC IGDS programme.
MSc Polymers, Polymer Manufacture & Product Manufacture: 1 year course open to holders of a science Honours degree. It is a European course based at North London, and in France and Spain.
MPhil and PhD: Awarded to suitably qualified graduates after a 2 or 3 year FT period of research and postgraduate study.

Higher National Diploma/Certificate in Polymer Technology: 2 year FT/PT courses. Entry is 1 A level pass or BTEC National Certificate.

NVQ Awards: The School is an approved centre and able to assess candidates and prepare candidates for assessment.

Plumbing

THE INSTITUTE OF PLUMBING

64 Station Lane
Hornchurch
Essex
RM12 6NB
United Kingdom
Tel: 01708 472791
Fax: 01708 448987
Email: info@plumbers.org.uk
Website: www.plumbers.org.uk/
www.registeredplumber.com

MEMBERSHIP:

Fellow (FIOP): Aged over 25 and working, for example, as a director manager or senior engineer in a consulting, manufacturing or installation company, with qualifications or experience equivalent to NVQ Level 4 or 5. Suitably qualified applicants can be registered as Engineering Technicians with the Engineering Council.

Member (MIP): Aged over 23, perhaps working as an established self-employed practitioner, partner, foreman, supervisor or technician, with qualifications or experience equivalent to NVQ Level 3. Suitably qualified applicants can be registered as Engineering Technicians with the Engineering Council.

Associate (AIP): Aged over 20 and working, for example, as a self-employed operative with qualifications or experience equivalent to NVQ Level 2.

Registered Plumber (RP): Description granted to applicants aged over 20 years who have suitable on-site experience.

Companion (CompIP): Open to anyone who is connected with the plumbing industry and supports the work of the Institute.

Trainee: Applicants will be studying for a qualification which will lead to a level of competence in one or more aspects of plumbing.

Industrial Associate: This category is for material and product manufacturers, plumbers' merchants, and professional and other organisations who support the objectives of the Institute.

Population Registration

THE INSTITUTE OF POPULATION REGISTRATION

The Register Office
Wycombe Area Office
Easton Street
High Wycombe
Bucks
HP11 1NH
United Kingdom
Tel: 01494 475385

The Institute consists of people engaged in the Births, Marriages and Deaths Registration Service and in work associated with the production of Vital, Health and Social Statistics, including the Census of Population.

Fellowship (FIR): Awarded to Members in recognition of outstanding service to the Institute.

Member (MIR): Must have been a Licentiate for at least 5 years and have produced a thesis on any registration-related topic which, in the opinion of the Management Committee, reaches the necessary standard of knowledge, research and professional competence.

Licentiate (LIR): Must at the time of their application be actively engaged in the profession. The Management Committee is currently considering how the Licentiate status will be awarded in the future.

Associate: Someone who is employed in the profession or an associated profession.

The Institute also elects as **Honorary Members** such people as in their opinion merit the honour.

THE INSTITUTE'S EXAMINATIONS:

The Institute recognises the Registrar General for England and Wales as the sole arbiter of registrars' qualifications and standards (in England and Wales) and has therefore suspended its examining role.

Printing

THE INSTITUTE OF PRINTING
The Mews, Hill House
Clanricarde Road
Tunbridge Wells
Kent
TN1 1PJ
United Kingdom
Tel: 01892 538118/518028
Fax: 01892 518028
Email: admin@iop.ftech.co.uk or
admin@instituteofprinting.org
Website: www.globalprint.com/uk/iop

MEMBERSHIP:

Honorary Fellow: Elected in recognition of outstanding service to printing or to the Institute.
Fellow (FIOP): Must have the qualifications necessary to become a Corporate Member. They must have been engaged for a sufficient period in an important position of responsibility in or connected with the industry and have made a distinctive contribution to the science, art and/or professional management of Printing.
Member (MIOP): Must have been engaged for at least 3 years in a relevant position of responsibility since becoming a Graduate Member; or have been engaged for at least 5 years in a relevant position of substantial responsibility or have been engaged in a position of relevant responsibility for at least 3 years and have attained a relevant degree or equivalent academic or vocational qualification or have contributed an original paper to an appropriate publication, relevant to the industry.
Associate (Assoc.IOP): Must have suitable experience in or connected with printing.
Graduate (GradIOP): Must have successfully completed a degree-level course approved by the Institute.
Student: Must be following, or intending to follow, an approved course of further education acceptable to the Council.

Production Engineering

INSTITUTE OF OPERATIONS MANAGEMENT
The University of Warwick Science Park
Sir William Lyons Road
Coventry
CV4 7EZ
United Kingdom
Tel: 024 76692266
Fax: 024 76692305
Email: iom@iomnet.org.uk
Website: www.iomnet.org.uk

MEMBERSHIP:

Fellow (FIOM): Must be over 30 years of age, and have at least 8 years' experience in the field, *or* have passed/been exempt from the exams prescribed by the Institute, and have a minimum of 4 years' relevant experience.
Member (MIOM): Must be over 22 years of age, and have at least 5 years' experience in the field, *or* have passed/been exempt from the exams prescribed by the Institute, and have a minimum of 2 years' relevant experience.
Associate: Must be 18 or over and either actively engaged or interested in Operations Management.
Student: Must be 18 or over and pursuing a relevant course of study.

EXAMINATIONS:

The Certificate in Operations Management (COM): Intended as an entry-level qualification, which aims to provide educational support for industry by providing a broad, general coverage of operations management and its role in supply chain management. It is intended to provide an introduction to the business environment in which all companies must operate, to the workings of the supply chain – from supplier to value adder, to distributor, to customer – and to the ways in which operations may be continuously improved. Ultimately, it aims to help companies and their personnel to improve business performance. Units cover: The Business; Demand and Supply Chain Management; and Improved Techniques. There is an optional industrial project (72 hours).
Diploma: This course is designed for the practitioner/professional manager working in the field. Modules include: The Business Environment; Manufacturing Planning & Control & Master Planning; Material & Capacity Requirements Planning; Inventory & Logistics Management; Shop Floor Control and Just in Time; and Managing Organisations. An NVQ in Management Level 4 may be awarded for the

appropriate elements if a competency based programme is followed (360 hrs).

Advanced Diploma: This is approached through an industrially based project and is aimed at those who will evaluate and develop present techniques and systems, or who will design and implement tomorrow's technologies.

THE INSTITUTION OF MANUFACTURING ENGINEERS

Rochester House
66 Little Ealing Lane
London
W5 4XX
United Kingdom
Tel: 020 8579 9411

The Institute of Manufacturing Engineers merged with the Institute of Electrical Engineers in September 1991. All regulations for membership are applicable as for the Institution of Electrical Engineers (q.v.).

Psychology

BRITISH PSYCHOLOGICAL SOCIETY

St Andrews House
48 Princess Road East
Leicester
LE1 7DR
United Kingdom
Tel: 0116 254 9568
Fax: 0116 247 0787
Email: mail@bps.org.uk
Website: www.bps.org.uk

(Incorporated by Royal Charter in 1965)

MEMBERSHIP:

Chartered Psychologist (CPsychol): Status granted to Members of the British Psychological Society who have been entered in the Register of Chartered Psychologists maintained by the Society under the terms of its Royal Charter of Incorporation. Entry in the Register is granted to Members who are judged to have reached a standard sufficient for professional practice in Psychology without supervision following at least 6 years' undergraduate education and postgraduate training in Psychology.

Fellowship (FBPsS): Awarded to Members of the Society in recognition of higher psychological qualifications and of an outstanding contribution to the advancement or dissemination of psychological knowledge or practice over at least 10 years.

Associateship Fellowship (AFBPsS): Awarded to Graduate Members of the Society who have either met the postgraduate requirement for registration as Chartered Psychologists and successfully completed a further period of study or practice of Psychology for at least 2 years, or have engaged in the application, discovery, development or dissemination of psychological knowledge or practice for at least 7 years.

Graduate Membership: Awarded to people who hold an approved university Honours degree in Psychology or a recognised equivalent, or an approved postgraduate qualification in Psychology.

Foreign Affiliates: Members of foreign psychological societies, mainly those which are affiliated to the International Union of Psychological Sciences, may be elected Foreign Affiliates.

Affiliate: Need have no technical qualifications in Psychology; he/she is interested in the Society's work but is not qualified to be elected as a Graduate Member.

Student Subscriber: An Honours degree student of Psychology in a university or other institution, or, in certain circumstances, a postgraduate student studying for a higher degree in Psychology.

EXAMINATIONS:

Qualifying Examination of the Society: Candidates must hold a degree from a recognised university or polytechnic or other institution. The exam comprises 1 written paper in each of the following: (a) Biological Foundations and Cognitive Processes; (b) Individual Differences, Social and Developmental Psychology; (c) Research Design and Quantative Methods in Psychology; (d) General Paper; (e) Advanced Option Paper and a practical component. A pass in the Qualifying Examination confers on the candidate eligibility for Graduate Membership of the Society and the Graduate Basis for Registration as a Chartered Psychologist.

Diploma in the Applied Psychology of Teaching: Candidates become eligible for registration as Chartered Psychologists as Teachers and Lecturers in Psychology. Before enrolment they must have the Graduate Basis for Registration and are normally required to have had 4 years' teaching experience under the guidance of a Chartered Psychologist who is a Teacher of Psychology. The Exam comprises: (a) 4 unseen written papers; (b) an Applied Teaching Assessment comprising (i) 4 case studies demonstrating the application of the theoretical material, (ii) 6 examples of the candidate's actual work on course structure and evaluation, eg samples of work assessed by the candidate, (iii) evidence of competence as a teacher from approved observers' reports on 4 occasions, and (iv) a video recording of an actual teaching session; (c) a dissertation; and (d) an oral examination at the discretion of the examiners. Candidates will normally be required to follow a 2 year FT or equivalent PT path leading to the Diploma.

Diploma in Counselling Psychology: Candidates must have the Graduate Basis for Registration. They are normally required to follow a 3 year FT or equivalent PT path leading to the Diploma, involving supervised counselling psychology practice. The exam is based on submitted reports of counselling work, unseen written exam papers, essays, reports of research projects and an oral exam.

Postgraduate Certificate in Occupational Psychology: Candidates, who must hold the Graduate Basis for Registration, may enter for this examination, which consists of 4 written papers taken over 2 days. The Certificate part-fulfils the requirements for registration with the Society as a Chartered Occupational Psychologist.

Diploma in Educational Psychology: Candidates must have the Graduate Basis for Registration, and will normally be allowed to enrol only if they have been accepted for employment as trainee educational psychologists in a psychological service. They are normally required to follow a 3 year training of continuous supervised practical experience and study. The exam comprises 3 unseen written papers, assessment of practical and research competence through submission of professional work portfolios, a small-scale research project, research dissertation, supervisors' reports and an oral exam.

Psychotherapy

BRITISH ASSOCIATION FOR COUNSELLING AND PSYCHOTHERAPY

1 Regent Place
Rugby
Warwickshire
CV21 2PJ
United Kingdom
Tel: 0870 4435252
Fax: 0870 4435160
Email: bacp@bacp.co.uk
Website: www.bacp.co.uk

MEMBERSHIP:

BAC membership is open to those practising Counselling or Psychotherapy, using counselling skills within another role or training in counselling. All BAC members are required to work in accordance with the Codes of Ethics and Practice. Membership alone is not a qualification.

There are currently 4 codes: for counsellors, for supervision of counsellors, for trainers and counselling skills.

ACCREDITATION:

Accreditation as an individual counsellor will be awarded to individual members who successfully demonstrate that they meet one of the following criteria: (a) 450 hours of formal counsellor training, comprised of 250 hours of theory and 200 hours of skills training, and at least 450 hours of supervised counselling practice over a minimum of 3 years; (b) completion of a BAC Accredited course plus supervised counselling practice as (a) above; (c) 10 unit combination of counsellor training (1 unit = 75 hours) and years of supervised practice (1 unit = 150 hours min per year); (d) 10 years of supervised counselling practice with a minimum of 150 practice hours per year. In all cases members must have an agreed ongoing arrangement for counselling supervision of $1\frac{1}{2}$ hours individual or equivalent monthly, have undertaken 40 hours of personal therapy or an equivalent activity, and give evidence of serious commitment to ongoing personal and professional development. This could be indicated by regular participation in further training, support study, etc. Accreditation is renewed on an annual basis.

United Kingdom Register of Counsellors: There are two forms of registration under this system: Independent for counsellors accredited by BAC and COSCA (Confederation of Scottish Counselling Agencies); Sponsored for counsellors working in counselling organisations that provide a counselling service.

BRITISH ASSOCIATION FOR THE PERSON CENTRED APPROACH (BAPCA)

Bm-BAPCA
London
WC1N 3XX
United Kingdom
Tel: 01989 770948
Email: enquires@bapca.org.uk
Website: www.bapca.org.uk

The association was founded in 1989 as a non-religious, non-profit-making organisation with the aim of advancing education in Client-Centred Psychotherapy and Counselling and the Person Centred Approach through the publishing of magazines, books, articles and its website, as well as co-operating with national and international organisations with similar goals and providing its members with opportunities to meet and exchange ideas. It brings together people who practice and support the Person Centred Approach in all areas of life, not just the 'helping professions' and worked-based activities. Members include clergy, community workers, counsellors, managers nurses, psychotherapists, social workers, teachers and the unwaged.

BRITISH ASSOCIATION OF PSYCHOTHERAPISTS (BAP)

37 Mapesbury Road
London
NW2 4HJ
United Kingdom
Tel: 020 8452 9823
Fax: 020 8452 5182
Email: mail@bap-psychotherapy.org
Website: www.bap-psychotherapy.org

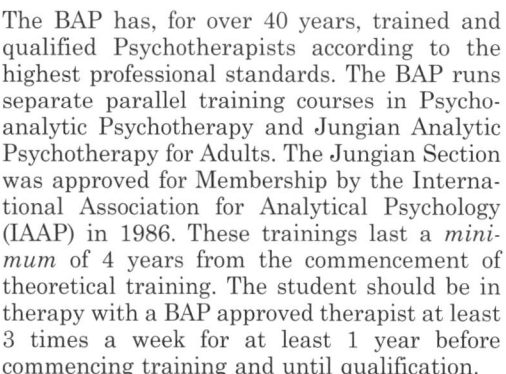

The BAP has, for over 40 years, trained and qualified Psychotherapists according to the highest professional standards. The BAP runs separate parallel training courses in Psychoanalytic Psychotherapy and Jungian Analytic Psychotherapy for Adults. The Jungian Section was approved for Membership by the International Association for Analytical Psychology (IAAP) in 1986. These trainings last a *minimum* of 4 years from the commencement of theoretical training. The student should be in therapy with a BAP approved therapist at least 3 times a week for at least 1 year before commencing training and until qualification.

A Training in Child and Adolescent Psychotherapy was begun in 1982 and recognised by the Association of Child Psychotherapists (ACP) in 1986; students can therefore expect to become eligible, upon qualification, for employment under the NHS. The training lasts a *minimum* of 4 years. In additon, the BAP offers a Training in Adult Psychotherapy for Child Psychotherapists already registered with the ACP. This training lasts a *minimum* of 2 years. Upon qualification, members of the BAP are eligible for registration nationally with the British Confederation of Psychotherapists and/or the IAAP or ACP.

In addition to its main professional courses, the Psychoanalytic, Jungian and Child Sections of the BAP offer shorter external courses of particular interest to workers in the helping professions who wish to extend their understanding of a psychodynamic way of working in their day-to-day work. Since 1997, the BAP, in association with the Department of Psychology at Birbeck College, has offered a Diploma/MSc course in the Psychodynamics of Human Development. This part-time course enables students to develop an understanding of Psychoanalytic or Jungian approaches to the study of human development, and to consider the contribution of recent research in child development.

External courses offered in 2002/2003 include: Assessment for Psychotherapy; Infant Observation Seminars – a Jungian Approach; Jungian Thought in the Modern World; Psychoanalytical Ideas and their Application; Counselling in Educational Settings.

Full details of all these courses can be obtained from the Secretary at the above address or from the BAP website.

Alongside its education programmes, the BAP also offers a Supervision Service and a Consultation Service for the media, and a prompt assessment and referral system for children, adolescents and adults requiring psychotherapy.

Public Administration and Local Government

THE INSTITUTE OF PUBLIC SECTOR MANAGEMENT

Bolton Enterprise Centre
Washington Street
Bolton
DN11 0XN
United Kingdom
Tel: 01204 385383
Email: info@ipsm.org.uk
Website: www.ipsm.org.uk

The Institute of Public Sector Management, established in 1983, provides a broad-based professional institute for managers employed in public, voluntary and 'not-for-profit' organisations.

There are many managers working in the public and charity sectors who can benefit from joining a professional body of like-minded officers who are interested in the promotion of best management practice. The IPSM aims to promote and advance efficient management and administration, develop the usefulness of the service provided by its members, and encourage the training and education of staff. Members are entitled to use the designatory letters IPSM and attend national and local conferences and seminars organised by the IPSM. They also have the opportunity to participate in the running of the Institute through the Council. The Institute provides members with a help-desk facility and is able to draw on a considerable bank of expertise across a wide range of disciplines, as well as providing a networking facility.

Full members must have an administrative qualification of at least BTEC Higher National Award standard. They must have been employed in the public, voluntary or community sector for at least 12 months prior to their application. Senior managers in their sectors are also eligible on the basis of their experience. Student membership is open to persons studying for qualifications recognised for full membership. The Institute has its own programme of awards and qualifications.

Purchasing and Supply

THE CHARTERED INSTITUTE OF PURCHASING AND SUPPLY

Easton House
Easton on the Hill
Stamford
Lincolnshire
PE9 3NZ
United Kingdom
Tel: 01780 756777
Fax: 01780 751610
Email: info@cips.org
Website: www.cips.org.

MEMBERSHIP:

Fellow (FCIPS): Fellowship is awarded by assessment and is defined thus: a **Corporate Member (MCIPS)** who, in the opinion of the Council of the Institute: (a) has demonstrated outstanding competence and achievement in purchasing and supply, a high level of professional knowledge and experience, and responsibility at a senior management level in an enterprise of significant size; *or* (b) has made or is making a significant contribution towards the advancement of the Purchasing and Supply profession.

Corporate Member (MCIPS): A person who has either achieved the Institute's Graduate Diploma qualification or has satisfied the Institute's criteria for assessment by alternative routes which require evidence of senior management experience.

Student or Associate: A person who either wishes to study for one of the CIPS qualifications, or is pursuing the professional competence route to Corporate Membership.

Affiliate: Those who have an interest in purchasing and supply chain management but do not wish to commit themselves to one of the assessment processes may join as an Affiliate.

EXAMINATIONS:

Graduate Diploma in Purchasing and Supply: Minimum entry qualifications are 5 GCSE passes, of which at least 2 must be at A level. The exams consist of a Foundation Stage and a Professional Stage. Many students pursue a BTEC Higher Award or a SCOTVEC equivalent to obtain substantial exemptions from the Institute's Foundation exams. Similarly those holding a recognised degree, diploma or other professional qualifications will be considered under the exemptions policy. Many colleges offer PT and FT study facilities and there are also correspondence courses. NVQ/SVQs in Procurement also provide a route to CIPS membership.

Certificate in Purchasing and Supply: Open access. Suitable for newcomers to Purchasing and Supply. Leads to the **Advanced Certificate in Purchasing and Supply** for those who want to develop their understanding of operational issues.

Quality Assurance

THE INSTITUTE OF QUALITY ASSURANCE

12 Grosvenor Crescent
London
SWlX 7EE
United Kingdom
Tel: 020 7245 6722
Fax: 020 7245 6788
Email: reception@iqa.org
Website: www.iqa.org

CORPORATE MEMBERS:

Honorary Fellow (HonFIQA): Limited in number. Someone who has rendered, or is in a position to render, conspicuous service to the Institute.

Fellow (FIQA): Stage 1: To meet the requirements of Member (MIQA) and in addition, to demonstrate extensive knowledge of sections 5–8 of the IQA Body of Knowledge.

Stage 2: Those meeting the requirements for stage one will be presented to the IQA's Board of Fellows, for consideration of Fellowship. Type of criteria will be: eminence in a particular field; status, eg senior manager in a large organisation; exceptional service to the Institute in a profession capacity.

Member (MIQA): There are two routes to becoming a Member of the IQA. The traditional way is through examinations and previous academic qualifications and training. The new Experiential Route considers those who have

THE CHARTERED INSTITUTE OF PURCHASING AND SUPPLY (CIPS)

THE CHARTERED INSTITUTE OF PURCHASING & SUPPLY

Easton House, Easton on the Hill, Stamford PE9 3NZ
Tel: 01780 756777, website: www.cips.org

If you choose a career in purchasing and supply management you will be dealing with different people and new challenges every day. You will be involved in the vital process of managing the supply of all your organisation's needs from essential services to critical products which enable the organisation to achieve its strategic goals.

There are many specialist areas within purchasing and supply management, and your role might cover:

- Devising purchasing strategies
- Identifying, managing and developing suppliers
- Sourcing the right goods and services, at the right price
- Negotiating contracts to achieve the best value for money
- Managing risks
- Supply chain management
- Systems implementation.

Purchasing and supply management is crucial to all organisations from commercial to public and voluntary, so you will have opportunities to work in any sector of the economy.

Demand for purchasing and supply management professionals continues to grow as organisations recognise they must contain their costs and understand their supply marketplaces in order to become more competitive. In a large organisation, reducing costs can have a significant impact on profits – and the opportunities and rewards are certainly there for people who can show flair and professionalism.

The average starting salary for a graduate trainee with no previous purchasing experience is around £17k. You can usually expect a promotion – and a rise to over £25k – within 12 to 18 months. Achieving the CIPS Graduate Diploma opens the door to greater responsibility and the potential for much higher pay.

The Chartered Institute of Purchasing and Supply (CIPS) has over 31,000 members worldwide and is Europe's largest purchasing and supply management organisation. It is recognised throughout the world as a highly respected representative body. Employers regard membership of CIPS as a strong indication of a person's professional ability and commitment.

If you join CIPS you will not only enhance your professional status, but can also tap into a wide range of support services such as technical information, training programmes, the CIPS recruitment service, careers advice and a free fortnightly magazine. You will also qualify for any members' discounts, including those offered by the CIPS Bookshop, which sells business books online.

Contact CIPS, Easton House, Easton on the Hill, Stamford PE9 3NZ
Tel: 01780 756777, website: www.cips.org

worked in the field and have gained a depth of knowledge of quality management.
Qualification Route: A degree or a recognised equivalent qualification. The IQA's A11 Introduction to Quality Assurance and A12 Principles of Techniques of Quality Management examinations or the IQA Diploma (DIPQ) and IQA Advanced Diploma (ADipQ) must have been successfully acquired, and the candidate must also have at least 5 years' experience in the field.
Experiential Route: To qualify through this route individuals must demonstrate an understanding of sections 1–4 of the IQA Body of Knowledge. This is assessed by submission of a portfolio of evidence and, if necessary, an interview.

NON-CORPORATE MEMBERS:

Companion of the IQA (CIQA): Eminent people are invited to become members in recognition of their contribution to Quality. Admission is the result of unanimous agreement between the President, the Director-General and one other nominated by the Council.

THE INSTITUTE OF MANAGEMENT SPECIALISTS CERTIFICATE AND DIPLOMA OF MERIT:

Associate of the IQA (AIQA): Open to individuals who have demonstrated quality responsibilities but who do not yet have the depth and breadth of knowledge and experience required for becoming a member.
Student: Open to those undergoing initial education and/or training in Quality-related topics.

EXAMINATIONS:

The Institute's exams consist of the IQA Diploma in Quality (DipQ). Existing qualification may give exeptions from parts of the above examinations. Please contact the Education Department for further details.

Radiography

THE SOCIETY AND THE COLLEGE OF RADIOGRAPHERS

207 Providence Square
Mill Street
London
SE1 2EW
United Kingdom
Tel: 020 7740 7200
Fax: 020 7740 7204
Email: carolinew@sor.org
Website: www.sor.org

Radiography comprises 2 disciplines: Diagnostic Radiography and Therapeutic Radiography. Diagnostic Radiographers are responsible for producing high-quality images on film and other recording materials which help to diagnose disease and the extent of injuries. Therapeutic Radiographers help to treat patients, many of whom have cancer, using ionising radiation and sometimes drugs. Employment in the NHS is open to State Registered Radiographers holding a degree in either Diagnostic Radiography or Therapeutic Radiography, the College's Diploma (DCR), or an overseas' qualification and clinical experience acceptable to the Radiographer's Board at the Council for Professional Supplementary to Medicine.
The profession is now an all-graduate-entry profession and the College's own Diploma (DCR) has been withdrawn as a route to qualification with effect from April 1995.
At least 50% of the curriculum is a clinical education programme within hospital departments though the academic and clinical components are fully integrated.
The entry requirements for all courses are the university general requirements (eg 2 A levels and 3 GCSEs grade C or above and various combinations of these including AS levels). BTEC HNC, and GNVQ are acceptable as is entry through an Access Course.
The majority of College specialist qualifications are being phased out in favour of post/graduate MSc courses.

Refrigeration Engineering

THE INSTITUTE OF REFRIGERATION
Kelvin House
76 Mill Lane
Carshalton
Surrey
SM5 2JR
United Kingdom
Tel: 020 8647 7033
Fax: 020 8773 0165
Email: ior@ior.org.uk
Website: www.ior.org.uk

Fellow (FInstR): A person who has been engaged for not less than 5 years in a position of special responsibility or leadership in Refrigeration or an allied field and has obtained a degree or equivalent in a subject approved by the Council; or has been engaged for not less than 10 years in a position of responsibility or leadership in Refrigeration or an allied field of which not less than 5 years has been in a position of special responsibility or leadership, and has obtained a National HD or equivalent qualification in a subject approved by the Council; or has been engaged for not less than 15 years in a position of responsibility or leadership in Refrigeration or an allied field, of which not less than 5 years has been in a position of special responsibility or leadership.
Member (MInstR): A person who has been engaged for not less than 3 years in a position of important responsibility or leadership in Refrigeration or an allied field and has obtained a degree or equivalent qualification in a subject approved by the Council; or has been engaged for not less than 5 years in a position of important responsibility or leadership in Refrigeration or an allied field and has obtained a National HC, S/NVQ Level 3 or equivalent qualification in a subject approved by the Council; or has been engaged for not less than 10 years in an important position of responsibility or leadership in refrigeration or an allied field.
Associate Member (AMInstR): A person who has been engaged for not less than 3 years in a position of some responsibility in Refrigeration or an allied field and has obtained a National Certificate or equivalent qualification in a subject approved by the Council; or has been engaged for not less than 5 years in a position of some responsibility in Refrigeration or an allied field and has obtained a C&G Craft Certificate, S/NVQ Level 3 or equivalent qualification in a subject approved by the Council; or has been engaged for not less than 7 years in a position of some responsibility in Refrigeration or an allied field.
Affiliate: A person who is actively involved in the science, art or application of Refrigeration or allied fields and who has not yet attained the condition for transfer to another grade of membership.
Student: A person who is receiving instruction at an approved institute of learning in subjects relevant to the science, art or application of Refrigeration or allied fields with a view to qualifying for a higher grade of membership in due course.

Retail

THE BOOKSELLERS ASSOCIATION OF GREAT BRITAIN AND IRELAND
272 Vauxhall Bridge Road
London
SW1V 1BA
United Kingdom
Tel: 020 7834 5477
Website: www.booksellers.org.uk

Membership is by subscription.
Diploma in Professional Bookselling: Launched in April 1996, this is designed for booksellers seeking a recognised qualification. It is a self-study programme of 15 modules covering all aspects of bookselling and is generally assessed by tutors accredited by the Booksellers' Association.

BOSS FEDERATION (BRITISH OFFICE SYSTEMS AND STATIONERY)
6 Wimpole Street
London
W1G 9SL
United Kingdom
Tel: 020 7637 7692
Fax: 020 7436 3137
Website: www.bossfed.co.uk

The Federation conducts exams in product knowledge to Diploma standards.
A minimum of 6 subject passes is required.
Diploma: For candidates who have been in the stationery and office machines trade for not less than 6 months.

THE BRITISH ANTIQUE DEALERS' ASSOCIATION
20 Rutland Gate
London
SW7 1BD
United Kingdom
Tel: 020 7589 4128
Fax: 020 7581 9083
Email: enquiry@bada.demon.co.uk
Website: www.bada.org

A member may be described as a 'Member of the British Antique Dealers' Association' or as a 'Member of the BADA'. (The use of designatory letters such as MBADA after the name is not permitted.) Applicants must be sponsored by at least 2 members and their eligibility is determined by reference to evidence that they are established in business in the Antique Trade and carry a stock of antiques; that they have carried on their business in the Antique Trade for not less than 3 years immediately before their application, unless the Council of the Association decides in a particular case on a shorter period; that they are persons of integrity or in the case of corporations, that they are under the control of such a person; that they have or command the degree of knowledge required to enable them to buy and when selling to describe the antique goods in which they deal.

THE CO-OPERATIVE COLLEGE
Stanford Hall
Loughborough
Leicestershire
LE12 5QR
United Kingdom
Tel: 01509 857218
Fax: 01509 857263
Email: joy.mcdonnell@co-opcollege.zee-web.co.uk
Website: www.co-op.ac.uk

Accelerated Accces Programme: A continuously assessed and examined 23 week residential course for mature students. It provides Social Science and Business pathways and leads to a HE Access Certificate. Students accepted qualify for FEFC scholarships.
Diploma in Management Studies (IM), **Certificate in Management Studies** and **Certificate in Supervisory Management** are both PT and by distance-learning, with a residential workshop.
NVQ/SVQ: A range of management, retail, customer service, training and development, human resource development and administration programmes, primarily at Levels 2, 3 and 4, to help meet the needs of the co-operative and mutual sectors.

A wide range of short courses particularly related to the co-operative and social economy sectors are also offered, including **Director and Member Training for Co-operatives**. A **Pension Fund Trustee Development Programme** has been introduced and **Credit Union Training** is also undertaken here at the Co-operative College.

THE GUILD OF ARCHITECTURAL IRONMONGERS
8 Stepney Green
London
E1 3JU
United Kingdom
Tel: 020 7790 3431
Fax: 020 7790 8517
Email: ironmongers@compuserve.com
Website: www.gai.org.uk

MEMBERSHIP:
Full Membership: Open to bona fide Architectural Ironmongers and Builders Merchants with an interest in ironmongery, who hold adequate stocks in relation to turnover of Architectural Ironmongery and are equipped to provide the technical expertise, delivery and other facilities for meeting the requirements of the districts served, and who comply with the rules. Full membership is also open to certain manufacturers who meet the membership criteria.
Subsidiary Membership: Only available to subsidiaries of Full Members.
Branch Membership: Only available to branches of Full Members.
Associate Membership: Available to manufacturers of any type of Architectural Ironmongery (or such other products as the Executive Committee may decide to be suitable) who carry on a business in a manner compatible with the interests and standing of Architectural Ironmongers.
Overseas Membership: Membership of the Guild is available to an overseas applicant who complies with the rules and who carries on business in a manner compatible with the interest of Architectural Ironmongers.
Institute Section: Open to individuals actively engaged in the business of Architectural Ironmongery who have *either* gained the GAI Diploma *or* had such practical training and a minimum of 10 years' experience.
Membership categories are Fellow, Member and Student. The Institute section has its own National and Regional Committees and holds meetings throughout the country for the membership.

EXAMINATIONS:
The Guild provides a 4 year course of training. Students are not permitted to take the second year course until they have passed the first year exam, or take the third year course until they have passed the second year exam. A Certificate is awarded on successful completion of the third year exam, and a GAI Diploma (DipGAI) is awarded on successful completion of the fourth year exam.

THE INSTITUTE OF BUILDERS' MERCHANTS
Parnall House
5 Parnall Road
Harlow
Essex
CM18 7PP
United Kingdom
Tel: 01279 419650
Fax: 01279 419650

To improve through lectures, classes and courses of instruction the technical and general knowledge of persons engaged in or about to engage in the trade of a Builders' Merchant; to award diplomas, certificates and other distinctions; to encourage and undertake research and invention.

MEMBERSHIP:
Fellow (FIBM): Entry is for those who have rendered outstanding service to the local branch or Institute and may be invited by the Governors to become a Fellow.
Member (MIBM): Applicants must have attained NVQ Level 4 at least, but other professional qualifications will be considered by the Membership Committee.
Associate (AInstBM): Applicants should have attained NVQ Level 3 at least, or have 3 years' work experience within the industry.
Corporate (CIBM): Applicants must hold a position in a profession or industry that is allied to or serves the Builders' Merchant trade.
Student Grade: This is open to anyone involved in Level 2 NVQs modern apprenticeships.

INSTITUTE OF GROCERY DISTRIBUTION
Letchmore Heath
Watford
Hertfordshire
WD2 8DQ
United Kingdom
Tel: 01923 851930
Fax: 01923 852531
Email: training@igd.org.uk

Individual Member (MIGD): Open to persons who have achieved success in the Post Graduate Certificate in Food & Grocery Industry Management.

EDUCATION COURSES:
Foundation Certificate in Management (accredited by Manchester Metropolitan University): An introduction to the food and grocery sector for junior and aspiring managers, consisting of 5 workshops, spread over a year.
Post Graduate Certificate in Food & Grocery Industry Management (validated by the University of Edinburgh and carrying 60 CATS points): A postgraduate programme tailored for aspiring middle managers in the industry. The course consists of 4 core units plus 2 option units, spread over a year.

THE INSTITUTE OF MASTERS OF WINE
Five King's House
Queen Street Place
London
EC4R 1QS
United Kingdom
Tel: 020 7236 4427
Fax: 020 7213 0499
Email: enquiries@imow.co.uk
Website: www.masters-of-wine.org

EXAMINATION FOR MEMBERSHIP:
The exam for membership is intended for people with advanced knowledge on all aspects of wine. Candidates are required to sit a 4 day examination consisting of both theory and practical papers. Once the theory and practical parts of the examination have been passed, the candidate must submit a dissertation, on the topic of their choice, providing the synopsis has been approved by the appropriate panel.

THE MEAT TRAINING COUNCIL

PO Box 141, Winterhill House
Snowdon Drive
Milton Keynes
MK6 1YY
United Kingdom
Tel: 01908 231062
Fax: 01908 231063
Email: info@meattraining.org.uk
Website: www.meattraining.org.uk

The Meat Training Council is the lead body, National Training Organisation (NTO) and awarding body for NVQ Levels 1, 2, 3 and 4 in Meat and Poultry. SVQs are awarded with the SQA. Professional membership is administered by the Worshipful Company of Butchers via its Guild of Freemen.

MEMBERSHIP:

Successful candidates are automatically eligible to join the Worshipful Company of Butchers Guild of Freemen.
Affiliate Grade (AffInstM): Achievement of the NVQ Level 2 qualification.
Associate Grade (AInstM): Success in the Advanced Certificate in Meat and Poultry or achievement of NVQ Level 3.
Graduate Member (GMInstM): Success in the Membership Exam or achievement of NVQ Level 4.

EXAMINATIONS:

Advanced Certificate in Meat and Poultry: This replaced the existing Associateship examination course from September 1999 onwards. It is a progression award/related vocational qualification designed to cover the underpinning knowledge and understanding content of the Council's S/NVQ Level 3 Meat and Poultry Processing. The award is based on 5 mandatory modules and 2 optional modules. The optional modules are designed to fit 6 industry sectors: abattoir, wholesale/catering, poultry, manufacturing, retail/supermarkets and enforcement. Awarded by the Council.
Graduate Membership Exam: Designed to enable those in the Meat industry to gain a senior qualification as a result of an intensive course of study. It gives an understanding of modern principles and techniques used by management with specific relevance to all sectors of the Meat industry; encourages a positive attitude towards management; helps people apply knowledge, skills and understanding gained from a study associated with a business environment; and develops skills in communicating. This course comprises compulsory core and optional specialist modules. Awarded by the Council.

Level 1: Entry-level qualification; Level 2: 4 qualifications; Level 3: Meat and Poultry Processing; Level 4: Meat Processing Management (Technical and Production). Designed for operational and technical skills, and all awarded by the Council.

THE SOCIETY OF SHOE FITTERS

Secretary: Mrs Laura West
The Anchorage, 28 Admirals Walk
Hingham
Norfolk
NR9 4JL
United Kingdom
Tel: 01953 851171
Fax: 01953 851171
Email: shoefitters@lineone.net
Website: www.shoefitters-uk.org

The Society is a professional institute engaged in the training of shoe fitters and assisting the public in obtaining fitting services. Entrance is by exam or specialised training course. Successful candidates become **Members (MSSF)** or **Fellows (FSSF)** of the Society of Shoe Fitters.

Road Safety

INSTITUTE OF ROAD SAFETY OFFICERS LTD

Pin Point
1–2 Rosslyn Crescent
Harrow
Middlesex
HA1 2SB
United Kingdom
Tel: 0870 010 4442
Fax: 0870 333 7772
Email: irso@dba.co.uk

The Institute of Road Safety Officers is the only professional body in the world dedicated to promoting the efficiency, specialised knowledge and career progression of Road Safety Officers. It is the Successor to the National Association of Road Safety Officers (NARSO), founded in 1957.

AIMS:

The objects for which the Institute was established are to provide a central organisation for all persons actively engaged in the promotion of Road Safety and to do such things as may be necessary to improve the status and further the interest of Road Safety Officers, including, *inter alia*, the following:
1. To Promote the efficiency and specialised knowledge of all those engaged upon Road

Safety work whether on behalf of Local Authorities, Police Authorities, Statutory Bodies, other organisations, commercial concerns or individually.
2. To improve the technique and effectiveness of education, training and publicity for Road Safety.
3. To arrange for an interchange of knowledge and experience of Road Safety matters between the members of the Institute.
4. To ensure that the specialised knowledge and experience of the Institute is available to other national organisations on behalf of the Institute.
5. To provide opportunities for association and interchange of thought and experience among the members and their friends and to hold conferences, discussions, lectures and the reading of papers; and for the acquisition and dissemination by these and other means of information connected with or useful to members.
6. To test by examination or otherwise the competence of persons desirous of becoming members or students, to improve the status of members and students, to award certificates, diplomas and other distinctions, and to institute and establish scholarships, grants, awards and other benefactions.
7. To establish and maintain a library and a collection of designs, drawings and other articles, and to print, publish and circulate papers, books and other literary matter connected with and useful to members.

MEMBERSHIP:

Fellow (FIRSO): Fellowships are conferred on members of the Institute who in the opinion of the Board of Fellows have made a significant contribution to the Road Safety profession.
Direct Member (MIRSO): This is available on application to holders of a relevant degree, Advanced Certifcate of Road Safety Studies, Edexel (BTEC) Professional Development Diploma in Accident and Safety Management from Manchester College of Art and Technology, Road Safety N/SVQ Levels 3 or 4, or non-relevant degree plus national Staff Training Phase II.
Associate (AMIRSO): For applicants with no Road Safety experience working within the area of Road Safety education, training and publicity or accident investigation; acceptance depends on a combination of work experience and qualifications.
Associate (1): Applicant appointed to a part-time post. Member grade available after 5 years' Associate experience.
Associate (2): Applicant appointed to a full-time post. Member grade available after 4 years' Associate experience.
Associate (3): Applicant has 2 years' experience and holds a non-relevant degree or certificate in Road Safety Studies or National Staff Training Phase II. Member grade available after 1 year's Associate experience.

QUALIFICATIONS:

Available from Manchester College of Arts and Technology, Openshaw Campus, Aston Old Road, Openshaw; tel: 0161 953 5995, x 3472, fax: 0161 953 3909.
The Edexel (BTEC) Professional Development Diploma in Accident and Safety Management is offered and leads to membership of the Institute of Road Safety Officers.

Road, Rail and Transport Engineering

SOCIETY OF OPERATIONS ENGINEERS

22 Greencoat Place
London
SW1P 1PR
United Kingdom
Tel: 020 7630 1111
Fax: 020 7630 6677
Email: membership@soe.org.uk
Website: www.soe.org.uk

The Society was formed in 1999 when the Institute of Plant Engineers (IPlantE) merged with the Institute of Road Transport Engineers (IRTE). The Society maintains the two professional sectors, IRTE and IPlantE.
The Society is associated with the Engineering Council UK and can register eligible members as Chartered Engineer (CEng), Incorporated Engineer (IEng) and Engineering Technician (EngTech).

MEMBERSHIP CLASSES:

Student: Studying or training in Engineering and below age 26.
Graduate: Qualified in relevant discipline but requiring further training and experience. Graduate members are expected to work towards attaining a higher class of membership.
Associate (AssocSOE + AssocIRTE or AssocIPlantE): Working in an Engineering-related occupation but not yet qualifying for any other class of membership.
Associate Member (AMSOE + AMIRTE or AMIPlantE): A good basic level of relevant academic achievement, training and experience in Engineering. May achieve Engineering Council registration as an EngTech.

Member (MSOE + MIRTE or MIPlantE): A balance of academic qualifications and/or extensive training and experience.
Fellow (FSOE + FIRTE or FIPlantE): A senior engineer with a high level of academic achievement and/or many years' training and experience.

INSTITUTE OF HIGHWAY INCORPORATED ENGINEERS

20 Queensberry Place
London
SW7 2DR
United Kingdom
Tel: 020 7823 9093
Fax: 020 7581 8087
Email: secretary@ihie.org.uk
Website: www.ihie.org.uk

In 1989 the Highway and Traffic Technicians Association changed its name to IHIE. Previous to 1972 the HTTA had been the Association of Highway Technicians, formed in 1965. IHIE is part of the NVQ awarding bodies for Transportation qualifications and Civil Engineering design. Enquiries to OUVS or Edexcel.
The Institute is a nominated and licensed institution with the EC and Fellows and Members may register with the Council as IEng or EngTech, as appropriate.
Fellow (FIHIE): Must satisfy the requirements of the EC for registration as an Incorporated Engineer, have passed a Professional Review, and hold a position of responsibility in Highways, Transportation or allied fields.
Member (MIHIE): Must satisfy the requirements of the EC for registration as an Engineering Technician, have passed the Technician Professional Review, and be employed in Highways, Transportation or allied fields. The minimum academic qualification is a BTEC NC in Civil Engineering Studies or equivalent.
Associate Member (AMIHE): Must have passed the first stage of the Incorporated Professional Review and satisfy EC academic entry requirements or have at least 10 years' experience.
Graduate Member: Must have an HNC, HND or degree; or have passed a Technician Initial Professional Development Assessment.
Student Member: Must be undergoing appropriate training, have undergone such training or be still studying.

THE INSTITUTE OF ROAD TRANSPORT ENGINEERS

22 Greencoat Place
London
SW1P 1PR
United Kingdom
Tel: 020 7630 1111
Fax: 020 7630 6677
Email: irte@irte.org
Website: www.irte.org

The Institute of Road Transport Engineers (IRTE) is a professional engineering institute on the list of Engineering Council Nominated Bodies. The Institute sets standards to improve engineering, commercial and management skill, knowledge and competence of all whose occupation or vocation is concerned with the design, production, operation and maintenance of road vehicles of all types used in the carriage of persons, passengers, goods and equipment. In partnership with government bodies and industry the Institute promotes improvement in the design, construction and use of all types of road transport vehicles. To promote continuing professional development the Institute encourages the training of its engineers to acquire theoretical and practical qualifications.

MEMBERSHIP:

Modern Apprentice: The Institute encourages young people in Road Transport Engineering to obtain professional recognition and support early in their careers. To this end an initiative has been launched, in recognition of the training being given, to encourage trainees undertaking a Modern Apprenticeship in Vehicle Maintenance and Repair to join the Institute and obtain the benefit from membership from the onset of their career.
Honorary Fellow: A person who has made a considerable contribution to the sphere of transport.
Fellow, Full Member and Associate Member: Road Transport Engineers who, in the opinion of the Council, merit admission to membership and satisfy the Institute with respect to the educational and vocational requirement as specified by the Council at the time of application.
Technician and Associate: Persons who, in the opinion of the Council, merit admission to membership and who satisfy the Institute with respect to the educational and vocational requirements as specified by the Council at the time of application but who have not had such a degree of responsibility or experience as would qualify them for admission as a Corporate Member.
Affiliate: A person who, in the opinion of the Council, merits admission to Affiliateship by

virtue of their occupation within the Road Transport or related industry.
Student: A person over 16 but not over 25 who is or will be pursuing such course of study as seen fit by the Council.

THE INSTITUTION OF HIGHWAYS AND TRANSPORTATION

6 Endsleigh Street
London
WC1H 0DZ
United Kingdom
Tel: 020 7387 2525
Fax: 020 7387 2808
Email: iht@iht.org
Website: www.iht.org.uk

(See also Transport, Road Transport Engineering, Works and Highway Engineering)
The Institution is currently an assessment centre for transportation NVQ/SVQs and offers assessment services for: Highway Maintenance Levels 3 and 4, Traffic Management & Systems Engineering Level 4, Transport Planning Levels 4 and 5, Transport & Technical Support Level 3 and Road Safety Levels 3 and 4.
The Institution is a Nominated Body of the Engineering Council and can offer Professional Review for registration as Incorporated and Chartered Engineers.

MEMBERSHIP:

Fellow (FIHT): Must hold a degree or qualification acceptable to the Institution and have held an important position of independent responsibility in connection with Highway or Transportation Engineering for at least 4 years *or* have at least 10 years' experience in Highways and/or Transportation, and have held an important senior position of independent responsibility in connection with Highways and Transportation for 4 years minimum.
Member (MIHT): Must hold an approved degree or professional qualification and have at least 2 years' post-qualification experience *or* be a registered chartered Incorporated Engineer *or* hold a recognised professional qualification and have at least 10 years' relevant work experience *or* have 80% NVQ/SVQ Level 4 or 50% NVQ/SVQ Level 5.
Associate Member (AMIHT): Must hold an approved degree and be engaged in Highway or Transportation work *or* have at least 5 years' relevant work experience *or* have 40% NVQ/SVQ Level 4 *or* 25% NVQ/SVQ Level 5.
Student: Must be at least 18 and be currently involved in an FT course of studies and/or in service training in Highways and Transportation.

Note: There is no entrance exam for any grade of membership.

INSTITUTION OF RAILWAY SIGNAL ENGINEERS

3rd Floor
Savoy Hill House
Savoy Hill
London
WC2R 0BS
United Kingdom
Tel: 020 7240 4935
Fax: 020 7240 3281
Email: training@irse.u-net.com
Website: www.irse.org

MEMBERSHIP:

Fellow (FIRSE): Must have been a Member for at least 3 years, with at least 5 years' superior responsibility; or be at least 35 years of age, engaged in the profession and have an appropriate knowledge of, and eminence in, the science of Railway Signalling and/or Telecommunications.
Member (MIRSE): Must be not less than 25, have been regularly trained, held a responsible position for at least 2 years and have satisfied the requirements of the Exam Regulations; or be not less than 28, have held a responsible position for at least 5 years and have the minimum educational qualifications applicable to a Chartered Engineer in an associated engineering discipline or its equivalent; or be not be less than 35, have had 10 years' experience in a position of responsibility in the profession and be holding a position of senior responsibility.
Associate Member: Must be not less than 23 years of age, have been engaged in the profession or an allied profession which has the necessary relevance to Railway Signalling and/or Telecommunications for a period of 2 years and have achieved an academic standard to the minimum level necessary to satisfy the Engineering Council's requirements for registration as an Incorporated Engineer; or alternatively have 7 years' experience in a position of responsibility in the profession.
Accredited Technician: Must not be less than 18 years of age, be actively engaged in the profession and hold an appropriate competency qualification as exemplified by an IRSE license.
Students: Must be aged 16–28, be employed and be receiving regular and practical training in some branch of the profession.

IRSE EXAMINATION REQUIREMENTS FOR CORPORATE MEMBERSHIP:

The aim of the IRSE Examination is to establish the professional competence of educationally qualified electrical, electronic and communications engineers in Railway Signalling and Communication Engineering. It is intended to test the main concepts of the subject material without bias to any one Railway Practice and it is designed to demonstrate that the student has reached the necessary professional educational standard required by a Signalling or Telecommunications Engineer for Corporate Membership of the Institution. This standard is typified by the exercising of judgement in the preparation, assessment, amendment or application of specifications and procedures, and is applicable to personnel engaged in the following activities:

1. Signalling/Telecommunications principles, practices, rules and regulations for the safe operation of railway traffic.
2. Design and development of Signalling/Telecommunications equipment and systems.
3. Preparation and understanding of the equipment drawings and specifications and/or design.
4. Planning, site installation and testing of Signalling/Telecommunications equipment and systems.
5. Practices related to assembly, wiring and testing of Signalling/Telecommunications equipment and systems.
6. Maintenance and servicing of Signalling/Telecommunications equipment and systems.

In order to meet the examination requirements for Corporate Membership, candidates must, within a period of 5 years, obtain a pass in Module 1, plus 3 of the remaining 6 optional modules. It is possible to obtain exemptions from individual modules where the candidate can demonstrate that he/she has passed an examination by a recognised body, which has substantially covered the syllabus of a particular IRSE examination module. Due to the specialised nature of the IRSE Examination, the scope for exemption is fairly limited. Claims for exemption must be made within 5 years of obtaining the particular qualification for which recognition is being claimed. The reason for this condition is that the exemption is based on information that may not be available where a qualification has been discontinued or changed.

Modules Available:

Module 1. Safety of Railway Signalling and Communications – No exemptions will be given.

Module 2. Signalling the Layout – Please apply, no exemptions currently agreed.

Module 3. Signalling Principles – Please apply, no exemptions currently agreed.

Module 4. Communications Principles – This is the most commonly sought after exemption. Many applicants for exemption claim that Telecommunications was part of their degree and that, on this basis, exemption should be granted. Unfortunately it is clear that the content of the Telecommunications element within a typical university Engineering degree is, at best, a basic overview. Occasionally, students study a Telecommunications topic for their final year project, but these tend to be a narrow specialisation in a particular field and the Council is not convinced that such study justifies module exemption. As a basic guideline, therefore, please do not ask for exemption to this module unless: your university study has been predominantly in Telecommunications; or your university study has included Telecommunications and your present career is Railway Telecommunications Engineering.

Module 5. Signalling & Control Equipment, Applications Engineering – Please apply, no exemptions currently agreed.

Module 6. Communications Equipment, Applications Engineering – Please apply, no exemptions currently agreed.

Module 7. Systems, Management & Engineering – Please apply, no exemptions currently agreed.

Security

INTERNATIONAL INSTITUTE OF SECURITY

Company Secretary
Suite 8, The Business Centre
57 Torquay Road
Paignton
Devon
TQ3 3DT
United kingdom
Tel: 01803 663275
Fax: 01803 663251
Email: iisec@btconnect.com

The Institute is a professional examining body specialising in subjects relating to security measures against loss through theft, fraud, fire, other damage and waste.

MEMBERSHIP:

Fellow (FII Sec): Fellowship is awarded on the basis of a thesis on a subject approved by the Board of Directors and undertaken after a specified period of Membership of 2 years. Also awarded to holders of an MSc or MA in Security Management from a recognised university with a minimum of 2 years' experience within the Security industry.
Diplomate (DIp II Sec): Diplomate is awarded to holders of a certificate or Diploma in Security Management at an undergraduate level, obtained from a recognised university, and who have a minimum of 2 years' experience within the Security industry.
Member (M II Sec): Certificate in Security Management level: available after successfully completing the Member level exam and subsequently registering with the Institute.
Graduate (Grad II Sec): Certificate in Security Management level: available after successfully completing the Graduate level exam (jointly accredited by the City & Guilds of London Institute) and subsequently registering with the Institute.

EXAMINATIONS:

Membership: Candidates must show that they have a comprehensive knowledge and experience of commercial or industrial security and the duties and responsibilities of a Chief or Senior Security Officer. Questions are based on the law as it concerns security practices, including its relation to fire, techniques and aids to security and the management/administration of a security department.
Graduateship: Questions are set on general security duties, including crime and fire prevention, security of premises and property, emergency situations, safety and English law. Additional modules are available to both Graduates and Members in Retail Security.

Shipbroking

THE INSTITUTE OF CHARTERED SHIPBROKERS

3 St Helen's Place
London
EC3A 6EJ
United Kingdom
Tel: 020 7628 5559
Fax: 020 7628 5445
Email: info@ics.org.uk
Website: www.ics.org.uk.

MEMBERSHIP:

Fellow (FICS): Must be at least 25, be a principal or director or hold a responsible position in Shipbroking and have passed the Qualifying Examinations.
Member (MICS): Must be at least 21, have (normally) 4 years' experience in Shipbroking and have passed the Qualifying Examinations.
Honorary Member: A person elected for outstanding services to the profession.
Retired Member: Those with less than 25 years' membership who, having retired from business life, pay a reduced subscription until they qualify for Life Membership.
Life Member: A retired Member with 25 or more years' membership.

EXAMINATIONS:

Qualifying Examination Structure:
Group 1: (All subjects required) Introduction to Shipping; Law of Carriage of Goods by Sea; Economics of Sea Transport & International Trade; Shipping Practice.
Candidates may select the following options in respect of Groups 2 and 3:

Option A: 2 subjects from Group 2 and 1 from Group 3;
Option B: 3 subjects from Group 2 and none from Group 3;
Option C: 1 subject from Group 2 and 2 from Group 3. If this option is the chosen, only 1 subject from Group C may be exempted, the other *must* be taken with this Institute.
Group 2: Dry Cargo Chartering; Ship Management; Tanker Chartering; Sale & Purchase; Liner Trades; Port Agency.
Group 3: Shipping Law; Marine Insurance; Financial & Management Accounting; International Through Transport.
Exemptions: Candidates with relevant professional or educational qualifications validated

by the Institute will be able to apply for exemptions, on a subject-for-subject basis, from all subjects except Shipping Practice in Group 1 and the specialist subjects comprising Group 2.
Foundation Diploma in Shipping Exam Structure: Comprises 2 subjects: Introduction to Shipping and 1 of the following specialist subjects – Dry Cargo Chartering; Ship Management; Tanker Chartering; Sale & Purchase; Liner Trades; Port Agency. Candidates must sit and pass both subjects during the same exam session in order to be awarded the Diploma.

Social Work

THE BRITISH ASSOCIATION OF SOCIAL WORKERS

16 Kent Street
Birmingham
B5 6RD
United Kingdom
Tel: 0121 622 3911
Fax: 0121 622 4860
Email: c.sedgwick@basw.co.uk.

With its continuing mission to campaign for and defend the values, principles and ethics of social work, BASW confronts the many challenges and opportunities facing social workers and the profession both at a national and international level. BASW members receive all the benefits of a first-class Advice and Representation Service, personal professional indemnity insurance, and the code of Ethics for Social Workers, as well as access to Parliament, the press, and over 75 professionl and public bodies. Venture Press, BASW's publishing house has numerous books in print, and BASW also publishes the internationally recognised journals *Professional Social Work*, *Practice*, and the prestigious *British Journal of Social Work*.

Sociology

THE INTERNATIONAL INSTITUTE OF SOCIAL ECONOMICS

Enholmes Hall
Patrington
Hull
East Yorkshire
HU12 0PR
United Kingdom
Tel: 01964 630033
Fax: 01964 631716
Email: hr24@dial.pipex.com

CORPORATE MEMBERSHIP:

Fellow (FIISE): Fellowship may be granted to persons already qualified as Members (see below) who have had at least another 10 years' approved experience; or who, being so qualified, have had at least 5 years' approved experience; or who have rendered outstanding service to the profession.
Member (MIISE): Membership may be granted to persons already qualified as Associate Members who have had at least 5 years' approved experience; or persons having a postgraduate degree or equivalent qualification in a course containing an approved balance of Social Economic subjects.
Associate Member (AMIISE): Associate Membership may be granted to persons whose first degree or equivalent qualification was obtained in a course containing an approved balance of Social Economic subjects; or who have at least a recognised first degree or an equivalent qualification, and an approved postgraduate degree or diploma in Social Economic subjects; or are considered to have suitable practical experience and alternative educational or other appropriate qualifications. Submission of an approved dissertation, research paper or published work will normally be required.

NON-CORPORATE MEMBERSHIP:

Affiliate Membership: Open to students on an approved course of study who would, on its satisfactory completion, be acceptable as Associate Members, or persons not otherwise qualified as Associate Members, Members or Fellows, but whose activities, experience, or academic work has provided significant contributions to the advancement of Social Economics, and who are elected by a majority of the Council.
Organisation Membership: May be granted to organisations either pursuing Social Economic objectives or wishing to see such objectives forwarded.

Speech and Language Therapy

ROYAL COLLEGE OF SPEECH AND LANGUAGE THERAPISTS
2 White Hart Yard
London
SE1 1NX
United Kingdom
Tel: 020 7378 1200
Fax: 020 7378 7254
Email: academic@rcslt.org
Website: www.rcslt.org

An undergraduate degree or postgraduate qualification from an accredited course is necessary to qualify as a Speech and Language Therapist. RCSLT issues to graduates the certificate which confers eligibility to practise in the National Health Service.

EXAMINATIONS:

3 and 4 year degree courses are offered at 15 universities and Higher Education institutions. Applications are made through UCAS. NHS Bursaries are available and there is no student contribution to fees. Pre-entry requirements vary from one educational establishment to another. If you are seriously interested in following a speech and language therapy career it is advisable to check at an early stage with the various establishments that your choice of A level subjects (or alternative exams) will be appropriate. Special arrangements may be negotiable for mature students.
There are 5 postgraduate courses (in London, Reading, Sheffield and Newcastle) for graduates from other disciplines who wish to gain a Speech and Language Therapy qualification. Accredited courses are run at the following institutions:
3 and 4 year undergraduate courses: Leeds Metropolitan University; De Montfort University; Manchester Metropolitan University; University of Strathclyde (Jordanhill Campus); Queen Margaret University College (Edinburgh); University of Central England in Birmingham; City University; Manchester University; Newcastle University; Reading University; Sheffield University; University of Wales Institute, Cardiff; University College, London; University of Ulster; College of St Mark & St John (Plymouth).
2 year postgraduate courses: City University; University College London; Newcastle University; Reading University; Sheffield University.

Statistics

THE ROYAL STATISTICAL SOCIETY
12 Errol Street
London
EC1Y 8LX
United Kingdom
Tel: 020 7638 8998
Fax: 020 7614 3905
Email: rss@rss.org.uk
Website: www.rss.org.uk

MEMBERSHIP:

Fellow: Fellowship is by election, but is open to anyone with a genuine interest in Statistics.
Chartered Statistician (CStat): Professional grade awarded to those with a good Honours degree (or equivalent) in Statistics, together with at least 5 years' responsible professional experience as a Statistician.
Graduate Statistician (GradStat): Professional grade awarded to those with a good Honours degree (or equivalent) in Statistics, but without the necessary professional experience to qualify as CStat.

EXAMINATIONS:

The Society merged with the Institute of Statisticians in 1993 and is continuing to operate the exams originally run under the name of the IOS. The aim of these exams is to provide a route into the Statistical profession for those in countries where few, if any, university courses are available, and for those in the UK who cannot pursue an undergraduate degree course, or who wish to convert from another discipline after some years' work.
The exams are held in May and there are 3 levels: **Ordinary Certificate** (2 papers), **Higher Certificate** (3 papers: Statistical Theory; Statistical Methods; Statistical Applications and Practice), and **Graduate Diploma** (4 compulsory papers: Applied Statistics I and II; Statistical Theory and Methods I and II; and an option paper with questions on economic statistics, econometrics, medical statistics, biometry, industrial statistics and operational research).

Stockbroking and Securities

THE UK SOCIETY OF INVESTMENT PROFESSIONALS (UKSIP)

21 Ironmonger Lane
London
EC2V 8EY
United Kingdom
Tel: 020 7796 3000
Fax: 020 7796 3333
Email: uksipstaff@uksip.org
Website: www.uksip.org

UKSIP was created on 1 August 2000 from the merger of two bodies, the Institute of Investment Management and Research, which was formed in 1955 as the Society of Investment Analysts, and the London Society of Investment Professional, which was established in 1986. The new body is a member society of the international organisation, the Association for the Investment Management and Research (AMIR), and students now study for the globally accepted chartered Financial Analyst qualification.

UKSIP, which has a membership of over 4000, has four classes of member: Regular, Affiliate, Student and Companion. There is also a Fellowship designation (FSIP), currently numbering about 50, for those senior professionals who have made a significant contribution to the Society or the Profession of Investment Management.

The Society is also responsible for the Investment Management Certificate, the threshold competence test for those wishing to become investment analysts or fund managers in the UK.

For further information on the society and membership visit www.uksip.org

Structural Engineering

THE INSTITUTION OF STRUCTURAL ENGINEERS

11 Upper Belgrave Street
London
SW1X 8BH
United Kingdom
Tel: 020 7235 4535
Fax: 020 7235 4294
Email: membership@istructe.org.uk
Website: www.istructe.org.uk

MEMBERSHIP:

The Institution authorises its corporate members to use the designatory initials **FIStructE** or **MIStructE**. Such corporate members may be registered by the Institution with the Engineering Council and thereby become additionally entitled to use the designation **CEng** (Chartered Engineer).

Fellow (FIStructE): Must be over 35, have passed the exam for Membership and subsequently have been engaged in a position of responsibility for at least 5 years. Alternatively, there is a direct entry route to Fellowship for individuals over 45, with an appropriate academic qualification, who have achieved a position of eminence in the profession.

Member (MIStructE): Must be at least 25, have an academic qualification equivalent to an accredited degree and have passed the Membership exam with relevant training and practical experience in Structural Engineering.

Graduate: A person who has normally obtained an accredited degree in Civil or Structural Engineering or an equivalent qualification and intends to study the profession of Structural Engineering.

Associate Member (AMIStructE): Must be at least 23, have relevant training and practical experience, and must possess appropriate academic qualifications equivalent to a 3 year degree, and have passed the Institution's exam for Associate Membership leading to registration as **IEng** (Incorporated Engineer).

Student: A person not less than 17 who is studying or intends to study the profession of Structural Engineering.

EXAMINATIONS:

Chartered Membership: Part 3 exam, a 7 hour paper on structural design and practice.

Associate Membership: Associate Membership exam, a 6 hour paper on structural engineering practice.

Surgical, Dental and Cardiological Technicians

THE BRITISH INSTITUTE OF DENTAL AND SURGICAL TECHNOLOGISTS

Department of Chemistry & Materials
Manchester Metropolitian University
Chester Street
Manchester
M1 5GD
United Kingdom
Tel: 0161 247 1418
Fax: 0161 247 6357
Website: www.bidst.mmu.ac.uk

ALL SECTIONS:

Life Member: Someone who has been a Fellow or Licentiate of the Institute for a continuous period of not less than 15 years, whose subscriptions have been paid up to date throughout the period of Membership, who has reached retirement age and is receiving no income, and who is recommended by the section committee.

SURGICAL SECTION:

Fellow (FBIDST): Fellowship will be awarded by Council only after 4 years in continuous membership at Licentiate grade to those who hold a relevant BTEC Higher Certificate, or CGLI Advanced Certificate, on either the reading of a paper at a recognised scientific meeting, or the publication of a paper in an approved scientific journal. This award is subject to recommendation or ratification by the Surgical Section Committee.
Licentiate (LBIDST): (a) An applicant who has passed the final exam in courses of education prescribed by the Council and is not less than 24; (b) someone of not less than 25 who has been practising as a Surgical Technologists for not less than 10 years.
Associate: An applicant who has experience or is undertaking a course of education but who in the opinion of the Council is not yet qualified for Licentiate.

DENTAL SECTION:

Fellow (FBIDST): Fellowship will be awarded by Council only after 5 years in continuous membership at Licentiate grade to those who hold a relevant BTEC Higher Certificate, or CGLI Advanced Certificate, on either the reading of a paper at a recognised scientific meeting, or the publication of a paper in an approved scientific journal. This award is subject to recommendation or ratification by the Central Dental Council.
Licentiate (LBIDST): (a) Someone who has successfully completed the full TEC, BTEC programme or SCOTEC Diploma programme; or (b) someone who holds the Final Certificate of the C&G; or (c) someone who holds the First Class Certificate of HM Forces; or (d) someone who has passed another exam recognised by the Institute for this grade of membership.
Associate: Someone who has successfully completed 8 units of the TEC, BTEC, or SCOTEC Certificate or Diploma programme, or who holds the CGLI Intermediate Certificate.

Surveying

ASSOCIATION OF BUILDING ENGINEERS

Lutyens House
Billing Brook Road
Weston Favell
Northampton
NN3 8NW
United Kingdom
Tel: 01604 404121
Fax: 01604 784220
Email: building.engineers@abe.org.uk
Website: www.abe.org.uk

The Association was founded in 1925 under the name of The Incorporated Association of Architects and Surveyors and is the professional body for those specialising in the technology of building.
Fellow (FBEng): Must not be less than 32 years of age and must have held a senior appointment in the construction industry for a period of at least 5 years.
Member (MBEng): Graduate holding an accredited classified Honours degree on satisfying the ABE Evaluation of Professional Competence (EPC). Exemption from the EPC is granted to corporate members of certain related professional bodies and to those over 35 years of age, holding a responsible position in a relevant organisation, having substantial experience, who satisfy an interview panel.
Graduate Member (Grad BEng): Must have at least one year's relevant experience and hold an accredited degree or one with classified Honours in a relevant discipline.
Associate Member (ABEng): Must have at least 2 years' experience in a professional office and hold a qualification of an academic standard not less than that of a BTEC HNC in Construction.
Student: Open to those enrolled on approved courses of study leading to MBEng.
NBA **Corporate Member (Fellow or Member)** is eligible to register as a Professional

Engineer (PEng) with the Society of Professional Engineers and thus entitled to register with the Union Internationale des Ingenieurs Professionnels and use the designation Ingenieur Professionnel Européen (IngPEur).

Swimming Instruction

HALLIWICK ASSOCIATION OF SWIMMING THERAPY

c/o ADKC Centre
Whitstable House
Silchester Road
London
W10 6SB
United Kingdom
Tel: 020 8968 7609
Fax: 020 8968 7609
Email: obk@obk.co.uk
Website: www.co.uk/halliwick/index.html

A voluntary Association which aims to teach swimming and safety in water, and to encourage confidence regardless of the severity of the disability. It exists to provide opportunities for recreational swimming to disabled people of all types and ages. The Association works through regional associations to which local clubs can affiliate, and provides **instructor training**. It organises regional and national galas. It also publishes books and has issued 3 videos.
Proficiency tests held by the Association are aligned to the Halliwick Concept. A high standard of teaching and exams is maintained. Courses for volunteers and professionals are already arranged in many parts of the country. Applications for others will be considered.

THE SWIMMING TEACHERS' ASSOCIATION

Anchor House
Birch Street
Walsall
West Midlands
WS2 8HZ
United Kingdom
Tel: 01922 645097
Fax: 01922 720628
Email: sta@sta.co.uk
Website: www.sta.co.uk

GRADES OF MEMBERSHIP:
Fellow Members, **Diploma Members**, **Qualified Members** and **Associate Members** are all entitled to vote. **Student Members** and **Honorary Associate Members** are not entitled to vote.

EXAMINATIONS:
Student Teachers' Certificate: This examination course is designed to provide preliminary training in swimming teaching for young people aged 14–18.
Basic Teachers' Certificate: This examination course is the introduction to swimming teacher training and the prerequisite for the Swimming Teachers' Certificate Examination.
Swimming Teachers' Certificate: This examination qualifies candidates to teach swimming.
Teachers' Certificate for Teaching Swimming: This 2 part examination course is designed specifically to train qualified school teachers to teach swimming to Key Stage 2 – TCTS(P) or Key Stages 3 and 4.
The National Aquatic Rescue Standard for Pool Lifeguards: A course to provide qualified Lifeguards. The award is valid for 24 months and carries a water test depth endorsement.
The National Aquatic Rescue Standard: A course to provide qualified poolside helpers. The award is valid for 24 months and carries a water test depth endorsement.
The National Aquatic Rescue Standard for Pool Attendants: A course to provide qualified poolside helpers. The award is valid for 24 months and carries a water test depth endorsement.
The National Aquatic Rescue Standard – Emergency Responders: A course to train those experienced in primary life support to act as emergency responders. This includes use of oxygen and automated defibrillation equipment.
The National Aquatic Rescue Standard – Spinal Module: A course to train those who hold practical lifeguarding skills in the knowledge and treatment required for suspected spinal injuries.
Parent and Child Module: A module for qualified swimming teachers that covers the special aspects of teaching babies and very young children.
Aquacise: A course for swimming teachers who wish to teach therapeutic water exercises, with particular emphasis on antenatal exercises, on remedial exercises following illness or operation and general water fitness exercises.
Disabilities Awareness Certificate: A course to train qualified helpers and qualified swimming teachers in the correct treatment and handling of those with more severe disabilities.
National Aquatic Rescue Standard – First Aid at Work: A range of First Aid courses including First Aid at Work and Appointed Persons Certificate, both of which comply with HSE requirements. An extension module to

First Aid at Work covers support in pregnancy, childbirth, febrile convulsions and use of specialised first aid equipment.

Tutors Course: The STA also runs courses to train tutors for the above examinations; within the regions seminars are regularly held on topics of interest to swimming teachers.

Taxation

THE ASSOCIATION OF TAXATION TECHNICIANS

12 Upper Belgrave Street
London
SW1X 8BB
United Kingdom
Tel: 020 7235 2544
Fax: 020 7235 4571
Email: info@att.co.uk
Website: www.att.org.uk

MEMBERSHIP:

Member (ATT): Membership is restricted to those who have passed either the Association's exam *and* who have a minimum of 2 years' acceptable current practical experience in UK taxation *or* to those who are Fellows or Associates of The Chartered Institute of Taxation.

EXAMINATIONS:

Candidates must meet the minimum educational requirements of 4 GCSEs (not craft subjects) at grade C or above, including English Language and Mathematics, or certain professional experience. Further details may be obtained from the Association. Candidates must have registered with the Association for at least 7 months before they may attempt the exams.

The exam covers Personal Taxation in the first paper and Taxation of Businesses in the second paper. In addition there are 2 papers on the Principles of Law and the Principles of Accounting. Exemptions for these 2 papers will be granted to those who have successfully studied Accounting or Law at A level or above.

Distinctions: Distinctions are awarded to candidates in the exam who achieve an exceptionally high standard. Such certificates are additional to various prize awards.

THE CHARTERED INSTITUTE OF TAXATION

12 Upper Belgrave Street
London
SW1X 8BB
United Kingdom
Tel: 020 7235 9381
Fax: 020 7235 2562
Email: post@ciot.org.uk
Website: www.tax.org.uk.

MEMBERSHIP:

Fellow (FTII): Fellowship is restricted to those who have submitted an acceptable thesis or body of work and who can produce satisfactory evidence of specialisation in taxation for at least 3 years prior to the date of their application. Theses or bodies of work may only be submitted by those who are already an Associate. Non-ATII qualified applicants are by invitation only.

Associate (ATII): Applicants must have passed the Associateship exam and have demonstrated 3 years' professional experience in UK taxation.

Subscribers: The Institute has a class of subscribers for certain limited technical information but they are not members of the Institute.

EXAMINATIONS:

Candidates must have been registered as a student with the Institute for 6 months and hold a Certificate of Eligibility. To obtain a Certificate of Eligibility a student must have passed the exam of The Association of Taxation Technicians or the qualifying exam for one of certain professional bodies. Further details may be obtained from the Education Department.

Associateship Exam: Covers practice ethics and administration, general taxation, interaction of taxes and 1 further paper from a choice of 4 options: general practice including owner-managed companies; taxation of individuals, trusts and estates; taxation of companies, their shareholders and employees; and indirect taxation.

Teaching/Education

THE COLLEGE OF TEACHERS

The British Psychological Society, Room 310
33 John Street
London
WC1N 2AT
United Kingdom
Tel: 020 7404 2008
Fax: 020 7404 2008
Email: gen@cot4.freeserve.co.uk
Website: www.collegeofteachers.ac.uk

HONORARY AWARDS:

Honorary Fellowship (FCoT): Chosen each year from among today's most distinguished practitioners of education.

Honorary Membership (MCoT): Given to those members or non-members who have given considerable time and help to the College in developing its various initiatives.

INDIVIDUAL MEMBERSHIP:

Ordinary Fellow (FCollP): The senior class of membership, reserved for those who have made an outstanding contribution to education. Minimum requirements for application: evidence of an outstanding contribution to education through high academic qualifications or a significant contribution to educational literature; tenure of a position of considerable responsibility in education (or 10 years in work demanding a knowledge of education). Holders of the Fellowship (FCP) qualification are normally eligible for election to this class of Membership. This grade is no longer available to new members.

Member (MCollP): The class of membership applicable to a practising educationist. Minimum requirements for application: a professional qualification and experience in teaching or the education service. Holders of the Associate (ACP), Licentiate (LCP) and DipASE qualifications are normally eligible for election to this class of membership. New members will be MCoT and cannot upgrade to FCollP.

Associate Member (AMCoT): For para-educationalists such as governors, support assistants, etc who are not qualified teachers.

ACADEMIC QUALIFICATIONS:

Under the terms of a supplemental Royal Charter which came into effect on 15 May 1998: the former 'College of Preceptors' became the 'College of Teachers'. The qualifications offered by the College will continue to be at the same levels as before. The College of Teachers is legally the same body as the former College of Preceptors, and so the only effective change is one of name. For the information of candidates, students, members, holders of qualifications, and others interested, the validity and standing of qualifications will not be affected. Do please contact the new College if you have any problems arising from this change of name, or anyone with whom you deal requires further information. The College will be pleased to provide any further assistance needed. The College of Preceptors qualifications were awarded pre-September 1999 and the qualifications of the College of Teachers post-September 1999.

Fellow (FCoT): An award at Masters' level conferred on the basis of a research thesis of about 50,000 words or for published work, professional papers or professional record. Candidates normally need to be graduates and experienced qualified teachers. For the FCoT by professional record, teachers will have to have responsibility for a major area, and the staff development within it.

Licentiate (LCoT): The College's qualification awarded to TESOL (Teaching English to Speakers of Other Languages) students at first degree level.

Associate (ACoT): The College's basic qualification for teachers. There is a Foundation Scheme (Mode A) in which the ACoT is awarded by exam, a range of schemes (Mode B) in which the ACoT is awarded by thesis, and ACoTs can also be awarded for approved courses conducted by institutions accredited by the College (Mode C). The College accredits 2 distance-learning institutions to offer an ACoT in the Theory & Methodology of Teaching English to Speakers of Other Languages (TESOL). The ACoT recognises significant work above the basic qualification level for teachers. Candidates normally need to be qualified teachers with at least 1 year's experience.

In 1990 Council approved the award of ACoTs with subsidiary designation (eg ACoT (Special Needs)) to candidates who are not necessarily teachers, but who qualify at ACoT level in fields related to education. Para-educationalists can also enter programmes under modes B and C. While awards are for life, the use of the Associate postnominal of ACoT is only permitted while holders remain in membership or Associate membership of the College.

Certificate of Educational Studies (COES): A first-level qualification instituted by Council in 1990 specifically for para-educationalists who are not qualified teachers but who play a significant role in education and for teachers at the start of their career to recognise their continuing professional development.

The College awards **Diplomas (DipCP)** and **Advanced Certificates (A.Cert)** to successful candidates from accredited courses. The current ones are all in the field of TEFL (Teaching English as a Foreign Language).

THE EDUCATIONAL INSTITUTE OF SCOTLAND

46 Moray Place
Edinburgh
EH3 6BH
United Kingdom
Tel: 0131 225 6244
Fax: 0131 220 3151
Email: egraham@eis.org.uk
Website: www.eis.org.uk

MEMBERSHIP:

Fellow of the EIS (FEIS): On the nomination of the Board of Examiners of the EIS, the Grade of Fellow may be conferred on:

1. Members of the EIS who have attained eminence as teachers or lecturers, who have rendered valuable service to the Institute and who have been recommended as being worthy of the honour of the Grade of Fellow by the local association or self-governing association to which they belong.
2. Members of the EIS of not less than 5 years' standing who present a thesis, not previously presented for any degree or diploma, which, in the judgement of the Board of Examiners, constitutes an original contribution to learning in relation to education. A thesis under this section shall be sent to the General Secretary not later than 1 October in each year.
3. Persons who have rendered signal service to education in Scotland or elsewhere. It shall be competent for local associations and self-governing associations to transmit to the General Secretary of the Institute on or before the last day of February in each year the names of persons who have rendered signal service to education and whom they wish to recommend as being worthy of the honour of the Grade of Fellow together with a statement of the nature and extent of their service to education.

Honorary Fellow (Hons FEIS): On the nomination of the Board of Examiners of the EIS, the Grade of Honorary Fellow may be conferred on persons who have rendered signal service to education in Scotland or elsewhere. Personal applications for the grade of Fellow or Honorary Fellow are not accepted except in the case of those presenting a thesis.

THE SOCIETY OF TEACHERS IN BUSINESS EDUCATION

88 Springfield Road
Millhouses
Sheffield
S7 2GF
United Kingdom
Tel: 0114 236 3659
Fax: 0114 235 2671
Email: stbesec@aol.com
Website: www.stbe.net

Fellow (FSBT): Shall be not less than 25 and shall be a Member or qualified to be a Member and shall have been engaged in teaching a Business subject for a consecutive period of not less than 3 years.

Member (MSBT): Shall be not less than 21 and shall hold (a) a teacher's certificate recognised by the Department for Education and Skills in respect of a Business subject or group of Business subjects, or (b) a teacher's certificate or diploma awarded by those examining bodies determined by the Society as being of a relevant standard, or (c) a degree of a university recognised by the Council provided evidence is produced of a knowledge of, and experience in, teaching 1 or more Business subjects, or (d) a certificate or diploma awarded by exam, by an appropriate professional body or other body as may from time to time be determined by the Council, provided that such a person can produce evidence of teaching 1 or more Business subjects.

Registered Student: A person studying for an exam leading to the award of an appropriate teacher's certificate or diploma and who intends to seek membership upon successful completion of this may be placed on the Society's List of Registered Students.

THE SOCIETY OF TEACHERS OF THE ALEXANDER TECHNIQUE

129 Camden Mews
London
NW1 9AH
United Kingdom
Tel: 020 7284 3338
Fax: 020 7482 5435
Email: info@stat.org.uk
Website: www.stat.org.uk

The Alexander Technique is a system of psycho-physical re-education. It teaches us a way of regaining our natural human birthright of upright, poised awareness in all activity. Restoration of natural poise brings relief from a range of conditions where excess muscular tension is a contributory factor. There is also an improvement in general well-being, both mental and physical.

TRAINING:

A 3 year FT training course is offered at a number (15) of Training Schools recognised and approved by the Society of Teachers of the Alexander Technique (STAT). Qualification is by continuous assessment leading to Professional Competence Certification by the Head of Training School and Full Membership of STAT, which is the professional body. Full Membership is restricted to those who have completed a 3 year FT course.

Application should be made to the Head of the Training Course chosen and admission is solely at the discretion of the Head of the Training Course. A complete list of Training Courses currently recognised by STAT can be obtained by writing to the Administrator, enclosing an A5 SAE. Some LEAs and charitable bodies make discretionary awards, but students must be prepared to make their own financial arrangements.

Technical Communications

THE BRITISH ASSOCIATION OF COMMUNICATORS IN BUSINESS

42 Borough High Street
London
SE1 1XW
United Kingdom
Tel: 020 7378 7139
Fax: 020 7378 7140
Email: enquiries@bacb.org
Website: www.bacb.org.uk

GRADES OF MEMBERSHIP:

Fellow (FCB): Fellows are elected by the Council and must be of the highest standing in the field of Internal Corporate Communication.
Member: (a) **(MCB Dip)** An Associate who has completed at least 2 years in Internal Corporate Communication and who has passed the Certificate and Diploma exams. (b) **(MCB)** One who has been engaged in Internal Corporate Communications for at least 10 years and has demonstrated his/her professional ability and competence to the satisfaction of the Membership Committee. Experience must include having had management responsibilities.
Associate Member: A person who is engaged in Corporate Communication.
Student: Must be enrolled in a formal course of relevant further education and/or be studying, by on-the-job training or otherwise for a relevant exam.

THE INSTITUTE OF SCIENTIFIC AND TECHNICAL COMMUNICATORS (ISTC LTD)

First Floor
17 Church Walk
St Neots
Cambs
PE19 1JH
United Kingdom
Tel: 01480 211550
Fax: 01480 211560
Email: istc@istc.org.uk
Website: www.istc.org.uk

CORPORATE MEMBERSHIP:

Fellow (FISTC): Must have been a Member for at least 2 years, have passed an appropriate exam and have exercised supervisory responsibility in the field of Scientific and Technical Communication for at least 4 years; or have exercised such responsibility for at least 3 years and have either suitable comprehensive knowledge or relevant special knowledge; or have appropriate professional education and experience and have submitted a thesis of an acceptable standard on a suitable subject.

In their evaluation the Institute is assisted by a panel of adjudicators. At their discretion a thesis may consist of or embody any work produced by the candidate during the 10 year period immediately prior to his/her application. A written thesis must be at least 6000 but not more than 12,000 words in length, and must be submitted within 1 year from the date of approval of the subject matter by the Council.
Member (MISTC): Must possess an acceptable qualification or have had equivalent experience in a branch of Science or Technology in which they are engaged as Communicators and have passed relevant exams, and have had at least 5 years' suitable experience (of which at least 2 years must have been in a responsible position in suitable practice); or have had at least 5 years' experience as above (3 years in a responsible position) and have either relevant comprehensive knowledge or relevant specialist knowledge.

NON-CORPORATE MEMBERSHIP:

Associate Member: Someone who wishes to be associated with the Institute to further their knowledge of Scientific and Technical Communication.
Student Member: Must either have enrolled in a formal course of relevant further education or be employed in the field of Technical

Communication and be studying, by on-the-job training or otherwise, for a relevant exam.

Textiles

THE TEXTILE INSTITUTE

4th Floor, St James's Buildings
Oxford Street
Manchester
M1 6FQ
United Kingdom
Tel: 0161 237 1188
Fax: 0161 236 1991
Email: tiihq@textileinst.org.uk
Website: www.texi.org

The Textile Institute covers all disciplines – from technology and production to design, development and marketing – relating to fibres and fabrics, clothing and footwear, interior and technical textiles.

MEMBERSHIP:

Fellow (CText FTI): Chartered Member of The Textile Institute. Applicants must be able to demonstrate that they have attained a standard of professional competence at least equal to that required for the Associateship, and that they have made a major personal creative contribution to: (a) an industrial or commercial operation or organisation in a Textile industry in ways that have a specific textile connotation; or (b) the advancement of knowledge through research, normally shown by publication; or (c) the advancement of technology in practice, as shown by developments in machinery, processes, or products; or (d) textile design; or (e) textile education, training, or communication.

Associate (CText ATI): Chartered Member of The Textile Institute who must have at least 2 years' approved experience in the Textile industries. Applicants must also: (a) have passed the prescribed exams of The Textile Institute; or (b) hold a TI-accredited degree or other approved qualification in a textile-related subject; or (c) hold an appropriate degree or equivalent qualification in a relevant discipline and be able to show evidence of a broad general knowledge of textiles in related areas and have at least 5 years' relevant professional experience after graduation; or (d) be able to show evidence of practice in the Textile industries or other relevant occupation that demonstrates a development of professional skill to a level comparable to an appropriate degree and its application over a period of at least 10 years and have a broad general knowledge of related textiles.

Licentiate (LTI): Must have at least 2 years' relevant experience. Applicants must also: (a) have passed the prescribed Textile Institute exams; or (b) hold a TI-accredited degree or diploma in a textile-related subject; or (c) hold an appropriate degree or diploma in a relevant discipline and be able to show evidence of a specialised knowledge of one aspect of textiles or a broad general knowledge of textiles; or (d) be able to show evidence of practice in the Textile industries or a related occupation that demonstrates the development of professional skill in a special area over a period of at least 10 years.

Personal Membership: Open to anyone interested in the Textile industries and in promoting the objects of the industries, of any nationality, anywhere in the world (the Textile Institute has members in 90 countries). Applicants for any of the professional qualifications must be personal members of the Institute and must remain in membership in order to retain use of their qualifications.

Company Patron Membership: Open to any company or organisation, enabling them to demonstrate their interest in, and commitment to, the Textile industries.

TRAINING:

A complete list of all degrees and other qualifications that are approved as satisfying the academic requirements for the award of ATI or LTI is available from the Institute.

Timber Technology

INSTITUTE OF WOOD SCIENCE

Stocking Lane
Hughenden Valley
High Wycombe
Buckinghamshire
HP14 4NU
United Kingdom
Tel: 01494 565374
Fax: 01494 565395
Email: iwscience@aol.com
Website: www.iwsc.org.uk

The Institute of Wood Science is the examining body for the UK timber trade, giving qualifications at Certificate (Intermediate) and Associate levels.

The syllabus of the Institute of Wood Science course is a comprehensive one, covering all aspects of wood technology, including utilisation. Both levels are based on a workbook concept and are designed to provide information leading to self-seeking study for completion. Several practical exercises are included to complement the theory.

For the **Certificate level** there are 5 modules and each module requires 60 hours' study, ie 30 hours' guided study and 30 hours' distance learning. The **Associate level** has a core module concerned with wood as a material and its handling and processing, and a project study with 1 additional module to complete the course requirement. There is no fixed time for completion of the course but it is expected to take no less than 1 year.

Successful students are awarded a nationally recognised professional qualification and membership of the IWSc. Those successful at Certificate level may use the letters **CMIWSc** and those at Associate level **AIWSc**.

Trading Standards

THE TRADING STANDARDS INSTITUTE

3/5 Hadleigh Business Centre
351 London Road
Hadleigh
Essex
SS7 2BT
United Kingdom
Tel: 0870 872 9000
Fax: 0870 872 9025
Email: institute@tsi.org.uk
Website: www.tradingstandards.gov.uk

MEMBERSHIP:

Fellow (FTSI): Fellowship may be granted to any member of at least 10 years' standing who has made an original contribution to knowledge or has rendered distinguished service to the Institute.
Life Member: Elected by Council in recognition of exceptional services to the Institute.
Member (MTSI): Candidates should have gained either a Diploma in Trading Standards or a Diploma in Consumer Affairs.
Associate Member (ATSI): A person employed in an occupation acceptable to the Management Board and who holds Part 1 of the Diploma in Trading Standards, or Part 1 of the Diploma in Consumer Affairs. A person who does not hold the appropriate qualification but whose length of service in their qualifying appointment is acceptable may also be admitted as an Associate.
Retired Member or Retired Associate: May continue to use the designatory letters awarded.
Student Member: A person who is registered as a student for the Diploma in Trading Standards, or the Diploma in Consumer Affairs.
Affiliate Member: A person who is not eligible for any other class of membership but who is desirous of promoting the interests and objectives of the Institute.
International Membership: Those persons resident outside the UK who share the aims and objectives of the Institute.
Corporate Affiliate: A body corporate who would not be entitled to any other form of membership.
President: An honorary post awarded by the Council of the Institute.
Honorary Member: An honorary post awarded by the Council of the Institute for distinguished attainment in associated work.

Training

THE CHARTERED INSTITUTE OF PERSONNEL AND DEVELOPMENT (CIPD)

CIPD House
35 Camp Road
Wimbledon
London
SW19 4UX
United Kingdom
Tel: 020 8971 9000
Fax: 020 8263 3333
Email: cipd@cipd.co.uk
Website: www.cipd.co.uk

FULL GRADES OF MEMBERSHIP:

Fellow (FCIPD): An applicant for Fellowship must be a Member of the Institute, have worked in Personnel and Development or one of its specialisms at a professional level for at least 10 years or are currently operating at a strategic level and have undertaken appropriate CPD (continuing professional development).
Member (MCIPD): An applicant for full Membership must be a Graduate of the Institute, have performed executive and/or advisory duties in Personnel and Development or one of its specialisms for at least 3 years, and have undertaken appropriate CPD.

OTHER GRADES OF MEMEBERSHIP:

Graduate (Graduate CIPD): Obtained by meeting the Institute's professional standards in 4 fields: Core Management, People Management and Development, a range of generalist or specialist electives, and a Management Report and CPD.

Licentiate (Licentiate CIPD): Obtained by meeting the Institute's professional standards in any 1, 2 or 3 of the above fields.

Associate (Associate CIPD): Obtained by gaining 1 of the Institute's Certificate-level qualifications, in Personnel Practice, Training Practice or Recruitment and Selection.

Affiliateship: Affiliateship is available to anyone and is particularly useful to those working in Personnel Development or one of its specialisms, those engaged in executive, advisory, teaching or research duties, and those in a profession or occupation where knowledge of the principles of Personnel and Development is desirable. Affiliateship offers the Institute's services, but does not confer any professional qualification or status. Discounted sub-grades are available for those engaged on a study or assessment programme leading to an CIPD qualification and/or membership.

PROFESSIONAL DEVELOPMENT SCHEME:

This incorporates 4 elements: Core Management, People Management and Development, a range of electives, of which 4 must be chosen, and a Management Report and CPD. The Institute also offers a Certificate in Personnel Practice, a Certificate in Training Practice and a Certificate in Recruitment and Selection, which are lower-level skills-based qualifications.

For further information on qualifications and assessments please contact the Membership Development or Professional Education departments at CIPD House.

Transport

THE INSTITUTE OF TRAFFIC ACCIDENT INVESTIGATORS

Gen Secretary: David W. Hutson
22 Valley Drive
West Park
Hartlepool
TS26 0AE
United Kingdom
Tel: 01429 427087
Fax: 01429 864489
Email: gensec@itai.org
Website: www.itai.org

A registered charity whose aims are to provide a means for communication, education, representation and regulation in the field of traffic accident investigation, thereby seeking to promote a professional approach to the subject.

ENTRY REQUIREMENTS:

Affiliate Membership: Open to any person with an interest in the subject of Accident Investigation.

Member (MITAI): Affiliates of at least 2 years' standing may apply for transfer to Member grade. Applicants must provide proof of their qualifications, personal involvement and experience in a specialist field that relates directly to accident investigation. Applicants are required to supply a portfolio containing clear evidence of their Continued Professional Development (CPD) completed for the previous 2 years, currently a minimum of 18 hours of study time per year. Applicants will require 2 Sponsors, each of whom should be Members of the Institute. 2 full files relating to 'Accident Investigation' must be submitted for assessment, at least 1 of which must have been completed within the previous 2 years and the other must not be more than 5 years old. All applicants are required to produce a 2500 word report, the basis of which will be to expand on their submitted work files.

INSTITUTE OF TRANSPORT ADMINISTRATION (IOTA)

Mill House
11 Nightingale Road
Horsham
West Sussex
RH12 2NW
United Kingdom
Tel: 01403 242412
Fax: 01403 242413
Email: director.iota@btclick.com
Website: www.iota.org.uk

QUALIFICATION FOR MEMBERSHIP:

Fellow (FInstTA): Granted to persons of special distinction and eminence from within the Institute and at the discretion of the National Council, to persons outside the Institute who have made an outstanding contribution to Transport.

Member (MInstTA): Granted to persons who have been an Associate Member for at least 2 years and have given proof of their ability to hold positions of high administrative responsibility within the Transport industry. Persons holding high executive appointments, possessing extensive experience in industry, commerce and transport may also be granted the grade of Member by the Council.

Associate Member (AMInstTA): Associate Membership may be granted to persons who

possess a minimum of 2 years' Transport experience at an adequate level. Persons of approved managerial status within the Transport industry may be granted Associate Membership by the Council.
Associate (AInstTA): Applicants who, while not necessarily employed directly in Transport Administration, fill ancillary appointments within the Transport industry.
Student: Open to men and women aged 16 and over who intend to make their careers in the Transport industry.

Travel and Tourism

CONFEDERATION OF

TOURISM · HOTEL · CATERING
MANAGEMENT

CONFEDERATION OF TOURISM, HOTEL AND CATERING MANAGEMENT

118–120 Great Titchfield Street
London
W1W 6SS
United Kingdom
Tel: 020 7612 0170
Fax: 020 7612 0170
Email: info@cthcm.com
Website: www.cthcm.com

The Confederation of Tourism Hotel and Catering Management was established in 1982 to provide recognised standards of management training appropriate to the needs of the hotel and travel industries, via its syllabi, examinations and awards. Those studying for the examinations of the Confederation are offered a structured learning process, encompassing both the theoretical and practical aspects of the industry, together with a clearly defined path of development through progressive grades of membership.

The Confederation offers four externally examined Diploma training programmes, each of which will normally take an academic year to complete, and four grades of membership each indicating a level of personal development.

TRAINING PROGRAMMES:

Diploma in Hotel Management: Aims to provide students with a broad understanding of the operational aspects of the international hotel industry, and a knowledge of the underlying principles involved. **Syllabus content:** Food and beverage operations, food science, hygiene and nutrition, front office operations, facilities and accommodation operations, hospitality costing and control, supervisory management, marketing, tourism, computing, business communication.
Advanced Diploma in Hotel Management: Aims to provide an understanding of the managerial, decision-making and leadership aspects of the international hotel industry and to develop independent research and study skills which will be required when working at senior managerial level in the industry. **Syllabus content:** Food and beverage management, food and beverage production, facilities and accommodation management, management accounting, human resource management, management research report.
Diploma in Travel Agency Management: Aims to provide students with a broad understanding of the operational aspects of travel agency management and airline ticketing, along with an understanding of the tourism industry. **Syllabus content:** Travel geography, the tourism industry, travel agency operations, fares and ticketing levels one and two, computer reservations systems, travel agency law, business computing, sales and marketing, finance for the travel industry.
Advanced Diploma in Tour Operation and Management: Aims to provide an understanding of the managerial, decision-making and leadership aspects of the international tour operation industry and to develop the independent research skills which will be required when working as a senior manager in the industry. **Syllabus content:** Tour operations, tour management, resort representation, advanced fares calculation, advanced computer reservation systems, brochure and website design.

ADMISSIONS REQUIREMENTS:

The selection of students for admission to the courses at Diploma level is at the discretion of individual educational establishments. No specific educational qualifications are required, although it is desirable for applicants to have completed formal secondary education.
For selection on to a course at Advanced Diploma level the applicant must have been successful in, or exempted from, the Diploma level course. Exemptions are granted at the discretion of the Confederation on the basis of previous education and experience.
Examination results and certificates: Each candidate will receive a record of performance in one of four grades for each component of the examination. The grades are Distinction, Credit, Pass and Referral. Qualifications are

awarded to those candidates who achieve at least a pass grade in all components of their course.

GRADES OF MEMBERSHIP:

Student Member: This classification is for those who have enrolled on a CTHCM course at a registered CTHCM centre.

Associate Member (AMCTHCM): Awarded to those who have passed or been exempted from the Diploma level examination. Holders of equivalent qualifications acceptable to the Confederation may also be granted associate membership.

Member (MCTHCM): Awarded to those who have passed or been exempted from the Advanced Diploma level examinations, and hold at least 2 years experience in the industry. Holders of equivalent qualifications acceptable to the Confederation may also be granted membership, as may those who have at least 10 years relevant experience.

Fellow (FCTHCM): Awarded at the discretion of the Confederation to those who have achieved positions of significant responsibility in the industry, or who have made notable contributions to the work of the Confederation.

ENGLISH HERITAGE

23 Savile Row
London
W1S 2ET
United Kingdom
Tel: 020 7973 3000
Fax: 020 7973 3883
Website: www.english-heritage.org.uk

Contact English Heritage for information on qualifications.

INSTITUTE OF TRAVEL AND TOURISM

113 Victoria Street
St Albans
Hertfordshire
AL1 3TJ
United Kingdom
Tel: 01727 854395
Fax: 01727 847415
Email: Membership@itt.co.uk
Website: www.itt.co.uk

MEMBERSHIP:

Fellow (FInstTT): Must pass the Institute's professional paper at Fellowship level or have been a Full Member for 10 years or 5 years and have made a substantial contribution to the institution or industry.

Full Member (MInstTT): Must pass the Institute's professional paper or have 5 years' experience in the Travel & Tourism industry at management level or hold a recognised qualification exempting them from it.

Details of the Institute's exemptions may be obtained from the Membership Department. A list of FT courses recognised for exemption is also available.

Associate Member (AInstTT): Must hold an accredited certificate from an Institute-approved college or COTAC II or other recognised qualifications or have 5 years' experience in the Travel & Tourism Industry.

Affiliate Member (Non-Corporate): Must hold Level I C&G Travel and Tourism qualifications, eg COTAC I, COTICC I or Airline I Qualification or Level 2 NVQ in Travel Services or Intermediate GNVQ in Leisure & Tourism.

Student Member (Non-Corporate): Must be studying at an Institute-approved college.

THE TOURISM MANAGEMENT INSTITUTE

c/o Hon Secretary: Stephen Watson MTMI
University College
Scarborough
YO11 3AZ
United Kingdom
Tel: 01723 362392
Fax: 01723 370815
Email: stephenw@ucscarb.ac.uk
Website: www.tmi.org.uk

The Tourism Management Institute is the professional institute for tourism destination management in the UK. Its mission is to advance tourism destination management for the economic, social and environmental benefit of recipient host communities.

Corporate membership of the Institute (Fellows, Members and Associates) is open to qualified professionals in tourism management, whereas non-corporate membership is for Students and Affiliates (commercial and educational bodies) whose activities are relevant and supportive to practitioners and the function of Tourism Management.

Veterinary Science

THE ROYAL COLLEGE OF VETERINARY SURGEONS

Belgravia House
62–64 Horseferry Road
London
SW1P 2AF
United Kingdom
Tel: 020 7222 2001
Fax: 020 7222 2004
Email: admin@rcvs.org.uk
Website: www.rcvs.org.uk

MEMBERSHIP:

Total Membership (all registers): 19,250. RCVS maintains a list of RCVS Recognised Specialists.

Member (MRCVS): To practise as a Veterinary Surgeon in Great Britain it is necessary to be registered with the Royal College of Veterinary Surgeons. Registration (other than temporary registration) carries with it membership of the Royal College. To qualify for membership the applicant must hold a veterinary degree granted by a British university or hold a veterinary qualification awarded by one of the Member States of the EU (and be a citizen of one of those Member States), or hold another overseas veterinary qualification which is currently recognised by the College for registration without further examination. All other veterinarians must pass the College's statutory examination for membership before being entitled to registration. The veterinary degree course lasts 5/6 years.

Members of the Royal College of Veterinary Surgeons (or holders of qualifications which would enable them to be registered by that College) are qualified to take up membership of The British Veterinary Association, 7 Mansfield Street, London W1M 0AT.

QUALIFICATIONS:

Certificates and Diplomas: The Royal College also has power to award postgraduate Certificates and Diplomas in a number of subjects, including cattle, sheep and fish health and production, pig medicine, poultry medicine and production, laboratory animal science, aspects of equine studies and small animal medicine and surgery, veterinary anaesthesia, ophthalmology, dermatology, cardiology, reproduction, public health and radiology, animal welfare science, ethics and law, state veterinary medicine, zoological medicine, by examination.

Fellow (FRCVS): The Diploma of Fellowship may be acquired, by members of the Royal College, not less than 5 years after graduation by thesis or not less than 20 years after graduation by meritorious contributions to learning.

Certificate in Veterinary Nursing: The RCVS Certificate in Veterinary Nursing and SVQ or NVQ Levels 2 and 3 may be awarded following 2 years' training in approved veterinary practices. Training is assessed in the workplace and also by examinations.

Diploma in Advanced Veterinary Nursing (Surgical or Medical): May be awarded following a further 2 years' study and training in veterinary practices and success in the relevant examination.

Veterinary Surgeons have a responsibility to ensure that they maintain and develop their professional knowledge and skills. The RCVS promotes the Continuing Professional Development (CPD) of its members and has a CPD record card scheme for all its members.

Only qualified veterinary nurses may be included on the List of Veterinary Nurses held by the Royal College of Veterinary Surgeons and thereby have the legal authority to undertake certain additional procedures allowed by the 1991 Amendment to Schedule III of the Veterinary Surgeons Act 1966.

SOCIETY OF PRACTISING VETERINARY SURGEONS

2 The Old Gunroom
Blagdon Estate
Seaton Burn
Newcastle
NE13 6DB
United Kingdom
Tel: 01670 789054
Fax: 01670 789359
Website: www.spvs.org.uk

The Society of Practising Veterinary Surgeons (SPVS) was founded in 1933 with the aim of promoting the interests of Veterinary Surgeons in private practice. The SPVS is a non-territorial division of the British Veterinary Association. Its remit is to advise on all aspects of managing the business of a clinical veterinary practice, be that financial, people management, design concepts, legal aspects, etc. We hold one-day, weekend and weeklong courses to cover such topics, also often including clinical seminars and workshops. The annual congress draws a wide cross-section of the veterinary profession and its associated suppliers and affiliated associations.

MEMBERSHIP:

Full Member: This is open to all practising Veterinary Surgeons and veterinary practitioners and entitles them to full voting rights.

Associate Member: Applicants must be working within a veterinary practice. This level of membership does not entitle voting rights. Applicants for this category of membership are required to submit their CV for consideration.
Graduate Member: This is open to those currently training as Veterinary Surgeons. This level of membership does not entitle the holder to voting rights.
Retired Member: Retired Veterinary Surgeons and veterinary practitioners are eligible to join at the discretion of Council.

Wastes Management

CHARTERED INSTITUTION OF WASTES MANAGEMENT
9 Saxon Court
St Peter's Gardens
Northampton
NN1 1SX
United Kingdom
Tel: 01604 620426
Fax: 01604 621339
Email: education@iwm.co.uk
Website: www.iwm.co.uk

CORPORATE MEMBERSHIP:

Fellow (FIWM): Conferred on a Member of at least 7 years' standing who has shown evidence of distinguished professional attainment in the sphere of Wastes Management.
Member (MIWM): Open to those who possess an appropriate degree, or other recognised qualification, have 4 years' relevant experience and have undergone a period of post-qualification vocational training.
Licentiate (LIWM): Open to those who possess an appropriate degree, have at least 1 year's relevant experience and have undergone a period of post-qualification vocational training.
NON-CORPORATE MEMBERSHIP:
Graduate Member (GradMIWM): Open to those with an appropriate degree and who are concerned with the Management of Wastes.
Associate Member (AssocMIWM): Minimum age 23 years, possessing 2 A levels or an HNC qualification, and with 5 years' experience in the Wastes Management industry.
Technician Member (TechMIWM): Minimum age 21 years, qualified to National Certificate level, and with 3 years' experience in the Wastes Management industry.
Affiliate Member: A person who is involved with Wastes Management, but is not eligible for any other grade of membership.

Student Member: Minimum age 16, a person undertaking a course of study and exams, both FT and PT, relevant to the Wastes Management industry.
Affiliated Organisation: Available to any company or organisation which is involved with the Wastes Management industry and which supports the aims and objectives of the Institution.

EXAMINATIONS:

Courses leading to qualifications in Wastes Management, accredited by the Institution, are available at HNC, first degree, PhD and MSc levels, at a number of colleges and universities in the UK. It is possible to study for a number of these on a PT or distance-learning basis. Up-to-date details of these, and information concerning the availability of such courses, should be obtained from the Education & Training Department at the Institution's offices. For further information telephone as above or e-mail education@iwm.co.uk

Watch and Clock Making and Repairing

THE BRITISH HOROLOGICAL INSTITUTE
Upton Hall
Upton
Newark
Nottinghamshire
NG23 5TE
United Kingdom
Tel: 01636 813795/6
Fax: 01636 812258
Email: clocks@bhi.co.uk
Website: www.bhi.co.uk

MEMBERSHIP:

Fellow (FBHI): May be conferred upon satisfaction of the following three requirements: (a) being a paid-up professional Member (MBHI), (b) completing a 5000 word dissertation or practical piece, (c) viva voce.
Member (MBHI): May be conferred upon (a) any Graduate Member (GradBHI) who has had experience equivalent to 5 years full time at the bench, or (b) any professional horologist who has passed the exams of both years of the Institute's Certificate in the Repair, Restoration and Conservation of Clocks/Watches and has had experience equivalent to 5 years full time at the bench.
Graduate Membership (GradBHI): May be conferred if (a) passed the Institute's Final grade exam in Technical Horology, (b) passed

the exams of both years of the Institute's Certificate in the Repair, Restoration and Conservation of Clocks/Watches, (c) obtained a West Dean College Postgraduate Diploma in the Restoration and Conservation of Antique Clocks, or (d) passed any such other exam as Council may consider appropriate.

Associateship: May be granted to any person having an interest in Horology, on payment of the appropriate annual subscription.

Student Membership: May be granted to any bona fide student of Horology who is serving a term of apprenticeship, or is Horology.

EXAMINATIONS

Exams in Technical Horology: The stages are Technical grade (1 year) and Final grade (2 years). FT and PT courses are available at some technical colleges and the Institute runs its own distance-learning course.

Welding

THE WELDING INSTITUTE

Granta Park
Great Abington
Cambridge
CB1 6AL
United Kingdom
Tel: 01223 891162
Fax: 01223 894219
Email: twi@twi.co.uk
Website: www.twi.co.uk

PROFESSIONAL MEMBERSHIP:

Honorary Fellow (HonFWeldI): Honorary Fellowship is conferred in respect of outstanding contributions to the theory or practice of Welding or an allied process, or in recognition for other special causes.

Fellow (FWeldI): Applicants must be over 35, hold an Engineering Council accredited degree (or be CEng), and have held an important relevant position of technical or scientific responsibility for not less than 10 years, or have made such noteworthy contribution to the technology of Welding or an allied process either in practice or in theory that their election will advance the interests of the Institute.

Senior Member (SenMWeldI): Applicants must be over 30, hold an Engineering Council accredited degree (or be CEng), have demonstrated a specified level of knowledge of Welding technology (various options available) and have undergone at least 2 years' training in engineering or in another appropriate field and, in addition, have had at least 2 years' responsible experience related to welding and joining technology.

Member (MWeldI): Applicants must be over 25, hold an Engineering Council accredited degree (or be CEng), have undergone at least 2 years' training in engineering or in another appropriate field and, in addition, have had at least 2 years' responsible experience related to welding and joining technology.

Incorporated Member (IncMWeldI): Applicants must be over 25, hold an approved SQA or Edexel HNC in Fabrication and Welding Engineering or another approved qualification and have had at least 2 years' training and 3 years' experience at the appropriate level with responsibilities for Welding or an allied process.

Technician (TechWeldI): Applicants must be over 21, hold an approved SQA/EdExcel Certificate in Fabrication and Welding Engineering or another approved qualification and have had at least 2 years' training and 1 year's experience at the apprioate level with responsibilities for Welding or some other field of science or technology or an allied process.

Graduate (GradWeldI): Applicants must hold an accredited first degree in Engineering or Materials, or an accredited BTEC or SQA National or Higher National Award or equivalent.

Senior Associate (SenAWeldI): Must be over 30, have been involved with Welding or allied activities for at least 10 years, and have held a post of responsibility for at least 5 of these.

REGISTRATION:

Corporate Membership: May qualify for registration as CEng. Incorporated Members are normally eligible for registration as IEng and Technicians as EngTech.

VOCATIONAL QUALIFICATIONS:

The Welding Institute is accredited by the UK Department of Trade and Industry to confer vocational qualifications under the Certification Scheme for Welding and Inspection Personnel. Categories of certification include Welding Engineers, Welding Technicians, Welding Inspectors, Welding Supervisors, Welding Technical Representatives, Welding Instructors, Underwater Inspectors and Non-Destructive Testing Personnel.

Welfare

THE COMMUNITY AND YOUTH WORK ASSOCIATION – YDA

General Secretary: C Shaw
'Roman End' Severn Street
Lincoln
LN1 1SJ
United Kingdom
Tel: 01522 524305
Fax: 0161 911 3296
Email: youthwork@msn.com

The Community and Youth Work Association incorporated as the Youth Development Association is a professional association international in a scope and activity for Youth and Community Workers, Connexions Personal Advisers and all working with young people. The Association is currently liaising on joint provisional qualifications and on the 'Youth Approved' kitemark scheme planned for 2003. The Association recognises the new Diploma for Personal Advisers and operates a short version of the Diploma in Youth Development for Personal Advisers, entitling them to become Members of the CYWA and/or Fellows of the YDA (FYDA).

MEMBERSHIP:

Fellowship (FCYW): Strictly limited to founder members, honorary representatives of longstanding and others whose work for the Association and Youth Work merits this award.
Membership (MCYW): Awarded to suitable applicants who are usually already Associates and have a number of years' experience in their field and to JNC-qualified workers after 3 years.
Associateship (ACYW): Available to those who have completed the Association's basic course or that of another acceptable agency or a local authority, and have suitable experience.
Affiliateship: Available for organisations and individuals who wish to receive publications, attend meetings and support the work of the Association or who are youth workers who do not wish to apply for another grade.
Student: Students preparing for full membership are registered as Affiliates.
The basic course covers an introduction to Youth and Community Studies, Current Issues in Community and Youth Work, and First Aid and Social and Economic Studies. Persons with an appropriate professional qualification may be exempted from these requirements.

EXAMINATION:
Diploma of Community Youth & Social Welfare: Operated jointly with the New Institute of Social Welfare (ISW) and replacing the Diploma in Youth Development and the ISW Dip. Assessment for entry takes into account DipSW/CQSW (CCETSW), CertYCW/DipHE (JNC for Youth Workers & Community Centre Wardens) and relevant NVQ/SVQ or RAMP accredited schemes (12 months).
Certificate in Youth and Community Work (CertYCW): The Association is currently liaising with Cert/DipHE awarders regarding the sponsorship of courses. (This does not indicate Association recognition of all DipHE.) (2 years)
Overseas Diploma: The Association welcomes international membership and operates a scheme for special assessment for overseas Associates (2 years).
College Diploma Endorsement Scheme: A scheme whereby college awards are endorsed for membership, it is open on a block basis to colleges approved by the Association guaranteeing levels of membership or offering a joint award.
Diploma in Management Studies (Youth Services): This postgraduate award is offered by flexi-study (12 months).

INSTITUTE OF SOCIAL WELFARE

Rear Vicarage
Stockport Road
Mossley
Lancs
OL5 0QY
United Kingdom
Tel: 01522 524305
Fax: 0161 911 3296
Email: youthwork@msn.com

Following the dissolution of the Institute of Social Welfare in 1990, the new Institute of Social Welfare was formed. The Broad Church Social Welfare policy of the former institute was adopted. The Institute has introduced a Diploma scheme as a route to post-qualification study. The ISW is a body of people drawn from different professions whose aim is the improvement of social and community services. It admits to membership workers in social services departments, hospitals, education welfare, race relations, the prison service, probation, youth service, day care, and residential and nursery services from state, voluntary and independent agencies. The Institute recognises the professional and the non-professional as essential colleagues in the network of care.

MEMBERSHIP

Fellowship (FISW): Members whom the Council consider have rendered distinctive service to social welfare, and all holders of the Institute's Diploma in Social Welfare.

Member (MISW): Persons engaged in the social services or as FT or PT officers of approved bodies or holders of professional qualifications approved by the Council of the Institute but not holding the Institute's own Diploma.

Affiliate: Any person or organisation wishing to further the aims of the Institute.

Overseas Associate: The Institute maintains a register of overseas qualified members by direct admission.

Diploma in Community Youth & Social Welfare: An opportunity for post-qualification/experience study by established professionals via an approved centre and a route to Fellowship (awarded with the YDA qv).

The Institute is working with the Community as Youth Work Association/The Youth Development Association to review qualifications to make them relevant to the 'Connexions' Personal Advisor career roles.

INSTITUTE OF WELFARE OFFICERS

3rd Floor, Newland House
137–139 Hagley Road
Edgbaston
Birmingham
B16 8UA
United Kingdom
Tel: 0121 454 8883
Fax: 0121 454 7873
Email: info@instituteofwelfare.co.uk
Website: www.instituteofwelfare.co.uk

CORPORATE MEMBERS:

Companion: Wholly within the gift of the Institute, and is the highest professional grade.

Fellow: Must have been a Member for at least 5 years, and must be holder of the Diploma in Welfare or its equivalent (ie must have been a practising Welfare Officer for at least 7 years).

Member: Must have been in post for at least 2 years as a practising Welfare Officer and hold the Diploma in Welfare Studies or equivalent.

Associate Member: Holder of the Certificate or Diploma in Welfare Studies but has less than 2 years' experience of Welfare practice.

EXAMINATIONS:

The Institute has published syllabus and exam regulations which can be obtained from the address above. All Corporate members in current practice are eligible for **Professional Accreditation**, the only such scheme available to welfare and social care professionals. There are clear requirements of practice, ethics and continued personal development which are subject to audit. Further details can be obtained from the above address.